Downtown Ladies

*Informal Commercial Importers,
a Haitian Anthropologist, and Self-Making
in Jamaica*

GINA A. ULYSSE

THE UNIVERSITY OF CHICAGO PRESS   CHICAGO AND LONDON

GINA A. ULYSSE is assistant professor in the department of anthropology and the African-American studies program at Wesleyan University.

The University of Chicago Press, Chicago 60637
The University of Chicago Press, Ltd., London
© 2007 by The University of Chicago
All rights reserved. Published 2007
Printed in the United States of America

16 15 14 13 12 11 10 09 08 07   1 2 3 4 5

ISBN-13: 978-0-226-84121-2 (cloth)
ISBN-13: 978-0-226-84122-9 (paper)
ISBN-10: 0-226-84121-9 (cloth)
ISBN-10: 0-226-84122-7 (paper)

Library of Congress Cataloging-in-Publication Data

Ulysse, Gina A.
    Downtown ladies : informal commercial importers, a Haitian anthropologist, and self-making in Jamaica / Gina A. Ulysse.
        p.   cm.
    Includes bibliographical references and index.
    ISBN-13: 978-0-226-84121-2 (cloth : alk. paper)
    ISBN-10: 0-226-84121-9 (cloth : alk. paper)
    ISBN-13: 978-0-226-84122-9 (pbk. : alk. paper)
    ISBN-10: 0-226-84122-7 (pbk. : alk. paper)   1. Street vendors—Jamaica.   2. Women merchants—Jamaica.   3. Informal sector (Economics)—Jamaica.   4. Imports—Jamaica.
I. Title.
    HF5459.J25U59   2007
    381'.18082097292—dc22

                                        2007022667

⊗ The paper used in this publication meets the minimum requirements of the American National Standard for Information Sciences—Permanence of Paper for Printed Library Materials, ANSI Z39.48-1992.

FOR LAMERCIE LAFRANCE & JULIETTE MARIE JAVE

Contents

Foreword

On October 2, 1995, a young graduate student in anthropology from the University of Michigan landed at the airport in Kingston, Jamaica. She had been there before as tourist and student, but this trip was different. For she was to do the fieldwork for her dissertation, that rite of passage into the higher ranks of an academic discipline. Haitian by birth, an activist for Haitian causes, a black woman in a largely white discipline, she was carrying both a Haitian passport and a United States permanent residency card. Her feelings were as divided as her identity. She was excited about her project but dreading her immersion in the "tough environment" of Kingston, in its "class and color divide, dense population, fast pace, congestion, gender dynamics, and continuous territorial wars."

To her surprise, the airport was unusually, raucously joyous. In a faraway Los Angeles courtroom, O. J. Simpson had just been acquitted of the murder of Nicole Simpson, his white ex-wife. Alone, unable to share in the exuberance, she collected her luggage with its survival tools for the next months: the books, papers, equipment, CDs, clothes, cosmetics. She maneuvered her way through customs, found an air-conditioned taxi, and drove through Kingston to her temporary home.

The young woman was Gina Ulysse, and *Downtown Ladies* is a major consequence of that fieldwork. Spacious in her concerns, Ulysse is attentive to both Jamaican material conditions and symbolic structures. Intellectually rich, ambitious, and innovative, her book significantly expands our knowledge of race and gender in postcolonial and developing countries, of the dynamic relations between globalization and comparatively small nation-states, of anthropology as a discipline, and of Ulysse herself. A performance artist and poet as well as an anthropologist, she insists on exploring her own subjectivity as well as the object of her research, the downtown ladies of Jamaica. Like her great and acknowledged predecessor Zora Neale Hurston, Ulysse suggests a different way of doing anthropology.

The downtown ladies are hard-working black businesswomen who negotiate the opportunities and vicissitudes of global and local markets. Conscious of the enduring power of history and custom, Ulysse constructs their past. From 1494 to 1655, Jamaica ("Xaymaca") was a Spanish colony that the British then captured. The indigenous population, the Arawak, had been eliminated. To build the sugar industry and trade, the British brought in indentured European servants and enslaved Africans, who became the vast majority of Jamaica's population. For reasons that are still debated, although no doubt none were altruistic, slaves were allowed to grow their own food on small plots of land. Although often in conflict with the authorities, some began to market their surplus within the colony. They were the forerunners of the higglers, who hawked and sold provisions.

Slaves were emancipated in 1838. To add to the labor force, planters began to bring in indentured workers from India, Java, and China, a move that increased tensions on the island. Economic and social conditions remained very difficult for blacks. As black men went off-island for work, black women assumed greater prominence as higglers. Indeed, as Ulysse points out, the market woman—wearing a long wide skirt and head wrap, selling her goods—was to become a highly publicized if obsolete icon of Caribbean black womanhood. The higgler was also measured against the stereotype of the tough, hard, uninhibited "rude gal." As World War II was ending, Britain began the transfer of power from its colonial administration to local politicians. In 1962 Jamaica achieved independence. Higgling remained one of the few occupations open to lower-class black females, who were heading over one-third of the households in the country.

Alert to commercial possibilities, the higglers became more international, entering independently into the export-import trade, deploying United States currency. They were given such adaptive labels as "foreign higglers," "traveling higglers," "international higglers," or "suitcase traders." They were also the unwilling legatees of the stringent codes of color and gender that slavery and colonialism had institutionalized. These codes profoundly linked darkness of skin with the lower classes and slavery; lightness of skin with the upper classes, femininity, and the status of "the lady." One of Ulysse's most fascinating sections focuses on the role of the beauty pageant as a contested site for staging the proper representation of Jamaican womanhood and her color.

The higglers also had to earn their living in the context of postcolonial Jamaican politics and the ferocious rivalry between two parties. One was the PNP, which was anti-imperialist, celebrated Jamaica's African roots, advocated democratic socialism and women's rights, and brought economic disaster. One recourse for survival was self-employment, in which the higglers were skilled. They could supply the Jamaican market with such foreign goods as household items, clothing, and footwear, and the foreign market with such Jamaican goods as T-shirts, reggae tapes, and rum.

In 1980, in a bloody election, the second party, the JLP, took power. It was far more accommodating to such neoliberal global agencies as the International Monetary Fund. In part to control a source of competition for businesses in the formal economy, the JLP began to regulate the foreign higglers. In 1982, they were given an official title, Informal Commercial Importers (ICIs). To find assistance in their confrontations with the government, the ICIs joined a group, the United Vendors Association (UVA). (The UVA organized its own beauty pageants for a short period.) Nevertheless, the ICIs became more subject to state control. They were, for example, to clear their imports through customs. In September 1983, the first arcade was built downtown for vendors of dry goods. By the end of the JLP's second term, the ICIs were integrated into the economy.

Ulysse is determined to bring the ICIs out of the shadows to which observers of women of color in developing countries often consign them, but with their identities self-defined and as "theorists of their own experience." No monolith, the ICIs have differences among themselves. Some find consolation and strength in religion; some do not. Some may have occupations, such as that of flight attendant, or a class status that enables them to operate discreetly and invisibly. Ulysse spends much of her time with those who must toil in public space and are visible—Miss T., Miss B., Mrs. B. She sits with them in their downtown arcade, a microcosm of the neighborhoods and struggles of lower- and working-class Kingston. She travels with them on a shopping trip to Miami, and is exhausted by their schedule.

Although Ulysse seeks the individuality of each ICI, she finds some common features. They like to be independent and self-employed, their own bosses. They believe that such self-directed activity will help them provide for their families and the economic security of their children. Hoping to pass their business from one generation to the next, they train apprentices, among them their children. The ICIs also embody a spirit of "friendly competition," helping each other out when they can.

Ulysse makes vivid the difficulties of the ICIs: the opaque but present state regulations, the rents in the arcades, the instability of the markets, the still present stigmas of class and color, the disdain of civil society, the accusations of being a lesbian or a mule in the pervasive drug trade or a prostitute. In a violent society, in which the codes of gender link masculinity and violence, the ICIs who work in public must also be "tuff." Developing protective shields, they internalize their vulnerability and pain. Yet, shrewdly and fluidly, they persist in creating their businesses, styles, and selfhood. Breakers and crossers of borders, they may work downtown, but they are ladies.

Ulysee is conscious of herself as another breaker and crosser of borders, and a "third world subaltern female." To analyze herself as such a person, one being educated at an acclaimed United States research university, she practices "reflexivity," a constant self-scrutiny. Why does she wear what she wears when she arrives in Kingston, the internationally branded clothes, the Coach bag, the Adidas sneakers? Why does she reside where she does in Kingston? Making Gina Ulysse as well as the downtown ladies the subject of her fieldwork, she is at once poignant, funny, and compelling. She maneuvers between being an outsider and an insider. By training, she is within anthropology, but because she is black by race, feminist by political conviction, and transnational in experience and perspective, she feels on the margins of the discipline. Her race is a point of connection with Jamaica, but her Haitian birth and United States education and life are points of disconnection. She knows that she can leave the daily discomforts and dangers the ICIs experience by returning to the United States. She is both "native" and "ethnographer." As native, she is granted some credibility by the ICIs, but as ethnographer, she is also suspected of being yet another academic visitor who will mine and extract the native material and then run. Feeling forced to invent herself as an anthropologist, Ulysse finds a method of trial and error, and learns from her own blunders.

Downtown Ladies helps to bring the genre of auto-ethnography into being. Ulysse has a double gift for us: first, her own voice and presence, and next, the voices and presence of these Jamaican businesswomen, the daughters of the higglers. They refuse to be victims. In the words of one ICI, Mrs. B., they will find the cracks in the foundations of global capitalism and move right through them. Do not sentimentalize or romanticize these women, but give them an irrevocable respect and admiration. They are, in truth, awesome.

Catharine R. Stimpson

New York University

Acknowledgments

Books that stem from dissertations undergo so many revisions that it is hard to know when to start the acknowledgment process. In the last decade, waves of people, ideas, and support came and went as "Uptown Ladies/Downtown Women" became *Downtown Ladies*.

At the inception, Ms. Mabel Tenn (formerly of Grace Kennedy Co.) gave the lecture that sparked my interest in this topic. Then Miss Tiny, a veteran ICI, has sustained it in spite of our continuous challenges. I also remain in great debt to Ruth Behar, my advisor at Michigan, who asked me "where are the women?" one day in March 1997. Her intellectual steering and ethnographic openness encouraged me to be empirically grounded and theoretically bold. Gracia Clark's imprint is part of the foundation of this project. I also thank Jeffrey Parsons and Fernando Coronil for their contributions. I owe special thanks to Earl Lewis, for seeing me complete my degree and for being my outside reader.

The Social Science Research Council and the American Council of Learned Societies as part of the Ford Foundation offered predissertation funding. At the doctoral level, research was funded by a grant from Inter-American Foundation in Latin America and the Caribbean. Additional support came from University of Michigan's Rackham Discretionary Grants, and the Office of Student Academic Multicultural Initiative and the Center for the Education of Women. At Wesleyan, project grants from Academic Affairs, Affirmative Action, and The Center for Faculty Career Development.

In Jamaica, Brenda Christie, Ras Historian, Mr. Desilva, Mrs. Brown, and Miss B were sources of inspiration and strength from whom I learned more than I can ever say. Numerous others also gave me their time, words, and experiences to commit to paper. I thank you individually and collectively for your insistence on defining yourselves. Thank you for your patience. Finally, here is the book that I promised. At the African Caribbean Institute of Jamaica, I found encouragement. Over the years, Mr. Bernard Jankee, Director of ACIJ, has never wavered in his commitment to this project. I can never repay him for hours of listening, steering, and last-minute help. The librarian Ms. Shernette Fullerton and the research officer Hazel McClune assisted in my research endeavors. At the University of the West Indies-Mona, I spent a semester and was fortunate to have extensive conversations and interviews with scholars across the disciplines, including Patricia Anderson, Anthony Bogues, Carolyn Cooper, Mark Figueroa, Norman Girvan, Elsie Le Franc, Elsa Leo-Rhynie, Rupert Lewis, Brian Meeks, Rex Nettleford, Jean Annie Paul, Betty Wilson, and Michael Witter. Postgrad student Ryan Williams became a most dependable cyber researcher.

Conversations with Colin F., Bruce Hart, and Kynan Cooke taught me much about the embattled sentiments of belonging and the subtleties of policing from another perspective. Sandy Grey-Alvaranga, Nesha Haniff, Myrtle Linton, Sara Manley, Kirk Meighoo, Lisa Ogilvie, Althea Perkins, Roderick Rainford, Frantz Rowe, and Kay Shackleford were supportive in numerous ways. Educator/performance artist Jean Small and filmmaker Mary Wells' friendships were instrumental to my overall success in Jamaica.

Additionally, at different stages, proposals and drafty drafts of chapters were commented on by Paula Auclair, David Graeber, Devaka Guna-wardena, Melissa Johnson, Katia Kolcio, Diane Laiken, Gina Langhout, Rupert Lewis, Elizabeth McAllister, Carole McGranahan, Rosario Montoya, Mari-Jose N'Zengou-Tayo, Baubie Paschal, Melanye Price, Melynda Price, Kate Ramsey, Cocomo Rock, Ashraf Rushdy, Jessica French Smith, Victoria Stahl, Betsy Traube, Serena Williams, and Evans Young. Thank you for your generosity.

Others offered notable friendship, mentoring, support, and guidance that I could not do without. I give thanks to the late Kendy Rudy (my first anthropology teacher), Basam Abed, Akos Ostor, Sandra Baker, Phanenca Babio, Andra Basu, Michael Benn, Chico Boyer, Doug Charles, Dianna Dozier, Ernestine Galloway, Demetrius Eudell, Ann duCille, Dawn-Elissa Fischer, Linc Keiser, Diane Kelly, Natalie Kellogg, Angelo and Batman, Charles and Susan Knight, Joe Belanger, Sassa Kraft, Jacqueline Mattis, Stephen Fowler, Kellyann Kowalski, Michelle Haynes, Evelyn Phillips, Jason McGill, Ella Maria Rae, Katie Hinds, Arlene Torres, Richard Wilk, Davian Wilcox, Kehaulani Kauanui, Kate Rushin, Mary Beth Bruce, Sharron Riley, Anu Sharma, Henoch Page, Billy Noah,

Audrey Simon, Jane White Lewis, Lorraine Gehrig, Jennifer Scott, Colin Wayne Leach, Opal Linton, Michelle Linton, Francisco Lopez, Renee Johnson-Thornton, Jill Reich, Jeff Utter, Sharon Whittle, Davian Wilcox, Krishna Winston, Evan Bissell, Irma McClaurin, Renee Romano, Gail Pemberton, and Jan Willis, and Wesleyan's Feminist and Gender and Sexuality Studies Salon. I also owe architect Catherine Johnson for her mapmaking.

At Wesleyan University, the relationship between teaching and scholarship was easy with sincerely interested students. I am especially thankful to the students who have taken my Black Feminist Thoughts and Practices course over the years. I benefited from in-depth dialogues with several of Wes's brightest. Questions and comments from Joanne Alcantara, Jenny Conrad, Danielle Dixon, Amy Fornari, Elizabeth "Zil" Jaeger, and Hetert Quebu-Waters forced me to take the work in directions I did not often see while keeping it accessible as they insisted I confront the heteronormativity I was re-creating.

Without research assistants Rachel Betton and Kendra Ing, the dissertation simply would not have made the crossing. I was lucky to be assigned Rachel as a mentee/student assistant through the Wesleyan University Scholar program. Kendra was equally invaluable and worked well beyond her job description. Her dedication to seeing the book through was nothing short of inspiring. Leslie Chapman and Kyrah Daniels took up where their seniors left off and proved to be as priceless at critical moments. I remain humbled by their love of the pursuit of knowledge and dedication to praxis.

My Wesleyan colleagues sociologist Alex Dupuy and writer Kristen Olson proved to be highly engaging interlocutors. Dupuy challenged me on every single point we disagreed on. I welcomed it with the awe I have for his dedication to Caribbean Studies. In Olson, I was fortunate to find a critical mind as open to reflexivity and storytelling as it is to explicating and understanding differences. Words are simply not enough to convey my gratitude to both of them. I am also indebted to Betsy Traube for her unwavering support for this project.

The two anonymous reviewers of the manuscript, who later revealed themselves as Faye V. Harrison and Mimi Sheller, made invaluable suggestions that required me to place this work and myself within a broader lineage and literature. Their insights and input definitely helped me strengthen my arguments and fine-tune this work. While I did not follow all of their suggestions, I am grateful for such thorough and extensive conversation with this work.

I am indebted to Kate Stimpson's foresight and recognition that the Women in Culture and Society series was ultimately the homespace for this work. I am grateful for her utter respect of my voice. At the University of Chicago Press, I am thankful to my editor Susan Bielstein and my assistant editor Anthony Burton for their commitment. My copyeditor Michael Koplow's skillful attention to detail taught me once again that writing, as Laurel Richardson writes, is indeed a method of inquiry.

On art: At the height of the research years, the creative works of Jamaican artists Petrona Morrison, Colin F., and Roberta Stoddart were necessary reminders of Jamaica's past. Stoddart's "God's Bride" and "Learning How to Glide" gave imagery to the visceral that social science too often denies.

On performance: Marc Arena, Kaneza Schaal, Chelsea Smith (my Greek chorus), and Andy Vernon-Jones helped me create. Without our performances, I simply could not remember why.

On food: In Jamaica, Guilt Trip restaurant in Liguanea, hosted by Colin and Donovan, provided the best meals in an oasis. In Middletown, O'Rourke's Diner and Typhoon were places I could always go to revise chapters at all hours. Ukrainian specialties were always in abundance at Bo and Katia's.

On smiles: Abe Josue, Cynthia B, Turquoise, Juliette Marie, and Zenon Kolcio supplied me with free laughter.

Had I not promised this book to my late grandmother and niece who is willing her own legacy, it would have been dedicated to the motivation I draw from Nesha Z. Haniff's pedagogy of action, Michel-Rolph Trouillot's scholarship, and Evans Young's social justice praxis.

Finally, my family has been a source of support. My mother Marthe Lucienne Simeon Ulysse, Katia D. Ulysse, James Jave, and especially Irmina Ulysse, who helped me to keep my eyes on the prize during the last stage. More thanks to Jean Robert Simeon, Elizabeth Charmant, Uncles Frank, Max, and Ivon Simeon, Tante Genevieve, Etienne and the extended Dumorne clan as well as Marie France Pierre, Ernst Pierre, and Elsie Demorseau for prayers that seem to traverse Queens to arrive wherever I may be.

This book is a libation. The first drop rushes out of a tin cup and will quickly be soaked by the waiting parched earth. I pour it onto the ground with maximum respect and in honor of all of those mentioned (and those whom I forgot to mention) as well as all the saints, all the dead, and the spirits *bo maman'm bo maman'm*.

Toward a Reflexive Political Economy within a Political Economy of Reflexivity[1]

"There isn't a foundation that don't have a crack in it...I told them... there's no foundation with no crack in it. We will look for it. If we have to we will wait and look for it. We will find it and we will go right through it."

Mrs. B. spoke these words in response to Jamaican government officials at a meeting in June 2004. They were discussing the implementation of a new customs clearance system that would severely curtail the business activities of Informal Commercial Importers (ICIs). She is a veteran ICI and a former officer of the United Vendors Association (UVA) who has been in this profession nearly twenty-five years. Mrs. B.'s foresight is a telling example of the savoir-faire of most ICIs. As she engagingly voiced her opinion, I quickly asked if I could take notes and quote her verbatim, because I knew these words should begin this book. Her statement is as enticing as it is thought-provoking. It captures how this ICI perceives the struggles all ICIs face as a group and how importers have historically dealt with their obstacles. Indeed, Mrs. B.'s analysis of their impending maneuvers through the structures that constrain them is not only apt, but it also evokes Foucault's notion of power and resistance. Her eloquently phrased viewpoint, in that sense, practically renders a Foucaultian analysis redundant. Needless to say, this third world, subaltern female in multiple shadows speaks. She can speak. However, as Spivak (1988) asks, can she be heard or read?

In asking this question, I inevitably implicate myself, the ethnographer as researcher and writer seeking to document various aspects of the lived experiences of ICIs such as Mrs. B. Can I/will I present Mrs. B. and her voice in a manner that does not perpetuate the silencing she and other ICIs often experience in Jamaica? The stereotyping of ICIs renders them hypervisible and causes them to be seldom listened to, let alone read. How do I travel with ICIs' lived experiences, take their tales across all sorts of borders (disciplinary, geographical, physical, national), as Ruth Behar (1993) has done, and tell their lives abroad? The late Jamaican-born black feminist poet June Jordan had addressed my dilemma quite directly when she pointedly said: "and the representative other/not obvious people or poets/worried a lot about just what you should do/if you fall into/such a difficult/such a representative slot" (1997:61).

As a third world subaltern female, I am indeed one of those representative others that Jordan defended. However, I not only represent otherness, but I now have the power as ethnographer to represent others like and unlike myself. This is of concern to me, because this project, in part, stems from my activist politics and from my commitment as a transnational black feminist anthropologist writing about Caribbean black females. Because I was born in the region, I am what the discipline refers to as a native anthropologist. For me, the difficulty of occupying this slot of "'representative other'" is many-fold. I present it here in terms of two interwoven threads. The first is the politics that brought me to anthropology the second is my position as a so-called native within the discipline.

Facing the Dangers of Self-Erasure

To better explicate this, it is useful to know that, for the most part, I decided to become an anthropologist to eventually contribute to helping my birth country, Haiti. At the mere age of eleven, full of internalized racism, I had naively vowed that I would never return to Haiti until things changed.[2] However, the more I learned, and began to see the world as a system, the less I blamed Haiti for all of its troubles.

From the doctoral process, I wanted the intellectual tools that would help me better understand and facilitate change in this country. Therefore, while I had some curiosity in the discursive exercises of intellectual inquiry, my primary interest in seeking the Ph.D. was quite action oriented. Consequently, during the course of earning my degree at the University of Michigan, my political interests oftentimes clashed with my graduate training. In fact, in the very first month of my first semester, on September 30, 1991, the elected president of Haiti, Jean-Bertrand Aristide, fled Port-au-Prince, ousted by a military-led coup d'etat. My sense of purpose began to fall apart and my heart bled. Even though I had not been to Haiti for fifteen years, there had been talk and excitement about this new president representing a change. Hope. I simply could not turn away, so I got involved. I raised the funds needed on campus and with support from Evans Young, assistant director of the Center for AfroAmerican and African Studies at that time, I organized a dialogue on the coup titled "Haiti: Political Crisis or Social Change?" with sociocultural anthropologist Michel-Rolph Trouillot and then cultural attaché Jean-Claude Martineau. The event was standing-room-only as concerned bodies filled the entire lobby of the building trying to hear these native Haitian intellectuals speak.

Soon afterwards, several UM faculty members, community organizers who had attended, and I founded the Haitian Solidarity Group. From then on, I led two lives at Michigan. In one, I was a graduate student. In the other, I was a political activist. The year 1991 was a defining one for me as I learned what kind of politics is acceptable for an academic to engage in. I confronted my choices in an embattled conversation with Nesha Haniff, a would-be mentor. I expressed my frustrations at feeling torn between my political commitments to Haiti and an intellectual training that I experienced as disassociating and where I felt completely erased. In addition, I could barely manage my time. She understood me only too well. She stopped me midsentence and plainly asked me what made me think that the academy would give me the space to be politically engaged in the manner that I wished, especially as a black female who, to prove myself, must work even harder. She ended her comments saying: "If you want to work for Haiti while you earn your degree, know that you will always have to do it on your own time." I left her office frustrated and tired. Yet I had accepted that from then on, my load would be even heavier.

I was ambivalent about conducting my research in Haiti. Several months before I had written to Michel-Rolph Trouillot (whom I did not know at the time) about how I could better serve Haiti in the future as an anthropologist. At the time, I was considering conducting fieldwork on black migratory patterns to Scandinavia. His advice was to study another country in the Caribbean, then to work on Haiti. That way, he wrote, I would gain a more complex perspective that I could bring to work there.

Then I would view Haiti as belonging to the region and not an oddity within it, as Haiti has been represented in the past. In addition, he stressed that I would then not make the mistakes that so-called native ethnographers tend to make. I appreciated his advice, though I still did not know where I would work. The 1991 coup, however, made my decision not to work in Haiti final, since I did not want to conduct fieldwork under fire where I would not be safe. I also knew then that whatever project I did undertake would be in the region and, inevitably, would engage the political.

Alter(ed)*native* Voices

Just how to do this type of work was not always clear to me. In the latter part of the seven-year process, I was exposed to and engaged radical feminists of color whose works confronted dominant racial politics of silencing anti-imperialist activism within and outside academia. These included writers such as Gloria Anzaldua, June Jordan, Audre Lorde, and Cherrie Moraga among others whose "in your face" lyrical offenses to mainstream white feminists demanded responses. I was even more interested in their conceptualization of academe as a site of struggle. I was better able to vocalize my experiences and greatest fears after reading Gloria Anzaldua's "Speaking in Tongues: A Letter to Third World Women Writers." In this piece, Anzaldua called out women of color to challenge patriarchal dominance and existing feminist perspectives that only further restrict us. She urges us to write in ways that would "keep the spirit of revolt and self alive" and "to become intimate with myself and you" (1983:168–169). Her call was about more than visibility. It was also to celebrate our differences in ways that render us fuller subjectivity. This is possible only with intimacy that is necessary to confront the boundary between self and other. Her words liberated me to face a looming threat. I was in danger of losing my voice and losing sight of my activism. From her words, I realized I would remain in danger as long as I did not confront the disjuncture between my training and my political commitments. I was better able to transform my frustration and worries into action, as Audre Lorde instructs, through writing (1984).

At the time, Behar was the sole experimental feminist anthropologist who blurred genres in the department. The dominant tone was one of conventionality and that is how I was trained. In my third year, I returned from the first study-abroad summer in Jamaica and took a course with her titled "Narratives on the Borderland." For the first time, I dabbled with experimental writing, not in my comfort zone as a spokenword poet, but as a would-be anthropologist. Despite this exposure and my attempts to resist the constraints set to redefine me politically, I still embarked on pre-dissertation and dissertation fieldwork (funded by the Social Science Research Council and the Inter-American Foundation, respectively) based on rather conventional anthropological approaches to political economy and development.

The most drastic of changes in the project occurred during my last year. I encountered Ruth Behar at the airport one Thursday afternoon. We sat together and talked and after I explained what I was working on, she asked me what happened to the women? Miss Tiny? Where are the moments on beautification, clothes, and toughness that I used to e-mail her about? They had been replaced by structures and patterns. There were no people. As I had been trained to, I trivialized these interactions with the ICIs as fieldwork trials that would eventually lead to more substantive information. I did not view these missives as "real" data. I had discarded these moments and wasn't even planning to write about them. A week later, we met in her office and she agreed to advise my project. She suggested I go back to the work I had done with her in another course on ethnographic writing. I switched advisors and began to rewrite my dissertation from a reflexive feminist perspective.

That is when it became evident to me that I was not only in danger of erasing the ICIs whom I observed, but of erasing myself as well. I revisited Anzaldua and, this time, took heed of her warring words: "By writing, I put order in the world, give it a handle so I can grasp it. I write because life does not appease my appetites and hunger. I write to record what others erase when I speak, to rewrite the stories others have miswritten about me, about you" (1987:169).

Although I embarked on this new road, I was still ambivalent about it, because I was often on the receiving end of backlash toward reflexivity. For many critics, reflexivity was too subjective and lacked emphasis on materiality. For others, it was navel gazing and confessional; hence, it was not theory. Barbara Christian articulated my concerns about the political and different ways of theorizing. Also aware of cultural politics, Christian in "Race for Theory," critiques French feminist literary criticism for its silence and erasure of voices of others who theorize differently. The disassociation that she found in their jargon-laden approach was another political maneuver. This was a way for white feminists to marginalize people of color and, in the process, claim the center, she concludes. Finally, Christian asked the most poignant question, "for whom are we doing what we are doing when we do literary criticism?" (1987:7).

Christian's answer to this question opened my eyes. She paraphrased novelist and essayist Alice Walker: "what I write and how I write is done in order to save my own life. And I mean that literally. For me literature is a way of knowing that I am not hallucinating, that whatever I feel/know *is*" (1994:357). I found the legitimacy I needed to claim and make a space for my voice (as a politically driven transnational black feminist anthropologist) and that of the ICIs who theorized their conditions in our conversations.

Contending feminists also critiqued the value of creative approaches. For instance, Margery Wolf argues that such approaches may build academic careers, but they could not change the material reality of subjects (1997). Her statement presumes that it is the task of feminist anthropologists to change the subjects' condition of existence, which may be the case for practicing anthropology, but it need not be the case of all ethnographic research. My aim is to shift or expand the ethnographer as well as the subjects' gaze on the researcher to cause a paradigm shift that has the potential to influence a symbolic change. I wish to disseminate new knowledge about ICIs in a manner that recognizes and respects their complex agency so that others who study them or other black females do not re-homogenize what is evidently textured subjectivities.

For me, reflexive ethnography was the genre that provided a solution for my dilemma within academia in general, and particularly within anthropology. Reflexivity becomes a new mode of academic activism, which seeks to interrupt the problem of ethnographic authority that arises when the focus is only on the subject. It reveals the cracks in the foundation or in the mirror (Ruby 1982). Put another way, by choosing to tell how the ethnographer comes to know what she knows, the tailored suit or monograph is exposed to be not as seamless as it appears. Rather, it is various pieces held together by all sorts of stitches, as a quilt. Reflexivity also allows me to unmask the political content of my encounter—I am there to learn about the region because of Haiti. Finally, this was a method through which I could foreground precisely how numerous individuals like Mrs. B., Miss T., and others contributed to what I write about them. While this may not change their daily lives in Jamaica, it would give them space with me to talk back.

My task was to recognize and engage ICIs as theorists of their experiences. In this way, this ethnography is a counternarrative articulated from what I call an *alter(ed)native* perspective to the conventionalities of the dominant discourse within anthropology. It is *alter* as in other and *native* as I was born in the region and am ascribed that identity. It is *alter(ed)* because of how my approach to this project has been modified both by my training and by my encounter with ICIs. The term connotes an anti- and postcolonial stance, with a conscious understanding that the continuities of history mean that there is no clean break with the past. With that in mind, alter(ed)*native* projects do not offer a new riposte or alternative view; rather they engage existing ones, though these have been altered. Alter(ed)native perspectives are those in which tools of domination are coopted and manipulated to serve particular anti- and postcolonial goals. To be very clear, it is the perspectives of Jamaicans that influenced the ways in which I "flip the script" on dominant discourses concerning "the other" and their worldview. In that sense, reflexivity, to me, would be the maestro. It would connect everyone and everything that gathered within my perception at the crossroads of observation. It would serve as a mediator of sorts, linking aspects of ICIs' public lives and their struggles and successes to me as "native" ethnographer, and all of us to the broader context in which I conducted this work within and outside of the discipline.

The Dissertation as Activism

From then on, I started to reeducate myself, to retool myself, slowly filling the gaps left by my prior academic training. To sort out what it means to be a black Haitian female in the academy, I began to actively seek mentors everywhere I could: in cyberspace, at conferences, and in associations. From their collective advice, I realized that my decision to produce activist work meant that I needed to take another decisive turn as I had that first semester in 1991. This time, it was about my professional career. I chose to define myself as a reflexive anthropologist and transnational black feminist. Even then I was wary of linking the two, as I had no contemporary black role model to follow. Zora Neale Hurston, a pioneer who is usually tokenized, was not even taught in my Traditions courses. She was mentioned in a lecture, but as I have come to learn since I began to teach in 1999, it is the presence of an anthropologist on the syllabus that marks one's work as relevant and legitimate anthropology.

Faye Harrison's *Decolonizing Anthropology* (1991b) was also absent on syllabi. I met Harrison when she came to give a talk at Michigan. After this, she began to point me in directions that would expand my knowledge of black anthropology. This new trajectory was significant, as it reinforced the complexities of my positioning that made being a representative other so difficult. Furthermore, in making these new discoveries, I gained a deeper understanding of the politics inherent in the complicated act of telling lives, particularly in relation to strategic silencing. While the literature was quick to discuss "partial truths" (Clifford 1986) of white anthropologists in core classes, I was more concerned with the exclusionary practices that discounted the voices of people of all colors.

Thus, the writing culture debate for me was less about issues of representation than it was about position. In other words, who gets to reveal what about whom? The crisis was, in fact, about power. More specifically, as Kamala Visweswaran writes, "the question is not whether anthropologists can represent people better, but whether we can be accountable to people's own struggles for self-representation and self-determination" (1994:32). She puts it another way and asks what would happen to this discipline if the other dropped out of anthropology and natives spoke back as sole author and not object (1994:32). Indeed, historically it is those in power who have told the story (Trouillot 1995). If the powerless spoke, and were heard, what would happen to the powerful? In the past, those who addressed the differences written on their bodies were relegated elsewhere in the name of objectivity. In that sense, a silencing (Trouillot 1995) and disavowal (Fischer 2004) of the past was a precondition to being recognized. When the natives spoke as John Gwaltney gave them spaces to in *Drylongso* (1980), they were rarely heard or read, and especially not within anthropology. This marginalization resulted in the disciplining of representative others as to the ways of the discipline and as to how to tell the lives of subjects if one is concerned with having a career as an anthropologist.

As an alter(ed)*native* who aspires to write about natives, I pondered over how to better engage and represent the partial silences that dominated me and forced me to confront my black feminist politics. I was concerned with two things: how much do I reflect on the processes and how do I problematize my position as both interlocutor and subject (Medicine 2001). In "Anthropology and the Savage Slot," Trouillot (1991) articulated a solution. Though his approach was conventionally disciplined, he argued for further deconstruction of the "native" concept within anthropology. This would inevitably reveal that we are all material and symbolic products, which would pluralize the "native" and in the process begin to destroy the "savage slot." Second, he stressed that the recent textual turn was rather limiting in its practice of reflexivity as it dismissed the pre-text, con-text, and content, all of which contribute to the reading of anthropological product, as isolated from the larger field in which its conditions of existence are generated (2003:25). Indeed, reflexivity often remained safe with its focus on interpersonal relations between researcher and subjects, thus going only so far. For various reasons, reflections by most scholars only flirted with the professional repercussions of "telling." As Kamala Visweswaran notes, reflexivity is viewed as improper (1994) precisely because, as David Graeber rightly argues, there are some auto-ethnographies that can never be for fear of committing academic suicide (2005:189). Despite the professional pitfalls and more fearful of committing epistemic suicide, I considered a reflexive approach a mediator that would help me become a mediator, given the difficulty of occupying this slot. As Mrs. B. said, "There is no foundation without a crack in it." By going through these cracks, I could look to find spaces through the discipline and not just on the margins from which to write.

Reflexive Political Economy

When I began my research on Jamaican Informal Commercial Importers (ICIs) in 1992, I was interested in development and political economy (narrowly defined). ICIs were an exciting and relevant topic, where development is concerned. They were predominantly females, often of working- and lower-class lineage, who participate in the "informal" economy and circumnavigate state-imposed restrictions, social marginalization, and civil society's disdain. In some cases, many not only succeeded but thrived; hence, they were a prime subject for contemporary research. With more data collection over a seven-year period, I came to understand them as both economic agents who now possessed and manipulated what Nesha Haniff refers to as the hegemonic U.S. dollar, as well as social actors engaged in battles to claim places and spaces in Kingston that they have been historically denied. I could not divide or split these two perspectives, as each informed the other. The articulation of the dialectic between these two positions was fueled by their individual family's history, though always within an even broader social and historical context.

The process of coming to this explication, however, was a tumultuous one that forced me to consider and unpack the multiple tensions that emerged as I grappled with issues concerning feminist epistemologies, research methods, and the politics of representation. I confronted these questions, as the realities I sought to document required that I cross and transcend disciplinary boundaries to gain a deeper understanding of traders who persistently strived to occupy and go through the cracks of global capitalism. It was after extensive field research that I came to understand the multiple ways that their self-making practices are nuanced responses to the daily-lived impact of global fluctuations. By self-making, I mean the various ways ICIs shape their gendered and racial/color identities through choices that affect how they view themselves and how others perceive them. ICIs' choices are linked and informed by time and place within the context of both Jamaica's broader racial/spatial cartography as well as the island's place within the world. Central to my approach is a reflexive stance that extends beyond representation to delve into material conditions. This perspective also engages the symbolic aspects of social position and location as well as the moral economy of authority and power (Thomas 2001). This reflexive political economy is practiced by the ICIs featured in this study. I elaborate on this concept in chapter 6.

For now, let me note that the reflexive political economy of both the researched and the researcher involves numerous factors and is grounded in a sense of personal history, or what Austin-Broos refers to as heritable identity (1994). This forms the basis of traders' self-perception and self-making practices as related to their place in local, national, and global dynamics. In our numerous conversations, ICIs in this study were constantly reflecting on their children or their parents as indicators of their place. This reflection was central to decision making; it was their motive. They kept one eye on the past and another on the future. In that sense, not only are they people with histories (Wolf 1982), but they also operate their businesses aware of the implications of their various historical connections. In 1992, when I asked two young ICIs why they were in the business, their answer was quite revealing: "because I want to have a house in the hills, too," one said. The awareness that they have been denied is precisely what drives many of them to wish and work for a big house. Most importantly, they seek to have one because others do, so why shouldn't they? It is that same reflection that influences their consumption patterns and where they invest their capital. For many, these constant evaluations reveal how they consider the multiple levels of constraints they confront in the world in which they operate. The limits that determine the course of their activities and lives are still best articulated by the old Marxian adage that man makes history, though not exactly as he chooses.

To consider ICIs' situation from a historical perspective, in their local setting, and to gain greater knowledge of the field that they maneuver, I converse mainly with Jamaican producers of intellectual and popular discourses. Thus, often North American theorists and scientists are eschewed in favor of regional scholars whose concern mirrors discussion in the North or even preceded the publications of North American and European scholars. My aim is twofold: to persist in pluralizing the native, and to frame ICIs within their broader history, particularly as they know and understand it. In *Global Transformations: Anthropology and the Modern World*, Trouillot makes a strong case for engaging locally produced scholarship. He notes, "anthropology has produced not only peoples without history, but peoples without historicity" (2003:136). He elaborates further and explains how contempt for local scholarly discourse often viewed as elitist only allows anthropologists to erase the knowledge that societies produce about themselves. In so doing, he argues, we not only homogenize the native, but also treat her as a noninterlocutor. To this end, I actively engage in dialogue primarily with local scholars. I also interact with the broader internationally produced scholarship that seeks to explicate Jamaican or thematically related conditions. The placement of this work at the center of these discussions has the potential to be illuminating in complex ways.

Racing Caribbean Gendered and Classed Notions

My attempts to engage in this conversation highlight some of the gaps in regional discourses that need to be filled. Through this engagement, I have come to recognize that Caribbean social scientists' notions of gendered subjectivities remains bound by theoretical gatekeeping concepts derived mostly from political economy and development paradigms. More specifically, in the last three decades, Caribbean studies on females have undergone a significant shift, from women to gender. Prior to the mid-1980s, the focus on women was ad hoc within the social sciences. There has been a consistent production in Caribbean literature and arts where such gendered productions are already categorized as feminine as feminist scholarship remains marginal and illegitimate.

In the work on Caribbean patterns of social organization, there have been numerous attempts to explain local class and racial hierarchies in relation to social and cultural pluralism (Brathwaite 1971, Smith 1965). The limits of these concepts have led others to argue that social stratification systems vary within the region. While many of the Caribbean societies may have rigid class systems, race and color were not always determinants of class, though in other cases these were correlated (Lowenthal 1972, Hoetink 1985).[3] Stuart Hall discusses how race is categorized in the Caribbean. He notes:

> In the Caribbean even where a strong white local elite is present, race is defined socially. Thus it enters into the mechanisms of social mobility and stratification via registrations: physical characteristics, pigmentation, in some indeterminate way, "culture." Of these colour is the most visible, the most manifest and hence the handiest way of identifying the different social groups. But colour itself is defined socially: and it too is a composite term. (1977:171)

Hence, the distinction between European and African features is ranked on the basis of a European standard. However, Hall continues, when these characteristics are combined with other systems of stratification (education, wealth, occupation, lifestyle, taste, appearance, values), they can socially "lighten" an individual. Others have focused on the saliency and social value of color and its meaningfulness as a category of analysis.[4] According to Lowenthal, the social value placed on color makes it a crucial determinant of status among the middle class and suffuses most of their relationships (1972). Since the majority of the population of Jamaica is black, the middle class occupies a liminal space because the hierarchical social order has been based on correlations between class and race/color. Recent disruptions of this order have exacerbated the fragility of their position. As a result, tensions between the lower and middle classes have manifested in numerous ways, particularly over definitions of class and gendered identities and other cultural productions.

The formulation of class that I employ here is a relational one that considers neo-Marxist perspectives.[5] According to Carl Stone, the "traditional Marxist emphasis on an inherent conflict between owners of production and wage labor is not appropriate [to the Jamaican case because]...of the fragmentation of interests based on differential benefits that accrue to various categories of wage labor and the owners of property" (1973:20). Stone maintains that there are multiple classes engaged in two levels of conflict. The first is conflict between institutionalized labor and management conducted through mass unions. The second and more explosive one "derives from the alienation of the more materially dispossessed segment of labour from their marginal relationship to the means of production.... Both levels of conflict are centered around the distribution of social and material resources rather than ownership and control of the means of production" (1973:21). In her work on the fictional Oceanview, Harrison deconstructs the lumpenproletariat and finds that it entails more class refractions with porous and arbitrary boundaries (1982). These groups are in constant re-formation given the articulation of the capitalist market. For that reason, I am partial to Bourdieu's (1986) deconstruction of capital, which posits a theory of various forms (social, cultural, and symbolic) that can be acquired, exchanged, and even converted. As Bourdieu's limited analysis clearly delineates, such transactions are not equally available to everybody, nor are they simply reducible to economic determinism (Bennett, Emmison, and Frow 1999, Goldstein 2003, Skeggs 2004). In spite of its neoclassical roots that emphasize a rational actor in constant pursuit of different forms of value through economization and maximization, Bourdieu's emphasis on the immaterial and non-economic is useful for me to make a different point. More specifically, it allows me to explain the refractions in raced and gendered experiences of class or how ICIs' complex positioning and uneven power inform their negotiations. In his analysis of Trinidadian factory workers, Kevin Yelvington asserts that "configurations of embodied social capital then both facilitate and preclude the acquisition of other forms of capital, including various forms of social capital, embodied and generalized" (1995:32). Similarly, I argue that it is the use and exchange of different types of capital, often for nonmaterial gain, by ICIs that forms the basis of their reflexive political economy. Thus, class as I present it here is intrinsically linked to race, gender, sexuality, and nationality. Or as Robin D. G. Kelley puts it, class is lived through race and gender (1997:109).

In the Jamaican case, class categories are far from definitive; they are no longer as specific to race or color as they used to be, especially because of social, economic, and political changes in the past decades. Nonetheless, the black majority of the population comprises the lower class among this group. The traditional or inherited middle class is comprised mostly of a brown population. This stratum also includes the Chinese and East Indians[6] as well as blacks. The upper class includes whites, browns, and Chinese, and the elite consists primarily of descendants of the plantocracy, other white immigrants, and Syrians and Jews, who have become honorary whites. Diane Austin-Broos (1984) attests to the way the white power structure of the colonial era has been replaced by a brown structure. This new dominating group controls the clientelist state system, which places emphasis on education, meritocracy, and achievement. The culture of each class is distinct, as these are characterized by the primary organizing principles of "inside" and "outside." Both of these class distinctions are ruled by a commitment to mobility. In many ways, the juxtaposition in this book of uptown and downtown Kingston as oppositional extends Austin-Broos's work. The key difference is that this work focuses almost entirely on the public lives of the traders. It examines their lives outside of their homes, in the open arenas in which they move. Thus, I raise fundamental questions concerning the relationship between gendered identity and spatial orders.

To address this complex subject, I use an interdisciplinary approach influenced by Michel-Rolph Trouillot's penchant for historicity. He insists that the contemporary Caribbean must be looked at through historic lenses that consider how the past manifests in the present (1988, 1991, 2003). As Trouillot has done in his study of Dominican peasantries, my aim is "to analyze the relations between contemporary market women and capitalism . . . [by taking] equally into account systematic features and historical particulars" (1988:286). In applying this methodologically, I critically engage culture, history, political economy, and feminisms. To date, there has been no substantive anthropological study of Jamaican ICIs. Indeed, as many have noted, the Caribbean lacks empirical work on independent international women traders (Le Franc 1989, Witter and Kirkton 1990). This book not only introduces these traders, but it also investigates the cultural complexities of linkages among local-national-global connections, politicoeconomic relations, and national and group identities. In the process, it reveals how sociocultural identity formations, which are responses to political, economic, and cultural structures, generate the local within the context of the global. In its consideration of self-making, this project departs from the literature on women and work, particularly in the informal economy, thus intersecting with recent Caribbean feminist questions. These call for nuancing discourses, which are based on essentialist notions of gender and power, particularly as these relate to identity, position, and location (Barriteau-Foster 1992; Mohammed 1994, 1998; Lewis 2003).

Within the social sciences, however, the feminist work in the English-speaking Caribbean employs a universal category of female: one that considers differences in class, race, ethnicity, and, to a lesser degree, color as well as other indexes. My work both builds on this literature and extends from it by stressing the importance of differences within gendered identities; specifically, by emphasizing the categories of lady and woman. I highlight the everyday impact of these social constructs through the processes by which they can be mediated. I emphasize the role of self-representation as a mediating factor in this dichotomy. In turn, I reveal the limits of local definitions of identities and how these affect individuals who exist inside, between, or outside of the borders of these distinctions. By foregrounding the concepts of lady and woman, this study further problematizes the differential impact of race/color, class, and gender on individuals at different moments in time and within various contexts.

Disciplined/De-sexualized Female Subjects

In Caribbean scholarship, the lines demarcating social sciences and literature and the humanities are quite rigid. Deconstruction of gender occurs in arts and literature and in political economy in the social sciences. Since the goal of this book is to both highlight and decipher the historical and contemporary codes that are written on the bodies of importers and that impact their movement, the category of ICI must first be deconstructed along the lines of gender. Inevitably, any in-depth analysis of gender ought to also examine sexuality. While I do not interrogate sexuality, I pay attention to the role that sexuality, or lack of sexuality, plays as a component in the performance of gendered identities in the world of ICIs. I point to its absence in part because I see the antigay and antilesbian sentiments in Jamaica as related to the intolerance of particular sets of raced and classed bodies. There is a general rejection of difference from an established norm that is best articulated in the discourse on sexuality. Whereas gays and lesbians cause gender trouble (Butler 1990), ICIs represent what I refer to as class trouble. To show the extent of this disruption for Jamaica, I advocate a corporeal approach to deconstructing the black female body (Grosz 1994) to expose its classed elements particularly in comportment. The theoretical common ground that I propose is that ICIs are othered like any other group that causes trouble in the order of things. Indeed, the very position of ICIs (as black working- and lower-class female participants in informal economic activities) in the local-global system cannot be understood without their deconstruction along the lines of the various categories they embody. In studies of the body, the emphasis is often on the discursive; here I use this approach as a foundation that materially grounds me to highlight the various ways that bodies are encoded with race, class, and gendered notions (Hall 1997a).

Ultimately, this project is about embodied intersectional identities and the deployment of capital. It focuses on and attempts to capture the moments in the lives of ICIs when color, race, class, and gendered meanings occur. These articulations demand analysis that argues for the significance of context. I shift between the historical past and ethnographic present, native and ethnographer, uptown and downtown, local and transnational to situate the work within the cracks in the foundation and on the margins (Behar 1993, Tsing 1993, 2005) and to provide a critique. In so doing, I intend not to view the lives of ICIs through a holistic lens, but rather to take a kaleidoscopic approach, like Weismantel (2001), to reveal the dynamics of the business, its participants, and the rhythm of the research across time. By viewing the traders from these multiple perspectives at different moments in time and in different spaces, I interrogate issues of location, position, and subjectivity. It must be noted here that in combining these approaches, it is to be expected that contradictions and tensions among them will be heightened, of which I am only too aware. Throughout the remaining chapters, the nuances of these theoretical approaches are further developed and interwoven with the ethnographic material.

To maintain a reflexive stance as I connect various disciplinary approaches, I weave narrative and analysis throughout the chapters. The theoretical questions posed by this study stem primarily from U.S. feminist studies in anthropology, literature, and Caribbean political economy. I also draw from cultural studies and practice theory. While I emphasize the role of ICIs as agents and actors, I also consciously abstain from reading their actions as resistance (Abu-Lughod 1990). I do this to avoid obscuring the complications in their actions. My interest instead is to tease out the complex and contradictory ways that ICIs go through the cracks in the foundation to explain how their identities are formed and the various institutions and mechanisms that reproduce these. In that same vein, I also do not refer to them as feminists, as this is an association that they would not readily welcome, let alone embrace.

However, I do want to stress that what I am doing is engaging in a transnational black feminist analysis that seeks to reveal the persistent power of race and the political economy of racism (Harrison 1995, Girvan 1991). It is an analysis that is rooted in the politics of daily life, which views all oppressions as interconnected and driven by local-global capitalist systems. This perspective remains best articulated by the Combahee River Collective statement, which states that "if Black women were free, it would mean that everyone else would have to be free since our freedom would necessitate the destruction of all the systems of oppression" (Hull et al. 1982:18).

Central to this radical feminist perspective is an emphasis on the interconnections among multiple forms of oppressions. Bodies, which are marked by or fit into multiple categories, experience oppression in complex ways that reveal how their various identities interlock. Cherrie Moraga and Gloria Anzaldua also took up this explication of oppression from the perspective of Chicana feminists. According to their theory, in the flesh, "the physical realities of our lives, our skin color, the land we grew upon, our sexual longings—all fuse to create a politics born out of necessity. Here we attempt to bridge the contradictions in our experience" (1983:23). As outsiders on the basis of race, gender, sexuality, and ideology, they experience even greater need to name themselves and tell their stories.

Given the significance of self-definition in black struggles, and knowing the power of representation and the politics of publication, my academic pursuits inevitably clash with my political yearning. My wish that ICIs speak for themselves is impeded by my scholarly obstructions. So, I apply traders' code-switching words and theories of themselves as dynamic and mobile Caribbean agents that further debunk static and romantic notions of the category local (Hall 1991, Kahn 2001, Wilk 1996). As a result, in many instances, we have partial dialogues. That this is significant to the ICIs was evident to me when I told several traders the current working title. "Yeahh it nice" they said. Downtown Ladies. Indeed, this title evokes both recognition and respect while it does not attempt to dislocate or relocate them.

Mapping out the Crossroads

My interest in this work stems from a realpolitik, yet the project itself is being made within the academy. This is a contradiction. In that sense, from its inception this book began occupying a space at the crossroads. As I seek a balance between these two sites and motives, I make references to and raise numerous issues that I do not pursue outside of the purview that is outlined below. These unexplored concerns are, at this point, beyond my proposed scope of this project, which simply seeks to introduce the topic of ICIs and, to paraphrase Mrs. B., to reveal how they go through the cracks inherent to all foundations. My goal is not to produce an all-encompassing study that reveals details of ICIs' business activities, explains how their work informs debates of production and reproduction or aspects of their personal lives, or shows how they can be subjects of economic "development." I consciously abstain from pursuing these topics, as they do not belong here. Rather, my focus is on the making of subjectivities. More specifically, I capture and explicate moments within which ICIs make themselves and find meaning in their lives as they collide with historical continuities and discontinuities at home and abroad. In that sense the subjects, this topic, and even the arguments therein are also in constant formation. They are being formed and transformed parallel to the changes occurring in the trade and the broader context that informs it. Hence, my hope is to weave a narrative that will not become yet another totalizing trope that poses the real danger of encapsulating ICIs into a slot of my making.

To keep this focus, in content and in form, I connect and disrupt various traditions to form a prism that will allow me to capture events in ways that mirror the topic and the subjects. Though my arguments flow throughout the text, I cross theoretical traditions that deepen my understanding of the terrains that ICIs traverse. These often clash. I do not attempt to resolve these tensions, as my purpose is to use them to create and frame moments of critical ethnographic engagement (Abu-Lughod 1990). Similarly, the chapters fluctuate between the ethnographic past and present and have their own closings. Indeed, while the positions and identities of ICIs persist, how traders deploy these do not. Likewise, the physical text would remain, while various aspects of my arguments have limited validity and would reflect their time. For these reasons, I refrain from writing a final conclusion, as there are cracks everywhere. An attempt to recast a foundation or freeze the frame would serve the purpose of providing ethnographic and theoretical coherence, which would only reinscribe the hegemonic concept of culture that I write against. Therein lies Audre Lorde's dilemma, of playing with the master's tools (1984). Finally, as this work is concerned with the politics and consequences of visibility both inside and outside of the academy, I take the liberty to randomly name and position all of my academic interlocutors (foreign and local). I do so in part to bring attention to our tendency to naturalize the presence and entitled power of the unmarked. In so doing, my hope is to highlight another significant point. The making of this ethnography stems from intersections of various intellectual, methodological, and inscriptive traditions. Hence, despite my political intention and dedication to the decolonizing anthropology project, this work is situated at the crossroads where the colonized, unevenly positioned, confronts the colonizer in conversation. Below, I outline my order of things.

In the first chapter, "Of Ladies and Women: Historicizing Gendered Class and Color Codes," I chronicle the significance of class and color codes in the construction of gendered identities, jumping back and forth between slavery and the present to show the continuities and discontinuities in the articulation of these codes. Based on analyses of historical examples of self-making and popular representations of females in various arenas, this chapter examines the historical connotation of the concepts of "lady" and "woman" as oppositional racial and color categories to argue that this dichotomy underlies how gender and class have been historically performed in the region, and in Jamaica in particular. I focus on how color, in these contexts, operates as a form of capital and decipher its rather complex value. This further highlights the impact of the class- and color-coded lady/woman continuum on the ICI—a construct that I argue has rendered her "out of place" in this larger gendered field, which she mediates through reflexive consumption practices, including what Douglass (1992) aptly calls a "culture of femininity."

In the second chapter, "From Higglering to Informal Commercial Importing," I provide a social history of the development of female market trading practices in Jamaica. It frames higglering within a broad political-economic context to elaborate on various aspects of the business and its subsequent official categorization as informal. This reveals higglering as a site of contestation since its very inception; it requires participants to constantly negotiate their activities with government, the formal sector, and civil society at large. This background sets the stage for understanding the position of the ICI as a new type of trader who emerged during the crises of the 1970s. I pay particular attention to the rise of neoliberalism in the 1980s to create an extensive field within which to view and assess the process by which ICIs were brought under state regulation. This series of policies includes the establishment of the paradoxical title of Informal Commercial Importer in 1982. I also discuss efforts by vendors to organize in response to these constraints. In conclusion, I argue that ICIs are not only misnamed, but their professional identities (based on stereotypes of race and class) are continually (re)formed through a series of government policies that are floating signifiers.

Chapter 3, "Caribbean Alter(ed)natives: An Auto-Ethnographic Quilt," outlines the larger social setting within which the study was undertaken through the ethnographer's maneuvers. I revisit Delmos Jones's "native anthropology" to foreground the transnational black feminist aspects of the work, by positioning and deconstructing myself, the researcher as a *regional native and local outsider* who is "out of place" in a range of classed uptown and downtown contexts. This placement is used to emphasize the coevalness, to use Johannes Fabian's term (1983), shared by the researcher and the researched. With a series of interwoven reflections on where one lives, hairstyles and clothing choices during fieldwork, I create a "polyrhythmic, non-symmetrical and non-linear" narrative that is more characteristic of African-American women's historiography through quilting (Barkley-Brown 1989). This quilt is used to tell a story that reveals the hidden material and symbolic meanings that are buried in anthropological methods that reinforce constructions of the other and therefore of the savage slot (Trouillot 1991, 2003).

Chapter 4, "Uptown Women/Downtown Ladies: Differences among ICIs," records profiles of ICIs from across the class and color structure. I classify these independent international traders on the basis of their selling location, particularly to demonstrate how visibility impacts upon traders' movements. I argue that the state-recognized category of ICI is an oversimplification based on an anachronistic image of traders from the late 1970s that has since become a stereotype. This chapter contributes to the larger debate on the impossibility of formalizing the informal economy through analysis of classed strategies (for example passing through customs) used by ICIs to circumvent state requirements (such as taxes and duties) that constrain their activities. I also consider the significance of this aptitude for border crossing within the context of mobilities and immobilities.[7]

In the fifth chapter, "Inside and Outside of the Arcade: My Downtown Dailies and Miss B.'s Tuffness," I take an in-depth look at the everyday activities of two ICIs, who sell inside and outside of the arcade where most of the research was conducted. I focus on different forms of gendered survival strategies, especially the embodiment and performance of tuffness (toughness) as a response to the symbolic violence of masculine domination (Bourdieu 2001), both uptown and downtown. The chapter also explores traders' relationships with each other and with the various organizations that represent them, both independent and state sponsored. I deconstruct the racial and social politics of space (Massey 1994, Rahier 1998): first, through a discussion of the emergence and maintenance of local arcades (built especially for ICIs to sell their goods) as spatial entities that reflect the larger class struggles that exist within Jamaican society; second, through an analysis of the place of the arcades within a social topography of downtown Kingston; and third, through the way in which several ICIs and I code switch between different self-made habitae by charting and navigating existing gender- and class-based spatial restrictions. The focus on this part of the capital city reveals it as an area that has been historically marginalized and is ruled by a class-specific racialized spatial order.

In chapter 6, "Shopping in Miami: Globalization, Saturated Markets, and the Reflexive Political Economy of ICIs," I document an ICI buying trip to Miami and use it as background to examine how traders transgress their "out-of-placeness" as they navigate the ins and outs of the world of import and export and international travel. I demonstrate that such negotiations are crucial to ICIs' self-making as certain kinds of modern black women and ladies who are distinct from the more traditional higglers. The buying patterns and apprenticeship systems that influence the continuous expansion of the trade and the saturation of the local market become the point of departure for a discussion of what I call a reflexive political economy, which in turn points to the social meaning of exchange among ICIs and between them and the broader world they occupy.

In the last chapter, "Style, Imported Blackness, and My Jelly Platform Shoes," I explore the deployment of personal style as what Bourdieu calls a "strategy of distinction" in the mediation of gendered class and color dynamics in Jamaica. I use a revelatory auto-ethnographic moment around a pair of jelly platform shoes to consider the author's self-presentation as disruptive to locally observed performances of color, class, and gender. I analyze the impact of such sensibilities on different patterns of consumption, distribution, and self-making among ICIs and their customers. I expose the liminality of new black middle-class status through discussion of ICIs' roles as distributors in rapidly changing trade. I conclude with an examination of local responses to the global flow of goods in terms of the impact of ICIs.

In the afterword, "Brawta," I speculate on ICIs' futures.

CHAPTER ONE

Of Ladies and Women: Historicizing Gendered Class and Color Codes

A woman is not born, but made.— Simone de Beauvoir

So great was the slave woman's desire to appear feminine and ladylike that many chose to wear dresses to work in the fields ... — bell hooks

A historical perspective on gendered mediations of class and color is necessary to gain a nuanced understanding of the predicament of contemporary Informal Commercial Importers (ICIs). Their work and self-making practices occur in a cultural and political-economic field that has a profound impact on how ICIs negotiate their daily lives, first, as black females who, as a group, are marginalized; and second, as participants in economic activities that are also treated as peripheral by the state and society at large. The material and symbolic meanings embedded in these practices can be traced back to the early days of slavery, when constructions of white, black, and colored females were based on the articulation of racialized gender myths and reinforced by patterns of labor. I employ the term "colored" as it was used during the period of slavery to connote any of the multiple combinations of mixed race. As the majority of ICIs in this study are working-class black (often dark-skinned) females, how they perform and fashion themselves is critical to both their definition of their social location and others' perception of their position. Their self-making practices unquestionably influence how they carry out different aspects of their business activities, from traveling to buying and selling.

The goal of this chapter is twofold. First, it is to historicize the interlocking gendered class and color codes that constitute the larger ideological terrain that ICIs navigate. Second, it is to show how these codes initially articulate the concepts of lady and woman and, subsequently, popular constructions of the higgler as the more traditional market woman. I argue that these codes create the discursive field within which ICIs maneuver, while it socially and conceptually incarcerates them. To capture the dynamism and pervasiveness of these interlocking codes, I take an unconventional approach to history by writing this chapter against linearity. That is, I purposely shift between the historical past and the ethnographic present in order to trace thematic continuities and discontinuities in the articulation of class and color codes at different moments in time.

More specifically, I map out the emergence of these codes in several arenas to reveal how they interconnect. I explore how they underlie various constructions of gendered ideals and their racial components during slavery. Then I illustrate how colored females deployed these codes in performances of class as they sought to mitigate the stigma associated with blackness and slavery. This is further reinforced by an exploration of how color operates as a visible form of capital with complex value. This emphasis on visibility is particularly crucial here, because in a relatively racially homogeneous society, distinction is chronically based on appearance. In later chapters, I discuss how going through the cracks is for ICIs structured in part through a politics of visibility. For now, I emphasize the nuances in gendered mediations of class and color codes to expose how these interlock to create cracks through which those who are outside or in-between the boundaries often move.

To show the persistent effectiveness of these codes in the present, I consider the sociohistorical significance of the symbolic meaning of black females as market traders in the region. Indeed, in historical and contemporary popular discourses, the higgler is, without doubt, the icon of black womanhood in the Caribbean region. As the ICI's predecessor, the higgler is the closest social marker of difference against whom the ICI is continually referenced. I argue that representations of the ICI as the ultimate "rude gal" are based on comparisons of her to the higgler. A rude gal is a tough, lawless, hard-hearted, uninhibited, and unrestrained female. She is the kind of woman who runs things. She's bad. Slackness (bawdy language and lyrics) flows out of her mouth as she speaks her mind, and she is not afraid of anyone. Historically, the higgler was viewed as a troublemaker. Now, she has been reconstructed as acquiescent. In the following chapter, this paradox becomes apparent through discussions of the emergence of the internal market and subsequent boom in independent international importing. More specifically, I will show how higglers, as precursors of ICIs, were initially perceived as out-of-place, coarse, rude, etc. These are the same terms that are often used to describe ICIs.

In addition, to emphasize the issue of traders' marginality and out-of-placeness, I focus on the ways in which perceptions of market traders are tied to the spaces they occupy as these either maintain or disturb the order of things. The higgler's business activities limit her sphere, as she moves locally from countryside to town to market and back again. The ICI, on the other hand, is transgressive in her movement. She bustles around the city and travels internationally. She disrupts racialized spatial orders as her business activities thrust her into arenas that were otherwise guarded social spaces (uptown suburbs, airports, hotels and shops abroad, etc.) of the middle and upper classes.[1] In addition, she has access to and manipulates foreign currency (in this case the hegemonic U.S. dollar) and can, therefore, afford the self-making practices that facilitate her becoming some kind of a lady.

Constructing Womanhood through Femininity

Poststructuralist feminist Judith Butler has argued that subjects are constructed through performance. She stresses that there is no self but routine presentations that are shaped by and re-inscribed through speech and other acts. More specifically, in terms of gender, she writes, "there is no gender outside of the expressions of gender...identity is performatively constituted by the very expressions that are said to be its results" (1990:25).[2] Julie Beattie puts it another way. She notes that while on the one hand, we are all always performing our cultural identities because they are all constructed, "on the other hand, these constructed subjectivities are institutionalized, made into structures that have an autonomy apart from the interactional performance" (2003:52). In that sense, she argues, there is a fixity to identities that allows for provisional or temporal selves. It is precisely with these ontological fragments that I am concerned. Identities are performed to create and re-create culturally constructed distinctions. Historically, such distinctions have been informed by ideologies of gender in accord with their concomitant racial, color, and class compositions that, in turn, reflect the larger historical and spatial contexts. As such, this quotidian performance has been based on both the embodiment and the fabrication of expressions of the self. By embodiment I mean the infinitesimal ways in which bodies simultaneously adopt, respond to, and reflect every aspect of their context. Nancy Scheper-Hughes offers a fitting definition. She writes, "Embodiment concerns the ways people come to inhabit their bodies . . . All of the mundane activities of working, eating, sleeping, having sex, and getting sick, and getting well are forms of body praxis and expressive of dynamic social, cultural and political relations" (1992:184–185).

In the advent of colonialism and slavery, when travel writers and armchair anthropologists sought to fill what Trouillot calls the "savage slot," performances required even more precision because dominant concepts of race were then framed in terms of "degrees of humanity" (Stoler 1996:41) or "Christian hierarchies of civility" (Trouillot 1995:77). Whites were considered to be human and everyone else was beneath them. According to Stuart Hall, conceptions of blackness were based on nature as opposed to culture. This emphasis on nature fixes blacks in permanent categories and also secures them through discursive practices that sustain this naturalization (1996, 1997a, 1997b). Existing concepts of white feminine beauty were bound up with notions of purity, delicacy, modesty, and physical frailty (Brody 1998, Bush 1981). In this discourse on race and gender, black females, who were placed at the lowest rung of the great chain of being, became the mediator between mankind and the animal kingdom. As Donna Haraway writes, "Colored female densely codes sex, animal, dark, dangerous, fecund, pathological" (1989:154). An example is Saarje Baartman, stolen from southern Africa and brought to Europe, where she became a display piece and an object of "scientific" study until well after her death (Gilman 1985, Sharpley-Whiting 1999). In travelogues, black females were further caricatured because they did not fit the ideal of beauty prevalent in Western Europe. These depicted black females as "mannish" beings, "accustomed to hard physical labour," and lacking morals and having an unrestrained sexuality that debased them as the archetypal female animal (Nugent 1904, Scott 1852, Stewart 1823, Trollope 1860). This ideology also justified their forced migration and then their subjugation in the New World. As Evelynn Hammonds and others contend, this colonization of the body of black females allowed for their subsequent devaluation. Regarded solely as property, without most rights, they were persistently sexually terrorized and exploited (Hammonds 1997:173). This gave rise to yet another prevalent myth about black females as the immoral temptresses or seducers of white men and the embodiment of evil. As the personification of uninhibited sexuality, black females (simultaneously feared and desired) were then juxtaposed against myths of white females as virtuous. Indeed, the nineteenth-century Cult of True Womanhood, which formed the dogmatic scenery against which gendered subjects performed and were understood, was not only implicitly based on whiteness, but constructed by contrasting the white plantation mistress to the black plantation slave (Carby 1987).

Thus, social constructions of gendered identities were closely tied to race. Indeed, distinctions between British and Creoles (those born in New World colonies) were recognizable. Nonetheless, all white females (whether born in the mother country or the colony) were considered to be "ladies," while black females were "women" or "girls" (Bush 1981). These categories were part of a social hierarchy in the cultural-industrial politics of class divisions at work in the empire particularly during British dominance in the Caribbean. By mid-nineteenth century, though Britain had turned its attention to India and Africa, Victorian ideals were reflected in this taxonomy that manifested itself in the colonies through racial, class, and color hierarchies. These were accompanied by their concomitant socioeconomic factors and expectations of behavior. The lady/woman polarity also demarcated and regulated the racialized spatial boundaries of the colonial order.[3] It allowed for the social marginalization of black females.

North American black feminist scholars such as Ann duCille (1996), bell hooks (1981), and Beverly Guy-Sheftall (1995) have argued well that these constructions placed black females outside the purview of the Cult of True Womanhood. According to the Cult of True Womanhood, primordial instinct or nature, which was accorded to men and black females, must be restrained. Thus, (black) woman then is to (white) lady as nature is to culture, albeit in this case black women represented nature at its basest point. To complicate this point even further, I argue that it is not womanhood per se that black females were denied by the Cult.[4] Indeed, their womanhood was reaffirmed with every single moment they were sexually exploited and/or used to procreate or breed another generation of forced laborers. Rather, they were specifically shorn of what we have come to regard as femininity, that is the desexualized demeanor that females (who are not born ladies) must mindfully cultivate in the moment to restrain their purported natural instincts. In short, it seems that white womanhood (or the very idea of being female) has been constructed through femininity. By this I mean that black females as the other of white females have been historically constructed and represented as nonfeminine throughout the black diaspora.

Literary scholar Natasha Barnes adds a Caribbean dimension to this phenomenon. She notes, "Femininity occurred in a racial landscape and is the jealously guarded domain of white females...it is wrapped in a mantle of respectability and civility that was denied to black people in general and black females in particular" (1994:474). In their claims for respectability in the region, black females used visible capital to mediate the stigma they inherited from enslavement. This capital, when properly deployed, became a signifier of the femininity they had been denied. And it is the search for respectability that has spurred those females, invested in this femininity, to shun being sexed in specific ways. In other instances, however, sexuality and sex became an element of trade. Historians have pointed out that slave owners and female narratives of slavery documented the willingness of certain black and colored females to trade sexual favors for clothing, ribbons, parasols, and anything else that would emphasize the femininity that was not ascribed to them (Beckles 1989, hooks 1981, Buckridge 2004). The significance of such symbols were particularly effective intraracially in asserting the fact that colored and even perhaps black females could be seen as ladies.

In the midst of this racial polarity, colored females (who, in a sense, adhered to performing whiteness) emerged as a favorite entity, for they mediated white purity (femininity) and black evil (femaleness). Indeed, whites often regarded colored females as comparatively more "civilized" than blacks, possessing the potential to be ladies. As a result, in some instances, white females perceived colored females of especially high stature as their competitors. Below I show that in asserting their differences from blacks, colored females highlighted the potential fluidity of this binary. They demonstrated the de facto continuum of these constructions as they revealed the material and symbolic values ascribed to whiteness. In the process of highlighting this, they reaffirmed the rigidity of the lady/woman binary as it was influenced by socioeconomic factors.[5] For those who were not seen as born ladies, and who did not possess the necessary types of capital, there were limits, since the necessary mediations for this self-making were quite costly.

Compounded by "race," class was one of the other factors that determined the position of ladies and women in these societies. These were, in turn, inextricably linked to ideas of labor and leisure (Thompson 1963) and differed considerably between urban and rural areas, where the division of labor, the size of the labor force, and its organization determined the type of work and the amount of time devoted to it. Among other things, this organization of people also justified the division of labor necessary for the capital accumulation brought about by mercantilism. A disproportionate number of black females were field hands in rural areas (Mathurin 1975, Senior 1991). They served as cooks, domestics, nannies, or hired laborers in the more urban centers.[6] Colored females often worked in the house and as store clerks and skilled laborers. At times, they occupied such positions by virtue of their birthright, that is, the privilege ascribed to them based on their paternity. However, the enslaved among this group always faced the possibility of being returned to the field. With this increased and more specialized labor force, the higher classes enjoyed even more extensive leisure.

White planter-class females were restricted to conjugal and maternal roles; working-class white females were active in management and other economic activities (Beckles 1995, Massiah 1986b). White females of humble origins, in the colonies, could aspire to the leisured, pampered position of those of higher status (Bush 1981:248). One's occupation, social position, and, later, property rights depended specifically upon one's blood quantum and how these genetic combinations were imagined to manifest somatically. The titles of many of these positions affirmed the social distinctions between ladies and women (e.g., ladies maids, cleaning woman, market women, washerwomen, etc.). It was in this context that the correlation between class and color—though a fluid boundary, given the various shades—became legally and socially legitimated. Thus, being colored, as opposed to black, emerged as a visible form of capital.

It must be noted that among British colonies in the Caribbean, the preoccupation with color gradations was not particular to Jamaica. The colonial system did recognize and categorize various possible types of interracial mixtures. Accordingly,

> The offspring of a white man and a black woman is a mulatto; the mulatto and the black produce a samba; from the mulatto and white comes the quadroon; from the quadroon and white comes the mustee; the child of a mustee by a white man is called a musteffino; while the children of the musteffino are free by law and rank as white persons, for all intent and purposes. (Henriques [1953] 1968:46)

Given these gradations, the boundaries of being colored were determined primarily on visibility. In this pigmentocracy (Lewis 1987) or shade-ism as the contemporary referent is named, not all the mixtures were equally colored. Greater value was ascribed to whiteness because it is property that has both symbolic and material privileges that last over time (Harris 1991). In other words, the lower one's black blood quantum, the higher one's social position among the black and colored populations. As I elaborate below, this internal hierarchy inevitably shaped a colored person's social and economic possibilities. In some instances, colored individuals received more deferential treatment than blacks from the planter and master class because of their racial proximity to whiteness (Brathwaite 1971, Heuman 1981, Curtin 1955). Simultaneously, if they caused disruptions, they could be demoted at any point. In part to continue reaping these benefits, a colored habitus emerged that appropriated the manners and customs of the dominant class. This pressure to conform, Bush argues, presented the colored population with opportunities for creative forms of resistance to slavery.[7] In occupying this perpetual and fragile state of liminality, they had to consistently distance themselves from the black masses (Brathwaite 1971). Those who could seek mobility through class performance did so by aspiring to and identifying with European ideals (e.g. ladylike behavior). They performed the manners of a higher class to be viewed as or to become less black. Thus, color was viewed as a manifestation of status and became a primary index of a person's worth.

Performing Class and Mediating Stigma

Following color, appearance was the primary way in which hierarchy was both made visible and recognized. As a marker of differences, owners and planters used dress or clothing in attempts to reinforce the social order among the enslaved population. Jamaican ordinances dictated that slaveholders clothe their laborers. According to the Slave Acts of 1792, it was mandatory that masters, owners, and possessors of slaves provide each slave with "proper and sufficient clothing approved by the justices and vestry of the parish" (McDonald 1993:111). Annually, they imported various quantities and qualities of cheap fabrics and clothing to the island. While across plantations and among owners there were differences in distribution, more often than not, these cloths and clothing were allotted to individuals based on the position they occupied within the plantation (Beckridge 2004). The more privileged received more than normal rations and/or special cloths from which they made their clothing. In addition, planters allocated accessories such as kerchief head-ties for females and hats or caps for males, and there were further differences in allotments to work gangs, as Jamaican planters did not supply field hands with shoes (McDonald 1993).

Individuals who received cloths cut them in distinct patterns that allowed them to perform class through their style. Style was used to make a cultural and socioeconomic statement.[8] As McDonald documented, enslaved people used style to undermine owners' attempts to mark them and to counter the stigma associated with enslavement (1993:111–125); that is the disgrace of being property and of being restricted from, and considered not able to, own property.[9] Those who could do so often acquired additional garments through purchase, trade, or thievery. Hence, accessories (such as jewelry and shoes) had value and became yet another indicator of status.

So stark were differences in appearance that numerous nineteenth-century travel writers documented the contrast in the mode of clothing of field hands, house slaves, and the freed population. Along with the social limits and racist ideologies of the time, these travel texts also revealed the importance of clothing in the competitive display that existed particularly among black, colored, and white females. As nineteenth-century British travel writer John Stewart writes:

> The females of color emulate, and even strive to excel, the white ladies in splendor, taste and expensiveness of dress, equipage and entertainment. At races, and other occasions, they spare no pains or expense to make an imposing display as if anxious to outstrip the whites in the race of fashion, gayety and pleasure. The latter are often outdone, in gaudy exhibition by these extravagant females. But the truth is, they do not aim at competition with them. To be surpassed in costly finery by a woman of color excites no uneasiness in a white female, though she would not wish to be eclipsed by one of her own *class*. (1823:331) (my italics)

Stewart explicated these displays of self-making practices vis-à-vis the racial hierarchy and pointed out that despite their attempts, colored females could not be in competition with white females. The latter were secure in a different class position, as it was reinforced by their race.

However, these colored females could and did compete with each other and with blacks. From the latter, they particularly strove to maintain social distance. Nineteenth-century English traveler Mrs. Carmichael documented more of these differentiations. Her social limits notwithstanding, she distinguished washerwomen in the countryside from house slaves in towns:

The appearance of those women was disgusting. Some of them, it's true, had apparently good clothes; but without one exception, the arms were drawn out of the sleeves, which, with the body of the gown, hung as useless appendages; while from the waist upwards, all was in a state of nudity: sundry necklaces, and a colored cotton kerchief with showy colours, completed their dress. As we entered town, although *we saw many well clothed*, yet several such disgusting spectacles were presented; and the little children, in by far the greater number of instances were literally in a state of nature. We observed several *colored* women (that is mulattos) at the doors and windows of houses the dresses of some of whom would have been elegant and graceful had they been more modest. (1833:10–11) (my italics)

Again there was a clear distinction among females of different races or colors. According to Mrs. Carmichael's judgment of taste, the colored female sexualization is writ large in their lack of modesty.

This observation ignores the fact that, in reality, these colored females were not necessarily trying to be like white ladies. They occupied a space on their own as reluctant or willing concubines of white males.[10] In some instances, these immodest dresses were used to attract would be benefactors. In that sense, they sought to compete with white females on terms that did not necessarily reflect the enforcing boundaries of the Cult of True Womanhood. The nuances in color and class performance demonstrate that, indeed, not all colored females were trying to be ladies.

In his writings, nineteenth-century traveler Anthony Trollope compared black women in Jamaica and white working-class women in Britain. He was astonished not only by the dressing methods of Negro women but also their sense of belonging and ease in such fineries:

Housemaids and haymakers in England do not wear their finery (of crinoline, long waists and flowing sleeves) as though they were at home in it. The Negro woman does not express this discomfort. She is never shame faced. Then she has very frequently a good figure, and having it, she knows how to make the best of it. She has a natural skill in dress, and will be seen with a bodice filled as though it had been made and laced in Paris. (1860:70)

Trollope was undoubtedly perplexed. He sets up a comparison noting that white working-class females in Britain were not at home in fineries, yet Negro females were. His observations implied that the latter certainly not only did not belong in fine clothes but also should not feel comfortable in them. In documenting this, Trollope ironically suggested that Negro women had some sort of "natural" affinity for quality. This remark points to the murkiness of social constructions of race particularly in relation to class and its privileges. Apparently, one of the social luxuries of whiteness was a sense of comfort and place with excellence. The inanity of naturalizing rank with race (as opposed to capital) is evident in that these Negro females were not only cross-dressing-across-class, but they did so with grace and managed, according to Trollope, essentially to succeed where lower-class white females could not.

English historian Catherine Hall offers an illuminating reading of Trollope's ambivalence towards females who ventured out of place. She notes that he was troubled by any disruption of the dominant gender order that unsettled the neatness and niceness of English homes (2002:220). She comments on a vignette of his published in *The Times* that ridiculed two young black females dressed in borrowed clothing playing princess. Hall's observations point to Trollope's fascination with racial cross-dressing, particularly given his known disdain for white working-class females disturbing gender dynamics: "These were mill girls, not the troubling Lancashire mill girls who dominated the streets of Northern towns with their clogs and their claims for independence, but black mill girls, dressed in all white and pretending to be ladies" (2002:221).

This practice of feigning position was as prevalent among poor white women during the nineteenth century in Britain. Carolyn Steedman points out that clothing has been a necessity for the mobility of any woman or girl child who wants to enter the social world. She notes, "A Birmingham eight year old of the 1860s lays money aside, week after week, to pay for a bonnet and dress so that she can go to a Band of Hope Fete; the parents of child workers in the Nottingham lace industry dressed their little girls in crinolines and ignored the lack of undergarments beneath" (1985:89). Appearance was much more important than propriety and modesty. As Steedman argues, the emphasis individuals placed on materials such as clothes reveals adherence to a set of social rules, social behavior, and social expectations. Dress, then, was key to performing a higher-class identity. Beverly Skeggs stresses that appearance became a signifier of conduct; to look was to be. "Appearance and conduct became markers of respectability though they had to be coded in the correct way" (1997:100).

In the colonies, within the constraints of slavery, clothing and appearance were quite noticeable to travelers. As various accounts revealed, the differences in the enslaved population's appearance was even more conspicuous during holiday festivities. The most popular was the Jonkonnu festival, which was held on various islands in the region during Christmas. During these festivities, the enslaved engaged in the competitive display of dress, dancing, and singing.

In everyday life, among females, difference was reinforced by the appropriation of European social identities. Those with ambiguous phenotypes (lighter skin) were especially able to manipulate their identities and construct themselves as ladies. If their physical characteristics and mannerisms blurred the boundaries between lady and woman, their performance needed to be even more precise. For unless they became ladies, they risked never attaining higher social status through marriage or by association.[11] However, this ability to remake oneself and become a lady had its limits, because colonial legislation supported by European racist ideologies and practices ultimately constrained colored females. An example of this tension is found in the case of Mary Seacole, colored widow traveler. In her autobiography, *The Wonderful Adventures of Mary Seacole* ([1857] 1988) she relates her experiences as a healer and adventurer while traveling in the Caribbean and Europe during the nineteenth century. Seacole uses various strategies to repeatedly distinguish herself as a middle-class lady from the black masses whom she referred to as "excited niggers" and "good for nothing blacks." She presents herself as being rather exemplary of Englishness, in part, by overvalorizing her Scottish parentage. Furthermore, she embraces the Victorian ideals of femininity of the Cult of True Womanhood as expressed by her preoccupation with "proper" female attire during her travels (Paquet 1992).

Although other colored individuals considered her a lady, among whites this aspect of her identity was less secure. In 1808, John Stewart observes "the brown female was rarely fully accepted into white society, if she has one drop of African blood in her veins it shuts her out from the society of white ladies as it is a moral stain in her character" (335). Yet, there is also evidence that colored ladies, at times, enjoyed even higher status than white females who failed to embody this higher state of being. Hilary Beckles provides some examples. He notes that in certain social circles brown females of ladylike character were more accepted than whites lacking these necessary social skills. This absence of manners, Beckles stresses caused quite a bit of embarrassment to British travelers (1998). The well-known nineteenth-century traveler Lady Nugent notes that perhaps the climate, the distance from European centers of civility and culture, and the proximity to the black population cause the abominable and improper behavior of many young white ladies (1904:68-69, 72, 201).

Indeed, it seems that the process of creolization occurring as the Old World conflated with the New also influenced the comportment of the entire population to such an extent that unladylike behavior was a point of distinction between white ladies of the empire and those from the colony (Brathwaite 1971). As a result of this division, on the occasions when white ladies sought companionship and "civil" white females of their class were unavailable in the region, racial lines were crossed. Such transgressions or crossings demonstrate that class was highly significant in the making of ladies, particularly for the colored who occupied that liminal space. The examples above show that this lady/woman continuum was fraught with contradictions, thus making it difficult to generalize. Class, as a factor, caused slippages that rendered race and color categories somewhat ambiguous. In some instances, the link between race and rank was futile, as class was a dominant factor in patterns of social organization. Yet in others still, it was race.

A similar tension regarding association and fraternization existed between the colored and black populations. Because of color proximity, the latter represented the greatest threat to the colored (or brown) population. In his study of this population, historian Gad Heuman notes that colored females established various educational societies such as the Society for the Diffusion of Useful Knowledge and the St. James Institute for Promoting General and Useful Knowledge (1981:14). Such organizations allowed brown members to differentiate themselves from blacks and to assimilate aspects of European civilization. Marriage and unions were yet another site where social distance was reinforced. According to John Bigelow:

> While the *entente cordiale* between whites and colored is strengthening daily, a different state of feeling exists between Negroes or Africans and the browns. The latter shun all connection by marriage with the former and can experience no more unpardonable insult than to be classified with them in any way. ([1851] 1970:260)

Undoubtedly, while the need to maintain this distance had its advantages, there are also numerous instances when coloreds and blacks forged alliances, particularly against the governing colonial authority.[12] However, I focus on the tensions between blacks and coloreds to stress the importance of this quest for distinction. This is to foreground the persistent power of whiteness and its privileges. There is a "possessive investment" (Lipsitz 1998) in being perceived as white.[13] Given this, for others without this visible capital, mediations are specifically materially based. Nowhere is this more prominent than in the color of beauty.

Color: Visible Capital

Jamaica is a (neo)colonial society. It was a Spanish colony from 1494 until the British captured it in 1655. The island gained independence in 1962, after it had been under British rule for over three hundred years. Among peoples of African descent, the British colonial system based inheritance of capital and property on recognized categories of various possible types of interracial mixtures. It is within the context of ownership of resources that color, as a marker of social and economic class, became the most important index of a person's worth in Jamaica. Currently, color gradations in Jamaica range from black to brown to red to high brown to *yella*. Even further distinctions are made among whites, Jamaica whites, and white Jamaicans. Whites are of "pure" European blood. White Jamaicans are those of European descent who were born on the island, and Jamaica whites are those who are phenotypically white but with questionable lineages.

As is evident above, Jamaica has been polarized between black and white since the earliest days of slavery, despite the persistent presence of a diverse population of Chinese, East Indians, and Syrians. The prominence of "colored" as a social category determined by both physical and cultural distinctions solidifies the black/white dichotomy. Moreover, most individuals habitually assess colored identity on the basis of the degree of African or European assimilation.[14] Hence, social analysts once distinguished between "two Jamaicas," one European and the other African (Curtin 1955), but within Jamaica as a whole, the latter has always been a rejected group. Color gradations have been used to maintain social distinctions. Common references are made between a pretty dark girl with good (European texture) or bad (African texture) hair.

Nowhere are the values ascribed to color more visible and significant than in beauty pageants, the public arena where femininity is reproduced often for national purposes. Color-coded beauty has its origins in the colonial past, where the demand for social order ruled these contests. During the eighteenth-century "set girls" parades, which preceded contemporary pageants in Jamaica, attested to this divide. At these events, both enslaved and free females, representing the principal social or racial categories of the colonies, were "set" against each other:

> There were brown sets, and black sets and sets of all the intermediate grada-
> tions of colour. They sang and they swam along the streets in the most luxuri-
> ous attitudes … but the colours were never blended in the same set—no blackie
> ever interloped with the browns, nor did any browns in any case mix with the
> sables—always keeping in mind,—black woman—brown lady. (Scott 1852:251–
> 252)

While the category of "colored" upset the racial divide between blacks and whites, boundaries were upheld to prevent even further intermixing. In the set girls pageants, the blending of sets would have disrupted the racial/spatial order of the day. As I discuss below, the color-based distinctions observed in these parades were perpetuated and are modified in current national beauty pageants. As white sociologist Mimi Sheller asserts, "Today as in the post-slavery period, color remains a measure of status" (2005:23).

The earliest winners of the Miss Jamaica contest that began in the early 1940s represented the white bias that excluded the black majority of the population, the Chinese, and the East Indians. By the late 1950s, other contests sprang up in an attempt to be more representative of the diverse population. One of them was the Ten Types, One People pageant held in 1955, and sponsored by the *Star*—the evening edition of the *Gleaner* (Jamaica's oldest daily paper). This pageant selected ten winners and gave them titles that corresponded to a pure or composite picture of the different races, ethnic variations, and colors of the people occupying the island.[15] Though the intention was to recognize the many races and ethnic groups that constituted the one Jamaican people, this pageant reified racial/color distinctions as separate points on a continuum of shades associated with different ethnic groups. Nonetheless, it took this multiracial approach for blackness to be publicly treated as beautiful, but only with chemically treated black hair. However, the pageant was short-lived, lasting only five years. With national independence in 1962 and the seeming disappearance of whites from the political scene, the brown population emerged as a dominating socioeconomic and political force. This group reinforced elements of racist ideologies and their position as superior to the black masses. The white and black opposition of the old social order was altered into a brown and black dichotomy. Yet whiteness loomed in the shadows. European facial features and skin color continued to reflect the ideal as a signifier of social position and access to various resources.

The Miss Jamaica contest, which came under the auspices of the government at this time, became the national beauty pageant and replicated the emergence of this "browning" as the beauty ideal. Prior to independence, resistance to the old social order had been in the making. Among the lower classes, there were formal and informal challenges. During the 1930s, as the Back to Africa movement raised black consciousness, one of Garvey's chief concerns was the image of black women in Jamaica. Honor Ford-Smith (1991) notes that while Garvey did not challenge the dominant ideology of gender relations, he felt that black women needed to be uplifted. Hence, in his poem "The Black Woman," he contested Eurocentric notions of beauty and Christianity. At the same time, this poem idealizes black females.

Black awareness continued with the birth and growth of Rastafari during the 1940s (Barrett 1977). Rastafari emerged as a radical opposition to white bias and the impoverishment and marginalization of the black masses locally and throughout the world. Finding their birthplace in Ethiopia, Rastafarians fashioned an everyday resistance via yet another black Jamaican identity that had its own beliefs, practices, and aesthetics. Rastafari overtly contested the European culture, which pervaded the urban centers of the island. As the movement became more popular, members were continually harassed and targeted by local government. Eventually, their persecution abated and some conditional social acceptance came with the use of Rastafari and reggae symbols by Jamaican political parties during the 1970s and with the international rise of Bob Marley as representative of reggae music. As an example of resistance against the norm, Rastafari also has its own limits. Its gender politics not only reinforce inequity, but also takes it to extremes. As Carolyn Cooper asserts, in Rastafari's biblical derivation, the female was ambivalently perceived as both deceitful and vulnerable (1993a:131). Because of this potential for evil, Rastafari subjugated females to their maternal roles and hailed them Mama Africa—in another mystification of both females and Africa.[16]

Rastafari was not the only opposition to the hegemonic order. Formal opposition came from within the black middle class as well with the formation of the Council on Afro-Jamaican Affairs (CAJA). Individual black professionals such as Dr. M. B. Douglas (a dentist who changed his name to Abeng Doonquah) and Mr. Vin Bennett, a manufacturer and chemist, were notably active members of CAJA. Through constitutional means, this organization sought to eradicate socioeconomic injustice in Jamaican society and to educate the black masses to be proud of their African heritage. Fundamental to their approach was the establishment of informal and formal ties with Africa. In 1964, this organization organized the first Miss Jamaica National Beauty Contest to counter the national pageant. Not only was the winner dark-skinned, but also her prize was a trip to attend Malawi's independence celebrations, and then to travel to Ghana, Nigeria, and Kenya as the guest of those governments. CAJA embraced the African continent primarily to alleviate the "racial separatism" that plagued Jamaica and, as stated in its newsletter, to raise the level of social and political consciousness of the Jamaican masses (Owusu 1996).

Despite these political visibilities, the white bias persisted in the national pageant. In 1967, judges removed the dark-skinned favorite contestant and her Afro hairdo from the final stage of the competition. Local journalists responded, noting that this rejection of the only contestant who represented the masses in particular was a "monster attack on a large group of people," and the chairman of the contest committee was charged with racial bias and snobbery. In other letters to the *Gleaner*, nonblacks who felt marginalized by this debate questioned their position within the nation as Jamaicans. The different views expressed on this incident foregrounded the realities of blackness in a country that professes a plural nationalism. According to Alva Ramsay, a journalist, this rejection, coupled with comments, and writings of politicians, intellectuals and reporters, was damaging to the morale of the country (1969).

It is within that context that the Miss Jamaica pageant had a moment of consciousness. The pageant succumbed to the waves of popular black awareness and protests (throughout the social structure) that brewed on the island. In the late 1960s and early 1970s, judges acknowledged black beauty with natural hair as the Miss Jamaica crown was placed upon the Afro-styled hair of two dark-skinned "ladies."[17] This mirrored some of the changes brought about by the black power movement pulsating throughout the black diaspora. In 1972, the Democratic Socialist government of Prime Minister Michael Manley, in a feminist move, emphasized the local need for gender equality and denounced the Miss Jamaica pageant as a "cattle parade." The pageant was not held for three years. It resumed in 1975, when the Miss Jamaica pageant was privatized. From then on, most winners were once again "Mahogany types—defined as Jamaica cocoa brown, neither full black nor very light-skinned" (Barnes 1994:479).

Since the majority of contestants are often racially mixed females, this new beauty ideal is usually well represented in first-tier pageants.[18]

Jamaican organizers have stressed that the winners have been those who have the potential to win international pageants. Indeed, to date, Jamaica is the most successful Caribbean country in the international beauty pageant industry. The island has won the much-coveted Miss World crown three times, and contestants usually rank highly in other international competitions.[19]

Consequently, the local beauty industry expanded. Numerous modeling agencies were founded to capitalize on this local-global demand for Jamaican beauties, including Attitude Model Agency, Best of the Best Model Agency, Creme de la Creme Modeling Agency, Jade Marc Models, and Sage Models. The more established ones include Pulse and Elite, which represent the majority of past and current winners. It must be noted that Spartan created Elite, the same locally owned company that had purchased the rights to the Miss Jamaica pageant. These agencies also include finishing schools, where young girls and ladies are taught "proper" comportment, table manners, grooming techniques, exercise routines, diction, and social conversation, among other skills. Miguel Models and a few other agencies started to represent darker-skinned females, thus challenging the European standard of the more institutionalized Pulse and Elite agencies. As of 2004, however, contestants from these smaller agencies have not won any major titles in Jamaica. They have had some success especially in regional pageants, where they are seen, ironically, as more representative of the island's majority black population.

The identity of pageant winners is a political issue that highlights the tensions at the roots of socioeconomic problems of the country. Winners who have caused the most uproar have been those of exclusively white parentage (whether European or Syrian—as members of this group have become honorary whites). Chinese contestants and winners have also stirred some controversy, whereas East Indians have enjoyed popular support. Tensions with the Chinese stem from black perception of them as belonging to the oppressive mechanism that exploits and marginalizes them.[20] On the other hand, the relationship between blacks and East Indians differs from island to island and from moment to moment.[21] As Miss Brenda confirms, pageants are about class status as well as social position. She was one of the organizers of Miss United Vendors Association (Miss UVA), an ICI beauty contest that was held for two years in 1988 and 1989. According to Miss Brenda, class status ultimately determines the winner.

She notes: "I don't believe a poor somebody can enter [Miss Jamaica] and win. You have to be up there. You have to be in a society class, because the things you require are expensive and you have to be up there. There are some pretty *girls* down here [downtown] but they would never win."

Because of the continued absence of dark-skinned females from national pageants, and the significance of color-coded beauty (for beauty is defined differently depending on the color of the individual) as another marker of class position, numerous tertiary contests have emerged throughout the island. These include Miss Caribbean Queen, Miss City of Montego Bay, and Miss Jamaica Independence. The Miss UVA pageant was held in conjunction with the organization's annual awards dinner. According to one organizer, this event was meant "to recognize and honor the hard work of vendors." Older traders were given certificates to recognize their seniority. Younger ICIs from different arcades[22] participated in the beauty contest, which, according to one of the organizers, was "done just like Miss World." A representative was chosen from each of the participating arcades, including Pearnel Charles, Constant Spring, Metropolitan, Oxford Mall, and Old Wolmers arcades. The contestants competed in categories that included evening dress, swimwear, and sportswear. The winner was crowned Miss UVA and was awarded prizes that were purchased with funds collected from vendors in all of the participating arcades. After two years, this event was discontinued. The renting of the ballroom of the Oceana Hotel and the other expenses were simply much too costly for the association.

As is common in the global beauty pageant industry, such local-national contests do not challenge or rival the more established local-international pageants (Wilk 1996, Oliver 2003). They are not as well-funded or well-sponsored, and they receive little or no media attention. Yet they persist because they feed a popular national interest in celebrating plural models of femininity while contradicting the definitions of beauty espoused by the primary pageants that disregard the black masses. Indeed, the Miss UVA competition countered the stereotype of the ICI, which I discuss in detail later, as an aggressive, loud black woman. The ICI's work requires a certain behavior, comportment, and presentation that are deemed unladylike, especially uptown. By crowning a Miss UVA, vendors created an arena to affirm their femininity and recognized the beautiful among them. They also recognized different body types. Although the winners did not include the large-size shape associated with the stereotyped ICI, the bodies of Miss UVA and the other crowned winners of the

different arcades departed from the thin, curvy body with just a little mus-
cle tone prized in national as well as global pageants. Furthermore, this
pageant opposed the public discourse that stereotyped ICIs and allowed
the traders to perform other facets of their gender identity publicly.

Beauty pageants are not only a lucrative industry. For contestants and
winners, they are vehicles for social and economic mobility both within
and outside of one's social milieu. Several contestants have won international contracts with top American and European modeling agencies.
At home, these models enjoy superstar status. They win instant fame
and recognition, notoriety, write-ups in society pages and roles in music
videos. In the media, they endorse local products, productions, and services. They also become trophy wives, as marriage with well-established
corporate leaders is a likely outcome. All of this occurs regardless of the
extent of their popularity abroad. Beauty is a highly prized commodity,
and it is a form of capital, as Lynn Chancer has aptly argued (1998), that
has historically facilitated unlimited access to resources and otherwise
scarce opportunities. In Jamaica, it is not beauty alone, but it is color.
In that sense, the beauty of color has racked up its value since slavery to
become what Stuart Hall refers to as a commodity of difference (1991).
In the aforementioned contexts, and as Trouillot (1991) has also shown in
Haiti, color has both exchange and use values.

These examples highlight the significance of color, as a symbol of both
material capital and symbolic capital in the region. Indeed, the high return associated with beauty (as a vehicle for admiration, recognition, and
socioeconomic betterment) is the reason that young girls cite winners of
pageants as their female role models.[23] Most girls will not have this opportunity given the value ascribed to color and the pervasiveness of lighter
skin as the national beauty ideal. In addition, the material and social capital that underwrites performance of this identity is outside the material
capabilities of the general population. With the history of pageants, most
Jamaicans comprehend that the correlations among beauty, femininity, and
whiteness (and now brownness by association) prevail. A dark-skinned
older ICI of working-class heritage once said that Miss Jamaica "has to
have tall [long] hair, she don't look like we." That is, she cannot look like
the majority black and often poor population.

In recent years, the greatest cultural challenge to this standard of the
color of beauty as personified by the young Jamaica cocoa-brown pageant
winner came from dancehall. This genre of popular music gave rise to alternative spaces and public events that both exhibited and fêted a working-

class black female body (though not necessarily always dark-skinned) as representative of downtown culture.[24] Historically, gender, race, and class codes and their complex multiplications were writ large on the black female body rendering it a complex cultural and political-economic transcript. As I will show below, that body also had its other.

Of Ladies . . . and Women

In a study of "white" elite families in Jamaica conducted during the mid-1980s, anthropologist Lisa Douglass shows how race, class, and color are central to the making of family within this group. She argues that these categories have gender and gendered components that still determine the marriage and infidelity patterns of elites of the island. She notes that family members and friends apply extreme pressure on individuals to be endogamous and therefore to maintain the existing class structure (1992). She further reveals that, among the elite, a cultural feminization of females, which stresses the continuity of the nineteenth-century ideal of (white or brown) ladyhood, is still widely practiced.

As Douglass notes, Jamaicans expect "any female who is white to be a lady and exhibit a consistent feminine demeanor . . . the fairer the female the greater likelihood that she is indeed a lady" (1992:247). A lady is, by definition, educated and refined, and to uphold the heteronormativity that governs gendered ideals, she should always be a wife. Her social status derives from matrimony and her devotion to her husband and family. Being a lady inevitably implies heterosexuality, devotion, and sometimes subservience to men and other family members. It must be noted that heterosexuality need not equal submission to patriarchy. Yet this performance of submission is central to how ladies are defined especially among the upper class. This compliance is yet another marker used to reinforce definitions of masculinity, which are also quite rigid. In a sense, masculinity is a counterpoint to femininity. Later, in chapter 5, I discuss how toughness is automatically ascribed to maleness in such a way that any alternative masculinity is seen as deviant. Hence, a male who is viewed as soft or sweet is seen as gay and therefore not masculine. Ironically, ladies who are tough are not necessarily sexualized in the same way. Douglass further stresses that the lady is expected to place her family's interests above her own. Other characteristics that are ascribed to her include femininity, which she exudes in all her attributes, from her diminutive size and unobtrusive manner, to her high heels and exquisite grooming, to her soft voice and careful diction. She does not use vulgar language or even patois. She distinguishes herself from all men and common women through body language ... A lady knows her place, when she goes out socially by night her husband escorts her, she avoids public transportation and must never walk. (Douglass 1992:246–249)

A lady also maintains a strict divide between public and private spaces. Walking on the streets not only brings her into a public arena, but also results in the unladylike conditions of being dusty and sweaty. Contact with the hot sun not only induces perspiration, but also damages and darkens sensitive white or light skin. Hence, ladies use private cars with air conditioning. This is just one of the many reasons that no other commodity holds greater importance in defining class status in Jamaica than the car.[25] Between the middle class and the upwardly mobile, individuals form car pools, which are a saving grace from the perceived humiliation of having to use the erratic and uncomfortable bus system.[26]

Furthermore, according to the *Gleaner*, a lady stands and sits with her legs together, and when she dances a lady does not "*wine*." That is, she avoids the expansive and explicit sexual hip movements of this dance style associated with ghetto women (Douglass 1992:245). The quintessential lady, to the middle and upper classes, is still the queen of England. Runners-up include Lady Bustamante, wife of Alexander Bustamante, Jamaica Labour Party (JLP) founder and independence movement leader; and the latest Miss Jamaica winner, who is seen as the epitome of the uptown girl, espousing middle- and upper-class ideals of beauty, femininity, and values. The extreme importance and high social status ascribed to beauty contest winners reinforce the fact that these pageants are critical sites in the reconstruction of female identities.

According to these categories, physically and socially the woman is the antithesis of the lady. She is strongly built, capable of hard work. She often shares the public space with men, and thus is no stranger to outburst and open conflict. She is most definitely the head of her household. She does not marry, for marriage is a costly act of status, as Raymond Smith (1973) asserts, a practice uncommon among the working and lower classes. Historically, the absence of marriage has been a point of concern particularly for the middle class.[27] Rather, the woman enters "visiting unions" with numerous men for whom she will bear children. Her ability to "breed," as they say in Jamaica, is central to her female identity. Edith Clarke's study of female-headed households conducted during the 1950s shows the connections among sexuality, procreation, and personal status in Jamaica. Clarke further stresses that the childless woman is an object of pity, contempt, and derision (1957:91–95).

Today, it is still common for young Jamaican working-class females to have their first child in their teens to establish their fertility and to escape accusations of barrenness (Elsa Leo-Rhynie 1993:12). This is particularly critical in the common law market, where the commodity being traded is paternity in exchange for care. Childbearing also establishes heterosexuality without the ritual of marriage that ladies are socially expected to perform. I understand this emphasis on (hetero)sexuality as a critical component of the manifestations of patriarchal power. It is through the female population that masculinity is constructed and defined. The importance of children in the construction of female identities prompts Massiah to argue that "women view themselves as mothers first, daughters second, and wives third" (1986:263). While Massiah's use of the term "women" is more general, her conclusion is more applicable to those of the lower rungs of the social structure. For the elite, as Douglass shows, the primary index of identification is the husband, to whom one is married (1992). Massiah further stresses that "no matter what mating forms women eventually enter, they declare their children as their primary responsibility and focus. The mother-child bond places the onus of being the provider on women, and in the final analysis renders men almost peripheral to the domestic sphere" (1986:263). Women, unlike ladies, are economically independent females who head their households. They are the primary breadwinners of the family.

In fact, by the end of slavery, black females comprised the majority of field laborers in Jamaica. In the immediate postemancipation period, 80 percent of the female population was employed in some sort of wage labor on plantations (Senior 1991). Women work because earning an income is linked to perceptions of her as both mother and woman. Furthermore, her sense of self and the esteem in which she is held in her community are also based on her abilities to provide.[28] Women's identities and self-worth as workers differ from that of ladies, whose identities, according to Douglass, stem primarily from their roles as wives, which implies a certain reverence to men. The lady maintains her household. The higher her socioeconomic status, the less likely that she works for money. If she does, it is in a respectable profession that allows her to keep spatial restrictions that govern her behavior. On the other hand, a woman's occupation and social location often thrust her into more public arenas. Typically, she is employed as a cleaning woman or helper, factory worker, washerwoman, or she is self-employed as a hairdresser, higgler, ICI, or seamstress, among other trades.

The Higgler: Icon of Black Womanhood

The most common gendered trade in the Caribbean is marketing, and more than any other figure the female market trader is fixed in popular imagination as the icon of black womanhood in the region. In paintings, posters, television advertisements, she sashays up and down the hills dressed in a long wide skirt, gathered and tucked into the waist to allow her freedom of movement. Her head, covered with a head wrap or madras kerchief, supports a wicker basket or wooden tray carrying her goods to market. Historically, her habiliment has marked her, as historian Steeve Buckridge outlines in his study of dress as a site of female resistance and accommodation in Jamaica. He notes that female peasants' "dress reflected their status within the broader society...Despite their poverty, peasant women accommodated European aesthetics in dress, when they could afford to, usually only on special occasions. For many of this class, the ritual of dressing up was important. In the fields and on the few surviving estates, unlike in urban areas, peasant women still wore osnaburg clothing as everyday dress" (2004:158). They were even more distinguished at the market, where, Buckridge notes, these female peasants' dress was a signifier of their social standing and occupation. He documents the significance of variations of head wraps among market traders, revealing that certain knots signaled marital status while others were symbolic of wealth and social standing within the market domain. Buckridge provides visual details of the bandanna, which deserve to be quoted at length. He writes:

> Among market women in Jamaica, bandanna head wrap was a coded dress form that conveyed marital status and occupation. It was a uniform marker that identified these women as traders and laborers, differentiating them from others. The head wrap was made by folding a squared piece of starched Madras cloth, as much as a yard in length, into a triangular shape and then placing the cloth over the head and knotting it at the back of the head. The knots were tied so as to leave two folds draped to the shoulders or centre of the back. The upper fold would be peaked and then curved to hang, suggesting the shape of

a rooster's tail. Some market women called this style the peacock, but the most common name was the cock's tail. The stiffer the fabric, the more pronounced the style and the easier it was to obtain the desired shape. To help stiffen it, cassava juice was boiled for a long time and used as a starch. (2004:164)

Buckridge's attention to this accessory is further evidence of how images of the higgler are fixed in a particular moment, especially since contemporary traders do not wear this bandanna.[29] Another indicator of the extensiveness of the higgler stereotype is the multiple referents such traders have acquired throughout the region. In Antigua and Guyana, the market trader is referred to as a *"huckster"* and *"hawker"*; in the Dominican Republic, a *"machanta"*; and in Haiti, as either a *"madansara"* or *"marchande."*[30] In St. Kitts, they are known as *"turn hands,"* and in Nevis and St. Lucia as *"speculator."* Copious documentation of this image from the earliest days of slavery to the present has made her symbolic of the region. Artists, travel writers, and visitors noticed and remarked on enslaved females walking great distances (sometimes fifteen to twenty miles) on the way to market with parcels on their heads.

In 1811, Gilbert Mathison notes that the enslaved "who either had no finery or were unwilling to wear it in going from plantation to provision ground to market and back, often wore work clothes" (1811:35). In *Domestic Manners and Social Condition of the White, Coloured, and Negro Population of the West Indies*, Mrs. A. C. Carmichael observed the following on a Sunday morning: "I saw, for the first time bands of Negroes proceeding from different estates, some with baskets, and others with wooden trays on their heads, carrying the surplus produce of their provision grounds to market" (1833:4). As Trollope noted, the black woman is particularly known for carrying things on her head. Indeed, the load on her head was often described in detail.

In *Two Years in the French West Indies* (1890), Lafcadio Hearn provided one of the most vivid accounts of this practice. In a descriptive sketch of Martinique entitled *Les Porteuses*, Hearn outlined the comportment of the *marchanne* as she carried goods on her head:

The erect carriage and steady swift walk of the women who bear burdens is especially likely to impress the artistic observer: it is the sight of such passers-by which gives, above all, the antique tone and color to his first sensations;—and the larger part of the female population of mixed race are practiced carriers. Nearly all the transportation of light merchandise, as well as of meats, fruits, vegetables, and food stuffs—to and from the interior—is effected upon human heads. At some of the ports the regular local packets are loaded and unloaded by women able to carry any trunk or box to its destination. (1890:103)

Hearn extensively discussed multiple aspects of being a porteuse from physical attributes to attire, to encounters during the exhausting and long journey to the market. But it is his lyrical focus on the details of how girls were trained as they mature to carry goods on their heads that warrants being quoted at length:

> At a very early age—perhaps at five years—she learns to carry small articles on her head,—a bowl of rice,—a *dobanne*, or a red earthen decanter, full of water, even an orange on a plate; and long before she is able to balance these perfectly without using her hands to steady them. (I have often seen children actually run with cans of water upon their heads, and never spill a drop.) At nine or ten she is able to carry thus a tolerably heavy basket or trait (a wooden tray with deep outward sloping sides) containing weight of from twenty to thirty pounds; and is able to accompany her mother, sister, or cousin on long peddling journeys,— walking barefoot twelve to fifteen miles a day. At sixteen or seventeen, she is a tall and robust girl, lithe, vigorous, tough,—all tendon and hard flesh;—she carries a tray or a basket of the largest size and a burden of one hundred and twenty to one hundred and fifty pounds weight;—she can now earn about thirty francs (about six dollars) a month, by walking fifty miles a day as an itinerant seller. (Hearn 1890:105)

In *Roaming through the West Indies*, Harry Franck observed: "Negro women with oval market baskets on their heads tramp energetically along the white highway" (1920:414). Early in the 1950s, McMillan provided another more contemporary representation from Jamaica of a higgler:

> To most visitors the market woman with her apron and tied-head, seated on her donkey, between the two paniers, which carry her goods, is the typical figure symbolizing Jamaica. Yet no more lively and pleasant figure could be seen— unless it is the same woman on foot bearing her basket on her head, perhaps full of blue and red lilies from the mountains... [At the market] the women wear bright coloured skirts and tie-heads, but generally the conventional *higgler*'s apron, a neutral colored pinafore with three pockets for copper, silver and notes. (McMillan 1957:35)

Clearly, not only was the market woman visible, but also observers were often struck by her demeanor, general comportment, and appearance. I believe that her status as the icon of black womanhood stems from this increasing visibility. Indeed, as the female peasant, she made significant economic contributions to the development of the local market. As Douglass notes, for the upper class, the higgler is the woman Jamaicans claim as their powerful matriarch. She is black, clever, assertive, and street smart. Douglass stresses that, to the white and brown elite and upper class, the higgler is actually viewed as a comical character, a caricature of woman whose reputed strength of character contrasts her actual lack of power (1992:249–250). What this image also illustrates is that the powerful matriarch (or strong black woman) is a limiting construct, an ontologically essentialist notion that rests on an ideal of strength that has been naturalized, but is informed by context. In chapter 5, I explore this point through further deconstruction of black female embodiment and performance of toughness or tuffness in local parlance.

Nonetheless, over the years, images of this trader have persisted and have undergone some changes. On Jamaica Tourist Board calendars and posters, she beckons tourists to "make it Jamaica again." She is presented at the market surrounded by baskets or behind a makeshift stall with a display of fruits, supposedly locally grown.[31] In 2004, at a Kingston tourist shop, I purchased a ceramic bank in the form of this higgler. This construct of the higgler is unchanging and ignores the contemporary impact of various global movements on the local.

In television ads, she smiles and promises would-be visitors that in Jamaica there is "no problem," or that they will be taken care of, as they will be showered with bounty. Perception of this higgler is but a continuity of historic ideas associated with African females. She is represented in the media as the national symbol of woman—a hard-working laborer. I contrast her likeness to Miss Jamaica, the beauty pageant winner who is the national symbol of lady—a person of leisure. However, one of the recent challenges to the lady/woman binary came from ICIs. It is undisputed that the economic crises of the 1980s and local-global political restructuring gave rise to this trader, who I argue occupies a seemingly liminal space between the beauty queen and the higgler as a certain kind of lady-woman.[32] ICIs represent a modern figure. As such, they contradict Jamaica's own external (tourist) image as a traditional, exotic island suspended in both time and space as symbolized by the higgler. Whereas the latter has a sense of place or belonging, the ICI is perceived as the ultimate rude gal—an in-your-face, tough, unlawful, uncompromising survivor who knows no boundaries.

Through her very existence, this trader re-created hegemonies as she disrupted orders and transgressed classed constructions of time, space, and place. Her debut occurred at a moment of time/space compression when global connections abounded with inequities and possibilities. The ICI emerged as a prime example of the incongruities in globalization. Needless to say, her entrance onto the local-global stage could not/would not be overlooked, for as Chandra Mohanty reminds us, "it is on the bodies and lives of women and girls from the Third World/South that global capitalism writes its script" (2003:235). As I have already shown, and will further demonstrate through a discussion of the ICIs' investments in beautification, Jamaican females have historically attempted their own reiteration of what is written on their bodies in ways that often fall outside the purview of capitalism's market-laden narratives. For these reasons, I liken the ICI to what Jamaican poet Louise Bennett calls a "cunny jamma oman,"[33] a quick-witted gendered agent who seeks to outmaneuver global capital by going within the cracks of multileveled structures of power that constrain her.

Enter the "Rude Gal"

Indeed, popular perceptions of the ICI as a rude gal stem from disdain towards her ability to manipulate capital and her disregard for social orders. For this, she is usually viewed as "out of place." Her business thrusts her as a consumer into spaces that are not the traditional domains of the working and lower classes. Individuals of such socioeconomic positions are often service providers. The common discourses on higglers and ICIs differ somewhat. Whereas the former are viewed as family matriarchs, the latter are perceived as bad modern women, rumored to be prostitutes, drug mules, and lesbians. There are multiple implications to being perceived as lesbians. Yet in Jamaica, as well as throughout other countries in the English-speaking Caribbean, the state operates as what M. Jacqui Alexander refers to as a heteropatriarchal apparatus that polices erotic autonomy (2006). Sexuality is not only policed by the state, which deems "homosexuality" illegal, but civilians also participate. In 1992, church pastors and parishioners alike took to the streets of Kingston with cutlasses, sticks, and bats when news broke out that gays and lesbians would hold a march. In 1997, a three-day riot broke out in a prison in Kingston when the commissioner of corrections, John Prescod, proposed the distribution of condoms to inmates to minimize the spread of HIV. At the end of the insurgence, six men were brutally killed and forty were injured. Those who were murdered are believed to have been gay.

Yet it is the antigay lyrics in dancehall that receive the most attention. Indeed, these are exemplary of larger cultural anxieties about sexuality (another marker of distinction) as a component of self-making. While these highly popular tracks often focus on males, they reaffirm and advocate an intolerance and vehement hatred for difference. I consider such sentiment another manifestation of the competitiveness, akin to what Peter J. Wilson (1973) refers to as the "crab antics," that underlies local social relations.[34] In that sense, the labeling of ICIs as lesbians is but another marker of otherness. Indeed, given Jamaica's patriarchal tendencies, the ultimate bad woman is one who is not only autonomous but also relegates men to the margins. Thus, the lesbian category not only masculinizes ICIs in their labor and class possibilities, but in their sexual desire as well. The lesbian category further marks ICIs as social pariahs. This notion of ICIs as lesbians stems partly from the fact that the majority of them are females who work together, travel together, and stay together. With the exception of their sons, most men (specifically their husbands or boyfriends) are only involved marginally in their business activities. This organization of labor is not a new phenomenon; it is one long observed among market traders in the Caribbean and the larger black diaspora.[35] Nonetheless, during the 1990s, because of their hypervisibility, these traders became stigmatized, in addition, as prostitutes and mules that transported AIDS, illegal drugs, and other commodities across their trading routes.

Indeed, especially among the younger population of traders, there are those who do earn their foreign exchange through prostitution. There are others who risk importing illegal commodities to reduce the impact of participating in a saturated market. In fact, in recent years, there are individuals who enter the trade solely for the sake of trafficking. Although these individuals are part of a growing minority, the majority of ICIs are dedicated workers. They practice their trade in an environment that is dominated by an unstable market, which requires that they work hard and be tough and resilient. Customarily, they are often heads of their households who primarily seek the autonomy of self-employment despite this business's volatile profit margin.[36] Most of the traders interviewed for this project stressed that they like to be their own boss. Ultimately, this is their primary reason for entering this trade. Furthermore, they engage in this business because they enjoy travel and the excitement of being a player (as distributors and consumers), no matter how small the scale, in the global market.

Most of the younger ICIs I encountered constructed their identities as different from higglers. Ironically, a notable number who became importers during the late 1970s were or had been local higglers or the children of higglers. They saw an economic opportunity and seized it. They became importers-exporters, taking all kinds of risks to respond to the felt needs of the Jamaican population. In 1982, when Prime Minister Edward Seaga officially labeled them "Informal Commercial Importers," a hierarchy of distinction emerged among traders. For many, this was formal recognition of their difference from more traditional higglers.[37] This title, many argued, emphasized the distinct demands of international trade over that of local marketing practices.

During the course of my research, it became quite evident that there was contestation among the ICIs I interviewed regarding their relationship to higglers and higglering. While a significant number did not object to being called higglers, or foreign higglers, many did not respond favorably at all. For others, it was an outright insult. I was swiftly reminded that "me no higgler, me an ICI."[38] Such responses were most common among younger traders, especially those who either previously worked in the formal sector or still do. In fact, this riposte was most common among lower- and middle-class participants who rejected this categorization yet secretly engage in importing to supplement their income and maintain their class position. As several ICIs quickly point out, they travel to foreign countries on a plane. They have to deal with conditions that are beyond the rural pursuits of the higgler. Furthermore, the higgler represents the peasant with its stigma of backwardness or lack of sophistication. Even her urban counterpart, the town higgler, has limited experiences in comparison to ICIs, who navigate the multisited world of international import and export and are often confronted with challenges posed by the state and big business.

As traders started to infiltrate new territories in attempts to carve out local and transnational spaces for themselves, a stereotype emerged from middle-class popular discourse of the ICI as a physically large black female who is loud, coarse, vulgar, and unsophisticated. She is often depicted wearing rather tight clothing and adorning herself in gold jewelry while lugging several large, heavy suitcases. During the mid-1980s, ICIs affinity for certain elements of hiphop culture further reinforced their working-class image. They sported the latest rude gal fashions with flaming hairpieces in bright colors (orange, blue, yellow, neons, etc.) accompanied by lots of cargo (jewelry), heavy gold chains, shackles, and anklets. Her embodiment of tuffness, coupled with the attitude and an extensive vocabulary of expletives, poised her to fight with anyone. She lies and cheats the government by not paying duties, and she overcharges her customers for the cheap wares that she imports.[39] In addition, her activities are viewed as polluting Jamaican culture. The ICI is considered a drain on the local economy. She takes hard currency abroad and floods the local market with cheap goods, allowing her to unfairly compete with established merchants.[40] Her success has allowed her to become the new nouveau riche, transcending her inherited class position.

Abroad and at home, the stereotypical ICI has been raced, classed, and gendered—perhaps all three, depending on the interlocutor.[41] I offer two examples as evidence. The first elaborates on her classed construction. The second stresses how she embodies the triumvirate. In "Learning to Love the IMF," an op-ed piece for the *New York Times* in 2000, E. M. Brown argues against the antiglobalization movement. He points to the ICI as exemplary of the democratizing power of the IMF. He writes:

> On a recent airplane flight to Jamaica, I sat next to a woman who was an informal commercial importer, or "higgler" in Jamaican parlance. She had been a housekeeper to a wealthy family, but had long dreamed of starting a dress shop. She borrowed start-up capital from an aunt in New York, and now she runs a boutique out of her home in Jamaica, selling clothes and makeup from an American discount chain to other aspiring members of the middle class. She is an unabashed social climber; she told me she had her eye on a house in her former employer's neighborhood. She is living proof that the new capitalists no longer know their place. (Brown 2000)

Several years earlier, in the 1980s, a Jamaican columnist, the late Morris Cargill, had another reaction to the ICIs' debut on the transnational stage. Upon their arrival, these traders quickly gained a reputation for their aggressive hustling in airports at home and abroad. Their presence on planes caused tensions that resulted in their being chastised in the media for their classed behavior and presentation. Cargill's commentary, one among a slew, echoed the cries of a middle-class in panic. He writes: "considering that so many Jamaican girls are slim and pretty one is bound to wonder whether higglers are the result of selective breeding." He proceeds to compare ICIs to Russian weightlifters whose fights are so brutal that none dare to intervene (Cargill, quoted in Douglass 1992:244–245).

First, let me point to Cargill's use of the term "higgler" as opposed to their official title. Over the years, in popular and official discourse, this slippage is rather common. A derogatory joke, it is a speech act that I argue continuously relegates the ICI to the margins. Since they have been brought under regulation, they are no longer "informal." I explore this issue in more detail in chapter 3. Second, Cargill's comparison of the higgler to the ideal Jamaican girl reinforces my earlier point about national ideals of beauty. The ICI is everything that the slim pretty Jamaican girl is not. They are clearly not even of the same generation. His comparison renders the ICI as woman, the lady's other. Third, this also raised a significant question about who should represent the nation, and how, abroad. Upon their ascent, popular responses to traders were framed in terms of issues of national representation. In these commentaries, ICIs were viewed as a national embarrassment who misrepresented the island when they traveled abroad. Finally, this narrative persisted and has had various effects. During the mid-1990s, when I was conducting my research, several middle- and upper-class individuals spoke of the early days when traders "did not know how to behave on planes" or "could barely fit the seats." This issue was of such grave concern that the United Vendors Association held a full-day seminar on issues of safety and behavioral patterns at the Oceana Hotel, downtown, on June 13, 1984.[42] One of the several underlying tones is that of the country bumpkin in town. Needless to say, since she came onto the scene, the ICI remained highly noticeable, unlike the higgler who now stays out of the way.

One of the consequences of this hypervisibility is that the ICI is not only "out of place," but is also perceived as not knowing her place. Knowing one's place is particularly important in Jamaica. The late prime minister Michael Manley's words complement Bourdieu's own understanding of practices of distancing to demarcate difference. He argues that class divisions are so deeply entrenched in Jamaica that only the upper strata of the society (the oligarchy and the establishment) "has certainty of place that is a highly developed, historical sense of privilege. This is often accompanied with a strong instinct for separation. To all who were below, the unspoken rule is 'keep your distance,' and 'know your place'" (1982:76–78). As the Brown editorial presupposes, the ICI's place was predetermined by history. As a former housekeeper who now has set her eyes on a house in her former employer's neighborhood, she is a threat to class order and to how elite Jamaicans would like Jamaica to be perceived in the international community.[43] She is a transgressive presence, albeit an economic one who cannot be contained. This says nothing of the social, economic, and political implications and consequences of her crossing. Brown disregards the reality of the market. The fact is that the actual number of ICIs with such success is relatively small, and the possibilities for social crossing are even more rare for those without the necessary cultural and social capital. As I show later, this stereotype of ICIs obscures the demographics of the business, yet it has become a social category on which national economic policies are continuously based.

The stereotypical ICI remains an affront to middle-class sensibilities. In truth, most of the traders I encountered at the arcade were unlike the higgler or the beauty queen. They were often far from acquiescent. Depending on the context, they were assertive, and at times highly suspicious of everyone. They have to be. Their business activities depend on their sharpness, confidence, and constant sense of self-preservation. To receive maximum respect, they must develop and maintain reputations that will deter potential offenders. On the street, in the arcade, at the airport or at customs, they must be alert. They often present themselves as tough women who have to be reckoned with to avoid being taken advantage of. As I discuss in chapter 6, this is particularly common when they travel alone. After all, their business activities take them into the world of international trade, a space dominated mostly by white men, oftentimes more educated than they are. Their primary goals are to avoid being exploited and to bring their merchandise home as cheaply as possible. At times, they accomplish this by deploying tactics that are manipulative and non-compliant. Other times, they do not. The more visible ICIs do not often fit the stereotype. In numerous cases, they actively try to counter it while at the same time use it subversively to ensure a profit. For my purposes here, I will give an example of the former by paying particular attention to ICIs' participation in what Lisa Douglass calls a "culture of femininity." Their activities, similar to those that Douglass found among the elite, serve to reinforce Simone de Beauvoir's assertion that a woman is not born, but made. In that same vein, I use this particular moment of ICIs' self-making to highlight the limits of my methodological training and how these could have further contributed to misrepresentations and constructions of traders. It took me a couple of years before I recognized that these moments were in fact the actual data I sought and not fieldwork trials as I initially thought of them.

"If It Is for Yourself, Nothing Is Too Expensive"

During late summer 1993, I experienced this beautification culture first-hand while conducting preliminary fieldwork with several ICIs. Miss Tiny, an ICI, insisted I accompany her to the hairdresser on Sundays. We arrived midmorning and remained until midafternoon. During this time, she had her hair and eyebrows done. She received a manicure and a pedicure. This beauty salon (an informal setup in someone's house) was frequented by ICIs of various ages from early twenties to fifties. During the beauty regimen, conversation revolved around the importance of grooming and taking care of oneself, the latest dance, DJs or reggae singers, men, and the foolishness of women who depend on them. The younger customers who often came in wearing the latest styles of clothing, shoes, or nail polish would turn the conversations towards fashion, or the latest fad and where to buy it. Miss Tiny, who continually expressed her dissatisfaction with my preference for baggy clothes, frequently chastised me for not getting my hair done, for wearing it out rather than pulled back in a bun, and for keeping my nails short and unpolished. While I engaged in these practices, I found them a waste of my time that was keeping me from doing "real research." I succumbed to these only because I realized, especially with Miss T., there would be no other conversation.

Soon, I started to get my hair done when I accompanied her. Then, I began to give myself manicures, with her encouragement, so my hands would "look nice and pretty." My principal objection was the amount of time that this beautification process required. At this salon, there was a consensus among the clients that we must make ourselves beautiful at any cost (this price includes time as well as money). As Miss T. always stressed, "If it is for yourself, nothing is too expensive." She would punctuate this statement with a dismissing laugh when I refuted her. Then she would restate herself, adding "ever" for emphasis. Without fail, every Sunday was grooming day (from twelve to nearly four o'clock). This process of beautification is of great significance and is central to both individual and group construction of a feminine identity, perceived sexual orientation, and economic status. It warrants further inquiry because it is not simply an investment in the making of oneself into a certain kind of female. It is evidence that this self has specific material and symbolic value, particularly in terms of the material capital spent on the beautifying process. Equally important, it is also an indicator of leisure time spent on self-making. In that vein, the beautification process echoes Stuart Hall's commentary on black diaspora cultures' use of the body as the only cultural capital we possess.

For these individuals, making oneself beautiful implied undergoing this process of getting made up—having the hair processed, getting the nails polished, and so on. This weekly ritual was important to these ICIs for several reasons. First, it is critical to self-making, as it is a direct investment in one's self-presentation. Second, these beautification processes are also a way to socially assert the femininity they have been historically denied. After all, their occupation relegates them to a public realm that requires a certain type of toughness of demeanor that is often read as natural.[44] Third, it distinguishes them from another static image of the higgler as unsophisticated, unfashionable, and cosmetically unmade (to be read also as unladylike, hence unfeminine). Both the ICI and the higgler, however, stand in sharp contrast to the lady, a figure against which the higgler has also been historically juxtaposed.

Hence, this beautification process in the salon not only reaffirms their femininity but also relocates it. Indeed, the distinction between a lady and a woman is not necessarily one of virtue, though that is implied. Rather lady and woman are class-based distinctions in self-making practices that compel the making, remaking, and even unmaking of certain classed subjectivities. Femininity, as I have shown earlier, is inextricably linked to color and class. It is a form of cultural capital that is loaded with hidden symbolic and material meanings that are predicated upon one's knowledge, access, management, and deployment of numerous resources. For working-class black females, such as the ICIs in this study, the performance of femininity entails clever manipulation of the interlocking gender, class, and color codes that have historically constrained them.

This performance is an act of self-definition that is fundamental to both U.S. black feminist thought and practice and Caribbean feminism.[45] For the former, the emphasis has been on how black females sought to reclaim the respectability they were denied. In the Caribbean region, the focus among scholars has been to explore how black females make themselves as rebels that demystified the performance of gendered norms (Mathurin 1975) or through extensive studies of strategies of economic survival (Bolles 1983, Harrison 1991a, Reddock 1998). In other cases, the focus is on the appropriation of stereotypes through subversion. Jamaican literary scholar Carolyn Cooper engages in this form of reclaiming. Her analysis of the hidden transcripts in historical oral/scribal discourses reveals another enslaved black female subjectivity (1993a). She is an agent with such awareness of the structures that impede her that she chooses to exploit her position and, in the process, claims to know no law and no sin. As I show later, this is applicable to the higgler as well as to the modern-day ICI. The continuity of the deployment of this tactic stems from their shared positions as black females who are socially marginalized and participate in a supposed peripheral economic activity.

In the examples of self-making outlined above, I emphasize both the material and symbolic components of gendered mediations of class and color codes. Historically, black females have been socially incarcerated in restrictive cultural and political-economic categories that have severely restricted the ways in which they go through the cracks. I have shown the impact of these restrictions by focusing on what facilitates their movement: capital. The different forms of capital deployed to assist in the crossings have a commonality (whether these were a madras kerchief, a pair of shoes, a fine or gaudy dress, salon-styled hair, manicures, etc.); they were all visible. Since slavery, gendered self-making practices have entailed mediation of class and color codes, which were based upon and understood primarily within the context of what is most visible: one's phenotype and appearance.

From Higglering to Informal Commercial Importing

Foreign higglers are part of a new set of survival economic adaptations to the world's emergent economic crisis for which the formal sectors are running out of conventional answers.—Carl Stone

The unchallenged trade by the higglers cannot continue—it will bury us!— Douglas Vaz

The historical development of informal commercial importing extends back to the earliest days of slavery, when the higgler emerged. The word *higgle* means to hawk or peddle provisions. This trading activity is popular throughout the entire Caribbean. Because it is so widespread, it has various names on other islands. In Jamaica, popular and colloquial use of "higgler" refers to any small-scale distributor, male or female. While this name applies to anyone who hawks, it has historically been gendered, and has a gendered connotation. In this study, I use "higgler" specifically to indicate a market trader or a middleperson who primarily distributes his or her own agricultural goods. Higglers are distinct from hawkers or vendors in that they are sellers who deal exclusively in farm provisions, locally grown or imported. The hawker or vendor trades in dry goods and/or cooked foods.

Tracing the evolution of the higgler in Jamaican history is synonymous with investigating the rise of the internal market system that developed alongside the colonial empire's extractive economy. From its emergence, higglering has been simultaneously a site of contestation and negotiation between the state and civil society (especially between the middle and upper classes), merchants and consumers, and individuals and their communities. Historically, these conflicts have arisen when the state attempts to regulate informal marketing activities that often compete with established merchants. In addition, despite ongoing tensions, higglering has proliferated. Opportunities continue to open, allowing marketers to participate in the local-global economy as they are enabled to challenge the social order. In the 1970s, other branches of higglering expanded as a significant number of new recruits infiltrated the burgeoning informal import/export market. State reaction to this growth in independent international trading not only replayed the battles of the colonial past, but also created new sites of struggles as both "space" and "place" became contested terrains.

In this chapter, I outline historical developments of independent marketing from higglering to the more recent informal commercial importing. I describe this expansion within a broader political-economic context to illustrate how interconnections between local and global relations impact participants. Hence, my intention here is not to provide a history of higglering per se, but to highlight the continuities and discontinuities in this trade and in the larger sociopolitical environment from which it stemmed. To achieve this, I divide this chapter into three parts. First, I trace the progression of higglering from its inception during slavery to its alterations after Jamaica's independence. Second, I evaluate a range of factors that influence and characterize Jamaica's contemporary market system and highlight differences and varieties among higglers. This provides a sociohistorical background that sets the stage for the arrival of ICIs. Until ICIs were given an official title, they were known interchangeably as "foreign higglers," "traveling higglers," "international higglers," or "suitcase traders." "Foreign" refers to anything abroad, in this case the location of traders' work. Finally, I outline the actual entrance of the vendors during the late 1970s and subsequent attempts by ruling Jamaican governments to regulate their activities. Foreign higglers emerged from a transnational socioeconomic field that continues to sustain their growth. Their relative success puts them in constant conflict with the state and big business. Over the years, higglers have organized in ad hoc and sometimes more formal fashion to respond to the government's efforts to control the boom in this occupation. I provide an account of one such organization, the United Vendors Association, founded in 1979 by several Garveyite Rastafari committed to black economic advancement. I conclude the chapter with a deconstruction of the paradoxes of formalization that includes a discussion of policies concerning ICIs as floating signifiers and considers the ways in which their given official title only relegated traders further to the social and political margins of Jamaican society.

Slavery/Emancipation and the Internal Market System

The British captured Xaymaca from Spain in 1655, nearly a century after they had established the Royal Africa Company to facilitate importing Africans for enslavement in the West Indian colonies. After fifty years, the native Arawak population had been wiped out—victims of the genocide so characteristic of most colonial encounters in the Caribbean. The forced migration of Africans for slaves and Europeans for indentured servitude increased the growth of sugar production. In the English Caribbean, Jamaica was the island with the largest sugar output. Production grew concomitantly with the importation of the enslaved labor force necessary to sustain this rapid growth. By 1768, the total population of the island was 187,700, of which slaves numbered 167,000, whites 17,000, and the colored and free black population, 3,700 (Heuman 1981:7).[1] To escalate the level of sugar production and maximize profits, planters implemented an arduous seasonal work cycle forcing the enslaved to labor eleven to eighteen hour days. To sustain this population at a low cost, property owners encouraged and established a food production system on their plantations.

The various causes of the enslaved's independent subsistence farming and other economic activities are topics that still fuel great debate among scholars, particularly historians. The point at which plots of land were allocated as provision grounds is contested, as are the circumstances that led to their distribution. However, many agree that planters were not overcome with humanistic or altruistic motives. Rather, as Sidney Mintz puts it, planters' decisions were simply based on "classical economic considerations of diminishing returns" (1974:192). They responded to the economic risks they faced. First, the poor quality of slaves' diet resulted in malnutrition and starvation, as well as a high mortality rate and loss of capital value as planters had to replace lost slaves (Craton 1977:2, Higman 1976:114). Allowing slaves to grow their own food on provision grounds reduced the planters' expenditures, which included importing food to feed their labor force. The imported food was supplemented with herring and saltfish, typically allotted to the enslaved.

Second, there was an abundance of land, and planters were willing to use it for provision grounds. As Jamaican topography is not wholly suitable to grow sugarcane, unprofitable plots were allocated to slaves to cultivate their aliments. On some plantations, there were "common grounds" used for the general food production for all residents of entire estates. The main provision grounds were usually located at great distances from the plantations. On the days they were granted free time for their own food production, slaves planted and tended to guinea corn, plantains, coconut, potatoes, maize, and yams. On other plantations, they also cultivated small "house plots" or "polinks" (small "garden spots" that adjoined their homes) in addition to their provision grounds. The cultivated surplus from these spots was often used for marketing purposes.[2] The provision ground system benefited planters in many ways. It was also a critical factor in the development of the enslaved population's informal economic activities, their identities, subjectivities, and consciousness as proto-peasants.

In 1662, seven years after the British took possession of the island, the first known market was established to serve free inhabitants in Spanish Town. In less than a quarter of a century, several other markets were operating. By 1720, numerous markets were established, formalized and maintained by colonial administrators throughout the island. This means that there may have been white higglers as well. However, slave higglers initially entered the market to sell their masters' goods. They were sent out to peddle wares. According to Lorna Simmonds, within the Kingston area "many female slaves seemed to have been involved almost exclusively in higglering and/or vending of some product . . . others described as domestics were hawking wares about the streets of towns for their masters, or more specifically for their mistress' benefit" (1985:5). Those employed as hawkers who were not supervised had ample opportunity to trade their own goods.

Nonetheless, details of the enslaveds' entry into the marketplace for their own exchanges are sparse.[3] Trading, however, had long existed among this population before they entered into the market proper. Some observers of these transactions noted that since they were not supervised in their own food production, the enslaved did as they wished with their surplus (Mintz 1974). Cultivators of different products engaged in exchange and redistribution with each other on their own terms. The managerial staff provided limited surveillance, and as a result they could not prevent such transactions between slaves of the same estate, or even adjacent ones (Mintz 1974). The first markets were managed by whites of the planter class to serve whites and the freed population. Eventually, the enslaved population took this system over, and, simultaneously, provision grounds and market-related activities became sites of continuous discord between the enslaved, masters, and landless whites, creating a legacy of conflict that still exists today. In fact, when slaves' food production rose, their rations were reduced and new responsibilities were piled on to cut into the time they had for marketing activities (Berlin and Morgan 1991:21).

Planters were threatened by the enslaved's entrepreneurial activities. As they became an integral part of the market, the enslaved faced greater opposition from planters and colonial administrators. On some plantations, owners prevented them from helping each other cultivate their grounds. Legislative measures were also established and enforced to restrict or prohibit their autonomous economic activities. For example, the enslaved could not participate in the market unless they carried a permit from their master-employer. To prevent them from dealing in stolen goods, restrictions were placed on the items they could sell. The provisions brought to market could only be food that they had produced. Initially, the enslaved were allowed to sell provisions such as fruits, fresh milk, poultry, and other small livestock. Certain provisions were perceived as implicit determinants of one's status. According to Mintz, "a slave with a carcass of beef was, prima facie, guilty of having slaughtered his owner's cattle" (1974:198). However, in the mid-1700s, the provisions the enslaved took to the market had expanded to include fish, poultry, pigs, and goats, and they not only traded, but also exchanged these for cash. As higglers became increasingly important to the local market, attempts to regulate their activities often were unsuccessful (Simmonds 1985:10).

The failure of the colonial authorities' attempts to regulate the enslaved's participation in the Sunday market resulted in the latter's domination of this venue. By the eighteenth century, an extensive market system emerged that was operated mostly by slaves. Throughout the island, market practices differed depending on the contrasting pattern of division of labor in rural and urban areas. In rural settings, where males and females worked as field hands, market activities were family oriented. Men, women, and children cultivated provision grounds and house plots. Since everyone participated in subsistence activities, it is very likely that they also performed specific market tasks. In towns, subjugated females served as domestics, cooks, nursemaids, and nannies, whereas males served as bakers, caulkers, carpenters, masons, silversmiths, and brick makers (Simmonds 1985:2–3). Many of them were taken away from their trade and sent to earn income for their owners. Urban slaves or freed people attended the market as customers, artisans, traders, and distributors. In that context, Simmonds asserts, rural slave higglers became an important link between the provision cultivator and the urban consumer:

> They facilitated the distribution of a wide variety of imports, local products and provision grounds during their time off... The rural female slave higglers provided the chief means by which the rural slave population was able to acquire the necessary and desired supplements to the basics provided by their owners, and some urban slaves were able to obtain the entire means for subsistence independent of their owners. (1985:8)

At times, among the enslaved, rural higglers actually held a monopoly on the supply of provisions sold to urban dwellers. This elicited serious complaints from whites, documented in journals and bulletins about the practices of higglers, because they controlled and increased prices of country provisions whenever they saw fit (Simmonds 1985:8).

As the market took on new importance to the enslaved, they participated with a fervor that caught the attention of many visitors to the island who recorded them in their travelogues.[4] For the enslaved population, the market had a variety of social meanings. It was a gathering place where they made contact with family and friends and found entertainment; the meeting at the market was also their opportunity for exchanging information. Hence, it is not surprising that rural dwellers walked as many as twenty-five miles carrying goods on their heads to attend the town Sunday market. During the later periods of slavery, this market was so well integrated into the Jamaican economy that it supplied meats, vegetables, and fruits to the enslaved population as well as to the freed population and whites. With the money earned, they bought food, clothing, furniture, tobacco, and other consumer goods. Sometimes, this income also helped defray the cost of manumission for themselves or their kin.[5] It has been estimated that by the late eighteenth century (around 1770) nearly 20 percent of the capital circulating in the island of Jamaica was actually owned by the enslaved (Mintz 1974:199). Marketing activities by this population became so essential to the stability of the island that some stringent laws restricting slaves' mobility were actually relaxed for Sunday marketing activities, with masters granting slaves permission to participate in markets even during the most tense times (Momsen 1988:218).

As Mintz notes, the provision grounds and independent economy were a social contradiction to the institution of slavery that was advantageous to both parties, but especially to planters because they reduced the

likelihood of rebellion or maroonage (Price 1996). Hence, they represented a "temporary solution" in this system of exploitation.[6] The material and psychosocial importance of slaves' higglering activities made
provision grounds paramount in emancipation debates, especially since
these grounds were arguably the property of those who tended them.
That is, they were treated as private and inheritable property, property
the enslaved could will to their children. In some cases, they were even
reimbursed when the properties were sold.[7] Unsurprisingly, during the
four-year apprenticeship[8] period, which followed the abolition of slavery,
house plots and provision grounds were crucial issues in negotiations
between the newly freed population and the former masters, who were
desperate for laborers. Many of the former masters used these grounds in
various ways to exploit the freedmen and freedwomen, who had become
dependent on the provisions they cultivated and their participation in the
internal market system. Former masters charged high rents, paid relatively
low wages for labor, and offered exploitative contracts (Bolland 1993)
that in many ways kept the new freedmen and freedwomen socioeconom-
ically enslaved.

After full emancipation on August 1, 1838, the newly freed population
faced a dilemma given the aforementioned factors and the insecurity
of land tenure from planters. Many were forced to seek other opportunities away from the estates where they had been enslaved (Bolland
1993). In other cases, many remained on plantations and negotiated with
planters to maintain access to their provision grounds (Besson 2002,
Marshall 1985, Scott 1985). Sheller elaborates on this: "There is evidence that
ex-slaves were attached to their houses, gardens and provision grounds,
which in many cases had valuable mature trees or ripening crops, not to
mention burial places of their ancestors" (1998:115). While free villages
continued to be established, primarily by Baptist missionaries, squatting,
especially on Crown lands, became a pervasive practice among the landless freed who were determined to acquire property (Besson 2002:89–93).
During this time, the small-farm sector grew rapidly. At the end of the apprenticeship period, planters charged exorbitant rents to the newly freed
population in order to extract labor from them (Holt 1992:107). At times,
they demanded double the rent from those who did not work on the property. In other cases, entire households, including women and children,
were charged rent for use of the provision grounds (Holt 1992, Morrissey
1989, Sheller 1998). In that sense, women were doubly exploited on the
basis of their race and gender. The newly freed departed from the larger

estates.[9] "They started small farms on the peripheries of plantation areas, wherever they could find land" (Marshall 1985:2). By the first year of the official census (1844), 80 percent of the island's workforce was engaged in agriculture (Eisner 1961). As these activities increased, so did divisions and patterns of labor.

Towards Independence: Specialized Higglering

By the middle of the nineteenth century, Jamaica was in a state of social transition and economic upheaval. The Apprenticeship Act had expired in 1838, and the decline of sugar production had influenced the plantation labor system.[10] Facing labor shortages and needing to keep wages down, planters, with the aid of the colonial administration, began to conscript and lure greater numbers of indentured laborers from India, Java, and China.[11] Since the late seventeenth century, several other groups of immigrants had also arrived on the island. These included Jewish and Lebanese/Syrian[12] immigrants who arrived initially as traders and quickly amassed capital and became merchants.[13] By the turn of the century, the number of East Indians had surpassed the population of whites; soon, the Chinese population became more numerous than the white population.

With this increased competition for work, dire socioeconomic conditions, and a limited definition of freedom, tensions arose between the newly freed population and the planter class. According to Jamaican historian Swithin Wilmott, one of the key issues causing the strain was the newly freed population's lack of access to ownership of property (1993). Owning land has historically been central to both legal and social concepts of citizenship (Maurer 2000). The denial of land and civil rights eventually resulted in insurrections and riots that brought black and brown populations together throughout the island and in other parts of the region. The most documented of these was the 1865 Paul Bogle insurrection (Robotham 1985). At issue was land. According to Woodville K. Marshall, "insecurity of land tenure, as well as relatively low wages for plantation labour, sometimes high rents, and low contracts reinforced many ex-slaves' determination to seek new and better opportunities away from estates" (1985:3). Squatting, especially near old provision grounds, continued to be rampant. Consequently, so did small farming, which caused rapid growth of the peasantry, increased petty trading activities, and heightened the "visibility" of females in the market place.

The issue of the visibility of females in the marketplace during this period ought to be viewed in relation to a series of dire socioeconomic conditions resulting from emancipation. The increasing role of Jamaican females in their household economy is due, in part, to the relative absence of a permanent male partner's income and the fact that female dominance of market activities is one of the Africanisms retained in the New World.[14] Indeed, during the mid to late nineteenth century, the Jamaican population had a higher number of females than males. This was the case even during slavery. The gap increased and contributed to the persistent gendering of the trade. Women's domination of the market was due to changes in the occupational structure, internal migration patterns due to urbanization (Edwards 1980), and external migration, among other factors. Men left the island in search of better wages and greater opportunities.[15] This migration trend is endemic to the region. Its roots can be traced back to the nineteenth century, when laborers migrated intraregionally to find better work. Decreased demand for skilled and unskilled laborers, both rural and urban, forced Jamaicans to move to other countries, where they became service workers.[16] Migration patterns reflect waves of travel to countries where employment opportunities and wages were greater and the work was temporary and would allow households to maintain their provision grounds or plots. During the 1950s, many men migrated to Panama, where wages on the Panama Railway were three times the earnings in Jamaica (McLean Petras 1988:68–70). This mass migration had other effects including a disproportionately high number of female-headed households. Furthermore, fewer opportunities for market-based employment of men on the island made a second dependable income in the home more important.

In her Ph.D. dissertation, "Role and Status of Rural Jamaican Women: Higglering and Mothering," based on research conducted in St. Mary during the 1970s, anthropologist Victoria Durant-Gonzalez found a direct correlation between women choosing higglering and men lacking employment. She writes:

> Economic pressures, combined with the lack of job opportunity and the familial role of mother, are influences that lead to higglering. These factors are so patterned among higglers that they can serve as a model for phasing into higglering and continuing to pursue this occupation. This model can be stated as the need for cash income, the lack of permanent work for men, limited job options open to women with limited salable skills, and children to provide for. (1976:172)

Nearly two decades later, sociologist Elsie Le Franc arrived at the same findings. She notes, "one of the more important reasons for the entry of women into higglering has indeed been the uncertainty and even absence of the economic contribution of a male partner... for a very long time higglering has had to substitute for, rather than simply supplement the male breadwinner's contribution" (1989:116). This also reinforces the lady/woman trope, as women are seen to take on the masculine role as well, thereby further distancing them from the femininity associated with ladies. This emphasis on one's income, the broadening of one's social base, and that sense of independence continue to keep this occupation popular among females. Another factor is that even in conjugal unions, females in the Caribbean have historically retained considerable autonomy, especially over economic matters. Thus, it wasn't surprising that this activity experienced a boom. According to Gisela Eisner, by the late nineteenth and early twentieth centuries, the number of petty traders/higglers increased rapidly. In 1861, there were 437 documented petty traders; by 1921, that number had increased to 4,164.[17]

At the turn of the twentieth century, as market trading activities surged, economic independence and social recognition continued to elude the poor black masses. They had little or no access to basic needs and resources and no possibilities for social mobility. Many aspects of their life conditions were similar to slavery. They were marginal and desperate. Their need for racial and class consciousness and socioeconomic and political independence was articulated by Marcus Garvey. In 1914, Garvey founded the Universal Negro Improvement Association (UNIA). Initially, the UNIA was a social welfare organization that sought to raise funds, feed the poor, and provide social services to the needy (Martin 1991). In 1916, the UNIA left Jamaica and relocated in New York. There it emerged as an international movement concerned with terminating the global exploitation of blacks and reuniting the black diaspora. Stressing the importance of self-reliance, Garvey advocated economic and social independence of peoples of African descent in the New World and repatriation to Africa. Under his motto "One Aim, One God, One Destiny," he mobilized masses of the black diaspora to participate in numerous economic activities. In 1928, Garvey returned to Jamaica with a more explicit black nationalist agenda. He formed the People's Political Party (PPP) and started a daily newspaper, *The Blackman*. His efforts failed under the colonial administration's pressures. According to Carl Stone, Garvey's emphasis on race contested the multiracial, nonethnic nationalism that was being professed by the new order of privileged ethnic minorities: mainly the Jews, browns, Chinese, and Lebanese (Stone 1991). He was seen as subversive to this power structure and was labeled a "dangerous element" that threatened the seeming unity of the island as propagated by the middle and upper classes. Garvey was eventually driven out of Jamaica for stirring up racial/color tensions.

Several years later, Garvey's efforts were validated in the labor riots of 1938, which echoed the cries of the 1865 rebellion led by Paul Bogle. The riots eventually resulted in changes to local political structures. It was out of this popular movement that Jamaica's two main political parties were formed. The two key figures were Alexander Bustamante and his cousin Norman Manley. After travels to Cuba, Panama, and the U.S., Bustamante returned home and established himself as a private moneylender. As such, he became aware of the abject poverty that plagued his nation. This prompted him to eventually become a fierce union organizer. Norman Manley was a Rhodes scholar and, at the time, Jamaica's leading lawyer. His interests were in promoting social and economic developments locally; he was not interested in politics (Post 1978). In the aftermath of the 1938 labor rebellion, he began to work on the formation of a political party concerned with the working class. The PNP was inaugurated with Bustamante, then a leading trade unionist at the platform, as a member of the party. In their own ways, they were strong leaders who agitated for the rights of the masses. After Bustamante formed the first trade union in Jamaica, tensions increased between the two leaders. Eventually, the labor organizer broke from the People's National Party (PNP) and founded the Jamaica Labour Party (JLP). Thus did the two government parties that continue to dominate Jamaican politics come to be. Both played significant roles in turning colonial authorities' attention to the desperate conditions of the masses. However, the relationship between these middle-class leaders and the masses foreshadows the character of their governments' relations with the majority population.

Between 1944 and 1962, throughout the transfer of power from the colonial administration to local politicians, a system of state clientelism emerged that propelled and sustained the dominant middle-class party leaders.[18] Across the social structure, party leaders manipulated resources and formulated a patron-client relationship with voters. This clientelism was a male-dominated system in which both the client and the patron were male, making policies and state initiatives patriarchal in character.

The middle class used clientelism as a mechanism to control and demobilize the lower classes, which had to seek advantages through clientelist structures (Edie 1991:20). With the elite and upper classes, this relationship manifested differently. However, among the poor, a vote cast for the right candidate could result in employment, food, bureaucratic favors, and help in time of crisis. At this time, the economic disparity was quite high, as 57 percent of the population was considered poor. For the black masses who occupied the lowest rung of the socioeconomic ladder, this interdependency was unviable. Only a limited number of them had access to education, which was the primary vehicle for social mobility.[19] With these restricted opportunities and no state advocate to turn to and no reliable welfare system, economic independence was a necessity.

For lower-class females, employment was even more crucial, as they headed over a third of all households in the country (Clarke 1957, Powell 1986, Momsen 1988). Higglering was one of the occupations that allowed them to maintain a livelihood. Erna Brodber confirmed this trend in her collection of life histories of Jamaican females at the turn of the twentieth century. An outstanding figure in her research was Mother Brown, who was born in 1861 and died in 1973. Mother Brown was a small farmer who cultivated yams, potatoes, and cassava on a plot of land with her mother. As she grew older, her own daughter took over management. Her family lived in Devon for generations. From there, they took provisions to the Mandeville market, leaving home on Fridays and staying over on Saturdays until they completed their sales. The women in Mother Brown's household had all different types of relationships with men. However, these men played only a peripheral role in their economic lives (Brodber 1986:30). According to Powell, "women do not separate earning an income from other aspects of their lives. Recent studies have shown that a woman's ability to provide for herself and her children is closely linked to her perceptions of her own worth and the esteem in which she is held by her community as both a mother and a woman" (1986:83). Even when men are present in their households, the women still consider the children their primary responsibility. Those who participate in higglering do so to replace the absent family wage of the male breadwinner and to fulfill societal expectations of their gender.

As an occupation, higglering had undergone few changes in the earlier parts of the twentieth century. The first two studies by anthropologists on higglering have contributed to our understanding of several aspects of the trade and its participants. The first study, by Margaret Katzin (1960), entailed a classification system of traders. Based on research conducted in Mandeville during the mid-1950s, her methods may be dated, as they sought to create a taxonomy and had limited social analysis. However, her typologies point to the specialization in higglering. She distinguished between urban and rural higglers mainly on the basis of residential location and the source of the goods they distributed:

A. Rural Residents

1. *Country People*; women who sell produce grown by someone in their own households.
2. *Weekend Country Higglers;* women from areas within 25 miles of Kingston, who buy wholesale in Coronation and sell there at retail.
3. *Country Higglers;* women who buy produce from growers near their rural homes and sell it in Coronation.
4. *Planter Higglers* or *Speculators;* mostly men who may grow part of their stock, but differ from country higglers principally because they cover wider distances to buy a large quantity of one commodity and transport it a greater distance, often over 50 miles, to market.

B. Kingston Residents.

1. *Tray Girls;* women who carry their total stock on a tray or flat basket.
2. *Weekend Town Higglers;* women who buy wholesale in Coronation and sell there at retail on Thursdays, Fridays and Saturdays.
3. *Town Higglers;* women who rent market stalls for which they pay a weekly fee that entitles them to sell at any time the market is open.
4. *Vendors;* town higglers who rent several stalls and specialize in one item, such as tomatoes. (Katzin 1960:298)

Twenty years later, Durant-Gonzalez (1976) came up with the following typology, in which the source of goods resurfaces as the primary criterion and the marketing location, both social and physical, of the buyer becomes irrelevant. She also pays particular attention to gender:

1. Farmer vendor—sells produce from her own or her husband's farm.
2. Farmer higgler—sells produce from other farms as well as her own.
3. Country higgler—only buys and sells, resides in the rural areas; comes to town during market days to sell her provisions.

4. Town higgler—only buys and sells, is a resident in the towns, and operates only within the towns.
5. Seller of locally manufactured goods.

Durant-Gonzales's typologies, though rigid, highlight how higglering, as a system or network of distribution, continues to be heterogeneous and complex and involves different groups of individuals who participate in various aspects of this network at different stages. Katzin's system of classification is particularly illuminating, as it considers both the position and location of participants from which one could infer subjectivities, since higglering has always been a class-specific phenomenon. More recently, several development-oriented studies have also created higgler profiles that include more personal demographics on participants. From these we learned that the local or traditional higgler is usually a rural female of African descent between the ages of twenty-nine and forty-nine who has achieved only a relatively low level of education, probably about three years of primary school.[20] Below is a profile of a town higgler from my own research conducted in 1993. This example highlights a particular higgler who fits into both of the classification systems noted above. She is a town resident who rents a stall in the market, where she sells the goods she buys from farmer higglers.

Miss J. is in her late forties. She is a town higgler (as defined by Katzin) who lives in Gordon Town (in the parish of St. Andrew) and orders her produce from country people in Trelawny. When she receives the goods she pays wholesale for them. She learned about the trade as a child, when she accompanied her grandmother, who was a higgler, to the market every weekend. Miss J. decided to become a higgler because "it was the best thing to try to do" to help out her family. She knew she would always make money in it. She has been a higgler for twenty years and had been in Papine for nineteen of those years. She used to sell outside of Papine, but the rain and constant thievery eventually forced her to obtain a space inside the market. Rental spaces are usually hard to come by, as family members pass these on to relatives. Papine market has nearly sixty stations. She pays a market fee weekly and taxes on the ground provisions she brings to market. She likes setting her own prices and being her own boss. The money she makes, she says, "really help[s] me with the kids."

Since meeting her in 1993, I have bought produce from Miss J. whenever I am in Jamaica. When I returned in 1995, she introduced me to her daughter, Miss E., who began to take over her business when Miss J. fell ill. Starting in 1995, the daughter began to accompany Miss J. to the market several times a week. Miss J. tends to customers while her daughter takes care of the money. Unlike her mother, who calculates in her head, Miss E. uses her calculator. Her daughter has completed both her primary and secondary education. Now in her early twenties, she is currently at a professional school learning a trade (accounting). She will inevitably replace Miss J., as the family depends on this income for subsistence, to finance the children's education, and for other expenses.[21] More importantly, eventually, she will inherit her mother's business as well as the stall at Papine market.

The empirical studies cited above, as well as my own research, confirm some of these earlier findings. In addition, these studies focused on the role of social networks in higglering, and I will discuss this important issue in greater detail in chapter 6. In the late 1950s, Katzin observed that higglers spend a great deal of time maintaining contact with customers. "Customer" is used here to refer to anyone she trades with, from the farmer trader to the servant or the lady who purchases her produce at the market. The actual business transaction lasts a short while; the rest of the time is spent adhering to local social expectations of politeness. Katzin describes such an encounter: "her supplier came to the gate . . . they chatted while the supplier selected and reaped the vegetables. Miss A. always kept her suppliers informed about the latest news in her own neighborhood and in Kingston. Her progress was slow because she stopped at the yard of everyone who had ever sold to her, even though she knew that some of them had nothing to offer at the moment, for she wanted to remind them that she would buy from them whenever they did have anything. Along the way she stopped to greet and chat with everyone she met" (1959:424–25).

Katzin found that higglering depends on a series of social networks in part because both higglers and consumers are dispensable. Indeed, there is always someone else to buy from or sell to. This is one of the reasons that customers often form bonds with the particular vendors they buy from consistently. Two decades later, Durant-Gonzalez's work would reconfirm Katzin's point. She maintained that the custom between traders and consumers is "You buy from me and I sell to you" or "You didn't buy from me, I won't sell to you" (1985:197). So buyers and sellers work to maintain the ties that assure their symbiotic economic activities. Among the newer traders, these social ties are particularly fragile. As I discuss in the next chapter, these loose bonds are also the result of a saturated market, which has radically increased competition.

Since the 1970s, higglering, within the Greater Kingston Metropolitan area, has become an even more specialized occupation (Le Franc 1989). Not only have several different types of traders disappeared and new ones emerged, but also the scale of business and type of activity have changed considerably among different groups of local vendors. During the 1980s Elsie Le Franc created her own list.[22] She notes that the more traditional higglers, that is, the farmer-vendors and farmer higglers, are a declining minority, while town higglers are increasing. Nonetheless, higglers in markets are still largely rural based, though fewer are involved in actual farming activities (1989:104). Now, these traders acquire their goods from farmer higglers, as illustrated in the profile of Miss J., or from wholesalers of imported goods on the Kingston wharf. The disappearance of the more conventional higgler is the result of several factors including a decline in agricultural production and a generational shift away from farming.[23] As I discuss later, these changes were exacerbated by interdependent global and local socioeconomic and political trends. Indeed, the most substantial change that occurred in this occupation in the latter part of the twentieth century was the emergence of international higglering. The increased growth of this branch of the trade and the hypervisibility of its practitioners eventually resulted in state regulation. It is undisputed that the PNP's attempt at socioeconomic decolonization, the global energy crisis of the 1970s, and local responses to these events intersected to give rise to this new group of independent international traders.

Politics of Change: Enter the Suitcase Trader

Globally, the 1970s were a turbulent time. In the aftermath of the Yom Kippur War (1973), OPEC overtly exercised its control over the price of oil to shock the industrialized West into recognizing its power. The embargo had lasting socioeconomic ramifications throughout the world. The Caribbean region was no exception. At this time, Jamaica was a relatively young nation, having gained its independence from Britain in 1962. During the early 1970s, the local economy reflected the impact of two decades of sustained growth. Jamaica had entered the bauxite market in the 1950s and soon became the world's leading exporter of this mineral. In addition, tourism was booming, though the industry was mostly foreign owned. With both incentives and support from the state, a local manufacturing sector developed (furniture, footwear, metal products, food, chemicals, and garments) that was heavily dependent on imported raw materials. Similarly, consumption patterns were mostly import based (Stone 1980:27). It was during this period of industrialization that Jamaica's trading patterns shifted from a British to a United States market.[24] The economy grew steadily between 1950 and 1962 at an average annual rate of 7.5 percent; from 1962 to 1968 by 5.1 percent; and from 1968 to 1973 by 6.1 percent (Levitt 1991:11). Postindependence Jamaica was experiencing a period of consistent growth. However, those who profited from the growth were the old plantocracy and the new elite.

With this rapid economic expansion came simultaneous shifts in the socioeconomic structure that only increased the economic disparity among the various strata of the population. Before independence, the social structure and labor force were rigidly coded by race, with few exceptions. British whites, local whites, or other persons with light complexions usually held top administrative and managerial positions within the private sector and government (Edie 1991, Henriques [1953] 1968, Nettleford 1972). Disenfranchised browns and blacks were dissatisfied with this order. Thus, one of the motives behind the state's movement towards industrialization was to establish national (local upper-class) ownership of industries (Edie 1991:39). With this project, new work opportunities in industry emerged along with a growing civil service and politics that facilitated the social mobility of browns and blacks. Now blacks had access to the ladder of mobility. Many among them had been educated in Britain as part of the first wave of migration to the metropole. As domestic spaces opened up for managers and administrators, they had the social and cultural capital to assume these positions.

Simultaneously, between 1962 and 1972, unemployment continued to rise from 12 percent to 24 percent. For youths and females, unemployment was well over 30 percent.[25] Modernization meant expansion of the bauxite industry, which eroded farming and forced rural residents to migrate to Kingston. These rural migrants were unable to find work in the capital city and became part of the surplus population of unemployed or underemployed who found opportunity in the informal sector.[26] The impoverished, dire conditions of population density and other socioeconomic factors generated what several scholars characterize as the ghettoization of certain parts of Kingston. In contrast, middle- and upper-class living standards flourished. As a result of this disparity, and the tensions between downtown ghetto dwellers and uptown suburbanites in Kingston, the crime and violence fueled by poverty became endemic. But the exaggerated economic disparity also gave rise to new forms of livelihood based on various degrees of hustling (from the petty to the fatal). This form of survival became a socioeconomic way of life, soon politicized, and constantly influenced the current racial/class/spatial order of Kingston. Within these confinements, alternative lifestyles emerged concomitant with subcultures in the downtown areas. Many aspects of these alternate lifestyles and subcultures revolved around what Jamaican economist Michael Witter (1977) calls a "hustling economy," including informal and sometimes illegal economic activities.[27] As life conditions worsened and crime rates rose, the opposition party (the People's National Party) diverged radically from the ruling party, the Jamaica Labour Party (JLP) and turned its focus away from economic growth and toward alleviation of the mass poverty and uplifting of the nation.

In 1972, the PNP came to power promising deliverance to the suffering black masses under the slogans of "Better Must Come" and "Power for the People." When it took office, the PNP government, led by Michael Manley, started redressing the socioeconomic imbalances caused by Jamaica's history as a dependent capitalist nation. There were several components to the PNP's plan. First, the party designed an anti-imperialist domestic policy independent of foreign control and responsive to the local majority. Second, the PNP plan promoted egalitarianism by expanding the number of opportunities available to the masses. Third, the approach was democratic socialist aimed at enhancing mass participation by changing the relationship between the state and its people. Finally, the policy celebrated Jamaica's African roots by promoting popular rediscovery of, and reinforcement of, black pride (Manley 1982:39).

The PNP's domestic policies included establishing a minimum wage and taking control of the import and export of goods and the outflow of income.[28] While these policies and programs were being implemented, the PNP introduced a number of "people programmes" and significant social reforms focusing on education, economic empowerment, and housing and land leasing that targeted benefits to youths, the landless, the rural poor, and others. Eventually, in 1974, the PNP was compelled to articulate a democratic socialist ideology. The government attempted to nationalize or "Jamaicanize" the economy; it also challenged the colonial system of local consumption patterns, which was highly dependent on imports (Stephens and Stephens 1986). Manley called on the people, especially the middle and upper classes, to curb what he referred to as their "felt needs" for foreign goods and to learn to appreciate local food and clothing to promote expansion of local production. To reinforce trade restrictions, the party eventually established a list of banned goods[29] that could not be imported to the island.

Manley and the PNP also began to advocate women's rights. Though females were not initially identified as a special interest group by the PNP, by 1973 the party had become increasingly committed to gender-specific issues.[30] Until then, there had been no legislation specific to females. The PNP addressed gender inequity in its policies by establishing a Women's Bureau, although it remained peripheral to the central administration.[31] This bureau became quite active in 1975, when it was transferred to the Prime Minister's Office and generated a number of gender-sensitive legislative initiatives and social programs even before the United Nations declaration of the Decade for Women (1975–1985). These initiatives included women's crisis centers and a Special Employment Program (SEP) of which women were the major beneficiaries. In addition, day care centers facilitated women's entry into the labor force, and the poor received both free uniforms for primary school students as well as meals from the School Feeding Programme. All socioeconomic classes benefited from free secondary and university education. Before these reforms, employers could dismiss workers without compensation. As a result of PNP policy, however, this was no longer permitted. The Equal Pay Act, the Status of Children Act, the National Minimum Wage Act, and the Social Security Programme Act, passed between 1973 and 1976, were attempts to alleviate the socioeconomic hardships of the lowest classes.[32]

These programs, while necessary to achieve socioeconomic equity and a just society, only drained national budgets. According to Norman Girvan, by 1976, the economy was under siege. "The Balance on service payments deteriorated (collapse of tourism), net transfers fell, official capital inflow fell and private capital flows turned negative as capital flight took place. The Bank of Jamaica lost $238 M in reserve funds and basically ran out of foreign exchange. On the fiscal side ... expenditure ballooned while revenue stayed flat in an election year marked by political violence, disinvestment and capital flight" (1998:4). Nonetheless, in December 1976, the PNP was reelected by a wide margin. Its fierce anti-imperialist campaign, echoing the spirit of resistance coming from other third world nations, was best articulated in Manley's famous "we are not for sale, we know where we are going" speech. In this defiant address, the prime minister eloquently expressed the frustration fermenting in third world nations all over the globe. He gave voice to a people's exasperation as a so-called postcolonial nation incarcerated by the continuities of neocolonialism. These were manifested in binding socioeconomic relations that uphold the divide between Western superpowers and the rest of the world. In taking this very public stand, the PNP was determined to take a third path.

In its insolent critique of neocolonialism, every topic was discussed. The PNP administration even addressed the issue of appearance as it considered dress as a form of resistance to imperialism. The party adopted various Rastafari dress codes that further enlisted support from the masses (Waters 1985). Manley himself pointed to the colonizing aspects of the three-piece suit, which is the preferred form of professional dress for Caribbean officials and dignitaries. He advocated the use of Kareba suits and the Cuban guayabera shirt (known in Jamaica as a bush jacket) instead. The prime minister's appeal for a decolonized mode of dress on the island deserves to be quoted at length:

> If you live in a tropical country that has acquired the jacket and tie as a style of dress that is not suited to your climate, you have made a number of unconscious concessions. First of all you own a style of dress, which is not suited to your climate. This is the first act of psychological surrender since common sense should dictate that the style of dress should reflect the reality of the physical environment. Further the fact that you did not question the relevance of another man's style of dress to your physical environment is a confession of a paralysis of judgment. Third, where the style of dress is inherently expensive, you have placed a strain upon the ability of your society to create external symbols of egalitarianism. Fourth, where the style of dress has become associated with the status symbols of class and the escape from economic reality through white collar syndrome, you have inhibited your own ability to identify reality and placed yet another psychological obstacle in the path of a realistic pursuit of your own social and economic possibilities. (Manley 1974:66)

Manley's multilevel analysis points to the broad and in-depth aspects of the aim of the PNP's project. I return to this in the last chapter.

With this new emphasis on socialism and anti-imperialism, the PNP formed a new friendship with Cuba. The alignment with Cuba, coupled with the implementation of socialist-oriented policies, led the U.S. and the international community to ostracize Jamaica. More local turmoil ensued. Multinational corporations, factories, and garment firms left Jamaica for even cheaper labor in countries such as Mexico and Haiti.[33]

Manley's socialist initiative not only alienated the U.S. and countries under its influence, but also caused mass migration of the local merchant class and professionals, who had easier access to foreign visas. They were conflicted about this new Jamaica, and many felt they did/could not belong. Thus, the island suffered massive capital flight and reduced levels of foreign investments.[34]

By this time, the global economy was in grave recession. In Jamaica, inflation soared as unemployment rose. According to economist Kari Polanyi Levitt, "The two oil shocks, the reaction of the private sector (local and foreign) to the PNP's socialist rhetoric and the realities of redistribution populist policies" had ramifications (Levitt 1991:18); six months later, as bauxite companies continued to cut back on production, the PNP's attempt to secure greater "Jamaicanization" of the economy slowly led the country directly into the arms of the IMF. The conditions of Structural Adjustment Loans (SALs) were contradictory to the PNP's socialist ideology and undermined the party's earlier attempts at reforms. Jamaica failed its performance test six months after the first agreement was signed. To gain eligibility for additional foreign loans, drastic economic readjustments were required. A 37.5 percent devaluation of the local currency was mandated, price controls—which had alleviated the effect of inflation on the very poor—were lifted, wage ceilings were imposed, and indirect taxes resulted in rising inflation and real wage decline. The PNP government could barely keep up with these IMF-imposed restrictions. Government expenditures increased slightly while revenue plunged due to declines in tourism, sugar, and bauxite earnings (Stephens and Stephens 1986:111). Within three years, Jamaica failed three more IMF performance tests. More adjustments were demanded. The economy failed to respond to these measures and continued to decline (Levitt 1991:24). Since the government had rejected IMF mandates such as devaluation, removal of restrictions on foreign trade, and economic liberalization, in 1979, the IMF suspended its agreement with Jamaica. Indeed, as many have argued, international lending agencies' development efforts are not designed to benefit the receiving country; rather, these are primarily focused on recirculation of the borrowed capital (Escobar 1995).

Prior to the oil crisis and Manley's social democratic policies, employment had been less than scarce for females.[35] As businesses and shops closed, manufacturing companies fled and female unemployment rose. Sweatshop employees lost their jobs; most of them, uneducated and without other marketable skills, turned to foreign higglering.[36] Poor urban females felt the impact of the structural adjustment programs. As their need for income intensified, self-employment was seen as the only survival strategy; it was the only social welfare net. The PNP's restriction on imports and the collapse of local industries had resulted in severe shortages. These shortages were exacerbated by the practice of removing merchandise from shelves and waiting for price increases before putting the items out again. In other cases, customers could purchase certain goods only in tandem with another less popular item, a practice referred to as "marrying goods." As there was an open market for foreign goods, unemployed females, many already active in independent trading, responded to consumer demands. Jamaica became an international provision ground as higglers exported produce such as thyme, scallions, june plums, and guineps, primarily to Cayman and Panama, where they sold these to earn foreign exchange. With this currency they purchased foodstuffs, like cereal and canned goods, or such articles as bric-a-brac, dry goods, and haberdashery. They imported these items to Jamaica, supplying consumers with items that were gone from the shelves of local stores and shops (Reid 1989:40). The flights to Cayman became known as "onion runs" because foreign higglers would import large amounts of this vegetable from the island (Taylor 1988:2). Among the items exported were manufactured goods such as T-shirts, reggae music tapes, rum, and Jamaican foods like water crackers, ackee, and Jamaican cheese. In turn, they imported household items, and eventually clothing and footwear, as well as status symbols like small appliances into Jamaica.

The foreign higglers identified, and traveled to, accessible destinations where there was demand for Jamaican products and the merchandise they sought was cheapest. Cayman was chosen as no visa was required and the airfare was relatively inexpensive. Visas for Curacao and Panama were not difficult to obtain, and purchases in Panama were duty free because of the free trade zone. There, they purchased clothing, shoes, cosmetics, and some household appliances. Haiti was a starting point, a trial run, especially for new recruits who traveled in groups and tested their skills (McFarlane-Gregory and Ruddock-Kelly 1993:3). In countries where they did not speak the language, they employed an interpreter who met them upon arrival and negotiated their prices. This individual often received an additional cut from business owners at the end of the day. Flights to their countries of destination throughout the region, were full of traders on their import-export missions. As their numbers grew rapidly, the sidewalks surrounding the main shopping areas downtown were loaded with the scarce goods that had disappeared from shops and supermarkets. In many instances, foreign higglers boldly squatted at the door of these nearly empty stores to sell their wares. In other cases, established businesses bought from these higglers and/or even sponsored their trips to replenish their stock.

To sell their goods, these traveling higglers surged uptown to more affluent areas "to set up makeshift display and storage stalls in the shopping plazas . . . [that] became known as 'bend down' plazas, a reference to the fact that customers must bend down to examine the goods for sale" (Taylor 1988:3). While the established business sector cried out and the upper classes (of civil society) expressed their anxieties and annoyance at the streets being blocked, the PNP government (looked on and) ignored these activities. Indeed, it was in no position to address this group of entrepreneurs who exemplified the PNP's self-reliance dictum. Foreign higglers were breaking the law that stipulated an annual J$500.00 limit on importing goods for personal consumption. According to Alicia Taylor, the PNP's disregard of the expansion of foreign higglering was likely to incur the wrath of its vocal lower-class supporters (1988:3). However, it must be noted that these traders' activities simultaneously contradicted and promoted the PNP's commitment to national self-reliance and economic independence, outlined in its Emergency Production Plan (EPP).[37] The entrepreneurial spirit of the foreign higglers was synonymous with the ruling party's aim, yet the independence they achieved required them to promulgate one of the most crippling legacies of colonialism, an import-based economy.

As the state passively looked on, this activity became more popular and salient. Teachers, insurance agents, managers, and others took personal flights abroad to purchase items they would retail back home in Jamaica. The pervasiveness and continuity of foreign higglering at this time is due to a series of historical factors. Marketing activities had been institutionalized in Jamaican everyday life; they involved mass populations, which the state could not service, and, as in the past, these new traders also provided products and a service to others that maintained social stability. Nonetheless, considering the extent and scale of the business, the more established business community became increasingly aggravated. Foreign higglering, like the provision ground system, which provided a temporary truce between slave and planter during slavery, aided the government. Suitcase trading, in a sense, replaced the government's social welfare system at a time of massive economic and social crisis. As the standard of living reached a level nearly 45 percent lower than during the 1970s, the established business community roared as foreign higglers became their fierce competitors. In response to these demands, the PNP did what governments often do; it appointed a committee to research the problem.

Neoliberalism: Regulating the Trade

As a result of trade deficits, Jamaica was near bankruptcy. With the economy in a slump, a third of the population out of work, and tense social conditions, Manley called elections a year ahead of schedule. While the PNP offered the nation a "non-IMF path," the opposition party—the JLP—promised "deliverance" and "equal rights and justice." The 1980 election was one of the bloodiest in Jamaica's history, with a politically motivated death toll between 980 and 1,000 (Stephens and Stephens 1986, Gaunst 1995). The JLP won the election by a landslide by pledging to steer the economy away from its previous "communist" path. It planned to achieve this through privatization, by liberalizing the economy, and by deregulating the export industry.

The new prime minister, Edward Seaga, called on the United States to assist Jamaica. In response, the U.S. proposed a recovery program in the Caribbean Basin Initiative (CBI)[38] and loans from international agencies. In 1981, the new government turned to the IMF, which recommended the country reduce its public spending, increase exports, deregulate foreign production, privatize state enterprises, and assess additional taxation. The government complied. However, despite drastic attempts to attract, and to appease the fear of, potential foreign donors, Jamaica could not entice these corporations to return; their attention was already focused elsewhere.

In 1983, the country failed yet another IMF test, but it had been granted other multilateral and bilateral loans from the World Bank, the IDB, and USAID with minimal conditions and even shorter strings attached. Economist Kari Levitt notes: "import controls were lifted and there was a surge of consumer goods and raw material imports, creating an artificial import-led, debt-fed expansion" (Levitt 1991:14). Local manufacturing declined as foreign higglering continued to boom. For example, footwear production dropped by 75.5 percent between 1976 and 1985. Garment manufacturing also decreased by 1987; there were less than 20 factories operating compared to 127 a decade before. The established business community continued to protest, demanding state control of foreign higglering. The political and economic power of this group, joined with other factors, such as international monetary loan conditions and local concern with street congestion, spurred the JLP to react.

Seaga, also the minister of finance and planning at the time, was proactive. He took a measure to the House of Representatives, asking that a no-funds import license be issued to foreign higglers. With a no-funds license, ICIs could not obtain foreign exchange from banks. This license, which was purported to remove obstacles that traders faced when importing their goods (the state-related logistics of moving goods), proved to be another challenge. These licenses differed from those allocated to established formal businesses, which required them to pay to import goods for commercial purposes and gave licensees automatic access to foreign currency at formal institutions. In December 1981, the government issued this licensing system, prepared by the Revenue Board. It was to take effect the following year. The goal was to register all foreign higglers alphabetically throughout the island by the end of December 1982. To obtain this license, traveling higglers had to present a passport, a registration certificate or letter of advice issued by the Revenue Board the previous year, customs duty receipts or import duties as determined from records of the Collector General, and an income tax reference number. Also, all back taxes on earlier importing activities had to be paid. The formalization process had begun.

As the Minister of Industry and Commerce, the Honorable Douglas Vaz, stressed (see epigraph to this chapter), foreign higglering was taking a serious toll on the business sector. Local manufacturing and commercial industries had never faced such fierce competition. Something had to be done. The licensing system went into effect on February 22, 1982. Any ICI who traveled after that date was expected to be licensed and to follow the new procedure to clear imports through customs. Imports had to be packed in locked containers that would be held at the Queen's Warehouse (of the Norman Manley International Airport) pending clearance. Duties would be assessed and, with proper documents, ICIs could collect their goods. Those who failed to follow these rules would be fined three times the value of their merchandise.

In November 1982, the State Revenue Board bestowed the official title of Informal Commercial Importer (ICI) on foreign higglers. The year 1983 marks the point when state regulation of foreign higglering began to be both consistently and aggressively enforced. Upon the arrival of ICIs at both airports, customs officers confiscated imports and held them until the importers paid the duties charged. The government also began to crack down on the trade by enlisting the police to seize vendors' merchandise and to remove them from the streets and storefronts. The Ministry of Local Government delegated this problem to the Urban Development Center, which oversees parks and markets throughout the island. Their primary concern was to satisfy all parties (established merchants, civil society, and the ICIs) and to relocate the growing number of ICIs. Their solution was to build an arcade especially for traders who congested Kingston streets. "Cities are mobile places and places of mobility" (Sheller and Urry 2006a:1), and ICIs interrupted downtown Kingston's metabolic flow. They were seen as impediments that arrested traffic, the transportation system, and the general stream of street activities. Their "unsightly" piles and makeshift stalls disordered the city's landscape, and the government maintained that consistent action would be taken to organize their activities in an orderly fashion.

Soon after, the government announced another measure. ICIs would now have legal access to an annual quota of foreign exchange. This was in response to vendors' complaints that they were restricted as smaller businesspersons. When the program was announced, it was documented in the *Gleaner* that ICIs under this new system would be able to secure funds at the parallel market rate from the commercial banks to make purchases (*Gleaner* 1983a). At this time, foreign currency was difficult to obtain. Noncommercial access to foreign exchange was limited to J$50 per individual annually at a rate of exchange of J$1.78 Jamaican dollar per US$1.

In addition, import quotas were introduced and assigned only to licensed ICIs by the Revenue Board. These had a monetary value of US $1,000–5,000 and permitted ICIs to import specific merchandise for an initial period of six months; this was the amount that an ICI could receive in foreign exchange for the entire year. The following is a list of permitted items issued by the trade administrator: burglar alarms, buttons, studs, press fasteners, balloons, cereals, cornflakes, Christmas tree decorations, cutlery, cameras, clocks, flowers (artificial), flashlights, fabric upholstery, footwear for children and women except sandals, hooks and eyes, hair clippers, hair dryers, laundry blue soap, lace edgings, lamp wicks, lawnmowers, locks and keys, mechanical lighters, manicure sets, vehicle parts (except brakes, filters, clutches, and radiators), nipples for bottles, needles, pins, pens (except ball point), pencils, powder puffs, radio receivers, citizen's band radios (license required from postmaster general), razors, steel wool, sporting equipment, scissors (tailors, dressmakers, others), sequins, tulle (lace), table glassware, umbrellas, wigs, and clothing accessories.[39] At the end of the six-month period, each ICI's case would be reviewed and new quotas would be issued. The total amount allotted to individuals was based on past records of importing, that is, on the duty paid by the ICIs over a period of time.

While this new licensing system offered some benefits for traders, there were just as many restrictions and hindrances. Needless to say, when the licensing deadline arrived (December 1982), only 1,768 vendors had registered on the island. This number was lower than the number of participants selling goods on streets throughout the Greater Kingston Metropolitan area and in other parishes in the country. Traders were rightly wary. The government had identified and was now focused on them as a new source of revenue. In the process, their business activities were being severely curtailed. The foreign exchange and import quotas, as well as the list of allowable import items, infringed upon ICIs' versatile buying practices and had the potential to undermine their markets. When ICIs began to import in the 1970s, it was in direct response to market demand. This new regulation sought to limit ICIs' ability to go through the existing cracks and threatened to crush their businesses.

As with most issues in Jamaica, this battle occurred in the public media, such as talk radio and newspapers. Newspaper columnists such as Carl Stone, Dawn Ritch, and Carl Wint took stands for or against this activity, which they viewed as a necessary strategy of the poor, a public nuisance, and a parasitic practice that disrupted the local socioeconomic order. *Gleaner* columnist Jennifer Ffrench's editorial on this issue, titled "Frustrating the Higgler," exposed the class conflict underlying this debate. She deserves to be quoted at length:

> If anyone had any doubts about the Government's policy towards higglers, now christened "Informal Commercial Importers" (ICIs) these should have been put to rest by what took place last week. When the Revenue Board can issue quotas for goods valued as low as $1000 for six months and on top of that eliminate many of the quick for profit items which the higglers used to sell, one must wonder if the intention is not, at first, to frustrate them and then force them out of business. Three weeks ago Industry and Commerce Minister indicated at a press briefing that the Government was "formalizing higglers", but little did anyone, in particular the higgler, suspect that this formalisation would be tantamount to virtually phasing them out of the system, which is where things seem to be heading. Whoever heard of higglers selling cameras and lawnmowers, not

to mention motor vehicle parts and citizen band radios? These are some of the items listed for their quotas, while ladies sandals and garments, which comprise a large part of the current sales of higglers have been excluded from the list of 48 items, which they are being allowed to import. (Ffrench 1983)

Her analysis detailed the impact that government regulation would have on this activity and its participants. She pointed to the impractical list of items vendors were now legally allowed to import, noting that the size of vendor stalls in the newly built arcade could not accommodate most of these. She concluded her piece by stating that the government must find another way to ensure that they balance their responses to demands from various interest groups in the society so that "everyone gets a chance to live. When all is said and done, the higglers certainly deserve that chance." This was a direct reference to the government's preferential treatment of big business. Then Ffrench asked the ultimate question: was the government's real intention to force ICIs out of the importing business?

Indeed, numerous vendors complained to their organizations that the process was hindering them from expanding and in some cases continuing their activities. They felt that they were being penalized for their previous informal importing activities. Records of the United Vendors Association document the experiences of several foreign higglers who explained how they were literally trapped into paying back taxes. According to these individuals, during their visits to the Collector General to obtain the recommendation letter, they were lured into conversation about their work in the trade. At the end of the conversation, they were told they owed a certain amount in revenue on the basis of their past activities. Most vendors stated they could not afford this. The UVA noted that only vendors with enough capital could pay their back duty in order to gain the legal license and remain in the business. The only option for others was to continue to operate illegally; some 40 percent of the ICIs in a 1990 sample were unregistered (Abbensetts 1990).

This new registration and licensing system was limiting, as it was intended to be. According to Seaga, those who had not paid past import duties were not eligible for the import license. Indeed, not all of the traveling higglers could register since they could not meet all the requirements of the law. This created more distinctions between traders who could afford to register and those who could not and therefore operated outside of the legal system. The government claimed this system would safeguard the activities of traders, as "goods will no longer be seized provided the imports are within the limits of the quota and do not include restricted items" (Revenue Board commissioner Canute Miller, quoted in *Gleaner* 1983b).

ICIs had found advocates among members of the Chamber of Commerce and intellectuals at the University of the West Indies, Mona campus. Their voices coupled with the outcry and mobilization of their organizations and ICIs' civil disobedience protests resulted in a small victory for traders. On June 21, 1983, the Ministry of Industry and Commerce announced it would no longer be issuing import quotas.

In September 1983, the first arcade built especially to accommodate the removal of dry goods vendors from the streets opened its doors. This arcade provided space for 580 ICIs. The *Star*, the *Gleaner's* evening edition, actually referred to these stalls as chicken coops. The government promised to build more arcades. In addition, mini-markets would also be built for food vendors who had taken to the streets along with ICIs. Makeshift food markets of shacks and stalls had sprung up all over the city. The minister of local government, Alva Ross, declared that he would clean up the area and bring this practice under control. The JLP administration remained persistent in achieving this goal. Early in 1984, the government declared that additional duties on imported goods would be imposed. In 1985, Metropolitan Parks and Markets, a subsidiary of the Urban Development Center, was created and directed by the Ministry of Local Government. The purpose of this agency was to monitor street vending and manage existing markets and the new arcades designated for ICIs. In 1986, the Constant Spring Arcade was built and provided spaces for 300 uptown traders. That same year, arsonists burned the first arcade. It was rebuilt in 1987 and renamed the Pearnel Charles arcade. Later that same year, an income tax number and national insurance number were required to obtain the newly issued business enterprise number (BENO). The activities of ICIs were being severely limited.[40] In the years that followed, more restrictions and policies were instituted, forcing traders to confront the state in innovative ways.

By the end of the JLP's second term in 1989, informal commercial importing had been as fully integrated into the economy as such activities can be. The management of informal economies is just another component of neoliberal globalization; it is necessary to pave the way for international funding institutions (Dupuy 2006). While on the one hand governments profess the well-meaning intent of their policies, on the other hand their actual effects only further impinge upon and constrict the lives of the poor, resulting in greater socioeconomic instability. According to economist James Bovard (1987), throughout the JLP's tenure in Parliament, the prime minister preached free enterprise, in accordance with international standards, while his government pursued rigorous interventions that increased state control of the Jamaican economy. From 1980 onwards, the government bought an oil refinery, hotels, and an aluminum melting plant, and created numerous state farms. The administration also interfered in various sectors of the economy and raised taxes to their highest level ever. One of these new taxes was a J$25,000 fee for the issuance of a shop operator's license and a shop operator agency permit. Bovard characterizes this period in Jamaica's history as yet another failed attempt at state-directed economic development. More specifically, Bovard emphasized the impact some of these measures had on the creation of small businesses, which he argued create far more new jobs than their large competitors (1987). Indeed, according to Stephens and Stephens, from both social and political perspectives, employment was the most crucial failure of this administration. More specifically, they note:

> In his 1981 budget speech, Seaga proclaimed his goal of creating 100,000 jobs over a period of three years.... However, after a decline from an annual average level of 27.3 per cent in 1980 to 25.9 per cent in 1981, unemployment increased again to an average of 27.4 per cent in 1982. In October 1982, unemployment stood at 27.9 per cent of the labor force, the second highest level ever recorded in Jamaica. In addition, under-employment grew as the percentage of employed people who worked less than 33 hours a week increased from 14.9 per cent in October 1980 to 19.4 per cent in October 1981 and 21.4 per cent in October 1982. (1986:262)

For the business of informal commercial importing, the unemployment crisis meant a flood of new recruits from across the social structure, especially from the middle class. Despite consistent government regulation, the trade served as a buffer against the realities of inflation. Importing allowed newcomers to "make a life" or "make do."[41] As I elaborate in the next chapter, policies affect traders unevenly. Middle- and upper-class traders who import informally often went unnoticed, while stereotyped lower-class ICIs were hypervisible. Inevitably, with increasing and continuous policies toward state regulation, ICIs' confrontations with government escalated. Traders needed official representation rather than ad hoc allies to address these restricting measures.

Traders Organize: United Vendors Association

The UVA was established at the end of PNP laissez-faire administrative policies toward foreign higglers and the commencement of the JLP's formalization process. According to UVA records:

> This association, which represents all categories of vendors (not just ICIs) was founded in the year 1979 in the midst of severe pressure from the businesses community (traditional) who continually attacked vendors on the basis of selling illegal goods of which they had no proof. This forced government to launch a campaign to remove vendors from the streets. The reasons given were that vendors were blocking the sidewalks, and KSAC [Kingston St. Andrew Corporation] backed by the police was used to intimidate and harass vendors to remove them from the sidewalks. The vendors maintained that due to the grave unemployment situation, they had no other alternative but to continue to sell on the sidewalks as no provision was being made for alternative accommodation. Many stalls were destroyed by the KSAC on more than one occasion. It was during this crisis that some vendors along with Ras Historian came together and had their first meeting in the Park and the UVA was inaugurated. Between 1979–1981 vendors under the leadership of the UVA were able to restrain both past and present administrations from unilaterally removing vendors from the sidewalks without providing alternative accommodation, since vendors were alleviating a burden off the shoulders of the government by providing their own employment. (UVA 1986a)

Sixty-one vendors were present at the meeting where members settled on a name for the organization, We the People United Vendors Association. They also decided on a formal structure and held an election for officers. There was a clear gender division of labor within the organization, as male vendors were nominated and accepted top stations, while females were named to the remaining secretarial and treasurer positions. The UVA, as it became known, was quite specific about its main goal. According to then acting chair Brother Neville Smith, "We are trying to get ourselves together to stand up for a better life, as vendors" (UVA 1980:4:2). To achieve their aim, they came up with the following objectives:

· Protect the interest of vendors and defend their rights;
· Organise vendors into a united body;
· Promote mutual respect among vendors;

- Negotiate on behalf of vendors, with all relevant authorities in all matters affecting and/or concerning vendors;
- Explore more profitable markets locally and abroad; and
- Develop and organise vendors into one cooperative movement in the areas of exports and imports.

Knowing the character of local politics, they established a strict rule to further ensure that the organization would maintain a nonpartisan stance, declaring that "no member is allowed to use the platform of this association to support, attract, or sympathise with any political party or to act in, or make any speech on behalf or in a partisan political way" (UVA 1982:10:12). In addition, between 1982 and 1985, the UVA ran an extensive popular education campaign specifically to address issues of partisan politics within the organization. In the beginning, vendors were concerned that the organization become and remain legitimately recognized by government so that it could indeed intervene and negotiate with the state and other relevant organizations on their behalf. As the UVA became legal, the organization was in a position to formally represent traders and to respond to various policies. It played a particularly significant role on the question of relocating ICIs. During its first decade, the UVA was quite active. It met regularly with vendors and mediated meetings, and initiated relationships with state officials, business leaders, and established businesses that sought to aid this new group of entrepreneurs. Without an office, the organization held its meetings at the Kingston Parish Church on King Street or in Coke Hall on Parade and Church Street. Members took minutes and documented attendance, which was often greater during tense times. Every three years elections were held, and new officers took office, although the gender hierarchy more or less remained.

The UVA was the source of information dissemination for all vendors. It provided ICIs with letters to obtain foreign exchange; it corresponded with various ministries concerning policies; it was in contact with embassies and airlines in attempts to pave the way and remove some of the obstacles impeding ICIs from carrying out their activities. The organization sought to be more than just an advocate for vendors. It was active in the community as well, organizing social events and making donations to homes for children and the elderly as well as sponsoring shows in its efforts to "promote the socio-economic well being of all vendors and their families." To achieve its goal, the UVA took an unrelenting approach to engage with government on any issues concerning ICIs.

While this may have been its goal, it is evident that during the 1980s, the ruling JLP party consistently rebuffed the UVA as it attempted to formally represent the interests of ICIs. UVA minutes and records also document a series of unanswered letters to government ministries as well as officials who failed to show up for planned meetings. Officials showed little regard for UVA input on the occasions when they met and were at the table. Nonetheless, it was in part, the organization's persistence that led to the government's relocation of ICIs to arcades as opposed to the complete removal of vendors from the streets. These newly built structures, however, caused problems of their own (from leaking that caused damage to vendors' goods to unsanitary conditions and lack of security).[42] Also, in the UVA's attempts to keep its business activities nonpartisan, they objected to the arcade being named after a PNP official.

While the government marginalized the UVA, this organization was being pursued by a series of businesses (such as airlines, customs clearing houses, insurance companies, travel agencies and others) that stood to capitalize on the impending expansion of this industry. Also, Sameer Younis, the president of the Chamber of Commerce at that time, was an advocate who attempted to recognize and engage this group. These interactions highlight the contentious character of the relationship between ICIs and the government, as they emphasize ICIs' (and their representatives') lack of power vis-à-vis the state. Thus, they were often at the mercy of the state apparatus that constrained and in some ways determined their businesses.

Policies as Floating Signifiers

Government policies concerning ICIs from that era are best viewed as what white French anthropologist Claude Levi-Strauss (1950) was the first to refer to as floating signifiers; that is, they have no meaning without context. Like race, which is not rooted in biology but is a social construct, these policies were sociolegal constructions. In many instances, they were not officially documented. As such, they were fluid and highly dependent on context, i.e., the government in power and the moment in time. Despite their multiple signification, however, it is imperative to note that these policies also had, and continue to have, both symbolic and material consequences. Materially, regulatory measures affect ICIs' economic decisions and their overall business potential. Their tax burden is very real and impacts their daily lives. I discuss the symbolic effects below particularly in reference to how the term "informal" in their official title serves to permanently socially incarcerate them. Ministries and other government-operated offices will hardly admit to possessing policies, let alone allow access to physical documentation that is supposedly public information.

From 1992 to 2004, I sought tangible copies of policies in the same manner that I sought to conquer all aspects of my actual fieldwork processes, but to no avail. Every time I tried, the process was the same. I would call the ministries or government offices and proceed to ask for information on ICI-related policies. The person on the line would send me to someone else, who in turn would send me elsewhere, and so on. The same thing happened when I went to the offices. When I was lucky, I would be pointed to the information office and allowed access to the library. On file, there was a study or two conducted by consultants for the purpose of relocating street vendors or studying informal economies. Depending on the office, the latter were often listed, but not available, or researchers and officers still employed treated these as their private property[43] and regulated who received access to such information. I often found myself engaged in a scavenger hunt for documentation. The redundancy of this process over a decade of conducting this research made me realize that accessing the actual policies in many ways was insignificant. Rather, from a sociocultural point of view, the fact that they were difficult to obtain is more noteworthy. Policies, it seems, exist in a virtual world. This reinforces my claim about their inconsistency, in terms of both their existence and their application.

The capriciousness of government regarding policies has turned the media, especially print media, into the most reliable source of state-related documentation. Indeed, as is evident below, more information has been published in the *Gleaner* than is accessible from clerks at ministries. This lack of transparency, in a sense, allows for the signifier (in this case, the policies) to not only have multiple referents, but also, regardless of their discursive fluidity, to continue to have drastic impact on the lives of those they target and contact. It is for this reason that I propose that ICIs occupy a subcategory as flexible citizens, to use Aihwa Ong's term. Ong uses this term to refer to "the strategies and effects of mobile managers, technocrats, and professionals seeking to both circumvent and benefit from different nation-state regimes by selecting different sites for investments, work, and family relocation" (1999:112). In other words, it is a concept that refers "to the cultural logics of capitalist accumulation, travel, and displacement that induce subjects to respond fluidly and opportunistically to changing political-economic conditions" (1999:6). I depart from Ong, however, and use her term to bring attention to the fluidity of ICIs' citizenship within their nation rather than as a transnational phenomenon. In doing so, my aim is to emphasize the fact that their status as Jamaican citizens is one that is in constant fluctuation. This is emblematic of their dialectic interactions with the state, which is more or less parasitic. Indeed, while they pay exorbitant taxes, unlike established businesspersons, they receive none of the recognition that comes with being incorporated into national fiscal policy. In that sense, they are not accorded full citizenship at home. This is possible because of the lack of transparency concerning policies, which allows the state (regardless of the party in power) to use the revenue collected from ICIs in multiple ways. As I show in the following chapter, policies may be fixed in their nonexistent discursive form, but their actual implementation is in fact quite the opposite. They are disproportionately applied to certain traders more than others, rendering the question of the informality of Informal Commercial Importers redundant.

An Official Paradox

The term "informal commercial importing" has been something of a paradox since it was first uttered by government officials. It is, in part, for this reason that the Jamaica Chamber of Commerce took an interest in ICIs. After all, they were being incorporated into national policies and their activities contributed tremendously to the Jamaican economy. As the JLP administration sought to formalize traders, ICIs found advocates among several established members of the formal sector who admired them for their entrepreneurial spirit and untrained business savvy. With increasing outcry from traders and their advocates, on September 8, 1983, an article appeared in the *Gleaner* that sided with ICIs and pointed to the JLP's deliberate efforts to pressure these new entrepreneurs out of the trade (Erskine 1983:1). A day later, Jamaica House issued a two-page statement from Prime Minister Edward Seaga defending his policies and responding to the article. He declared that the purpose of the formalization of foreign higglers was to give them status as small businesspeople who no longer operated on the fringes of the economy. Seaga wrote, "An article appeared in Thursday's *Gleaner* titled 'Government's treatment of ICIs irks

Businessmen' which reveals a lack of up to date information on the subject which requires that I should repeat here information which has been made public from time to time on Government's policy with regard to professionalizing various types of activities in the small business sector." Seaga stressed, "The program of transforming certain types of higglering into a more professional operation in place of the often illegitimate, sometimes rowdy, and frequently disorganized activities which have been the pattern until recently, has been under my personal supervision as part of the overall policy of raising the level of recognition of small business activity" (1983:1). While the prime minister argued that this policy was designed to regulate an economic activity that was out of control, both his rhetoric and the government's subsequent actions clearly point to efforts to domesticate the unruly foreign higglers. Similar to attempts by masters and planters during slavery and its aftermath, the racial/spatial order was being demarcated to keep everyone in their place.

The prime minister recapitulated the conditions and cracks of the old system that higglers went through. Then he outlined the actual measures taken by his government to redress this situation. This is one of the most detailed official statements concerning policies on ICIs ever made public. I reprint most of it here. According to the prime minister,

> under the former system, higglers:
> 1.) operated without licenses;
> 2.) imported goods, which were prohibited for which they were fined and the goods later released to them;
> 3.) practiced wide-scale under-valuing of imports;
> 4.) jammed the passenger arrival lounge at the airports with goods in large quantities, which should have been handled as freight;
> 5.) sold goods on the sidewalks in an unsightly and disorganised market place which scarred the face of the city with shacks and other undesirable structures.

After a period of re-organisation, the following measures were instituted which have considerably changed the pattern of operation of higglering. The measures included the designation of higglers as Informal Commercial Importers (ICIs) in keeping with their new status of operation as small business people working on a more orderly and business like basis:

> i.) An amount was earmarked for the issue of import quotas against which licenses are now issued to ICIs based on funds, which they obtain on the

parallel market. The quota determined on the basis of previous levels of trading as established by customs receipts, with a minimum amount for first time traders or those who did not have adequate records.

ii.) Only goods which are normally importable can now be imported. Imports which are illegal can no longer be imported.

iii.) All goods on arrival are placed in special iron containers at the airport designed for the purpose and having two locks. These containers are transferred to the Queen's warehouse in another section of the airport and another appointment given to the ICIs to attend and clear the containers which are then stripped by Customs just as in the case of goods arriving for imports by major importers, contrary to the views expressed in the article.

iv.) This has minimized the under-invoicing of goods and has facilitated the correct levels of import duties. This has not been possible under the heavy pressure which customs officers had to endure while attempting to value and clear higgler imports along with normal passenger baggage under the previous disorderly system.

v.) A tax is levied on each ICI based on the size of their quota issued and evidence of tax receipts must be tendered and taxes paid on previous sales, before new quotas are issued. There are no exceptions to this rule. Because quotas are based on levels of import duties, the temptation to under quote the value of goods to reduce the payment of import duties is also minimized.

vi.) A more orderly system of sales has now been instituted for ICIs in place of the unsightly rag-tag system on the main streets in downtown Kingston by the erection of the new market place for their activity.

vii.) The system is not yet working to the full extent desired but the results so far are very heartening and satisfying on all sides. As a consequence, these hard working persevering small traders are no longer operating on the fringe of the economy, and sometimes illegally, but have been given status, recognition and a rightful role as small business people capable of operating in a professional manner.

The prime minister concluded with a warning message to those in the formal sector siding with traders: "The lesson to be learned from this is that these small traders, who have had in the past to push and shove their way to deriving benefits and getting recognition, can now be much more *organised and disciplined*, then other elements of the business community should take note of their responsiveness in asking themselves the question whether they are as responsive to good order in the proper conduct of business affairs" (ibid. 16) (my italics).

As the JLP administration's policies were to professionalize small traders so they no longer operated on the "fringes of the economy", it is evident this plan was implemented rather successfully. This brings up a crucial question about the "informality" of the Informal Commercial Importer. It has been stated that "informal" is a reference to the fact that it began as an illegal activity. In 2004, the commissioner of customs noted, "The informality is because they are nomads of sorts, without a permanent establishment." This does not explain why this term continues to apply to traders who occupy stalls in an arcade, which gives them a fixed location.

However, from the 1980s onwards, ICIs have been slowly incorporated into national fiscal policies and are now fully integrated in the economy. Most traders I interviewed noted that the new title gave them respect, especially as it distinguished them from the higgler and made them into "professionals." I believe this label has also had some negative consequences for ICIs. It obscured the fact that "informal" traders remained stigmatized for the conditions that gave rise to the trade, especially given the fact that they were so heavily regulated. This term also obscures ICIs' contributions to the national economy and the broader market and social stability. The consequences of this marginality are explored in later chapters. First, it must be noted that the execution of policies was uneven and had a differential impact, especially on ICIs who fit the stereotype and were easily recognized. Thus, the government's regulation measures were exclusionary, as they applied only to visible ICIs, creating a bureaucratic abyss. This is just another example of capitalism's key concern, captured in the phrase "what the traffic will bear." Government heavily taxes a group of "flexible citizens" who have limited political power at the levels of policy making and implementation and virtually no representation.

CHAPTER THREE

Caribbean Alter(ed)*natives*: An Auto-Ethnographic Quilt[1]

Me don't want to talk. ... I don't want to talk to you! I'm in a book already. —Miss Tiny

Once we pluralize the native, the category itself becomes untenable and the savage slot becomes open to deconstruction. —Michel-Rolph Trouillot

Expectations Here and There

... A nd when the "native" subjects have talked to one too many researchers, they know. They know that, despite good intentions, ethnographers arrive to collect information and stories about their lives, which will be reorganized and interpreted in a document with which the ethnographers will build their careers. It is a document that various scholars, who seek to "reinvent," "decolonize," or "recapture" anthropology, claim has the potential to intellectually, socially, and politically incarcerate subjects within yet another "savage slot," because anthropology depends on it.[2] My purpose here as both "native" and "ethnographer" (to use disciplinary terms) is to situate myself on the margins and write critically against that structure.

When I returned to Jamaica to begin dissertation fieldwork in October 1995, I was reluctant to meet with the United Vendors Association (UVA) officials and the traders I had come to know over the years, because I had told them I would return early the previous spring. I was unable to do so because of funding complications that delayed my departure. The primary trader in the project was surprised to see me.

"Me didn't think you'd come," she said.

"But I told you I would. I told you I would get a grant and come back to do this work," I replied. She did not hold it against me, but I was aware that she expected that I, like the white researchers she experienced before me, would not keep my word.

When I first began my conversations with the UVA officials, they pointedly asked me for money. This demand was eventually changed into a request to make a monetary contribution to the association. Since I had planned to volunteer my time and administrative skills, I offered them instead. I did not want to do a direct monetary exchange for a story; I was concerned about what kind of information money could buy. These officials quickly reminded me of previous researchers: "them never write, or come back or send the thesis like they say they will." The trader who I had the most contact with during earlier fieldwork made it very clear to me that she did not want to be part of my research since she was already in a book. After several visits and kept promises, she changed her mind.

I had to confront the fact that the traders and UVA organizers, as well as the government officials I interviewed, had a particular understanding of the social relationship between researcher and subjects. Indeed, one too many consultants, graduate students, and undergraduate students had come through the arcades, taken their stories, and told them they would come back, but never returned. Over time, a lack of trust inhered in these relationships. This mistrust had a profound impact on my work, because it determined the quality, and even the quantity, of data collected from narratives and field observations as well as the documents to which I was given access.[3] Based on previous interactions with foreign researchers, no one expected to see the end product of the research to which they contributed. But even more, this mistrust indicated their belief that the academy does not value, or even consider, researchers' relationships with subjects. Rather, in the cases when these relationships continue, it is primarily due to considerable commitment and effort on the part of the individual researcher. In the Kingston case, ICIs noted continual exploitative experiences by local and foreign researchers. Given numerous state-funded, development-oriented studies that yielded no tangible results, ICIs also critically understood institutional politics. Their complex knowledge resulted in deployments of agency by subjects in ways that Caribbean ethnography has yet to acknowledge.

Perhaps nothing asserts this agency more poignantly than this chapter's epigraph from Miss Tiny. It not only indicates the coevalness,[4] to use Johannes Fabian's term, that she (as subject) and I (as researcher) share;

it also shows how our coevalness compresses within the space we inhabit. In that sense as subjects, we coexist on the same temporal and spatial planes. Miss Tiny's initial reluctance was due to the fact that she was already in a book and, along with several other traders whom I interviewed, had been studied by others. At my insistence that she is but a chapter in that other book as opposed to the subject of a whole book, which I hope to write some time later, she proceeded to elaborate on the reasons for her disinterest.

"I don't want to talk about mi business because mi in a book already. I don't need another book." She enunciated every letter of every single word. Over the years, I learned that such articulation was an indication of her getting cross. "You no understand Jamaican?" she teased me, and then continued. "The book is sellin' everywhere, you know. I see it at the airport in Miami, in New York, Toronto."

"Even in Michigan," I added.

"But mi no get nothing. Mi no get no money."

In defense of the writer I responded, "I don't think anyone else gets anything, Miss Tiny. Everyone else in the book would have to get something, not just you ... "

To that, Miss Tiny laughed.

Later, I inferred that she knew very well that there would be no financial compensation for her contribution. Yet she wanted me to know that she knows what happens with the work. Perhaps she wanted it clear between us that she did not need me as much as I needed her. And she never lets me forget this. This moment pointed to my dependency (as a researcher) on Miss Tiny, which created complex fieldwork dynamics that feminist anthropologists have been grappling with in their attempts to write culture against the discipline's hegemony.[5] The body of work by Zora Neale Hurston notwithstanding, it is only recently that Caribbean feminist ethnographers have begun to engage with this concern (Simmonds 2001, Slocum 2001).

My purpose in this chapter is to make an auto-ethnographic quilt that tells a nonlinear, polyrhythmic story. This quilt is made out of a series of reflections to position myself in relation to my fieldwork mediations and negotiations in Kingston and Ann Arbor to highlight the complexities inherent in the categories of native and native ethnographer, which were bestowed upon me. To achieve this, I will de-essentialize the black female subject by pointing to how, as with the ICIs, differences in my experiences varied on the basis of gender, class, color, age, marital status, maternity, and nationality. This will show that the subjects, St. Clair Drake's black folks who inhabit here and there, are in fact what Trouillot considers symbolic and material products (Drake 1991, Trouillot 1991). In so doing, my aim is simply to pluralize the native and to embark upon a deconstruction of the "savage slot," as Trouillot challenges ethnographers to do.

Destroying the Savage Slot

On October 2, 1995, I arrived in Kingston for my dissertation fieldwork. I descended from the plane wearing makeup (which I don't normally wear), dressed in a crisp, white linen shirt purchased from Banana Republic, a year-old pair of sage linen pants purchased from Garnet Hill, with a new pair of khaki suede Adidas sneakers. My posture bent by the weight of my well-worn Coach briefcase, which was stuffed with my wallet (large enough to carry a passport and an airline ticket), a vinyl case containing twenty-four of my favorite CDs, files of correspondence from the African Caribbean Institute of Jamaica and the Inter-American Foundation, and letters of introduction from the University of Michigan's anthropology department. My carry-on was filled mostly with books, including one on natural healing for women. It also had a bottle of Dr. Bach's rescue remedy (homeopathic flower essences), another bottle of stress relief aromatherapy, and a duty-free bag (containing Chanel Vamp lipstick and nail polish a medium-sized Jean Paul Gaultier perfume, and a small bottle of Gap Earth perfumes).

By this time, I had been to Kingston enough times to be well acquainted with the layout of the airport. I waited in line for an immigration officer, who gave me a two-week visitor stamp. Then I identified a porter to find my baggage. I was pushing my heaping cart of suitcases to get in line for customs when the airport exploded with screams of joy, loud stomping, pretend gun salute ("Pow! pow! buyaka, buyaka!"—verbal mimicry of gunshots that are usually done at dancehall sessions by the attendees to express satisfaction with performers) and high-fives. Several of the porters and the passengers were slapping the walls. Almost everyone was rejoicing: airport workers, returnees, Informal Commercial Importers, young, old, men and women of different classes in various types of apparel. I turned around, trying to determine the cause of this excitement. My heart was pounding against the wall of my chest, as I had no idea what was happening or why. I noticed that I was among only a few, including the white people, who had blank or frightened looks on their faces and were not participating in this enjoyment.

The jury had deliberated and found O. J. Simpson not guilty. I had been so caught up in preparing for fieldwork, that I had forgotten what day it was. Great, I thought, as I became conscious of my own anxiety about getting through customs and self-conscious of the fact that my face was one of the blank ones, without a smile. I was confused and immobile and did not even try to sort the ironies that filled this moment. I thought of the differential value ascribed to white and black females and lack of attention paid to gender-based violence on this island. I thought of my overstuffed bags, my suitcases that were weighed down by the bottles of wine, the tape recorder, the audiotapes, the radio–CD player, the batteries, the short-wave radio, the beauty products, and the clothing. I thought of the paradox of Jamaicans, who become black in the United States but are brown, high brown, or red in their own country, identifying with a man who remade himself by distancing from his own blackness. I thought of the social worth of white womanhood knowing that there would not have even been such a high-profile chase, let alone a trial had Nicole been black. I suddenly felt the vulnerability of my being a young dark-skinned single female Haitian citizen with an unrecognizable family name.[6] I silently cursed, and then soon smiled as I quickly realized that I had just been given the distraction I needed to *pass* through customs without any difficulties.

I approached the young male customs clerk and greeted him with a broader smile than usual. He said he knew O. J. was innocent and that there was no way he would have been convicted.

"Especially not after Rodney King," I added.

He asked what was in my bags. I told him I had stuff I needed to conduct research on ICIs for eighteen months. Did I have electrical appliances? he continued.

"Just things I need for research," I replied, but this time batting my eyelashes and pouting my rouged lips, as flirtation has its methodological uses. Lastly, he asked if I was carrying food. "Of course not; I like Jamaican food as it is," I honestly responded. We smiled. He stamped my customs form. I left and found yet another porter, who got me a JUTA taxi[7] that took me to the Pegasus Hotel for tea, where I waited until I could join the "lady" with whom I would be staying until I found my own apartment.

Having been to Jamaica on research trips in 1993 and in 1994, I did not look forward to experiencing and confronting the subtle and aggressive forms of colorism, classism, and gender discrimination that I had been subjected to every day on previous trips. This was exacerbated because I failed to adhere to local customs. Prior to leaving Ann Arbor that October, I had decided that, this time, I would not only observe my social position, I also would behave accordingly. That is, I would perform the role of researcher with a U.S. dollars–sponsored grant. By observing class and color codes and some of their gendered components, I would perform my perceived class, which would allow me to mediate colorism and to some extent command respect at the outset. In assuming my expected social place, I was expected to do less work and to employ local workers. I was determined to make this return to Jamaica as painless as possible, the best experience that grant money could buy.

In truth, though I was thoroughly excited about the project, I absolutely dreaded being in Kingston. Because of its rigid class and color divide, dense population, fast pace, congestion, gender dynamics, and continuous territorial wars, I experienced Kingston as a tough environment and affectionately dubbed it "New York City to the hundredth power." Being there required extensive emotional labor that I had to minimize to carry on the work with limited distractions.

I leaned back in the air-conditioned taxi as we drove away from the Norman Manley International Airport towards central Kingston. As we skirted around the dilapidated houses, shops, and other buildings of Harbour View, I thought back to an evening in June 1994. I was in Kingston conducting archival research and reestablishing contacts when I came home after an outing to find the LAPD's infamous low-speed chase of O. J. Simpson in the white Bronco on two of the three local channels. In addition to the shock of the event itself, I remember being anxious and paralyzed, unable to reconcile feelings of being displaced by this "intrusive" U.S. media frenzy in "my" "field site" (in Kingston). At the time, I thought of nothing else. Looking out of the taxi window, I absorbed the stark contrast between the ostentatious, pillar-adorned mansions that formed the skyline of Beverly Hills, the garbage-strewn areas below in Mountain View, and the numerous LA-style apartment complexes that hid behind thick-gated walls that had sprung up like wildflowers in a year's time.

Characteristically, contemporary Jamaica is something of a trompe l'oeil (literal translation, "deceives the eye").[8] Since independence in 1962, governments have constructed the island's image to provide the local and global worlds with visions of Jamaica that are quite contradictory. The local nationalist version comprises a plural society of Jamaicans of various races, colors, and classes that is united despite ongoing tensions. In the global arena, this description differs, as its primary purpose is to feed the island's tourism industry. This anachronistic image, which is seen mostly abroad, consists of happy-go-lucky blacks (sometimes with locks) on the coast eagerly awaiting visitors (Sheller 2003). This representation completely obscures the very plurality that underlies the local vision. However, in both cases, the relatively small white population is more or less barely discernible. Yet in reality, as most members of this population form the upper echelon, they are far from being invisible. Rather, they loom in the background, as the political and economic puppeteers of those in power.[9] These visions are not merely incongruous. As in a trompe l'oeil, the reality they purport to reflect is another illusion. Indeed, beyond the popular nationalist rhetoric, class and color divide this "one love" nation. As I discuss later, while the economic disparity among Jamaicans is less extreme than that of other countries of the region, the traditional middle class, who are the social gatekeepers of Jamaican "culture," continue to buffer the disparity between the small, mostly white and brown elite and the larger black masses. Yet this divide is entrenched and prominent enough to contradict the united plural population implied by the national motto, "out of many, one people."

Indeed, certain parts of the capital are reminiscent of North America, with peach-colored, terra-cotta-tiled malls and streets lined with the latest imported sport utility vehicles. The island's proximity to the U.S. facilitates both the import and export of cultural elements, albeit asymmetrically. Despite many visible similarities to the U.S., however, life in Kingston is a Jamaican experience. Pondering issues of distance, time, and space between east and west, north and south, I wondered what distanced "my" field site from the U.S., particularly since fiber-optic technology nullified almost any argument that stressed time.[10]

Time and a Multitude of Others

This site, "the field," where anthropologists conduct their research, is neither spatially nor temporally bound. "The field," as a concept, is defined once a site is chosen and researched in university libraries that house previous definitions of this site by established professionals who have made their careers on these very definitions. As grant proposals are written, this definition of "the field" expands. Indeed, when we decide to go, for how long, what we take and don't take with us, and personal expectations of the place are all markers of "the field." What we do upon our return continues to impact the individuals from whom we collected data. As Deborah D'Amico-Samuels explains, terms such as "out in the field" and "back from the field" help to maintain the distance between anthropologists and their research subjects. She asks how one demarcates fieldwork as a location when her field research is on gender, color, and class in Jamaica, she writes her dissertation in New York, and participates in a seminar in Trinidad? Which of these, if any, is more legitimate? (1991:69–73). In that sense, I concur with D'Amico-Samuels's conclusion that "the field is everywhere." Hence, as a concept, it is not a fixed territory. It exists in our imagination as well as out there on the ground.

The different markers used to delineate this fictive space are rendered obscure in urban areas, especially since globalization manifests differently in rural settings (Behar 1993; Tsing 1993, 2005; Mendez 2005; Smith 2001; Yelvington 1995). As I show later, consumption patterns (as effects of global movements) occur in juxtaposed and contradictory ways that reveal the clash between local and global. These are particularly evident in urban settings where communication dissemination often originates. Talk radio shows, newspapers, and TV shows are all located in major cities in Jamaica. Capital cities are cosmopolitan areas where the seat of government is located. Trade and cultural interpretation of economic, political, and social flows occur on multiple levels in this setting (Sassen 1991). In addition, internal and external migration and telecommunications are often instrumental in connecting cities to their larger contexts. Furthermore, as Enoch Page has argued, telecommunications consumption is not only classed, but raced and instrumental in the dissemination of particular images of blackness that reinforce the dominance of white public space (1999). In the 1970s, the satellite dish invaded the country. It soon became a toy of the very rich. The dish, a class symbol, soon played a key role in the redefinition of Jamaican culture. Since becoming more affordable, the dish has slowly infiltrated every crevice left open by the absence of, or the limited appeal of, the Jamaica Broadcasting Corporation (JBC), now called Television Jamaica (TVJ). Those who could afford to do so hired an electrician to run lines from the hill to smaller houses in the valley. Eventually, to compete with the dish, the television stations JBC and later CVM (a station founded by Community Television, Videomax, and Mediamix Limited) began to import television series and talk shows from the United States.

The mass media are crucial to the time-space compression. David Harvey observes: "Mass television ownership coupled with satellite communication makes it possible to experience a rush of images from different spaces into a series of images on a television screen. The whole world can watch the Olympic Games, the World Cup, the fall of a dictator, a political summit, a deadly tragedy ... " (1989:293). As of late 1993, Jamaican television daily offered *The Today Show,* the *Oprah, Montel,* and *Sally Jesse Raphael* talk shows, and others. On the radio, excerpts of NPR and the BBC report were heard daily, as well as the American Top 40 on Sundays. The field, as Appadurai notes, must be analyzed within the context of these transnational cultural movements as a new cosmopolitanism that thrives, competes with, and feeds on these transactions (1991:192). To ignore these cultural movements is to deny the impact, however minimal or strong, they have had on Jamaica and Jamaicans as a result of both U.S. imperialism and other global processes.

Concepts of the field must consider the impact on the local social order of the flow of individuals as well as commodities. In Jamaica, rural dwellers are lured to urban areas and foreign lands. Urbanites are also fixated on, and actively seek, visas to Britain, Canada, or the United States in search of the opportunities, fame, or money that will distinguish a "special" individual from the masses. Indeed, for the majority of the population, migration (both internal and external) is the only means to a better life, other than increased income through higher education or illegal activities, and is thus the preferred choice for some. It is fair to estimate that most Jamaicans have a relative or a friend who lives or has lived abroad. The activities of ICIs take them to London, Miami, New York, Panama City, Port-au-Prince, and Toronto, among other cities in the Jamaican and Caribbean diasporas. Friends and relatives in these cities sometimes play a role in their businesses. Migration and travel have historically influenced local and transnational social relations. These days, according to Appadurai, the result is that more persons in more parts of the world consider a wider set of possible lives than they ever did before. He notes, "Fantasy is now a social practice; it enters in a host of ways into the fabrication of social lives for many people in many societies" (1991:7–8). This is the reason that imagination is integral to my research, particularly since displacement and dislocation have historically been a part of Jamaican identity.

Jamaicans' desires or fantasies about the U.S. determine their daily social practices and aspirations in several ways. The U.S. is where many lower- and working-class individuals hope to migrate to find work and/or to get an education. Eventually, they return home with U.S. dollars as well as other material and social capital that gives them greater access to resources such as property and better schools for their children, which they could not have afforded on Jamaican wages. For the middle class, the Jamaican diaspora extends farther than Britain, Canada, and the United States to other parts of Europe and Africa. Abroad, they acquire a higher education that facilitates their socioeconomic mobility upon returning home and increases or stabilizes their social status. Among the elite, there are Miami Jamaicans with dual residences. They work, shop, and get their medical treatments in the Sunshine State and spend weekends socializing in their island homes. Indeed, the fact that opportunity is driving migrant movements need not mean that socioeconomic and political ties to homelands are severed. On the contrary, anthropologists have found quite the reverse (e.g., Glick-Schiller and Fouron 2001, Ong 1999, Thomas 2004). As both Basch, Glick-Schiller, and Blanc (1994) and Rouse (1991) have found, such attachments create and maintain new diasporic communities. Such connections have strengthened concomitant with the increasing movement of capital, goods, and people or perhaps, it could be said, because of this flow (Dupuy 2001). Nonetheless, the global South remains highly dependent on the North, prompting us to (re)consider the era of globalization in terms of what Trouillot calls a "fragmented globality," a world in which "inequality both reflects and reproduces the economic polarization that divides continents, countries and populations" (2003:63). As poverty levels persist in the entire region, remittances (money sent home from abroad) and seasonal migrant labor account for significant percentages of the local GDP. In 1990, remittances represented 3.2 percent of Jamaica's local GDP. Within a decade, that number had increased to 13.6 percent (International Monetary Fund 2003). In this context, the U.S. visa, which is difficult to acquire on the island, has become yet another status symbol of social and economic position.[11] During my research years, the official number of Jamaicans migrating to the U.S. alone exceeded 40,000 annually. The number of immigrants who are illegally crossing these borders is not known, but it is estimated to be even greater due to the economic engine driving this process.

This relationship that exists between Jamaicans and United States citizens is not one-sided. An increasing number of North Americans flock to the island to, as Mimi Sheller terms it, "consume the Caribbean" (2003). They come in search of both sun and pleasure during music festivals, such as the Reggae Sunsplash and Sunfest, during high tourist seasons and college and university spring breaks. An even larger population is familiar with the island through some knowledge of and/or consumption of the better-known symbols of Rastafari, Bob Marley and the "celestial" herb ganja (marijuana). Within the U.S., the presence of Jamaican migrants in African-American communities has led to reciprocal consumption of aspects of each other's popular culture, resulting in collaborative music projects between hiphop rappers and dancehall DJs. Independent international traders have been instrumental in this cultural exchange as importers, exporters, and consumers of popular culture.

The cultural movements that traverse Kingston, New York, and Miami are the result of Jamaican and North American desire for, and consumption of, different elements of dancehall and hiphop such as clothing, hairstyles, jewelry, and lyrics. Besides migration, this desire is partially fueled by the satellite dish and the VCR in middle- and upper-class homes. The VCR has made the rapid transportation of the latest styles in both countries possible. During my fieldwork in the mid 1990s, bootleg copies of Biggie's fashion shows (he was one of dancehall's top clothing designers at that time) made their way to Brooklyn in one day, or the latest Video Soul or MTV buzz clips could be seen before record companies formally released these albums on the island. Television plays an even more significant role in this transnational culture flow.

Telecommunications technology has influenced the transnational flow of hiphop and dancehall and its related economic transactions as carried out by participants in formal and informal economies. In this context, independent traders such as ICIs who distribute these popular commodities are contributing to this seemingly closing cultural gap between certain cities in the U.S. and Jamaica. They import clothing, shoes, and other accessories, which Jamaicans sport daily with uncanny resemblance to B-boys and B-girls (original term for break dancers) in the U.S. At times, despite the tropical weather and the architecture, certain streets of downtown Kingston resembled Flatbush Avenue or Fulton Street in Brooklyn.

Between 1992 and 1998, when I was conducting this research, I viewed these visible nuances as elements of the trompe l'oeil. As I stated above, parts of Kingston seemed like the United States. However, these similarities remain on the surface. Thick descriptions would reveal that this consumption and these transnational movements have had a rather limited impact on the national culture. Their effects on the old social order are infinitesimal, as I show later. As such, they fool the eye. These deceptions are symptomatic of a larger analytical problem that renders the region difficult for anthropologists to place. Trouillot rightly argues that, with its predominantly diverse population, the Caribbean region is "not western enough to fit the concerns of sociologists. Yet it is not 'native' enough to fit fully into the Savage slot where anthropologists found their preferred subjects" (1992:20). Moreover, he notes, given a history of persistent contact with the old world, this new world was hardly the place to look for primitives. Needless to say, the Caribbean is undeniably complex, as its very existence questions the West/non-West dichotomy and the category of native that anthropology is premised upon (Trouillot 1992). It is this incongruity that prompts Trouillot to further claim that the region's inescapable heterogeneity has always posed fundamental questions for anthropological theory that anthropologists have chosen to ignore. Deborah Thomas and Karla Slocum push Trouillot's argument even further, asserting that the distinctive complexity of the region makes it an important site to examine the contradictory ways that the global manifests within the local (Slocum and Thomas 2003). Indeed, this characteristic of Caribbean heterogeneity is a conundrum that I attempt to decipher by exploring its particular consequences for me as a Haitian ethnographer.[12] Below, I explore more specifically how I negotiated the Caribbean diversity that I uniquely embody and positioned myself throughout the fieldwork process in Jamaica.

Regional Native, Local Outsider

Disavowal of the region's homogeneity had manifestations that influenced various aspects of my fieldwork process from Ann Arbor to Kingston. At Michigan, my Haitian identity and my interest in Jamaica were often confounded both inside and outside of the anthropology department. Usually, I was mistaken for Jamaican or individuals assumed that my research was in Haiti. This suggests a parochial view of native anthropologists, limited by the assumption that they study only their birth countries. Kath Weston, who is considered a native anthropologist for studying same-sex families, puts it very well: "the discipline is implicated in constructing the native as an internally homogeneous category. When she embarks on a career in anthropology, she is likely to be seen as native first and ethnographer second" (1997a:171). Indeed, being viewed simply as "native" proved to be the fulcrum of power, identity, and authority issues that I had to confront at every stage of the project in both key sites. This perception stems from disciplinary views of the archetypal anthropologist as white and male. In turn, this influences the marginal position that women and people of color occupy in the academy.[13] An archeology of the project's development explicates the full extent of this dilemma and the complexities of my negotiations.

I identified my research topic as a first-year graduate student on a six-week study-abroad program in 1992. I returned to Jamaica in 1993 for six months as a Social Science Research Council (SSRC) predissertation fellow and then again in 1994 with my own funds (on credit). I went back in 1995 to conduct dissertation research funded by the Inter-American Foundation (IAF).

I returned in 1994 without outside funding because of the sensitivity of my topic, the importance of continuity in building relationships with the people I studied,[14] and the expectations I discussed earlier. Also, I had developed a sense of accountability and was rather naively determined to not re-create the cycle of exploitation, of which the traders and NGO workers never failed to remind me. Several of the ICIs explicitly told me that they expected more from me because I was black. They had different expectations and were wary of "the white people who come here ask questions and leave." I was often reminded, "Dem say they will return and show us the book but dem never come back." Though I worried about this new responsibility, I did not feel constrained by it. I quickly told them that I would write a dissertation and then a book from multiple perspectives that could contain information that they might not agree with or even appreciate. But I did stress that I would work to maintain my end of the relationship. I promised them that they would see the end results of my work and that if they found some of my arguments useful, they could use the work for their benefit.

Since the discipline is not premised on researchers maintaining relationships with their "subjects," to honor this commitment, I chose another path at an early point in my career.[15] This placed me in a situation where I became what reggae's great songwriter Robert Nesta Marley referred to as a "duppy conqueror"[16] (conqueror of ghosts) who would follow the often-silenced black anthropological tradition of questioning the discipline's Eurocentrism. The particular ghost that I chose to confront is bias towards native anthropologists and exactly what constitutes fieldwork for them. This preconception (in the field, the discipline and in the academy) manifested itself in many ways. What is of importance here is the assumption of an over-familiarity with Jamaica. It is worthy of discussion as it re-affirms Trouillot's assertion that anthropology does not know what to do with the region's heterogeneity (1992). Also, it reveals the complexities of situated knowledge (Haraway 1991) and conjures up questions about what exactly constitutes local knowledge when there are varieties of locals and knowledge.

Up until 1994, I had spent a total of seven months in Jamaica. I was quite far from understanding, let alone mastering, Jamaican patois, the language of most of the ICIs. Furthermore, those seven months did not grant me automatic "insider" status, nor did the fact that I was born in the region.

Indeed, this nativeness, as it had been bestowed upon me in Ann Arbor, seemed to transcend geographies and different colonial histories. I hailed from a former French colony that freed itself through what Trouillot (1995) calls an "unthinkable" revolution, two centuries before in 1804, while my work was on an island that had received its independence from the British only three decades ago, in 1962. This "nativeness" ascribed to me obscures the fact that participant-observation is (inter)subjective. My specific social location informs the processes I undergo to gather data. Since ethnography is premised upon methodologically driven data collection, the native ethnographer is viewed as having an advantage because this individual already knows local ways, and thus has easy access. While this notion has been textually defeated, it continues to undergird anthropological practices.

The native researcher is in a no-win situation. Everyone thinks they know. Ironically, as Delmos Jones (1970) found, the general assumption of locals was that the native ethnographer already knows the rules. Feminist anthropologist Kirin Narayan (1995) makes a different point that pushes my argument further. She asserts that class and other differences increasingly widen the divide and purported shared experiences between native subjects and researchers; moreover, these native scholars are often trained elsewhere, in universities in the North, away from their sites of research. Those scholars who assumed I was Jamaican shared the assumption that I worked at home. This assumption had various implications that I return to later. Having an entrée in the field is still perceived unfavorably by the discipline because investments in the "culture" category reinforce participation-observation as the primary method of data collection (Trouillot 2003). In principle, fieldwork is about collecting, a vestige of its imperialist past, which often entailed grueling processes of negotiations between researchers and their subjects to gain information. Hence, having easy access to material raises fundamental questions about constructions of the field, the fieldworker, and the making of ethnography. The implication is that the native ethnographer does not have to work as hard.[17]

Renato Rosaldo offers a humorous explanation with his notion of the Lone Ethnographer. The rise of classic norms in anthropology, he notes, is almost synonymous with the arrival of the "Lone Ethnographer who rode into the sunset in search of 'his native.'" After undergoing a series of trials, he encountered the object of his quest in a distant land. There, he underwent his rite of passage by enduring the ultimate ordeal of "fieldwork." After collecting "the data," the Lone Ethnographer returned home and wrote a "true" account of the "culture" (1989:30). For this Lone Ethnographer, field research required the eventual conquering of every space. It is a moment during which the anthropologist is tested by the natives and eventually overcomes obstacles. For the native ethnographer, already familiar with the society, fieldwork lacks the challenges that make this project about conquering. In truth, it was me who was outmaneuvered by interactions in the field. What I learned, I learned through trial and error. In addition, my collection of data was almost always about negotiating my own sense of being out of place. Sometimes, I was viewed as a Jamaican. Initially, fieldwork was about establishing my identity—first, as an anthropologist, then as a regional native who is also a local outsider. As a young black female who eschewed class codes, I did not live up to "the deep-seated archetypal images of the 'real fieldworker,' or the 'real anthropologist' that constitute a significant part of the common sense (in the Gramscian use of the term) of the discipline" (Gupta and Ferguson 1997:12). My conversations with Jamaican individuals across class lines revealed more about this.[18] Furthermore, I hardly felt the sense of belonging or the ease of being a "native" that I feel, only in certain contexts, when I am in Haiti, despite an initial seventeen-year absence.

Another disciplinary bias is disregard for the emotional labor that accompanies the work of anthropologists. In the past, cultural anthropologists struggled to acknowledge the impact of this aspect of working with subjects. In recent years, anthropologists have attempted to address this complex issue.[19] While the varieties and specificities of this dilemma have been revealed, for black female ethnographers reflexivity abounds with career risks. Given our historical positions within the discipline (Harrison and Harrison 1999), it is not accidental that phases of our careers were not comprehensively engaged until recently (Bolles 2001, Harrison 1999, McClaurin 2001b). Indeed, reflecting (which is viewed as telling by positivists and others invested in the order of things) on disciplinary constraints and fieldwork practice is cautiously undertaken, as critics still question the validity of raising such epistemological questions (Salzman 2002). There are still partial silences, which require analysis, as they are but manifestations of the persistent power of race (Harrison 1995), racial formation (Omi and Winant 1994), and the possessive investment in whiteness (Lipsitz 1998) within the discipline.

For black females, reflexivity carries its own set of implications. In "Theorizing a Black Feminist Self in Anthropology," McClaurin writes, "contrary to Marcus and Fischer's argument that native scholars lose critical insights when we become trained, we cannot form the voices of critiques they so desire primarily because the discipline does not want to hear us—and so many of us languish in silence, hiding our critiques" (2001b: 59). In spite of Audre Lorde's warning that silence will not protect us (1984), our historical silences on certain subjects have allowed many to be taken seriously and, in some ways, have sheltered careers. Simultaneously, these survival strategies have also reified gendered ideals and reinforced the stereotype of the black superwoman. There is a political economy to reflexivity (Ulysse 2003). Indeed, who is reflexive, what they reflect on, where they reflect, and at which point do they begin to reflect are all subject to professional evaluation in the process of making careers. This monitoring of disciplinary ways not only upholds conventional forms, methods, and writings, but in the process also influences decisions about what types of work black anthropologists do or ought to do. As in Jamaica, where there is a possessive investment in hegemonic ideals, in the U.S.—the other site where I work—there are also ideal constructions of black anthropologists.

Indeed, those who seek to attain tenure as well as those with the power to bestow it (as the main marker of professional achievement) uphold these constructions. This is a structural practice that has had significant impact, especially on up-and-coming black anthropologists. Often, they do not seek to produce creative ethnographies. Their projects that blur genres and are more humanistic are usually kept distinct from their scientific works; reflexive works in particular are published only after the publication of the more conventional work necessary to secure promotion. This reveals and reinforces the value ascribed to more conventional ethnographies, especially those that do not reflect on the political (within the discipline). Such works are the foundation for career building; they are more likely to be cited and recognized. The policing occurs on all fronts and manifests itself in different ways. Junior scholars like me are protectively encouraged to observe professional dictum and not air our private structural struggles in public or in print, where they will have lasting effects and repercussions. Even though well-meaning, this advice also maintains the pattern of erasure. Silence is just another structure of power. Therein lies the frustration of black anthropologists who must then, generation after generation, re-expose the continuities of these patterns (Baker 1998, Harrison and Harrison 1999). Their works are often viewed as "too angry" and "emotional" and less objective than conventional works that uphold academic authority, thus reinforcing the myth of objectivity.[20] Since the marked are usually seen as representative of their race, not only are black anthropologists homogenized, and homogenize themselves, but similar to the ICIs, we are professionally confined by constructions that obscure differences among us. The multiplicity of our positions, subjectivities, and voices accounts for the differences in our works.

Nonetheless, among black anthropologists, those who are heard usually speak in the dominant language using the widely accepted form. Overtly political projects are seen as less scholarly, which disavows the black tradition of knowledge production for racial vindication (Baker 1998, Harrison and Harrison 1999, McClaurin 2001b). Black anthropologists in the U.S. and elsewhere in the black diaspora have historically engaged in conducting work purposely aimed at correcting racial misconstructions and misrepresentations. Indeed, the primary work was Antenor Firmin's monumental *De L'Egalite des Races Humaines* (The Equality of Human Races, 1885), which was a riposte to Arthur de Gobineau's *Essai sur l'Inegalite des Races Humaines* (The Inequality of Human Races, 1853–1855). Firmin wrote this work to debunk the nineteenth-century racist practices of anthropometry and craniology that dominated his time (Fluehr-Lobban 2000). This work would be silenced and disavowed until over 115 years later. In the twentieth century, other Haitian scholars and writers such as Jean Price-Mars ([1928] 1983) and Jacques Roumain (1978) wrote political novels on problems of race and class, based on extensive fieldwork and archival data collection. According to Leith Mullings, it is the time spent revisiting issues deemed illegitimate that keeps black anthropologists from pursuing new concerns (1997). Thus, in addition to field research, native anthropologists who engage in corrective work are often burdened with other responsibilities as well (Jacobs-Huey 2002).

Yet the assumption is that native ethnographers do not face hardships nor have to make the sacrifices that nonnatives do. During my preliminary research phase in 1993, my daily experiences in Kingston attested to how the "fieldwork" process was at best inconsistent, as I embodied more identities than I was aware of, let alone knew how to negotiate. At worst, it was an intellectual nightmare as the theoretical approaches and methodological tools I brought from graduate school often failed to capture the subject under research. And within this never-ending nightmare, I was often emotionally overtaxed. I attempted to transcend the limits of various social positions ascribed to me while juggling the theoretical concepts of "insider," "native," and "Western feminist," which I was ascribed by virtue of being a black female from the region pursuing a research project on females. In reality, while I had more than general knowledge of the region, I lacked familiarity with my specific settings.

One of my challenges was to refrain from making suppositions about Jamaica based on what I know of Haiti or other countries in the region. My most fruitful approach, which I eventually took after many small blunders, was to simply pretend that I know very little. However, feigning ignorance was not always easy especially as I was, periodically, regionalized and even localized. At times I faltered, as I discuss in chapter 5, and I was amazed by similarities and contradictions. The parallels between Haiti and Jamaica were particularly significant given that the former is often viewed as such an oddity in the region. When I sought detachment, I reverted back to my graduate training. I had been trained to become a (white) gentleman (Guinier, Fine, and Balin 1997), so I behaved like a white male ethnographer—that is, as if my social location did not matter. More often than not, however, I was not accorded the impunity that usually comes with white skin.

In reality, I occupied the margins as what I call a regional native and local outsider. I was as difficult to place in Jamaica as I was in Ann Arbor. Numerous times, Jamaicans would automatically speak to me in patois, assuming I was a local. Other times, higglers at the Coronation Market would ask me where I was from because, as they say, "You look like we, but you no Jamaican." This pleased me, as it gave me a sense of belonging. When I responded I was from Haiti, I was shocked by the response "You don't look like one dem boat people dem." These reactions were often classed. My working- and lower-class interlocutors downtown were familiar with Haitians only through media portrayals. Several times, during the course of more extensive fieldwork (in 1994, 1995, and 1996), a number of Haitians washed ashore the island's north coast on their desperate voyages to Miami. I was not one of the boat people. Far from being a refugee fleeing political persecution, I came to Jamaica (with class privileges) to pursue an intellectual enterprise. What made my experience different from that of a white or black person? To answer the question simply, it is our respective positions as these have been historically defined. For example, a black female (of my skin tone and same social position and class lineage) from the U.S. is of higher status than I because of the increasing value of her citizenship.

My experiences were distinct, I would argue, for two interrelated reasons. I was some sort-of local in a society where remnants of colonialism (e.g., the stigma associated with blackness, as symbolic of enslavement, inferiority, and inequity) persist. In addition, as a Haitian, I occupied yet another category. I was marked predominantly as a refugee by the lower classes and to an unknown class by the middle and upper classes. My acquaintances and friends among near-elite Jamaicans, at some point, thought my father was a diplomat. What connected the various responses and perceptions of me was the fact that I disrupted class and color codes. I have an unfamiliar surname and I am dark skinned, yet I possess social, material, and cultural capital that are associated with those of the upper classes.[21] Since my class identity was not written on my body, the discord between my class and color required that I strictly observe the codes on which performances of identities are founded historically if I wanted my class to be known.

My first trip to Jamaica was in 1985, as a bona fide sun worshiper—a tourist. When I returned in 1992, with the UM Center for AfroAmerican and African Studies program, I was randomly reminded by sneering remarks from the hotel staff (especially the darker-skinned waitpersons) that people as dark as I am do not seek the sun. Also, I became more aware of uses of umbrellas and hats to preserve one's lightness. One of the program's assignments was to unpack the local meanings of color. Through this exercise, I became more sensitized to color and class categories. Middle- and upper-class interviewees (of light shades) noted that class was the most important category of identity in Jamaica. The lower the class of individuals I interviewed, the more they stressed the prominence of color. A dark-skinned waiter noted that his family encouraged him to seek a light-skinned girl for marriage to achieve status by "lifting up" the pigment of his children. With lighter skin, his children would have greater opportunities for socioeconomic advancement. At this point in the research, my sample was far from representative. The differences in their responses may have been indicators of social class, but they also revealed how color and class operated depending on the individual and the researcher.

"Out of Place" in Papine

In 1993, I returned to Kingston for predissertation fieldwork. I lived in Papine to observe and document the day-to-day activities of the agricultural market of the same name. This area also has access to transportation through its bus terminus. Papine is a working-class neighborhood, part residential and part industrial, that is located north of the university and at the foot of Upper St. Andrew, one of the wealthiest areas in Kingston. There was a Gillette factory and warehouse, a car garage, a plaza, a medical clinic, a jerk center (eatery), a Chinese eatery, a soft drink depository, a couple of bars, and several small shops where "bun and cheese" and the local Red Stripe beer and cigarettes could always be found. The neighborhood was always lively, especially in the morning and late afternoon as buses rushed back and forth to all parts of the capital. In my backyard, the more destitute lived in shacks scattered in the ravine below. The residences adjacent to mine each housed several families. In the remaining houses, rooms were rented mostly to single men. I lived in this neighborhood in a two-room apartment with running water, a kitchen, and a verandah. Rose, whom I employed to wash my clothes, told me she lived in a room the same size as my living room with her three kids and her boyfriend.

I was living an upper middle-class life in a predominantly working-class neighborhood. Given the exchange rate at the time, the SSRC fellowship afforded me a comfortable life. My daily activities included courses at the University of the West Indies during the day and frequent visits to the arcade where the ICIs I knew worked. I also went to the gym regularly. For entertainment, I attended art exhibition openings, a few dancehall sessions with friends, theater productions at the Creative Arts Center, concerts at local hotels, and university events. Initially, I used public transport, but after three months of unpleasant experiences (harassment) on the bus and at bus stops, and after a bus blew up a block from my street, I began to use taxis. The efficient way to use taxis is to become familiar with specific drivers and request them from the dispatchers. I chose drivers using various references. At the Papine market, I bought fresh produce several times a week from the same higgler and her daughter. For other items, I shopped at Sovereign Mall, a supermarket, which then epitomized middle-class consumption in Jamaica. The store itself is over eight thousand square feet and has an extensive wine shop (though the best wine is still available from embassy personnel and expatriates who are invisible

ICIs) and a deli with an ice cream bar. Two television screens showed the latest music videos all day. Shoppers could find most items available in the U.S. Both socially and economically, this life was quite different from the one I led in Ann Arbor, especially as a graduate student, since here I could afford more with the hegemonic U.S. dollar.

The life I led in Papine set me apart from people in the community where I lived, though it did not set me apart from most of the ICIs with whom I worked. These individuals aspired to a higher class, that is, to be bourgeois. In my daily activities, the discord between my imputed and subjective positions was foregrounded, making me more aware of my fragmented selves. My socioeconomic status was constantly challenged in various temporal and spatial contexts, whether I was on the streets, on the way to school, at the university, at the gym, at the Consortium, in the arcades, at Carlo's Cafe, at Sovereign Mall, in taxis, at the market, in the museum, or at the bank. Individual responses to me were so inconsistent that I rarely experienced a sense of continuity in my daily encounters. While these encounters left me frazzled and at times bitter, I remained committed to the project hoping that at some point I would expose and address these moments. The "Afrophobia" that I experienced and witnessed impacted me ambivalently, yet violently. In its popular use, the term "Afrophobia" refers to the hairstyle. I use it here in the same way as Dennis Greene (1997), as analogous to blackness and to refer to both a fear of black people and of being black.[22] Wherever the location in Jamaica, these occurrences varied and were no different from incidents of race-based discrimination practices that would occur in the U.S. They were, however, much more frequent and quite overt. On the one hand, I was demoralized.[23] On the other, I became more dedicated to pursuing the project to get answers, to understand the particularities of Jamaican society that incubated, bred, and continues to breed what I then viewed simply as persistent self-deprecation. During these initial trips, I clearly did not comprehend the dialectics of class and color dynamics.

After I left Jamaica, I had numerous conversations with individuals from the region about my experiences. Through these dialogues, I learned that although the symbolic violence of these encounters was, as I sensed, informed by color, they were exacerbated by inconsistencies in my performance of class. The discontinuities in my interactions were the result of my failing to adhere to existing boundaries and codes as observed by people of my obvious color and perceived class. I came to understand responses to these as evidence of disjunctures in my everyday self-making practices.

"Why You Do Dat to Your Head?"

In Kingston, with the SSRC grant, I was in a much higher economic class than I occupied as a graduate student in the U.S. However, by Jamaican standards, I seldom presented myself or behaved as a member of the black middle class. For dark-skinned females of the middle class, color is mediated through observance of the culture of femininity and dress discussed in chapter 1. One of the ultimate symbols of ladyhood is her well-groomed hair. At the time, my hair was permed or "colonized"—a term I used much to the shock of the females I encountered.

I decided to stop processing my hair after a self-loathing experience at a middle-class beauty salon in upper Barbican. For years, I had been ambivalent about processing my hair. At times, I would go months without a touch-up, a reapplication of the perm to keep my hair straight. That summer, I waited the longest I ever had. At the salon, the hairdresser berated me for this. "Why you wait so long for a touch-up?" she asked. "Look it how tough your hair is," she commented as she pulled and pulled my tresses to get rid of the kinks. By the time she was done, my hair, fashioned in a bob, was bone straight. I looked in the mirror and was not at ease with what I perceived as a disjuncture. Several months later, in early December 1994, I got my hair cut to a low Afro at another salon in Liguanea. None of the female hairdressers would agree to cut my hair, which at the time was about shoulder length. They were concerned about what my reaction would be once the hair had been cut. Finally, the barber on duty agreed to cut it. In the barber chair, I sat contently and became a spectacle as workers and patrons alike came to the front room to see that silly "Yankee gal" cutting off all that pretty hair. Each comment became more frustrating. "Do you know how long it will take to grow back?" an older client asked me. "I don't want to have this hair," I responded apologetically. My reply fell into an abyss. Soon after the cut, a female hairdresser stopped by and asked if I was going to "texturize" the new 'fro, that is soften it with more chemicals. Yet I had cut off the hair precisely to get rid of all of the chemicals.

At that time in Jamaica, this natural hairstyle had a greater symbolic significance, one that went beyond aesthetics. Because of both Rastafari and the black power movement of the 1970s, natural hair had value as an anti- and postcolonial symbol. Individuals, across classes, were amazed that I had cut off all that hair. Many perceived my new short hair as a sign of social resistance to gender norms because it defied the hegemonic standard of beauty, femininity, and even sexuality. For dark-skinned females,

the texture and especially the length of one's hair was a charged signifier. At the time, lower-class women who had low (cropped) hair were often labeled rebel women, as they did not adhere to the more "respected"
gendered norms, instead adopting a more masculine persona. This breaking of gendered norms, which in some ways celebrates a black nationalist
identity (through the acceptance of natural, i.e., unprocessed, hair), also
exacerbates the local Afrophobia. It reinforces the old colonial stereotype
of the black woman, which is often juxtaposed against the brown middle-
class ideal of lady (cultured or refined).

Individual males perceived this hair as an affront to their masculinity.
In my discussions with other females with similar hairstyles, I learned that
random men had a tendency to react violently to their cropped hairdo.
Indeed, I was often asked "Why you do that to your head?" or "Why a
pretty girl like you do a ting like dat?" The interrogators were always men,
whether in taxis, in offices, or on the streets. Since long hair (regardless of
form: natural, permed, locks, or weaves) is the decisive symbol of femininity, sometimes there were follow-up questions concerning my sexuality.
"Do you have a man?" suggesting that I was a lesbian. This association
is a crucial indicator of the politics of visibility given the rampant homo-
phobia that keeps gays and lesbians more or less closeted from the gaze of
the heteronormative state and civil society. This comment also suggests an
unnaturalness, as an unfeminine female is danger, to use Mary Douglas's
(1966) metaphor, among the pure. "Him like it? What him say?" they
would ask, in turn, questioning the masculinity of any man who would
be with me. The tone of the query is evident. Gender norms being what
they are in the region, what type of man would desire an unfeminine or
masculine female with short hair, without the main symbol of femininity?
In any case, such questions point to hegemonic ideals used to discipline
dissent.

Occasionally, I responded to these comments. Other times, I did not,
keeping my interlocutors guessing. When I chose to engage, my riposte was
a lingering distasteful cut-eye.[24] Until low hair became fashionable later in
1994, the females who wore this style were either lower- and working-class
rebels or middle-class artists, conscious deviants, and "yardies," a term once
used to refer to Jamaicans who have returned home from abroad. Since the
1980s, "yardies" has come to connote criminality (Skelton 1998). It was
these moments that forced me to question to what extent unambiguously
dark-skinned Jamaican working-class females were scrutinized and policed
by others when they disregarded the social order. Because of the ICIs'

recurring disruption of the order of things, I wondered if they experienced the constant policing I did and, if so, how it was manifested for them and how it affected their demeanor. As black females have done historically, did they also perform other identities to facilitate their everyday life? To make do with their demanding business? Did these performances extend to the arcade? When they traveled abroad? How, if at all, were their responses informed by their new access to capital and material accumulation?

My love for the sun and this cropped hair gave me yet another identity in Jamaica. Too often I was asked, especially by working-class individuals, if I were African, implying that "black" and "natural" are synonymous with Africa. Sometimes, I purposely replied "aren't we all?" which pleased the Rastas and discombobulated the more European-identified inquirers. That my natural appearance was equated with being African is quite ironic as people on that continent also suffer from the same "white bias" that plagues the Caribbean. Bleaching creams, hair straighteners, and hair extensions are just as popular in Africa, indicative of white bias and Afrophobia there too. As I discuss in the remaining chapters, white bias and Afrophobia are, and have been, historically linked to a fear of economic ostracism and, in most cases, social ostracism as well. For disrupting the old colonial order of things has its price. Such action could lead to a social death, or what Walter Rodney refers to as class suicide (1969).[25]

Field Methods: Cross-Dressing-Across-Class

In 1993, unbeknownst to me, in certain circles, I was on the verge of social self-termination. I had failed to perform class, that is, to wear the locally recognized symbols that would properly signal my socioeconomic position. Without this mediation, my class identity was fixed by my skin color and its concomitant stigma. Hence, I was placed on the lower rungs of the social ladder, particularly in those spaces that were more rigidly policed by social gatekeepers. Yet my North American-accented English, foreign mode of dress, and overall demeanor were inconsistent with the class position I assumed, working-class, and the one that was ascribed to me, upper middle-class. Living where I did in Papine, yet dressing as I did, I was a walking contradiction.

In January 1994, I had a conversation with Trouillot in which we discussed the dilemma of black anthropologists and the point at which they enter the field. He recounted his experiences in Dominica, where he conducted his dissertation fieldwork. He spoke of the difficulties he faced in getting appointments with ministers for his research. He noted that he would arrive at the ministries dressed in accord with the weather and proceeded to wait in line to see these officials. While waiting, he wittingly observed twelve Frenchmen, ten Americans, and three British students, casually dressed, who would proceed up the stairs to the offices of the same ministers who were "unavailable" to him. Once he ceased cross-dressing-across-class and changed his clothing to a formal three-piece suit, those ministers were no longer occupied.

Similarly, I was in another country in the region where members of the black middle class habitually display their economic status, often ostentatiously, depending on the aesthetic, in order to be ascribed a particular position and to be treated with basic respect. Trouillot had cautioned me to enter the field from the top and not from the bottom. Then I would reaffirm my class position based upon my education and source of income. The fact is that I am a dark-skinned, single female who looked even younger than she was in a region that valued status and its myriad manifestations. Entering at the top would have facilitated my research and helped me mediate the multiple intersections that I embodied. Indeed, race, color, class, gender, marital status, and generational stratifications, which are indices of station in the region, also determine the larger context within which one's research occurs. This was confirmed when I returned to Jamaica in 1994. Patricia Anderson, a sociologist at the Mona campus of the University of the West Indies (UWI) questioned me about how I presented myself during that first trip.[26] In her final analysis, she exposed me to the consequences of the disjunctures in my self-making practices. Through her, I learned that as I dressed down or cross-dressed-across-class, my mediations of capital were invisible. She concluded that for locals, I simply blurred too many boundaries, which rendered me totally out of place. Both Trouillot's and my experience attest that the blurring of boundaries has its dangers for blacks.

Given the experiences recounted above, I prepared for the final phase of fieldwork in 1995 adamant about minimizing any visible inconsistencies. Knowing that skin color must be mediated with the "appropriate" class markers, I specifically requested funding (which I did not receive) for status symbols on several of my field research grant applications. I wanted to document the fact that as a dark-skinned female in Jamaica, my negotiation processes differed from those of others with more privilege. I entered the field racially stigmatized without the political or social luxury ascribed to whiteness. Indeed, as discussed earlier, whiteness is property. The cultural capital (education and elite university affiliation) and symbols that I did possess were invisible markers, and hence had limited value. In addition, though I am a native of sorts, individuals often localized me. I was expected to "know better" and, as a result, to act accordingly. This perception of me was specific to context. It revealed the spatial organization that underlies social relations. In other words, it depended on whom I was with and where we were.

After weeks of sun worshipping, my skin became quite dark. I was often addressed as local, especially when accompanied by whites, who were automatically perceived as tourists or foreigners. This occurred constantly, especially during my study-abroad programs in 1992 and 1993. In uptown and downtown Kingston, Port Antonio, and on the north coast, waiters and others in tourist areas addressed me as the local tour guide of white North American colleagues. Once at Coronation Market in Kingston, street vendors approached me, asking me to entice my white Jamaican friends to purchase their wares from them. These examples not only highlight the pitfalls of my failure to visibly assert my socioeconomic status, but they also indicate how the visibility and invisibility of various forms of capital operate in conjunction with cross-class and -color fraternization. I return to this issue in the final chapter. Hence, my request for certain items was an early attempt to engage in what I call a reflexive political economy in praxis. My goal was to forecast the influence of the researcher's socioeconomic position on different aspects of the project and to point to anthropology's normative notions of the "researcher," "the field," and "methods" (Harrison 1991b, Gupta and Ferguson 1997) in order to unpack some of the intersecting gender, class, and racial codes embedded therein.

These biased concepts unquestionably perpetuate race and class privilege by ignoring and even exploiting existing baseline inequalities on the ground in the field. In the Caribbean and elsewhere in the black diaspora, white skin has been upheld across racial lines as the ultimate status symbol, allowing individuals a range of privileges including gender and class. Most will have access to resources and the advantage of flaunting ignorance of social expectations with little to no consequences. Without a doubt, these are different for a black female depending on her shade. In the region, particularly among the middle and lower classes, white anthropologists are ascribed immediate social status and power regardless of presentation. Generally, reflexivity is not a common practice among Caribbean ethnographers. While anthropologists of color tend to cross the boundary, their white counterparts working in cultural settings where color/race matters rarely (with the exception of Goldstein 2003) reflect on how their whiteness operates in the field.[27] White anthropologists may be ridiculed for their foolishness (disregard of social order), but they are often forgiven for not adhering to these social norms. The socioeconomic status of white anthropologists and their abilities are doubted differently, if at all, as Edwidge Danticat noted "their skin itself is their three-piece suit."

In addition, as I indicated above, native anthropologists in these circumstances not only must adhere to social norms, but are often also expected by subjects to be more responsible and ethical. There may be a gender component to this. To diversify black anthropologists, let me note that individual positioning and choices ultimately determine the character of researchers' relationships with subjects and how these are ultimately presented textually.[28] For those who practice more engaged research, the negotiations differ. Racial and color proximity when working among one's "skinfolk," to use Zora Neale Hurston's term (1979), sometimes heightens the possible dangers of anonymity that could make data gathering in certain contexts improbable.[29] Initially, I had tremendous difficulty getting access to certain high-ranking government officials on my own. I am certain that the work I carried out with Metropolitan Parks and Markets (MPM) would have been virtually impossible had it not been for my upper-class networks. This inevitably highlights the class-based access that I had as an outsider compared to the more restricted resources of the marginal masses.

In 1995, prior to leaving to pursue my fieldwork, I purchased power.[30] These material and symbolic items included silver jewelry with lapis lazuli and Giorgio Armani designer glasses that were clearly "foreign" and costly. The clothing included numerous tailored pieces (especially for the interviews with upper-class government officials) and simple skirts and pants, as well as other items that symbolically affirmed a stable middle-class position. These objects, carefully chosen, comprised a particular classed aesthetic. I observed and respected certain gendered rules and brought back a rather stylish "ladies" wardrobe, several pairs of high-heeled shoes, perfume, make-up, etc. Similar to the colored and black females who sought symbols to assert their denied femininity during slavery, these items allowed me to perform class and mediate the ways that blackness has been stigmatized. I also brought a pair of Adidas loafers for those long days when living in Kingston became unbearable, as they did in 1993. Indeed, performing the lady entails high heels, which require a presence and comportment that could become taxing over time. Instead of renting in Papine, I sought housing in a middle-class neighborhood. I lived in the New Kingston area, halfway between the university and downtown, in a studio that gave me physical comfort and a sense of safety. My choices were reflexive consumption practices meant to present a mediated self to counter the myriad manifestations of class and color stigma.

At the arcades downtown, I wore long floral skirts and linen shirts or blouses that covered my arms. I tied my head with a scarf. This got me the respect of the older men and the socially conscious younger men (who dubbed me their African Princess or Roots Lady).[31] Simultaneously, this mode of dress annoyed several of the ICIs, who thought I must be soft (spineless) because I hid my body under all those clothes; I did not accentuate it like many of them do. Both of these responses suggest a sexualized construction of the black female based upon the lady/woman binary discussed in chapter 1. Yet I was never referred to as a woman by either of these two groups. While ladies may accentuate their bodies, they do not cover their figures. Such practices are associated with religious observances. It is precisely this affinity that the ICIs were objecting to. When I wore anything that revealed even my calves, I dreaded going downtown, especially to my primary field site, where numerous young men worked and lingered around the arcade posing. They would grab me, demanding that I talk with them because "dem like me." I would have to assert myself by performing tuffness in a manner I resented. In chapter 5, I examine the embodiment of a corporeal shield as a necessary component of self-making among those who work or live downtown.

To complicate matters, the UVA was managed by two older Rastafari who were not pleased when I tried to dress in accordance with the tropical weather. They objected when I wore pants or anything that showed any skin and when I continued to get my hair cut very low. Their disdain for my cropped, rebel hairstyle stemmed from Rastafari doctrine, which honors one's locks as a crown of glory and prohibits the cutting of one's hair. They wanted me to become a Rasta, especially since they felt I showed a lot of potential: I often openly expressed my politics, and my research wardrobe consisted of long skirts and blouses, which reflected a Rastafari aesthetic.

Sometimes I conformed to these gendered self-making sensibilities. This conventionality highlighted the complexities of the multiplicity of gendered identities that are the result of class and color crossings. Sometimes, I tied my head with a scarf and went downtown, which meant I had to decide to not go to certain places uptown such as the bank, the super market, the university, or the café, where this accessory was usually frowned upon because of its class code. Historically, the head-tie or tie-head (scarf) is an accessory, a marker of working-class status in the English-speaking Caribbean (Robertson 1995:113). More recently it has been associated with certain social or religious groups (popular with Rastafari and Pentecostals among others). Headscarves are visible uptown among more Afrocentric and black nationalist middle-class females, especially in various African cloths. Like any other ethnic-identified accessory, this headdress has different significations for black or brown, Chinese, Indian, or white females. The darker the skin, the more this accoutrement necessitates the "appropriate" jewelry and clothing to mediate an unquestionable middle-class and/or uptown identity.

When I did wear head-ties, several of the ICIs I knew expressed their disapproval: "You like dem Rastas too much." They were very concerned that I was getting too close to the dreads. For these black females of working-class or lower-class lineages who do not possess the social and cultural capital that I do, visible mediations of color and class codes are even more crucial. Their constant warning regarding my proximity to Rastafari also signified their own recognition of this association as a form of class suicide. My devaluation would inevitably impact them, as my questionable class position would lessen the status they derived from my research interest in them.

These issues made me increasingly conscious of the symbolic politics of the ethnographer's identities, especially with regard to the limits and problems of how, through appearance and embodiment, one navigates the racialized spatial orders of field sites. These issues are brought under analysis here to give greater consideration to what Emma Tarlo (1994) refers to as the problem of what to wear. I wish to complicate this question even further by emphasizing another aspect. Where does one go because of what one is wearing? The visibility of clothing renders dressing a significant component of class performance and negotiations. As a result, a dressing method is required. My tendency was to rebel by cross-dressing-across-class.

Like gender cross-dressing, which disrupts the social categories of male and female, cross-dressing-across-class confounds socioeconomic orders.[32] Whereas the former has long been considered an anomaly, Marjorie Garber (1992) has argued that transvestism is an uncanny intervention that represents a space of anxiety about fixed and changing identities and throws into question gender norms. She locates transvestism "at the juncture of 'class' and 'gender,' and increasingly through its agency gender and class were revealed to be commutable, if not equivalent. To transgress one set of boundaries was to call into question the inviolability of both, and of the set of social codes—already under attack—by which such categories were policed and maintained" (1992:32). In that sense she argues, the transvestite (also a trompe l'oeil) represents not just a category crisis, but a "crisis of category" itself. Indeed, cross-dressers offer a performance of the performance. By this I mean that they are performing a gender that they are seeing performed. Their aesthetics, which also fall in between categories help to illuminate some of the manifestations of my cross-dressing-across-class. More specifically, how did I collapse class? Where did I fit in this ordered world? As I show below, nothing highlights the social construction of both gender and class more than when this performance is exaggerated. As a result of my dressing methods, I also represented a crisis in category as I stood at the intersections of the crossroads of class, color, gender, sexuality, and nationality constantly in flux because of my ability to manipulate different types of capital. Indeed, I disrupted existing hierarchies. I caused class trouble as I confounded various codes and their concomitant historical ideals.

Sometimes I simply did not adhere to local class and gendered expectations. I wore what I would on a college campus in Ann Arbor to try to maintain some sense of equilibrium. By not always conforming, I did not lose myself as Kondo (1990) did and found some solace in the process of living against the culture. During these times, my senses were more acute. Reactions to me were evidence of my disruption of class and color codes. Nevertheless, I was not always aware of the basis of my cultural faux pas. Did wearing Doc Martens with faded jeans and a kente wrap cause a stir at the National Dance Theatre Company performance lobby because they were pitchy-patchy,[33] to use local vernacular? Indeed, these items were respectively symbolic of dancehall, punk, and Afrocentricity. I was forced to figure out what caused the reaction (the frowns, glares, stares, and even whispers). Was it the untidy aesthetic? Was it the mixed capital signs? Was it how these intersected with my color and/or perceived class? Regardless, my "inappropriate" performance created a disorder. To appropriate Butler, it was causing class as opposed to gender trouble. My "playful disruption" of the categories reinforced their severity (Butler 1990). While my performance went against the norm, it did force me to see and experience Jamaica from a range of classed perspectives. However, all of these occurrences differed depending on context. While the disruptions varied, responses to them were consistent. Without a doubt, they were systematically specific.

These reactions reveal that the "native" position ascribed to me in Ann Arbor certainly did not translate smoothly to Kingston. As a result of my appearance, my ability to immerse myself in the field or "go native," as they say, was inhibited or compromised by the fact that I am simultaneously a regional native and local outsider as well as an ethnographer. This forced me out of place, which inevitably had methodological implications. The numerous sites where fieldwork was conducted required that I shift among multiple positions at various times in different spaces that emphasized the incongruities in the intersections of gender, race, color, class, sexuality, nationality, and generation. In other words, I was actively code switching. My corporeal performances were determined by my context. They depended on who my interlocutors were, where I was, and what I wanted to find out.

Alter(ed)*native* Ethnographer

Given the persistence of these discontinuities in my interactions, eventually I began to use them as a research tool. Through a process of trial and error, I sought to research informal commercial importers and the broader environment that created them. Knowing the difficulty that both local and foreign researchers have in collecting data from ICIs, I considered several methodological approaches. In terms of participant-observation, I briefly considered becoming an informal importer for a year to gain firsthand experience of the trade. This option and others were challenging on multiple levels. Foremost, in becoming an ICI, I would be perpetuating the belief that ethnographic authority can be gained only by becoming an insider—that is, that insider privilege is an actual condition of nativeness and that knowledge gained in this fashion is superior to others.[34] Furthermore, given the overt and subtle nuances of Jamaican self-making practices, there are raced, classed, and gendered obstacles that limited the possibility of my partaking in all parts of this process.[35] Going native in my case, as a black female, where the majority of the population is also black, becomes a rather complex endeavor. There is no native, but a plurality of locals in different colors, classes, genders, and gendered identities. The question remained, if I were to follow my training, which of these would I be? Which type of native could I become,

given that there are different classes and multiple shades or color gradations of natives?

Despite my color, my middle-class position set me apart from the
working-class individuals in the arcades. As I stress above, and will discuss in greater detail in subsequent chapters, my complex positioning at
times limited the extent of my participation. As my interest was in documenting and analyzing the experiences of ICIs of a particular social location and economic position, I could not fully participate as one of them.[36]
Had I become an ICI, the knowledge gained would, in fact, be inconsistent with what I sought to learn. My actual experience would be based
upon responses to the incongruity between who I am and who others perceive me to be. I could have abided by my social position, but that would
have hindered different aspects of the data-gathering process unless I attempted to pass by performing yet another class identity. I could have
chosen to alter my speech, mannerisms, and presentation and sold goods
on the street or in an arcade like a working-class ICI. Taking on another
identity would soon make me even more suspect and would highlight yet
another ethical problem, my real motive for conducting the research.[37]

Undoubtedly, the traders would likely perceive this approach as a
mockery of their reality, since the majority of them did not have my options. Most ICIs enter this occupation to survive and gain respect. I would
be viewed as yet another researcher who sought their knowledge entirely
for personal gain. Given the copious research projects undertaken in the
Greater Kingston Metropolitan area, the general consensus regarding researchers is that they do not reciprocate. This is reconfirmed every time
I return to Kingston and mention my respondents by name. Individuals
are surprised that I maintain contact with traders. Local scholars are even
more distrusted by traders, as they often consult for the state.[38] Another
popular opinion among locals is that the data collected is for the U.S. government. To address this concern, I explained that dissertations are public
documents that I could not control, though I would choose what would be
included in this work. I had been encouraged by my mentors to find ways
to give something back to the traders and the UVA. Throughout fieldwork and beyond, I became active in the UVA. I attended meetings and,
on occasion, even spoke on their behalf. Hence as a participant-observer,
I used a methodological approach, which at times entailed conscious interactions and interventions.

My decisions were informed by my purpose in undertaking this project.
I sought to diagnose the basis of social inequality in Jamaica and to inter-
pret the various causes of its persistence in order to understand how these

can be redressed. From that perspective, while I remained troubled by the category "native," I was dedicated to the activist component of the native anthropology project first outlined by Delmos Jones (1970). More specifically, Jones wrote, "I am an intrinsic part of the social situation that I am attempting to study. As part of that situation, I must also be part of an attempt to forge a solution" (1970:255). As I stated earlier, my decision to enter the discipline was politically motivated and is tied to my commitment to Haiti. I shared Jones's ideals and believed that solutions could be found by going beyond Geertz's native's point of view (1976). I wanted to engage all of the natives (informal commercial importers, government officials, and local and regional scholars who have been formulating theories of their condition, as well as popular commentators and other organic intellectuals) to the extent that this was possible.[39] Given that native voices are often limited in anthropological texts, engaging locally produced scholarship and organic intellectuals entailed embarking on a more politically engaged anthropology that must extend the parameters of ethnography to include the very context of its production, which facilitated disavowal of such knowledge.

Building on the Du Boisian legacy of work and praxis in anthropology, Faye Harrison suggests that ethnographers turn their heightened and intensified different sensibilities, visions and understandings into a useful research instrument (1991b). From this place of multiple consciousnesses, she argues, the researcher can play a strategic role in the struggle to decolonize anthropology and the imperialist project from which the discipline arose. While I worked in Jamaica, my logic and intuition were "rooted in some combination and inter-penetration of national, racial, sexual, and class oppressions," as Harrison describes it (1991b:90). This awareness did not disappear when I returned to Michigan. I was living, working, and conducting my work in Anzaldua's borderlands (1987); the margins that I occupied were constantly shifting. This space, bell hooks suggests, can be used strategically to develop a critical black voice and to build feminist solidarity for political work (1990).

When I cross-dressed-across-class or performed class against culture, my senses and sensibilities about self-making and social relations in Jamaica were quite heightened. This in turn fostered greater understanding of the environment in which I conducted my research, as well as the socioeconomic and political economy of the ethnographic project itself. In addition, my performance highlighted how the research process is an embodied endeavor, one in which lived and felt experience, through all the senses, is integral to both the data collection process and the knowledge produced (Stoller 1989, Weismantel 2001). For U.S.-based black feminist anthropologists, acknowledgment of this relationship between knowledge and experience has been somewhat limiting. By this I mean that those who focus on such concerns are often constrained to reproduce hegemonic (or tenurable) ethnographies if they are interested in professional advancement within the discipline. Thus, work on epistemological questions is often addressed in separate articles that reflect upon fieldwork experiences.[40] Regardless of this choice, as Bolles has aptly argued, in the citation game that propels careers, black feminist anthropologists remain the least cited, especially by white feminists who tend to regard their work mostly as experiential (2001). In "New Voices of Diversity, Academic Relations of Production, and the Free Market," Harrison takes this point even further. She contends that theoretical contributions of black feminists are continuously erased through consistent devaluation of writing that does not reinforce disciplinary hegemony. These exchanges, she asserts, are symptomatic of the division of labor within academic relations of production (1999). Black feminist anthropologists occupy a position as "outsiders-within" the discipline (Hill-Collins [1991] 2000). Unsurprisingly, as a result, historically, many have turned to other disciplines and/or to the arts to extend the full range of their expression (Harrison and Harrison 1999). In general, such works have been neglected and brought under the rubric of humanism, or adopted altogether by other disciplines.[41] In part, because of what Catherine Lutz calls the gender of theory (1995), reflections on the intersections of embodied knowledge are still relegated to the margins, outside of dominant discourses. When the object of reflection is race and class within the academy, and the larger politics that shape intellectual production, such discussions are treated as trivial, and not ethnographic. The panoptic lens extends only so far when the self is the object of the gaze.

As Bruce Knauft stresses, disregard for the cultural politics within anthropology is duplicitous. It neglects the fact that the academy in general, and anthropology in particular, also has its own culture. The representation of cultural contestation is not simply a concern for the field among the people we study. Hegemonies (of voice and perspectives) are maintained by disciplinary practices as well (1996:250-252). I use a reflexive voice to consider the interconnections between aspects of fieldwork often hidden in conventional ethnographies as well as the broader political environment in which ethnographies are made.

Indeed, as Ruth Behar asserts, reflexivity is susceptible to the charge that it is simply self-serving and superficial. This, she argues, "stems from an unwillingness to even consider the possibility that a personal voice can lead the reader to the enormous sea of serious social issues" (1996:22). This, I argue, extends to reflections on the discipline as well. For black feminist anthropologists, the implications of this dismissal are even shoddier.[42] According to Narayan (1995), native anthropologists do face a particular dilemma (as both products and subjects of the discipline), which they must maneuver and that also constrains them. Kath Weston (1997a) puts it quite simply:

> social relations inside and outside of the profession pull her [the native ethnographer] toward the poles of her assigned identity, denying her the option of representing herself as a complex, integrated, compound figure. Instead of writing as "I, Native Ethnographer"—or some equally compound subject position— she ends up positioned as either "I, Native," or "I, Ethnographer." The nuance of the two as they are bound up together is lost. (1997a:171)

To retrieve this complex voice, I use auto-ethnography to reflect on my interactions and relations with subjects and the dynamic power that binds us. As Irma McClaurin notes, "auto-ethnography is simultaneously autobiographical and communal, as the self encounters the collective" (2001b:69). The above reflexive moments make explicit the connections between the immersed subject (I, native) and the purported detached observer (I, ethnographer). It also begins to forge the intimacy Anzaldua (1987) suggested. With the particularities of how my Haitian nationality played out in Jamaica, I have revealed some of the complexities inherent in the category of the native.

As I stated in the introduction, my goal is to pluralize the native. I have done so by interweaving a tale out of various auto-ethnographic reflections. First, by pointing to the reasons for the ICIs' expectations of me (as a group that has been overstudied), and mine of them, I have revealed that we shared time, space, and place. Second, as a regional native and local outsider, I occupied a state of displacement on the border, as Haitian national and U.S. resident, that informed my interactions with diverse groups of locals.[43] Third, I was initially oblivious of the gendered components of the articulation of class and color codes. My disregard was most evident in my early dressing methods, which revealed my class performances to be incongruous in ways that symbolized class trouble or what I call socioeconomic disorder. Later, I will show how my use of codes notably diverges from that of most ICIs due to our different social positions.

Through these observations, I seek to de-essentialize black female subjectivity to show divisions based on class, color, age, and nationality. Whether I was with higglers, ICIs, government officials, scholars, and others on the street, at the arcade, on buses, in taxis, at the university, or at the supermarket, I constantly crossed shifting class and color lines. My crossing required performances that informed aspects of the various methodological approaches used in this project. At times, the boundaries between native and ethnographer were obscure. The lines were blurred as the categories I embody necessitated conciliations of class and color codes that have both historical and contemporary referents. Thus, these mediations compelled my temporal crossings at various times in ways quite different from the ICIs whom I studied.

CHAPTER FOUR

Uptown Women/Downtown Ladies: Differences among ICIs

Ha fi big up all di ICI who juggle out a street
Hard, hard fi mek a end meet
Yard or a broad naa tek no defeat
(I have to pay homage to all the ICIs who peddle in the streets
Who work hard to make ends meet
At home or abroad they take no defeat.)
          —Buju Banton, DJ and singer (1995)

Why pay for the trip? You should make the ticket pay for itself. —Miss M., flight attendant and ICI

Rereading the ICI Stereotype

In both official and popular discourse, no distinction is made among Informal Commercial Importers. They are simply lumped together into a stereotype of ICIs that has both material and symbolic aspects. Materially, they are viewed as small-scale traders of a homogeneous socioeconomic group who conduct the same activities. These demographics have changed since their emergence. Similar to higglering, which became more specialized over time, independent international trading is a complex business that requires expert workers at various stages, from traveling to buying and selling. Symbolically, ICIs are perceived as thieves who lie, cheat the government, and import knockoffs, for which they charge exorbitant prices. This stereotype has numerous implications for ICIs as businesspersons and as black females. Understanding the influence of the stereotypes further reveals the intricate web that constrains them socially, economically, and politically. Stereotypes, in general, reinforce what Stuart Hall calls "the racialized regime of representation." As he puts it: "stereotyping reduces, essentializes, naturalizes and fixes difference. In addition, stereotyping also practices closure and exclusion [by] symbolically fixing boundaries and excluding everything which does not belong" (1997a:258). That exclusionary practice is relevant here, as the stereotype obscures the participants of this trade.

In this chapter, I highlight the heterogeneity inherent in the business and among its participants through many profiles of ICIs from across the social structure including lower-, working-, and middle-class traders. In presenting this variety, my goal is to reveal that informal commercial importing is in fact a pervasive practice that cuts across class and color lines.[1] On this basis, I argue that the category ICI constitutes a diverse group of vendors and that their businesses vary in degrees of formality and informality, which renders the concept of informal economy redundant. I will discuss a number of factors that contribute to this crossing of economic boundaries such as the scale of their operations, their subcontracting activities with established businesses, the value of their commodities, and the class of their consumers. In so doing, I expose the dilemmas created by official policies that are based on the popular anachronistic image of the ICI.

Indeed, over the years, the state-recognized stereotype of the ICI became a meaningful category that has served Jamaican governments (regardless of the party in power) in several ways. First, by virtue of ICIs' avid participation in independent economic activities, ICIs conceal the realities of Jamaica's unemployment rate; they obscure the ways the state fails to provide for its citizens. Second, they benefit the state economically. They are heavily taxed, pay various fees, and yet receive little to no protection or services from the state, which continues to enact measures that further constrict their activities. Indeed, ICI policies are developed on a rather limited purview of the business and its practitioners. Because of this narrow definition, these policies target only ICIs who fit into the stereotype. As a result, formalization is disproportionately implemented, rendering state attempts to regulate this activity inherently ineffective. This flaw leads to a more comprehensive question: can informal economic activities be formalized? The answer is negative, due to the inherent heterogeneity and dynamics between formal and informal activities. I argue further that ICIs are mere scapegoats, often blamed for Jamaica's flailing economy because of their socioeconomic location. Thus, they are politically powerless to counter the exploitative taxation that's imposed on them.

As I demonstrate below, informal commercial importing is a multi-faceted activity that draws in a diversity of participants including novices, recurring temporary retailers, and veteran market traders. Anthropologists continue to grapple with how to explain such multiplicity in this sector of the economy (Browne 2004, Seligman 2004, Weismantel 2001). As is evident in chapter 2, in the past scholars tended to use classification systems that eventually outlived expansion of the business and its inevitable trans-formations. To encapsulate the wide range of specialization, expertise, and position among ICIs, I use a simple system that categorizes traders according to their level of detection, that is, how socially visible or invisible they are and whether they are likely to be perceived as importers by oth-ers.

Visibility is based foremost on the location where ICIs sell their mer-chandise, which often reflects both their social positions and that of their customers. The basis and degree of their visibility usually correlates with the supposed formality or informality of their economic practices. I use this criterion to emphasize how their business activity is noticeable to the state apparatus that monitors and regulates the stereotype. On the one hand, there are the visible ICIs who fit the state-recognized category. As discussed in chapter 2, they tend to be more detectable since they embody and perform characteristics of this image in appearance as well as through their trading and importing patterns. In addition, their business activities occur in very public arenas such as the arcade and the streets. Consequently, they are more easily targeted and policed.

Invisible ICIs, on the other hand, operate out of their homes, offices, ho-tels, and even formal commercial establishments such as specialty shops, stores, and supermarkets. They are not perceived as ICIs by government officials primarily because of the small scale of their activities. In some instances, they are invisible because their style of presentation and per-formance of color and class are incongruous with that of the stereotypical ICI. The boundary between visibility and invisibility is no more fixed than the standard determining formality and informality. Not all visible ICIs purchase goods only in large quantities and not all invisible ICIs import only distinctive items on a small scale. Nonetheless, like the lady/woman polarity discussed in chapter 1, these ideals are likely to have greater effect on those who fit them and differential effects upon those who do not.

"The Full Has Never Been Told"

Below, I record profiles of persons who engage in informal commercial importing at different levels and who cross the formal and informal boundary. Not everyone presented here considers herself an ICI. Older traders often call themselves higglers or ICIs interchangeably. Among the profiles presented, rejection of the title is often based on class position. The majority of visible ICIs proudly refer to themselves as such. Among invisible ICIs, however, the label is not prized. Middle-class professional females rarely publicly use this identification. Often, their scale of operation may be less than a full-time occupation. For many, informal commercial importing is simply a sideline in which they participate sporadically or seasonally. They often refer to their activities as shopping or buying a little of this and that. Others reject this label outright. The higher the class, regardless of informality, the more likely they are to call and consider themselves importers, whether or not they are officially registered. This rejection of the term "ICI," I argue, stems from the social stigma associated with traders. Indeed, because she is hypervisible, the stereotypical ICI cannot afford to be unregistered.[2]

Before I begin, it is important to note that these profiles were created during predissertation and dissertation fieldwork between 1993 and 1996. Since then, I have returned to Jamaica several times and found that a number of the individuals presented here are in different places economically and geographically. In part to protect traders' identities as much as possible, I paraphrase them. They are quoted mostly in the analysis section that includes details about their various strategies. The process of gaining the data to construct these profiles was quite a challenge, as ICIs are rightly distrustful of researchers, particularly since their conversations often result in more stringent policies.

In addition, so far, ICIs have not seen the result of their contributions in print, particularly their contributions to academic projects. It took me months to get certain individuals to speak with me candidly at the arcade. As I discuss in greater detail in the next chapter, downtown has its own code of silence. Everyone abides by it. To break through this wall takes a considerable amount of time and, more crucially, a network of persons willing to intercede on your behalf.

Uptown was another matter. Most of my profiles came from individuals who also imported informally but did not identify as informal importers. I told the vendors I was doing research on ICIs. Ironically, they were often the ones who offered the most information. Once I explained that I viewed them as ICIs, many stopped sharing information. They recognize and admit the social and class privileges they have, which allows them to import without difficulties, while more visible ICIs are targeted. Others did not want to be included at all. I rarely pressed for specific details. Because I had the time, my interview techniques were quite simple. I let them tell me whatever story they wanted me to tell.

The length of the profiles is usually a good indication of the extent of the communication I had with a particular person. In some instances, they are short, because I document rather generic information about these persons to keep details they would not share publicly about their personal affairs private. In others, there is an indication of what type of information they were willing to disclose. In both categories, I wrote profiles of individuals who did not want to speak with me after very brief conversations. They often spoke with me as a favor to other ICIs I have come to know over the years. They were often suspicious of me and would not interact with me when I approached them alone without my contacts. So I began to buy shoes, lots of shoes, from ICIs to get better acquainted with the traders within the areas of the arcade I frequented. Among invisible ICIs, the shorter profiles were done on persons from whom I purchased items or obtained a service. In some cases I spoke with these vendors only a couple times. I did not pursue these traders as much as the arcade-based ICIs who were my primary interest. My goal was to understand how black females confront and respond to socioeconomic and political structures. For this reason, I emphasize their color and class identities to reinforce their fluid connection and stress how government regulation impacted the stereotypical ICI.

Visible ICIs

Profile 1. Miss T. is dark skinned and comes from a traditionally lower-class family. She describes herself as black. Currently in her early sixties, she started out in the business during the early 1980s. Her foreign higglering activities were preceded by a long history of informal economic activities that have made her one of the arcade's most experienced and fascinating traders. She has been almost every kind of vendor existing within the continuum of the trade. Her knowledge in this area, she quickly admits, she received from her mother, who was also a higgler. At a very young age, like most children of higglers, she accompanied her mother to market on weekends, thus learning about the trade. In her midteens, she left her mother's home for Kingston to pursue her own economic activities. In the last forty-seven years, she has been a tray girl, a food shop owner, a fish vendor, and finally an ICI.

She began her career as an Informal Commercial Importer as a result of the misfortunes of being a street vendor. The van that she used to both transport and refrigerate her fish was stolen. Like most of the old-timers, she began by exporting produce to Panama and importing goods in high demand in Jamaica. On several occasions, she also traveled to Haiti, where she bought plastic goods. On those trips, she would meet a friend, an interpreter, who accompanied her, since she doesn't speak Kreyol. He negotiated her purchases. She buys in gross for both wholesale and retail purposes. She is an expert buyer who also purchases for other traders. She buys various goods including cereal, paper products, bric-a-brac, clothes, and shoes. The wide variety of goods ensures that there will always be something to trade.

An Anglican since childhood, Miss T. believes her many trials and successes are the result of having chosen God. "From the moment you open your business, you have to put God in front ... You either open your business with God or the devil." Her continued dedication, after twice losing everything in fires in her arcade stall (occupied since 1985), stems from an unfailing belief that God, who gave her the knowledge to do her work, will always take care of her. As she notes "God comes first in everything. If not for God, me cannot sell."

Over the years, she has primarily sold shoes and some clothing. I have repeatedly visited her in the arcade during days when she could not sell a single pair of shoes or even a roll of toilet paper as there were no buyers. A person who does not accept defeat, she often reminds me that "in life, like in the business, some days are good and some days are bad. But with God all things are possible." She used to attend the Wednesday Falmouth market until it closed in 1997. The Falmouth market was primarily a wholesale market that promised some income, especially during the low buying season. She accumulated enough capital to purchase a pickup truck to minimize the exhaustion, discomfort and lack of safety of these trips. Before that, she, like other ICIs, rode on semi-trailers that carry higglers and ICIs to markets. Though she travels as her funds permit, she often expresses a desire to quit the business, since it is no longer profitable. With past profits from the trade, she purchased her home and pays for the education of her grandchildren. Despite the hard work, she notes that the business allows her to enjoy herself. An oldies music fanatic, she frequently attends shows. The trade also enables her to buy things that she wants and needs for herself and to travel to visit her children, who reside abroad.

Profile 2. Miss B. is in her early forties. She is from a working-class family. She is categorized as brown or red by local standards, yet she describes herself as black. She started in the business twenty years ago as a stall attendant for a friend. At the time, she was working in a garment factory. She left the factory job and began to go on buying trips six years ago. Before that period, she did not consider herself an ICI. She entered the trade for the same reasons as most ICIs—self-reliance and a better income. She travels with a friend to Miami during the winter months and to New York during the summer months. She sells shoes because she is "lucky with shoes." She has been in the Pearnel Charles arcade for twenty years now and has weathered the loss of merchandise during three fires and numerous break-ins. She used to go to the weekly wholesale market at Falmouth but stopped last year because it was no longer worth the hassle.

Profile 3. Mrs. B. is in her early forties. She is dark skinned and from a lower-class background. She describes herself as black. She is originally from Kingston. Her mother, she says, was a higgler. She became a foreign higgler before the factory where she had been employed closed in the early 1980s. She decided to become an importer because she realized she could make more money. The mother of four children, all in school, she needed an increase in income to keep up with the rising inflation rate. On a tourist visa, she made her first buying trip. She traveled to New York City with a friend and bought shoes and bags as well as cosmetics, which she brought back and sold on the streets downtown. She did well. She had also brought back some synthetic hair packets (used for weaves), which sold well. She continued to buy shoes and bags and, over time, began to invest more in hair since that gave her a quick turnover. In the last ten years, she has primarily imported hair, handbags, backpacks, and shoes. She has been able to purchase a van to help with the transport of goods.

One of the most successful ICIs I know, she has her goods in several stalls in two arcades, Old Wolmers and Pearnel Charles, and employs at least four workers to mind them. She provides them with health insurance and even gives them paid vacation time. She has a pleasant demeanor but is tough when she needs to be. During fieldwork, I often visited traders in the Pearnel Charles arcade first. Then I would leave, cross the street to Old Wolmers arcade, and visit Mrs. B. She often parks outside of this arcade. She sits in the van among the boxes of hair in different shades of black, brown, red, and blond. These tresses also come in different lengths and varieties of styles including straight, curly, and wavy. She is also surrounded by nylon and leather backpacks.

I have sat with her many times, and I have seen her switch from the Queen's English to Jamaican patois, from being sweet to tough, depending on the customer and the circumstance. Her clientele includes laborers as well as professionals and hardcore dancehall fans. When customers approach Mrs. B., she can quickly tell who is not accustomed to the arcade. She often sends one of her workers along with them to navigate. When I asked her why she does this, she replied "some customers need to feel special." Her business is so lucrative that she travels at least three times a month, primarily to New York. A devout Pentecostal, she likes "being natural," as her denomination teaches. She places God above everything and will give you a sermon if you raise the Lord's name in vain. She says, "I like this occupation because it makes me independent and makes me a person of substance." She confided that she often loses on her investments, but in the end it's all worth it.

Profile 4. Mrs. M. is dark skinned and from a working-class family. She considers herself black and is in her midfifties. She became an ICI in the early 1980s. She is originally from the country and has lived in Kingston since the 1960s when she came to look for work. She has held various jobs in the manufacturing industry. When her factory closed in the late 1980s, she began to work in her sister's stall in the arcade. Her sister and a friend brought back merchandise, which they encouraged her to sell for herself. She decided to go into the business after she had saved the startup money. She took a trip to Miami with another friend who took her in as an apprentice and taught her the business—what to buy, where to buy, where to stay, etc. She doesn't like to travel; she prefers to go to places that are close to home so that she can come back the same day. She doesn't like the business these days, because "the taxes are killing we." The everyday physical demands of the business have also taken a toll on her health. During the mid-1990s, she reduced her traveling activities and goes to the arcade less and less.

Profile 5. Mr. Y. is in his forties. He is very light in skin shade. He is of working-class origins. He considers himself black. His mother was a higgler. He began to import in the late 1980s. He sells mostly men's clothing and operates a stall in the arcade. He specializes in quality clothing for men. He will quickly tell you that he doesn't buy knockoffs. He entered the business to be his own boss. He travels mostly to Panama and New York. He says he likes the trade because he likes the traveling and being independent. He does not like the hassles of customs, and he claims the business is tougher now than before.

Profile 6. Miss G. is twenty-five years old. She is dark skinned from a working-class family. In conversations, she often refers to herself as a black woman. When I asked her what it is like to be an ICI, she quickly responded that she wasn't an ICI, but she worked for one. She minds the stall for a trader, a friend of her mother's, who owns several stalls. She has worked for her for four years now. She tells me she earns more on this job than she would in the free trade zone. Though she is an employee, she enjoys a sense of independence. She says she is saving her money so she can go into business for herself and operate her own stall. She says she is satisfied working for an ICI because her employer is understanding and pays her well.

Profile 7. Mrs. C. is fifty-two years old. She is dark skinned and describes herself as black. She comes from a lower-class family and considers herself a lady. She is the mother of four children—a daughter and three sons—and a grandmother of five. She started in the business fourteen years ago, after disagreements with her former employer at a factory. Along with six other women and one man from her church, she went on her first buying trip to Panama during the early 1980s. The man who had initiated them in the trade has since left it. He taught them from whom to buy and where to go. She went on two more trips with the group before branching out on her own. A couple years after she started her own business, she began to travel to Miami and New York, where she continued to buy clothes and shoes because "that's the main market." She likes the traveling and being her own boss, which allows her to do everything on her own time. As her business grew, she began to travel more frequently, especially to Panama.

She loves the business. "There is pleasure in going and choosing something and bringing it back and someone else likes it...the customer enjoys it as much as you enjoyed buying it." She points out that trading is not an easy business to be in because you take a lot of risks. She credits her longevity in importing to being a good Christian and working with God: "I try to be a good businessperson...you don't do it just for the love of money but you have Christ with you and having Christ with you means a lot." She withstands all of the ups and downs of the market with a fighting spirit and copious economic activities "because you can't depend on just one thing" to maintain a family.

Profile 8. Mr. M. is a dark-skinned man in his early twenties; he considers himself black. He comes from a new middle-class family. His mother is an ICI. He started to work with her when he was younger, watching the stall and helping out. When he finished school, he began to accompany his mother on buying trips. She fell ill in the early 1990s. To keep from losing her business, she sent him on a buying trip, since he had experience traveling with her. At that point, he began to branch out on his own. He knows just where to go, and she has taught him what to buy. He said that he didn't think he wanted to be an ICI, especially since he does not enjoy the traveling. But he likes being his own boss. Besides, he stands to inherit the business from his mother (Mrs. C., in profile 7). His brother, who sometimes tends the stall with him, is also an apprentice.

Invisible ICIs

Profile 9. Miss V. is in her late thirties. She is very fair skinned and would be socially classified as high-brown because of her long straight hair and freckles. She considers herself brown and is of lower-class origin. She moved from the country to live with family and attended one of the top secondary schools for girls in Kingston. She is now a well-established business owner. After our initial conversation, I pressed her for a formal interview. She was reluctant, saying that I really needed to talk to the other traders who had to deal with all the hassles and could not avoid problems with customs. In the early 1980s, she worked as a flight attendant. She decided to get into import-export after she noticed the foreign higglers on her flights. She realized this business could help her reach her goals of obtaining higher education.

At that time, Jamaica was burdened with import restrictions. She began to export local rum and liquor to Miami and to other Caribbean islands, where she flew as a flight attendant. On her return trips, she imported alcoholic beverages such as Jack Daniels and cognac for several hoteliers on the north coast. This was very lucrative. At times she diversified and exported other products depending on customer demand. She continued to import and export for three years, investing most of her profits in farming, as she intended eventually to leave the business. She admits that her social position facilitated her activities. With her frequent travels, she was able to import on a small scale consistently. She told me "I didn't have any problems. I knew the airport employees. They knew me." She notes "since everyone was doing it in the beginning, no one cared." By the time the trade was under regulation, she had decreased her activities and was attending business school in the United States. She also purchased a small operating farm. She stopped importing entirely when she finished her degree and began to pursue her dream of becoming a property developer.

Profile 10. Miss F. is dark-skinned and from a lower middle-class family. She considers herself black and is in her late fifties. She is a full-time informal trader. She started in the early 1980s by chance. As an entertainer, she traveled frequently to the U.S. and Europe. During these trips, she would "pick up this and that" and sell them to friends when she returned. She says, "I had a good time doing it and it was working. People liked what I bought, so I decided to make several trips specifically to shop. I went to New York because my cousin lives there and she has a car. She drove me to different stores where I bought things on sale. I sell them back in Jamaica for the original price. Then I began to go to the wholesale district, and sometimes they would give me a discount on the wholesale price. Then I could have a higher markup. Sometimes it was as much as 200 percent depending on the goods." When she retired from dancing, she entered the trade full-time. She began to sell out of a special room in her home and has been doing so for the past fifteen years. She stopped traveling when she identified a wholesaler from whom she could buy goods. Her overhead costs were reduced since she no longer traveled.

In the mid-1980s, she also began to sell perfume both at home and to established stores. She bought the product in bulk from a wholesaler who had an exclusive contract with her, thus giving her a monopoly on perfume. According to Miss F., "the markup on perfume is not very high, but you always make money and when you wholesale to a store, you make a lump sum at a given time." However, that did not last long. Others soon got into this market, and it became quite competitive. She found other wholesalers, including someone in England who buys throughout Europe and comes to Jamaica twice a year. Her stock is always upscale and turns over quickly. She gets her merchandise from the New York buyer who purchases items from exclusive wholesalers, as well as Bloomingdale's and Saks Fifth Avenue. The quality of her products is very appealing to her clientele, who are primarily interested in "better" clothing. She sells "boutique style" clothing, mostly to upper middle-class customers. These include managers, doctors, lawyers, and entertainers. There are some who are into tailored pieces and others who are interested strictly in designer clothing. Some of the brands she has distributed included Calvin Klein, Liz Claiborne, Marks & Spencer, Nicole Miller, Versace, and Tag. She never has more than one piece of a particular style of clothing. Her shoes are always of the finest Italian leather.

She usually carries a combination of goods like clothing, perfume, and accessories, as well as household items, including furniture. Perfume, she says, "has the quickest turnover. It doesn't last forever and since everybody wants to smell sweet at some time, they are always buying it." She sells it for cash only, never on credit. The clothing she sells on credit for two months maximum. The furniture is slowest to obtain, sometimes taking up to six months to arrive, but when it comes in, it is always solid money. With this combination, Miss F. always experiences cash flow.

Profile 11. Miss R. is dark skinned and calls herself a black woman. She comes from a lower-class family. Though she is in her late thirties, she is a tray girl, of sorts, selling cigarettes, newspapers, and crackers, sitting on a stool on the corner of the lane every morning until midafternoon, when classes end. She is the mother of two young children whom she must send to school. Her mother is a higgler at Coronation Market. At the end of market day, her mother often joins her on the street corner to allow her to run errands or pick up goods to sell the next day. For example, during crab season, Miss R. buys crabs and cooks them to sell to pedestrians. During mango season, she picks up a few. With the profit she earns, she will travel to Cayman or Panama, where she will buy "a little of this and a little of that," which she gives to a friend to sell for her in the arcade or outside of the market. She also sells some of these imported goods in her home. On average, she goes on two trips a year, one for the Christmas season and the other for Easter.

Profile 12. Miss C. is a high-brown lady whose face is decorated with freckles. She is in her midthirties. She was born into a middle-class family and considers herself brown. She is married and has a child. Recently she returned to Jamaica after living in Britain for over twenty years. She is currently employed as a massage therapist in an exclusive beauty salon uptown. She travels mostly to Miami and New York to buy beauty products and costume jewelry. Occasionally, she travels to England to buy aromatherapy products, which are quite expensive in Jamaica. Her clientele are mostly females who come to the salon. When the owner is not on the premises and while known customers are sitting in the waiting room, she passes around a small pouch of jewelry or a flat tray with nail polish or a small basket of perfumes and oils. She returns later to check whether anyone wants to make a purchase. Buyers are not issued credit. She likes the quick turnover, she says. When she travels, she always buys enough to return with a full suitcase. Sometimes she buys additional things, such as clothing for friends who will buy from her. She likes to travel and considers this activity necessary to accumulate the capital necessary to acquire her own salon.

Profile 13. Miss S. is twenty-nine years old. She is a single, not quite dark-skinned lady (as she would call herself) from a traditional lower-class family. She identifies herself as brown. She is a young professional in a management position at an established firm in Kingston. Two years ago, when personal problems affected her income, she decided to start importing so that she could maintain her lifestyle. Her first trip was to Miami with a friend. To minimize their expenditures, they stayed with another friend who drove them around to different stores such as JCPenney and Kmart, where they bought sportswear such as knit shirts and dresses and tights on sale, along with some toiletries. She bought no more than three similar pieces but always in different colors. She sells primarily to coworkers or friends who socialize together. They would not want to purchase the same item as a friend. She brought her best pieces to work in a duffel bag, which she showed to coworkers during tea break or lunch. The buyers would pay for their goods with cash or on credit over two months in accord with her work pay schedule. She reinvested the profits in her Valentine's Day trip. She went to New York alone and stayed with a friend. She shopped in the wholesale clothing district. This trip she focused mostly on gifts, such as watches and perfume gift sets, as well as clothing.

She also shopped for numerous personal items and requests and shipped those items home in a barrel. When she arrived, several friends dropped by her place to see what she had brought back. Several had requested specific items, which they paid for as soon as she presented them. She realized that accessories and perfume were the first things to go. On her next trip, she purchased mostly these items. She travels rather sporadically since this is an activity she conducts to supplement her income as needed.

Profile 14. Miss X. is what Jamaicans call high brown. She was born in an upper-class family. She also considers herself brown, or in local parlance, a browning. Educated at one of Kingston's finest girls' schools, she has been working as a flight attendant for over fifteen years. During her frequent trips, she purchases all sorts of items including perfume, jewelry, clothing, and shoes. She sells out of her home and will bring her wares to customers' homes when she returns from her trips. Her activities grew, and eventually she began to operate a small shop on the north coast. In an upper-class area, she owns a quaint boutique stocked entirely with items she imports informally during weekly airline trips. On a visit to her shop, I once told her about an upcoming trip to Guatemala. She asked me to look for small items that she could sell in her shop. I was taken aback. "Just don't bring too many. Gina, look for things that no one else would have that are of quality." "Like what?" I asked her. "Oh you know... anything... you've got good taste. Look at your lapis earrings and jewelry... purses, belts. Gina! Why pay for the trip? Make the ticket pay for itself. Why should you pay for it?" And that is often the strategy that governs the practice for neophyte part-timers. Such vendors often start by needing to cover the cost of the trip, and then expand their activities to make more profit.

Profile 15. Miss O. is dark skinned and comes from an upper-class family. As a result of her stellar class lineage, she is considered brown even though she identifies as black. She grew up in a wealthy Kingston suburb and attended one of the top girls' schools in Jamaica. She is a young professional currently living abroad. As is common among those in her social milieu, she migrated and earned her higher degree abroad. The topic of her master's thesis was informal commercial importing. She returned home to conduct her research. From her subjects, she said she learned about the multiple opportunities in the business; she decided to become an ICI. Among friends and families, she became something of a rebel, someone who rejected expectations and embraced the way of the masses. She borrowed money from a family member to begin importing. She went on buying trips and brought things back that she sold mostly to friends of friends and later to stores. After a number of trips, her activities were taking off to such an extent that she employed others and began to import on a larger scale. Eventually, she returned abroad. Though she has left the trade, whenever she travels home, the ticket always pays for itself.

Differences among Traders

As these profiles show, vendors participating in informal commercial activities come from a range of socioeconomic positions. They cut across class, color, and gender lines. While they import different merchandise on various scales and sell to different customers, these individuals enter the trade for similar reasons. They choose independent trading to gain greater control of their lives and to be their own bosses. Among older invisible ICIs, there are some obvious continuities. They tend to follow family tradition. The younger ones enter the trade after work in free trade zone factories or equally low-paying and demanding work in the service sector. For most of these traders, the business is not a vehicle for mobility per se, but a means through which they can earn a consistent livelihood. The economic activities of Miss J., who has a tray and sits on a street corner near the arcade, vary seasonally. She has come to depend on the income she earns doing these different activities, and she spends accordingly. For now, she is satisfied with the size of her business, as it will take her several years to expand. Nonetheless, even now, she is able to maintain her family.

When I met Miss L. in 1993, she was a helper who planned to get into the business. Since I have known her, she has been talking about entering the trade. For a couple years, she talked about needing to raise the start-up funds to go on her first buying trip. She contacted a distant cousin abroad for help, to no avail. She had hoped that someone would sponsor her. Two years later, she hadn't given up her dream. She would continue this way until she could save enough to set herself up with a stall somewhere. As Elsie Le Franc (1989) argued, due to the crossing of boundaries, informal commercial importing was likely to become just another form of disguised wage labor. In my research, I found that for most of the arcade ICIs, the occupation is just that. New recruits brought increasing competition and a saturated market. There is cognizance among newcomers that it is structurally impossible for everyone to make it big in the business. Despite this overcrowding, many seek the trade for the flexibility and independence it offers. This sense of freedom should not be underestimated. It is the reason that marketers throughout the region continue to flood this occupation.[3] Simultaneously, there are also those who strive for much more. They aim to succeed and, in most cases, they have not only surpassed society's expectations, as E. M. Brown's op-ed in the *New York Times* (2000) stated, but they have also managed to propel their children and grandchildren into another economic stratum. As is the case throughout the region, their new material agency may not necessarily lead to upward social mobility (Brown 1994; Carnegie 1981; Gordon, Anderson, and Robotham 1997; Mantz 2003). I would argue that individual traders are motivated by their very own freedom dreams (Kelley 2003).

Mrs. B.'s motive, from the time I met her, has been to be able to retire early to the country, away from the harshness of Kingston. She focused on expanding her business enough to send others on trips so that she stopped traveling altogether. She hoped to be able to live comfortably from her investments. She managed this and, in the process, was able to employ several family members and friends. When I asked what she didn't like about the business, she replied, "It rough." While she enjoyed certain aspects of the business, she noted that it took a considerable toll on her body: "Going up and down to get mi things released from customs. Sometimes mi tired. But I have to go." She continued, "If it wasn't for this, I wouldn't have mi van. I couldn't send my children to school and buy my place in the country." For these ICIs who value autonomy above all else, the gains are the outcome of the hardship. While many among them dislike how rough the business is and the increasing competition as "everyone wants to be a ICI," they don't plan to leave it or to do something else.

The fact that informal commercial importing consistently draws new recruits is evident in the profiles of invisible ICIs. Middle-class traders do not necessarily come from families in the informal sector. Yet these individuals have similarities with the old-timers. They participate in importing for everyday survival, greater economic independence, and the possibilities of capital accumulation. Like traders who occupy stalls in the arcade, on the streets, in stores, or in offices they identify a market and respond directly to customer demand. They purchase various goods to have constant incoming cash by selling items that have a quick turnover, so they are never without. They reinvest their profits to expand their businesses. A key difference with these traders is their willingness to mix their business activities with their private and work lives. In the examples cited, several of the middle-class ICIs involved friends in their businesses and counted them as customers. Friends and coworkers form their customer base. Most of the arcade ICIs I encountered were quite clear about not crossing such boundaries, even when their children are involved. In a sense, they do not take their work home. And when they do, the lines are clear. When money exchanges hands, it is not personal. Business is business. Among arcade ICIs there were those who were adamant about not working with family and friends, others who trusted no one but kin, and still others who only dealt with business associates. In most of these cases, there was often a story about being robbed while staying over at a friend's on a buying trip or about a family member who borrowed money and never paid it back and so on.

It is precisely because of the scope of difference that state definition and regulation of informal commercial importing unfairly targets those who are the most visible, for the state has a stake in policing their economic practices as well as their bodies. In a study conducted for the Jamaican government's policy review, researchers Donna McFarlane-Gregory and Thalia Ruddock-Kelly proposed a new definition of ICI that would include everyone involved in importing: from the person who travels, to the individual who sells goods imported by other ICIs or shipped by partners or relatives who reside abroad, to the person who sells goods produced in Jamaica abroad (1993:20). This definition considers the extensive and complex networks central to this activity and would inevitably increase the size of the population of traders who ought to pay duties and taxes on imports. Indeed, the process of formalization implemented since the 1980s was comprised of measures that reach only a small sector of the entire informal commercial importing population. The limited effects of these regulation attempts point not only to the dynamism of informal economies, but also to the fact that such activities exist across the social structure and simply cannot be contained. Others have found that it is virtually impossible to formalize informal sectors.[4]

Government attempts to institute such economic policies often take the form of conditions on international monetary loans that purport to promote development. In Ghana, Gracia Clark has found that structural adjustment policies have had direct effects on market women's practices (2001). Florence Babb finds a similar trend in Peru with respect to privatization of market spaces (2001). As Victor Tokman concludes, the informal sector operates between underground and illegality (1992). He argues that informal producers obtain access to what they evaluate as important while minimizing the risks associated with illegality. As a result, nonobservance of regulations becomes a relative matter. He further stresses that national economic policies are often well-intentioned, but usually ill-conceived, like tax systems that result in widespread evasion (1992:16–22). While I disagree with Tokman's assessment of the state's intention, he does make a relevant point. Informal economic activities are practiced on a much grander scale than policies can reach. Consequently, governments siphon revenues from whom they can: usually, the least powerful among poorer constituencies without political representation. While the majority of visible ICIs are but petty traders, the image representing the myth of traders as thieves who overcharge for products and continuously attempt to circumvent regulation prevails. The stereotype allows government to continue to target those they can. By focusing on this particular group of ICIs, the state, through its systematic practices, plays a significant role in reinforcing existing class hierarchies and privileges.

Nonetheless, formalization has also had some contradictory effects. It brought details of this activity to the public and, in the process, attracted new recruits. According to a former general manager of Metropolitan Parks and Markets (MPM), "Once government formalized vendors in the early 1980s, people who did not have formal education, known skills, went into selling because of the increased accessibility. Over the years when technical training was limiting people from other jobs they went into selling." The occupation continues to expand as a social welfare net. In addition, rumors of ICIs getting rich and buying houses with cash resulted in an increase in the number of registered traders to 12,000 by 1988. The ICI is no longer a lower-class city dweller with low levels of education and skills. New infiltrators come from across the classes. Many of these neophytes come directly from the formal sector. According to Egbert Reid, the new influx included registered nurses, policemen, schoolteachers, telephone operators, and insurance agents (1989:40). Over the years, the number of males who have entered this occupation, which is dominated by females, has also increased. The number of unregistered ICIs is far greater than the registered.

Passing through Customs

In 1996, Dustan Whittingham, president of the Jamaica Higglers and Sidewalk Vendors Association (an organization founded in 1986), estimated that the total number of ICIs (both registered and unregistered) was close to 300,000. Even then, that number was an underestimate, as the persistence of a volatile economy, high inflation, lack of jobs, and low incomes in the formal sector made informal commercial importing attractive across a broad spectrum of the population. Everyone in Jamaica knows someone who brings things to Jamaica to sell, whether it is computer parts (especially memory chips, which are quite expensive in specialty shops), auto parts, Greek and Italian extra virgin olive oil, or expensive European facial beauty products. Most of these traders are unseen because they are not located in arcades or on the streets. They operate in sites that are invisible to the public and the state, such as their homes, offices, hotels, and stores. These invisible ICIs are employed persons in the formal sector and include the helper, the domestic servant, the cleaning lady, the assistant secretary, the museum attendant, the university student, the insurance agent, the bank teller, the hairdresser, the beauty parlor owner, the flight attendant, the professor, the expatriate, the NGO worker, and the embassy employee, even the ambassador and his wife who have customs clearance.[5] Those of the lowest classes import as a sideline to supplement their low incomes. For those in the middle, it is often a means by which to maintain one's social status, which is primarily based on consumption patterns. Individuals in the highest bracket usually aim to build capital. Their business activities differ from those of visible ICIs in that they target specific markets at particular times of year. Because of these differences, there are all sorts of advantages to being undetectable.

However, not everyone benefits equally from this obscurity. As I have already argued, history has marked all bodies with class and color codes that, when performed correctly, add up to various capital signs. These facilitate or hinder individual crossings, especially for the most invisible of all informal commercial importers. The stereotype of ICI as a loud, large buxom black woman dragging several large overstuffed suitcases also has her "other" in the form of the middle-class lady of leisure. The following are defining characteristics of this invisible ICI:

1. She is a lady (she may be dark skinned, but she is socially brown or on the border of that category).
2. She is highly educated.
3. Her association and social networks reflect her inherited class position.
4. She sells in her office or home, or sometimes even operates a shop.
5. Her buying trip is disguised as leisure or business rather than importing.
6. Her stock contains greater variety and styles. Most of these items are of higher economic value.
7. She supplies formal sector businesses and/or is sponsored by an establishment.
8. The higher her class, the more exclusive her market and the more expensive the goods she sells.
9. Her customers are high-ranking professionals who, for social reasons, must maintain their consumption of distinction (this will be discussed in later chapters).

The government simply cannot regulate the activities of this type of ICI in the same way as the visible ones because their scale of operation is often much too small. These middle-class ICIs import status symbols, such as "better" shoes, clothing, cosmetics, fabrics, home furnishings, and jewelry.

Because distinction is key to middle- and upper-class identities, they do not import in volume; hence, they are not identified as commercial. They travel regularly, and often seasonally, sometimes prior to holidays such as Christmas, Easter, Valentine's Day, or to holidays observed on which merchants offer big discounts in the country of destination (for example, the Fourth of July, Memorial Day, Labor Day, and the day after Thanksgiving in the U.S.). They inform their customers of their date of departure so that they may make requests for specific purchases. Abroad, they stay with friends and family to cut their total expenditures. They return home with little or no hassle from customs, depending on the time of year. They do not face the hostility that visible ICIs do, if they face any at all. Within their milieu, however, there are social disadvantages. The higher their class position, the more likely they are to encounter disdain, especially from older females invested in archaic notions of being a lady. They lose status among those who frown upon their having to hustle, an indication of their financial insecurity. "Wow...you should have seen her in those days. She was something else. She was not afraid. She was out there traveling, shopping, bringing lots of great things from the States and England even. Sure I bought from her. We all did. You have to admire how she just took charge...I admire her...But I could never..." Miss P. and I were talking about a close friend who once was an active and invisible ICI. That friend sold most of her goods to her friends. She did not have a shop, but conducted transactions in her home or brought her merchandise directly to customers. In her class position, certain types of entrepreneurial activities were deemed acceptable (such as having a boutique or selling to established merchants). Others were not. Having to work and, especially in this capacity, had its own stigmas for those in the higher echelon. It is in such contexts, with the persistence of the lady/woman ideals, that an uptown lady becomes a downtown woman.

When I began my research, I first spoke with Miss H. She is one of the flight attendants who insisted that I did not need to hear her life story as much as I needed to hear those of the ICIs at the arcade because, as she said, "I didn't have any problems. I could have continued with it, but it was tiring." She continued, "These ladies have to deal with customs and the way they treat them...they would not talk to me like that!" Government officials cannot legally identify persons like Miss H. as ICIs, thus they cannot question the volume of their "personal luggage." Such ICIs sell their wares to friends of friends or peers who pay in cash or installments from their paycheck in private, outside of public and government scrutiny. They are able to carry out their business activities in part because societal standards expect them to travel and to be avid consumers. Another invisible ICI, Miss B., noted that when her business expanded, she avoided the hassles of customs by taking girlfriends on buying trips. They became her private couriers. She purchased their airline tickets, and sometimes they stayed with her or visited their friends or family members. In exchange for this free trip, Miss B. had two additional suitcase spaces per friend. She filled them with merchandise, and they all flew back to Kingston. Upon their return home, they breezed through customs as young upper middle-class ladies returning from a weekend abroad shopping. While the existence of such ICIs points to the flaws inherent in regulation, it also offers a commentary on class and color performance.

The question is, who can pass through customs and how? And what exactly facilitates this crossing? The act of passing, Nella Larsen ([1929] 1997) so viscerally alerted us, requires that one perform class properly so as not to disrupt the order of cultural markers assigned to class and color codes. For this reason, the visible working-class ICI is more likely to be targeted for duties than her upper-class counterpart. This ICI's appearance and habitus render her class visible in the same manner as the middle- or upper-class trader. Since the occupation itself is a class signifier, the higher the class of an individual, the more likely she is able to continuously pass through customs without being identified as an ICI.[6] Passing, it seems, depends on a number of factors. These include her identity as a lady, which presupposes her class position and makes her off-limits to customs officials who are below her in stature. As I discussed earlier, class taboos in social relations dictate that persons of different classes "know their place" and keep their appropriate distance. Individuals across the social structure generally observe these norms.

It must be stressed, however, that it is precisely because the ICI disregarded this order that she was labeled a rude gal. Her disruption is the lady's gain. Paradoxically, her disorder reinforces what it means to be a lady and indirectly allows this invisible ICI to pass. As I indicated above, the unsuspected lady ICI passed, as she is expected to be a frequent traveler and avid consumer because of her class. Such traders are able to operate under guises protected by both their social status and their class. Thus, duty collecting leaves a lot of discretion for the customs agent, where cultural factors influence decisions. Both of the customs officers I interviewed asserted that persons who are not licensed, card-carrying ICIs are able to pass through customs because the official guideline on what constitutes commercial goods is quite specific. However, the decision regarding who pays duties and taxes on excess goods, as I illustrate in chapter 6, is quite random.

Socioeconomic Politics of Visibility

It was that randomness in product selection, in part, that allowed foreign higglers to outrival established business owners when they first began this activity in the late 1970s. They brought things that people wanted, as Miss Tiny noted earlier. At the advent of the formalization process, they were able to pass through customs, because the PNP government overlooked their activities. Once they became subject to the JLP's panoptic gaze in the 1980s, traders' capacities to outmaneuver this new system of regulation (dictated by international funding agencies to implement neoliberal policies) was severely limited. They have had to learn new tactics. In 2004, a customs administrator informed me that his office is especially knowledgeable of ICIs' methods of avoiding duties. He notes, "they can't cheat because we know all their tricks." Indeed, they do. Over the years, government has become more proficient. It has developed a risk assessment system to detect those who, among the stereotyped, attempt to undercut customs. According to customs, they now have an extensive research department and a verification unit that conducts extensive examination of all products imported into Jamaica. I would add that their reach is still limited, as invisible ICIs are still importing under the radar.[7] The information retrieved is logged into their system. This data is complemented with an index of prices that is updated every six months. So when ICIs declare their goods, the value and quality of the products invoiced can be checked to avoid underinvoicing. The administrator did note that there is the occasional ICI who attempts to pass red peas for hair, as the latter is more costly. However, such deception is easily exposed upon weighing the container. Most ICIs are well aware of customs' increasing aptitude in dealing with their tactics. As a result, traders have developed a relationship with the state in which they expect government to continuously overtax them. In turn, ICIs constantly adapt by seeking creative ways to endure this challenge. Nonetheless, not all ICIs are capable, let alone willing, to engage in outmaneuvering the regulatory system. As Miss Z. noted, "it's too much work."

During the late 1970s and early 1980s, foreign higglers would arrive at airports early and look for business travelers without personal baggage and entice them to claim their boxes of merchandise so that they could avoid hassle and duty. These higglers preyed on the sympathy of the traveler, whose kindness would supposedly help her feed her children or nurse her sick mother. Several ICIs I interviewed had used this tactic and others to circumvent constraining state regulations. These strategies point to traders' consciousness of their position and location within the local-global context and how this awareness informs their possibilities for action. To avoid government duties, traders constantly deployed the stereotype of the poor, ignorant higgler.

One of the most well-known examples of this deployment of the stereotype is that of the ICI who arrives at the customs station in Kingston's Norman Manley International Airport and starts to curse and cry once the official opens her boxes to find only left shoes without their mates. She cries that the wholesaler in Panama cheated her. She continues to moan, because she has lost her investment. This money she had borrowed to start her little business was taken. The shoes are worthless without their match. Out of sympathy and fear of a commotion, the customs officer allows her to pass through customs without having to pay duties. Meanwhile, in Montego Bay at the Sangster International Airport, her partner claims the same story with the right shoes. The two ICIs meet after the ordeal and reunite the shoes. Their quick wit and savvy made the front page of the *Gleaner* (*Gleaner* 1990). This deployment only reified the stereotype. However, in the submissiveness to the performance of this identity, there are hidden transcripts. As James Scott notes, "in playing dumb, subordinates make creative use of the stereotypes intended to stigmatize them. If they are thought of as stupid and a direct refusal is dangerous, then they can screen refusal with ignorance" (1990:132). Issues of national and international security had their impact on this practice. Strangers are less likely to take responsibility for luggage from persons unknown to them. As a result, ICIs have had to be even more resourceful in their circumvention tactics. More recently, when they pack their goods they put the more expensive items in the bottom part of the barrel. The hope is that the agent will examine only the items on the surface of the barrel. As I learned from customs officials, they have caught on to this practice. It is also well known that traders continue to obtain foreign exchange mostly from unofficial sources on the parallel market to avoid documentation of the full extent of their activities. Given the excessive taxation, the saturated market, and the low purchasing power of consumers, their survival or success in the business depends on their ability to undermine regulation.

No one is able to undercut official guidelines more than traders who import on a small scale. Invisible importers of distinctive high-quality items earn even more. When an ICI suitcase is opened, customs agents automatically look for quantity because commercial goods are defined solely by volume. The smaller the number of items in a suitcase, the more likely this importer is to avoid duties, though that is not always the case. An invisible middle-class trader noted that once she was stopped at customs and the official, expressing his suspicion of her commercial activities, pointedly asked her, "You think me a idiot?" She had made several trips that month and had seen the same agent upon each return. She noted she did not have any "arrangements" with anyone at the airport. He charged her duty on her "personal" items. She paid the duty she was charged on the goods and still made a profit. The anxiety of getting caught is one of the reasons that she has stopped traveling altogether.

State practices of controlling their borders regulate racialized class and gender performances that warrant further examination. The idea of people passing through customs and national borders has its correlation in ideas about racial and class passing. However, these connections are rather fluid. They are another site that reveals the disjunctures and disruptions that are caused when certain bodies attempt to multiply various types of capital. For example, a customs officer was sensitized to my attempt to smuggle the electronic equipment precisely because black middle-class individuals tend to do so. I also could not pass at the scale of the urban street or maze of the market stall, as I explain in the next chapter. Similarly, because ICIs exist across the class structure, their movement in and out of local, national, and transnational regulatory regimes at borders has much to reveal concerning the more relational aspect of mobilities and immobilities. I return to this point later, in the brawta (afterword). The ways in which ICIs fashion their border control practices are grounded in their performances of positions. That said, their methods differ according to the individuals and depend on context. Whether or not they succeed depends upon how ingenious a tactic they use, who they know, and who the officer is at the time.

I also encountered those who have never been caught by customs. One ICI told me she has the kind of personality that allows her to get through. This ability to pass through customs with nothing to declare is one of the key problems with regulation. With the focus on the stereotype, government policy has yet to address this issue. According to several officers, it is especially difficult to charge duties to the "stoosh" or uppity uptown ladies who travel frequently and import on a small scale. One noted, "You see them come through once a week, but you can't charge them because they don't have the right volume for commercial goods." A veteran customs officer stressed that these ladies are often offended when officials try to suggest they are importing goods for commerce. And when they are caught, the implications are rather minimal. They are only charged duties on their goods. Their merchandise is not confiscated, and they face no legal repercussions that could impede them from continuing their activities. In most cases, their importing activities are supplementary. Needless to say, government policies are implemented unevenly and reinforce existing socioeconomic boundaries.

In short, customs' official guidelines for taxes and duties are both unrestricted and constrained by government definitions, depending on the volume and the type of the goods. As I have discussed above, the wave of new recruits highlights the consistency of the trade across class and color lines. However, the articulation of class and color categories allows for variation in the ways that traders practice the trade. This in turn leads to both benefits and challenges for different vendors. Nowhere is this more apparent than in the process of clearing goods through customs. For visible ICIs, this is an ordeal that requires that they follow a tediously bureaucratic and expensive procedure to avoid hassles. The prevalent belief is that this vendor intends to deceive the state. In that sense, she remains stigmatized by the same conditions that brought her into being. She remains a fixed image in popular and official imagination. Consequently, she is hypervisible and thus unable to circumvent the system regulating her in the same manner that it did decades ago. She must adapt. This ICI simply cannot be unregistered, and furthermore she is the most heavily regulated. She remains the target because her body, comportment, and performance are coded with inscriptions from the past that continue to affect her present. The area where her corporeal performances are most complex and simultaneously unrecognized is downtown Kingston in the arcade.

CHAPTER FIVE

Inside and Outside of the Arcade: My Downtown Dailies and Miss B.'s Tuffness

You have to be tough! If you are not tough, you won't make it in Kingston.— Nesha Haniff

It's really rough. Sometimes, I'm just tired.— Miss B.

When I began this project, my intent was to create a social map of the Pearnel Charles (PC) arcade that would explain social relations among traders, customers, and officials of Metropolitan Parks and Markets (MPM). However, by the time I felt comfortable enough to walk around, after multiple visits to Miss T., I realized the arcade is a complex building with accessible spaces as well as cleavages and crevices that are not as open as they appear. A rectangular concrete structure with vent windows on all four sides, PC arcade measures 20,000 square feet. The main entrance is in front on the street facing the lower parts of South Parade. There is another doorway in back on Mark Lane. The inside layout is like a grid with 580 metal stalls built mostly with chicken wire fences in various clusters depending on the row. The stalls vary in size but most measure approximately five by ten feet and are often lit by a single lightbulb extending from exposed electrical wires. Two restrooms in the building are lit mostly by rectangular floodlights that barely brighten their intended areas. Poorly ventilated and with narrow side entrances, the arcade is usually quite hot.

The surrounding fringes of the arcade often have little or no light. In these dark bends, it is difficult to see what commodities are being sold inside the stalls. In search of coolness, bodies often block the small entryways;

stools, chairs, and standing fans, surrounded by crowds of people, may also bar entry. I found these areas impenetrable. Initially, to get a sense of the entire arcade, I would canvass the building. I rushed at first. Then I began to pretend I was shopping. My comportment and discomfort signaled my "out of placeness." With time, I began to walk a bit more slowly. All the while, I sensed I was trespassing. I should not be lingering there. As I walked by, individuals stared and often I heard them ask: "What dat foreign girl want?" Perhaps I wanted to sell my U.S. dollars? Or I would hear laughter and/or a series of muffled whispers. People were used to seeing me roaming around the center of the arcade where the ICIs I knew were mostly located. My anxieties about those other parts of the arcade had two sources. First, I was steeped in classed perceptions of downtown as a danger zone. While not without basis, as I show below, this view limited/conditioned/shaped the risks I was willing to take for research purposes. Second, no ICI or UVA official had introduced me to traders in these corners. The absence of a liaison made it difficult for me to establish rapport with ICIs downtown. From their perspective, I was just another suspicious intruder. While the arcade itself is far from dangerous, other areas there require someone to facilitate entry for research. Respecting boundaries in this setting is crucial because certain parts of downtown have their own rules.

I soon abandoned the idea of working in the whole arcade, as I realized that by limiting my area of observation, I would be able to collect more consistent data. Besides, initially Miss T. would not introduce me to traders in other areas, and I decided venturing out on my own would take too much time. I repeatedly asked her to introduce me, and she would say yes, but not follow through. Four months after my arrival, Miss T. finally introduced me to another ICI, who in turn, introduced me to another. From these connections, I built a larger network of potential research subjects. I was concerned, as these ICIs introduced me only to their friends. Initially, I attributed Miss T.'s unwillingness to her desire to remain my primary source of information. But over time I began to realize that there were other reasons. Eventually, I recognized their reluctance to introduce me to others was symptomatic of their own suspicion of strangers. Not everyone in the arcade knows everyone else. Traders in my network often reminded me "all kinda of tings a gwan in the arcade."

I view the arcade as a microcosm of downtown. It consists of multiple enclaves and includes pockets closed to outsiders. Many of the factions found in this locale are based on divisions and tensions between JLP and PNP supporters. Also, they are built in neighborhoods entrenched in decades of politically motivated territorial wars. When these structures are built, the party in power usually maintains its clientelist practices. For example, acquiring a stall and maintaining its security are charged with political meanings. Cultural divides (on the bases of religion) are usually re-created there as well. Thus arcades are not only simple civil spaces but politicized enclaves as well. In the beginning, vendor organizations attempted rather successfully to encourage and maintain a sense of bipartisanship among all vendors. Recently, divisiveness has also been curtailed by the fact that over the years, both political parties have targeted ICIs for increased duties and taxes. As a result, there is a political accord that is often reinforced during times of protest against the state. Indeed, ICIs of any faction share a disdain for national policies and suspicion of outsiders, who might be working for the local or U.S. government.

Strangers to the arcade are easily identifiable by their appearances,[1] unless their performance of class allows them to successfully pass. The arcade clientele is the working class and the underclass. Middle-class buyers tend to shop in stores and/or buy from middle-class ICIs. Middle-class persons (unrelated to traders) who come through the arcades and linger are government employees, development workers, or student researchers, people from whom ICIs have yet to benefit.[2] Traders know that government officials and researchers are collecting data for policy decisions that will affect them. Hence, ICIs' reluctance to engage with unfamiliar persons is often a preemptive means of protecting their activities. Over the years, their suspicion has increased concomitantly with the rising number of traders becoming involved in more illicit trafficking. Thus, the presence of North American researchers has taken an entirely different set of meanings downtown, particularly since U.S. policies in the "war on drugs" are implemented differently in third world territories.

To situate downtown within a broader socioeconomic and political setting, I sketch the expansion of the capital city and the ghettoization of specific parts in relation to the development of the persistent violence that permeates central and western parts of Kingston. I highlight the significance of the connections between space, place, and social relations among traders, customers, organizations, and civil society at large. Following Doreen Massey, I view space not as a "flat," static surface but as a moment in the intersection of configured social relations that is dynamic, because the social relations that create it are themselves dynamic (1994:168–169). I show how the history of spatial relations downtown both shape and are shaped by the making of masculinity in this area. Consequently, I argue that a gendered habitus of "tuffness" emerged among those who must inhabit this space. Indeed, male responses to these conditions have contributed to constructing spaces of masculine domination (Bourdieu 2001, Harrison 1997b) that influence female behavior as well. I argue that for females, an embodied demeanor of tuffness is indispensable to navigate the streets of Kingston, especially downtown. In conclusion, I relate Miss B.'s performance of tuffness to the naturalization of the "black superwoman" or "tough black woman."

I present my "research dailies" of two ICIs: one sells inside, the other displays her wares outside of the arcade. In cinema dailies or daily shots are the unedited footage typically viewed the same day they are filmed. The sections on the inside and outside of the arcade were written as I went home in the taxi or as soon as I arrived there, as I did not take notes at the arcade. I present them here "as is," without additional camera work to get the scene right, as what my senses captured during those days of January 11–13, 1996. I use these snapshots to demonstrate the everyday activities of the trade and individual dynamics of being and working downtown. I consider the larger context within which arcades are situated to show the ontological effects of this environment on ICIs.

My concept of Kingston (including its environs and the arcades) is based on the formulations of urban space put forth by sociologists Mimi Sheller and John Urry. In their introduction to *Technologies of the City*, "Mobile Cities, Urban Mobilities," they refute the sedentarist models of urban studies that "fix space as a kind of bounded geographical location in and out of which people move, but which has a kind of givenness" (2006a:4). They contend that "cities have new urban logics, technical systems and discursive orderings ... Questions of security, violence, fear and terror [are] being translated into new infrastructures of mobility, surveillance and selective immobility or more precisely demobilization" (ibid.). A case study of contemporary Kingston offers a particular perspective on this British model.

Kingston

Jamaica measures 4,400 square miles; at its widest point, the island measures 150 miles wide (from east to west) and 51 miles long (from north to south). Half of the land is 1,000 feet above sea level, and the Blue Mountains at their highest peak are almost 7,000 feet above sea level. The island

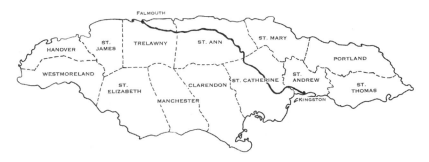

FIGURE I. Map of Jamaica with parishes.

is divided into fourteen parishes, which are further divided into smaller settlements called districts (see figure 1). Today, nearly half of the island's population of 2.8 million resides in Kingston, the capital and largest city. Situated on the southeastern part of the island, it is a major seaport. It shares municipal administration with St. Andrew to form the Kingston St. Andrew Corporation, also known as KSAC.

Kingston was founded in 1692 after an earthquake destroyed Port Royal, the island's main port of entry at the time. According to Mary Carley, this site was part of a single property purchased from an absentee proprietor. The design was planned in checkerboard fashion, with streets and lanes that meet at right angles (1962:152). In 1693, Kingston became a parish. Colonial offices, including the Receiver General, the Island Secretary, and the Naval Agent and its deputies, were transferred to this new location. In 1703, a devastating fire killed over 1,500 people and gutted Port Royal. Kingston, the only other commercial center at this time, became the primary port. For a brief period, the colonial administration, which occupied Spanish Town, left and relocated to Kingston. In 1758, however, these offices returned to Spanish Town. During this time, the population of Kingston doubled as a result of internal migration from sugar plantations and the arrival of immigrants from Europe and of slaves from Africa. In 1802, Kingston was granted autonomy over its affairs. By 1845, as sugar prices fell, the decline in overseas trade that had sustained the city took a toll on the island's economy. Twenty years later, after the Morant Bay Rebellion, the corporation of Kingston was dissolved. In 1872, Kingston became the capital when the government abandoned Spanish Town.

By the early twentieth century, Kingston's population grew with some sporadic fluctuations. In 1921, the population was 117,000 (Clarke 1975:1–6, 29–38). As internal migration to this area increased, whites moved further away from the corporate area to the northern parts of Upper St. Andrew, which had gained considerable status as a residential area. In May 1923, the administrations of St. Andrew and Kingston were consolidated with the formation of KSAC (Kingston St. Andrew Corporation). The largest incoming groups to KSAC were blacks and coloreds. Between 1921 and 1943, they accounted for over 90 percent of the city's growth. More specifically, 32,900 colored and 78,020 blacks had migrated. The Chinese and East Indian populations also increased (Clarke 1975:62–63). Tenement yards were constructed throughout the city, mainly to accommodate this influx. Within several years, racial/spatial enclaves were formed in the capital. Blacks comprised 60 percent of the total population and were mostly found in West Kingston (certain parts of which became squatter camps), the area adjacent to Half-Way-Tree, as well as some enclaves in East Kingston. The coloreds were concentrated mostly in East Kingston, though they were present in some parts of West Kingston, as well. Many also lived in the suburbs north of Half-Way-Tree.

The Jewish merchant population comprised 0.4 percent of the city's total population. They were located mostly in the middle-class and elite suburbs of the Half-Way-Tree area and East Kingston. The Syrians and Syrian coloreds who comprised 0.3 and 0.05 percent, respectively, were concentrated in St. Andrew and in the better suburbs of East and West Kingston. The Chinese and Chinese coloreds were 1.8 and 1.3 percent, respectively, of Kingston's population. The former were clustered in China town, that is, on West Street, Princes Street, and Orange Street. They lived mostly in this area; the Chinese coloreds were also found in East Kingston. The East Indians made up 2 percent of the population, while East Indian coloreds comprised 0.07 percent. The former were confined to the West Kingston area while the latter lived along Spanish Town Road, within the environs of the northwestern city limits (Clarke 1975:60–73). With these rapid demographic shifts in population density and racial patterns of migration, the socioeconomic lines dividing the city became increasingly salient.

By the 1950s, the geographical divisions of Kingston reflected the socio-economic characteristics of a particular racial/spatial order with multiple dimensions. Uptown/downtown is one of these divisions and is clearly demarcated by two main streets, Half-Way-Tree and Crossroads. Uptown, in the northern part of the city, is more lush and green and consists primarily of suburban enclaves. The northeast section of the city includes the suburbs of Beverly Hills, Mona Heights (where the University of the

FIGURE 2. Uptown/downtown violent areas.

West Indies is located), Gordon Town, and Upper St. Andrew (where the Jamaican elite live). Barbican, Cherry Gardens, and Stony Hill are several of the more central and northwestern middle-/upper-class pockets within the city (see figure 2). However, throughout several of these areas there are further divisions. For example, lower classes dwell within these pockets, and it is not uncommon to find shacks within the valleys of these hills.

The division of the downtown area is particularly complex because it is based on relations between supporters of the two main political parties, the JLP and the PNP. The sections include Jones Town, Dung Hill, Tivoli (formerly Back O' Wall), Rema in the west, and Nannyville, Telaviv, and Southside to the east.[3] As Faye Harrison notes, these boundaries are somewhat volatile because they are "loci of safety, danger, neutrality [which] are contingent and subject to recodification" (1997b:466). Most

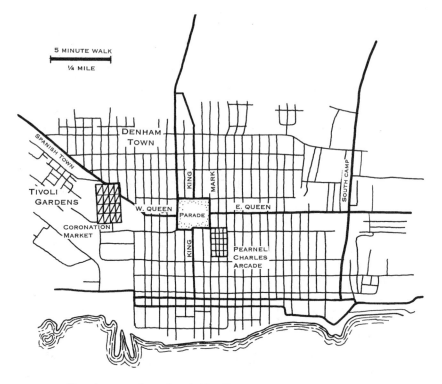

FIGURE 3. Downtown arcades and market locations.

of the arcades are located within a half-mile radius of King Street, the center of downtown's commercial district, which in itself is surrounded by the most dangerous paramilitary political constituencies and several police stations (see figure 3). Indeed, these "tribal" boundaries have been volatile for years because of tension between the two parties, their supporters, and gangs. In recent years, the relationship between certain apparatuses of the state and downtown factions has become tenuous at best. There has been increasing aggression from the state, which has violated international human rights laws. Since the early 1980s, Jamaica remains on Amnesty International's human rights violations list for extrajudicial executions. As most Kingstonians will alert foreigners, "The general rule of the Jamaican police is to shoot first and ask questions later." Order has increasingly deteriorated since the 1980s. As I discuss below, this loss of power is inextricably linked to the ambiguous roles that political parties played in constructing these constituencies during the early 1970s. In the trenches, life was desperate for sufferers. Yet among the sufferers, there were those with another consciousness, those who not only saw the enemy, but hoped for vengeance. To use Bob Marley's lyrical theories, they were the small axe, sharp and ready to cut down the trees of Babylon that flourished uptown.

Hustlin' Sufferahs and Silence

The more destitute parts of downtown were ghettoized during the twentieth century as a result of several natural disasters, including hurricanes in 1903 and 1951 and a severe earthquake and fire in 1907. The latter destroyed the eastern and southern sections of the city, burning through the entire commercial area to the south of Parade. About 1,500 people were killed. Because of these disasters, new attempts to develop the lower parts of the city focused primarily on Parade and ignored the outskirts of the city, where a growing number of dissidents and poor people lived. The relocation of several main government offices (such as the Headquarters House) and upscale social clubs (such as the yacht club) also contributed to deterioration. In addition, the government responded to the rapid population growth by constructing several housing developments that failed to meet the increasing demand. Shantytowns of tenements and squatter yards grew throughout the western areas, exacerbating the already desperate conditions.

These overpopulated enclaves have historically offered refuge for the rebels and the marginal. During slavery, runaway slaves and freed blacks migrated to these sections of town (Clark 1975). Many Rastafari communities were also founded in these areas. The notorious Jamaican drug posses of the 1980s, who succeeded the Johnny-too-bad of the rude bwais (boys) gangs, emerged from these poverty-stricken ghettos during the 1950s and 1960s. Young, out of work, frustrated, and desperate men embarked on a life of rape and pillage to counter their desperation and hunger, often in fatal fashion. As South African literary theorist Grant Farred puts it, "The rude boys tried to overcome their externally imposed structural disenfranchisement through horizontal violence" (2003:227). They were also known for their swaggering postures, rhetoric, and flashy dress styles. Their dispositions reflected an everyday life of poverty-generated desperation. They were influenced in part by the hero worship prevalent in spaghetti western movies and by Rastafari doctrine, which emphasizes the devastating impact of white/brown colonial oppression of the black majority.

In the 1970s, this antihero was best captured in movies. Perry Henzell's film *The Harder They Come* depicted the economic realities of life in downtown ghettos. In this film, the lead character Ivan (played by Jimmy Cliff), a young man from the country, migrates to the capital after his grandmother's death. His mother spurns him. A preacher offers him refuge and informal work, but eventually fires him. Ivan tries to use his musical talent to find a way out of his desperation, but he is exploited by the music industry, which is controlled by uptown browns. Unable to find other work, he turns to his only option in Jamaica's then emerging transnational informal economy: the ganja trade. When he questions its hierarchy, he is betrayed and soon becomes a hardened criminal, chased by both the local police and ganja traffickers. He dies at the end of the film, as heroes of westerns often do. The most daring aspect of the film was its revelation of the complex ties among downtown gangs, uptown state officials, and the brown middle class to drug trading and the militarization of local constituencies for personal gain.

In fact, it is undisputed that government parties, through their patronage system, facilitated the politicization of the rude bwais. These youth gangs were awarded cash, short-term jobs, and guns. In return, they assured the electoral support of local voters, protected local residents from armed enemy insurgents, and enforced the will of the party. This process of politicization has been primarily attributed to area leaders' attempts to control their constituencies to assure future votes in the late 1960s (Harrison 1987, Small 1995). Regardless of origin, in the end both political parties had armed their supporters and created a new paramilitary system. As this relationship between party loyalists and their patrons deepened, an internal decision-making body, which oversees the distribution of resources and the maintenance of order, was formed. Political scientist Carl Stone called these "political machines," and their formal hierarchical structures, "garrison communities" (1980).[4] Over the years, they have become states within a state that not only undermine but also often substitute for government's role as provider and protector of citizens. The clientelist system of the late 1960s and 1970s was being eroded by an internal power structure with a different source of income led by influential gang leaders with badness-honor reputations known as dons.[5] The new chiefs were no longer the politicians. According to Stone, it is dons who dictated the terms of relations to politicians. They extorted money from the private sector with impunity. The intricate network from which their power stemmed was such that they were above the law (1973, 1980, 1989).

By the mid-1980s, garrison communities and their internal political armies had become systematically entrenched in the transnational traffic of contraband, drugs, immigrants, and consumer items. Rude bwai posses extended throughout North America and Britain, and ganja sustained the local economy, becoming the most consistently traded commodity, especially during moments of economic crises (Griffith 1997; Harrison 1987, 1988, 1989, 1990, 1997b, 2005).[6] The movement of ganja decreased as the cocaine market boomed. Jamaica's strategic location made it a key transshipment point for trafficking from Colombia. With high unemployment and no social welfare net, it is not surprising that disenfranchised young men became so central to the flow of drugs in and out of the region. This phenomenon is just another facet of the global recirculation of capital with its concomitant racial division of labor that is now anchored in what Keith Nurse (2005) aptly refers to as the masculinization of poverty. Smaller than the feminization of poverty, he writes, this complementary trend targets young men of the underclass who are at risk as globalization increasingly favors a feminized labor force. For these young men who are vulnerable to being swept into criminal activity (Harrison 1989), self-making becomes intrinsically linked to violence. They resort to this "more dangerous anti-social behavior largely because male socialization encourages and rewards violence" (Nurse 2005:8). Moreover, Nurse believes that "societies' expectations of men (e.g. breadwinner role) and men's adherence to traditional conceptions of masculinity" reinforces this social expectation, which is "sadly out of step with the new gendered reality of the region" (2005:9). Sociologist Linden Lewis also calls for a need to unpack constructions of Caribbean masculinity. He argues for an analysis that distinguishes between hegemonic masculinity (which often embraces certain misogynist tendencies) and other subordinated forms of masculinity (2003:108). It has indeed been said that Jamaican posses were selected by Colombian cartels precisely because of their reputation as cop killers. This may be fact or just another urban myth. What is undisputed, however, is that one's street credibility depends upon the measure of one's badness-honor.[7] Participants are embroiled in a perpetual cycle of reputation building based on gang violence and battles with police that is propelled and sustained by the ever-expanding illegal drugs market.

During the mid to late 1990s, demand made trafficking an attractive alternative to work for those open to such options. Foreign governments' attempts to expunge this activity from their borders resulted in differential legal consequences, especially for those at the bottom rung of the ladder in the business. North American and British policies were to deport suspected and captured gang members back to the island. Deportees now possessed advanced military equipment, skills, and economic backing (from the powdered cocaine and crack trade), which facilitated their entries and reentries into the U.S., Canada, and Britain. As a result, in Jamaica, internal territorial and tribal wars, as well as battles with the state, are now being fought with even bigger and faster guns.

Many areas became battlegrounds as the new influx of deportees rewrote and toughened downtown codes of conduct. Already barren from the mass capital flight of the 1970s and underdevelopment, certain areas of western Kingston became ghost towns while others turned into firing ranges with sporadic gunfire throughout the day and constant shots at night.[8] For local dwellers, this is simply part of daily life that necessitates various survival strategies, including the performance of silence. Within a local-diasporic context, no one wants to be an informant. Indeed, there is always some consequence for telling. When one speaks out, others view it as foolish interference and disregard of complex power plays or even betrayal. At the very least the purported snitch would receive a lick. Death could be the outcome depending on the significance of the issue. I was consistently reminded of the danger of speaking about what did not concern me. Indeed, the links between police, drug traffickers and government officials were such that one simply could not decipher who, if anyone, was safe.

In 1997, this rule was reiterated in *Dancehall Queen*. In this movie, the local gangster had simply warned his potential victims by whispering, "You walk you live, you talk you bombaclaat dead!" For people downtown, this code of conduct is a reality with which they must cope. These constant threats are among the reasons why uptown individuals are afraid of getting caught downtown, especially after business hours. Yet danger too has its specificities depending on the symbolic and socioeconomic value of the stranded. It is within this milieu that arcades for ICIs were built (see figure 3).

Gun(men), Violence, and the State

Over the years, government has routinely deployed the military in the downtown area in attempts to reestablish order and regain the power that the police once monopolized. For example, in the spring of 1994, murders and robberies were at a high point, which impacted the business community. Businessmen claimed to have lost millions of dollars. Later that summer, a gang-related feud between factions in Hannah Town and Matthews Lane (not too far from the arcade) led to an exchange of gunfire that left five dead and four injured, including one ICI in the PC arcade. The following spring, a resurgence of violent crimes and murders turned the main shopping streets of downtown into a ghost town. Prominent business leaders called for the army. During a two-week period in mid-June 1994, over twelve people were killed. The prime minister promised to "saturate the area with security personnel from the police and the army" (Blair and Sinclair 1995). Surprisingly, the state managed to simultaneously criminalize the violence, street congestion, and illegal vending. In addition to discharging the military, it hoped to also relocate vendors. The removal of street vendors was seen as a crucial part of securing the downtown area (Blair and Sinclair 1995). Conveniently, vendors are framed as the source of violence rather than targets in need of protection. This is also an excuse to protect conventional business and stores.

In mid-August 1996, a mother, her six-year-old child, and another bystander were the victims of a reprisal killing in the North Street area. Later that year, in October, the military was deployed in problem areas. During a most successful raid for firearms, gunmen, and drugs, the soldiers killed a gunman. His body was placed atop a military vehicle with his face up and arms extended like a crucifix and driven throughout several other problem areas as a trophy and a warning to those who defy the state. The sheer brutality of this act only reaffirmed the perception that, to the government, certain downtown areas have had foreign territories. They were uncontrollable and insular and hence must be conquered by drastic means such as crucifixion. The use of this potent Christian symbol, however, had a reverse effect. It rallied civilians, especially uptown, who were concerned with the increasing unchecked power of the state.

In August 1997, the police fired on gunmen in Tivoli Gardens (the JLP stronghold) from a helicopter. Nine years later, the facts surrounding this case remain unclear. These troubling incidents would not occur uptown; they highlight the fact that certain downtown areas are under siege. The crucified gunman is a symbol of the sociopolitical realities of space. It is a reminder of the class components of the racial/spatial order that divides Kingston. With or without state sanction, this act was an affront, a declaration. State officials eventually denounced it, and it became part of a lengthy list of violations. The incident was not forgotten. In 2000, the JLP opposition leader, former prime minister Edward Seaga, had a memorial constructed in honor of the victims. In order to squelch potential social unrest and to answer questions posed by Jamaicans for Justice (JFJ), the government ordered an inquiry of these events.

It must be noted that these human rights violations are business as usual in Jamaica. The rivalry between the two main government parties (PNP and JLP) has historically been enacted on the bodies of the working-class and lumpenproletariat gangs. Those entangled in and often victimized by these battles are usually poor downtown dwellers. Downtown areas are volatile and the violence and criminality that ensue therein are often quite complex. They involve multiple actors and parties on multiple levels pertaining to official and illicit actions. The frequency and unpredictability of these events have created an atmosphere where safety for workers and residents is scarce.

Among the local intelligentsia and popular media commentators on daily talk radio shows, there is a general sense of dejection about downtown. Concerned individuals are fed up with gang violence and state-based abuse of downtown citizens. There is a perception that gang wars are merely the result of misguided men, without long-term vision, who fail to recognize their true worth. Indeed, life was undervalued in Jamaica. During my research years (1994–1996), the word on the street was that a person could be killed for J$500. This devaluation was the result of the increasing use of crack cocaine by new addicts in Kingston and its environs. Sarah Manley put it best when she said, "Life is cheap in Jamaica, and Jamaicans don't like anything cheap." In 1999, in response to this boom in aggression, uptown communities organized and formed Jamaicans for Justice, which defines itself as

> a non-profit, non-partisan, non-violent, volunteer citizens' rights action group, founded in 1999. It advocates for fundamental change in all spheres of Jamaican life—judicial, economic, social and political—in order to improve the lives of Jamaican citizens. JFJ believes that justice is the bedrock of any civilised and progressive society, and all Jamaicans must have equal access to fair, correct and impartial treatment.[9]

JFJ believes "that the majority of Jamaicans are decent, law abiding citizens; that each person is innocent until proven guilty in a Court of Law; [and] that each citizen deserves respect, freedom and the right to enjoy a peaceful existence."[10] The membership of this group is predominantly middle- and upper-class browns. Their efforts in the last five years have brought attention to the concerns of disenfranchised citizens. However, the social distance between this advocacy group and its clients has resulted in disparagement of the JFJ. This distance is not simply due to social divergences between the classes; it is continually reinforced by the spatial recomposition of downtown.

Social geographer Doreen Massey notes that the geography of social structure is a geography of class relations and not just a map of social classes (1994:22). She argues that spaces have both social and economic dimensions. Cartographic representations give them an absolute dimension that renders them static. More specifically, she writes, "space is created out of the vast intricacies, the incredible complexities, of the interlocking and the non-interlocking, and the networks of relations at every scale from local to global. What makes a particular view of these social relations specifically spatial is their simultaneity. It is a simultaneity, also, which has extension and configuration...space is a moment in the intersection of configured social relations" (1994:265). Social structure must be understood within the context of these relations. Since these relations are predicated upon the sociohistorical and spatial restructuring of employment, they are full of power and meaning that are set in specific moments in time (Massey 1994:80–87). Below, I present multiple examples of group interactions (especially between police and civil society) downtown that support Massey's thesis.

State responses to the violent incidents reaffirm how the space and place of the masses within the social order are not only marginal, but also immaterial. In times of unrest, the government's first recourse is to manage street vending. The removal of vendors is viewed as central to securing downtown streets. In that sense, vendors' bodies become boundary markers that are used to demarcate safety. Their next step is to deploy the military and extend surveillance in an attempt to reassert state power. This occurs when prominent persons have been killed and/or when the business class, citing the effects of increasing violence on its livelihood, exercises its political clout to demand action from the government. Otherwise, warring factions are continuously ignored as the poor and lumpenproletariat persist in gunning each other down.

In her work on downtown areas, Faye Harrison (1987, 1988, 1989) stresses that such occurrences must be placed within a wider international context. She contends that these human rights violations must be viewed in light of the policing of the drug crisis exclusively in ghetto localities. This policing is the result of militarization of the Jamaican state as encouraged by

neoliberal policies such as the Caribbean Basin Initiative (CBI), promoted by Reagan, in the early 1980s.[11] These global recompositions are
also responsible for the urban restructuring that occurs throughout mobile
cities (Brenner 2004).

In part due to the violence and the important role of space in the making of subjectivities, Jamaicans across social classes are familiar with the
sociocultural topography and observe racial/spatial orders. There are
exceptions, especially among the younger populations who contest these
boundaries. They cross the uptown and downtown line socially to participate in downtown culture both in order to (re)claim their identities
as Jamaicans and to assert their masculine identities. In fact, their consumption of dancehall has brought Jamaicans across class lines into a single
space more than any other form of popular culture. Indeed, Passa Passa—
the after-party event held weekly on Wednesday nights on Spanish Town
Road in Tivoli Gardens—draws people across color and class lines, and
most surprisingly even political affiliations.[12] Despite these temporary
crossings, however, most Kingstonians live their lives in accord with this
spatial divide. In the last decade the economic gains of the new black middle class from the informal economy have facilitated downtown dwellers'
crossings to uptown to satisfy their new consumption patterns. This economic crossing of class lines, however, is reciprocated mostly at the agricultural market.

Nonetheless, the middle and upper classes that work downtown habitually drive to their homes uptown in their rolled-up, tinted-window cars.
Socially, they only cross the uptown/downtown line to attend cultural
events at the Ward Theatre and the National Gallery of Art, which are
located south of the border. Still, when an event (such as the Pantomime)
is attended by a cross-class group of individuals, the price of tickets and
location of seats often uphold existing social boundaries (more expensive
seats and boxes in the front). Lower-class individuals venture uptown
mostly to work as domestic helpers, clerks, or gardeners. At the end of
their workday, they are often seen walking down the hills to the bus stops,
where they will catch a ride home. The lower classes seldom venture
uptown to socialize, though many travel on Sundays to attend church
services. They have limited buying power. As a result, most of them
cannot afford to shop above Half-Way-Tree and Crossroads; they buy
what they need at markets, arcades, and shops located downtown.

Historically, the main location of Kingston's commercial activity has
been downtown. At the turn of the twentieth century, local markets flourished despite the problems in local-international trade. As white British

geographer Colin Clarke notes, internal trade was divided between retailing and wholesaling activities. In Kingston, the internal trade system consisted of three main branches: provisions markets, which were manned by Afro-Jamaicans; the grocery trade, which had been introduced by the Chinese; and dry goods, which was the specialization of Syrian and Jewish peddlers. Provision markets were located at the foot of King Street and West Queen Street; the grocery stores on King Street and West Street; and dry goods were sold primarily in the northern area south of Parade (1975:38). By the 1950s, these areas of specialization and their racial/ethnic correlation remained. They were disrupted in the late 1970s by the arrival of foreign higglers, who would later enter the import-export market en masse and compete with the traditional merchants including the Chinese, Syrians, and Jews. As many females participated in informal economic activities to alleviate their families' abject poverty, sufferers hustled and scuffled to live in the toughest parts of central and western Kingston.

Research Dailies: In/Outside the Arcade

If downtown marks the lower rung of the racial/spatial divide of Kingston, then the arcade symbolically represents some of the subdivisions within this area. Arcades are generally class-specific territories with boundaries seldom transgressed.[13] In downtown arcades, shoppers are mostly lower-class individuals who live or work in the area or uptown. These include those who work in government offices, banks, and insurance companies. During my fieldwork, I became quite aware of who came into the arcade and who didn't (especially when I was in the van outside with Miss B.). Very few middle-class customers shopped there themselves. I was repeatedly told by middle-class friends that they never go to arcades and would never buy from a "higgler," because it is widely believed that goods in arcades are not of good quality, thus not worth the exorbitant price that traders charge. On the rare occasions when upwardly mobile or middle-class female buyers came through the arcade, they were usually accompanied by either older female family members or men. They would walk through rather quickly or remain outside.[14] While it is socially accepted to go to market to buy provisions directly from country farms, such allowable transgression does not extend to the arcade.

The same can be said about food shopping patterns. On Thursdays and Saturdays (wholesale days), it was not uncommon to see uptown ladies at Coronation Market buying their produce directly from farmer higglers. On other days, they frequented grocery stores on Hope Road or Constant Spring Road or near Knutsford Boulevard. It had become relatively common to see working-class individuals shopping at the Sovereign supermarket, or younger persons in the food court of the mall or at the movies. Their consistent presence at Sovereign in the last five years resulted in mall managers issuing a dress code in 1997. This code, which prohibited the preferred dress of the lower-class or downtown youths, was clearly meant to keep them away from the mall. This clearly pointed to the significance of style as a marker of class, as well as to the politics of the racial/spatial order and to class anxieties about possible transgressions. Not surprisingly, Sovereign supermarket's dress code failed to keep the young black youths from returning. Over the next several months, mall managers prohibited nonlicensed taxis from entering to drop off customers. They also placed guards at the three entrances of the supermarket to enforce this new rule.

While uptown boundaries are often explicitly articulated, downtown lines and codes of conduct are not as blatant. Words of warning remain unspoken, yet known to all. Their utterance often implies that action will follow. In the arcade downtown, ICIs and their customers as well as government officials know and abide by the rules.

The pace of life in the arcade depends on the business cycle. The busiest time of the year is December. August and September follow, as they come just before the beginning of the school term. May and June are the third highest because of graduation. During these peak times, there is always activity in the arcade area, and customers do buy from traders. During slow seasons, many traders keep irregular hours, except on Saturday, the busiest shopping day of the week.

ICIs located in the center of the arcade have difficulty attracting customers. The issue of location is very complex and has caused tensions among traders and between traders and MPM. ICIs on the outside of the arcade get to customers first. One of the ways traders deal with this competition is by hiring *goosekillers*—sales agents (young men) who roam the streets carrying the items for sale—to attract and solicit customers before they even enter the arcade. As more traders inside the arcade hired these agents, the competition was brought outside. As a result, traders whose businesses thrived were the ones who were the most accessible and sold a variety of popular items.

Day 1. Outside the arcade, I sit with Miss B. in her van while she sorts through a box of synthetic hair. She is sitting on top of another box surrounded by hair, leather and synthetic bags, and nylon backpacks. As she sorts through the packets, she tells me that I need to talk to other ICIs so that I get a range of different views, not just hers. A customer approaches. She tells me to stop talking and attends to this customer. Miss B. hands her several packets of the wavy black hair, which the customer folds into her bag. The customer pays and we resume our conversation. She tells me that things are tough because there are too many people getting into the business and there is more competition. She quickly adds that she should not say this since the business has been good to her and more people need to try their luck at it. A man stops by and greets her. She gets out of the van to go talk to him.

She returns and calls over one of her workers. This older ICI is probably in her late fifties. Miss B. hands her the keys to the van and asks her to put on the radio, because she wants to listen to the news. The older ICI fidgets around on the front seat and puts the key in the ignition. A few minutes later, Miss B. asks her, "What's the matter? You can't turn on the radio? How many times do I have to tell you, you have to learn how to drive? You a woman. You must drive." She makes her way through the boxes and bags and sits on the front seat. She turns on the radio. "You have to drive for yourself, man. You can't be waiting upon your son. You have to drive." She comes back to the box and resumes her sorting. I ask if she wants help. She says no. I fidget around a bit with my backpack. She says don't worry. Nobody's going to take my bag. Since I dress like a student no one will bother me.

Minutes later, another ICI from one of the adjacent arcades comes to talk to Miss B. She has been having some problems with a goosekiller. Miss B. steps out of the van and talks to her. I turn my eyes away from them as she whispers to Miss B. Miss B. goes to call another ICI to accompany her to the police station, then to MPM, and finally to the *Gleaner*. People need to know what is going on in the arcade. It turns out the goosekiller in question urinated on this ICI while she was conducting her business in the arcade the previous day. Several other random shoppers stop by and ask her for prices or whether she sells particular brands or styles of hair. Always cordial and with a smile, she responds by first calling everyone darling or sweetheart. Another customer approaches the van. Miss B. gets out, tells me she'll soon come back. She calls a worker and asks him to accompany her and her niece inside the arcade. She returns to the box and before I even ask her, she tells me that you have to treat your customers special. After another hour, I returned to the UVA office.

Day 2. I arrive at the arcade at 11 a.m. today. Miss T. has just arrived. She unlocks the gate and tells me to sit on the stool inside the stall. I sit down. Some of the shelves are empty because her stall was broken into last week. Her goosekiller comes in, and they unpack several boxes of clothing that are piled on top of each other in the corner where she stores her goods. They are men's T-shirts and sport shirts, which are still on their hangers. She takes them out and hangs them vertically outside of her stall, all in a row like most other traders do. She also hangs several from the grid in the ceiling so that the shirts are hung from above. We chat. No one comes by. She tells me she is buying her ticket on Monday. I ask her for the travel agent. She gives me the name and number, and then asks me if I want to call her on her cellular phone. I did not know she had a cellular phone. She hands it over to me. But I do not know how to operate it. She says I must be an idiot, "How you come from foreign and you don't know how you use a cellular?" I tell her that in the States only people with money have a cellular phone. She laughs, which I found annoying, and then she proceeds to instruct me on how to use the phone. The whole time she is laughing at me; I feel distant from her and I kept thinking about our class differences and status symbols.

From the way she is talking, I realize that she is planning on traveling with somebody—Miss Z., an ICI whose stall is on the other side. Over the time I have spent visiting her, I observe that she has had no interactions with the other traders on her row. None whatsoever. They don't even say good morning. Across from her, the other ICI sits on her chair, her back facing the entrance to the arcade. Then she moves her chair inside the stall.

While I was with Miss T. today, she has had three customers. She has sold two pairs of shoes; one of them to a young man who doesn't even haggle over the price. The other two customers haggle the price down. She starts saying she doesn't have time. "Don't touch my shoes if you're not buying," she warns him. He looks at the shoes then asks how much. She gives him a price. He quickly asks if she would take any less. She says, "No! If you don't want it, just go on." He makes another offer. She laughs and says she will only take off fifty dollars from her original price. He takes out money from his pocket and pays her. She gives the goosekiller his cut and hands over a couple bills to another man behind him who is outside but whom I had not noticed before. A man in a nearby stall starts to curse at the customer and calls him a "fuckery" because he bought the shoes from Miss T. and not from him. Apparently, the buyer had approached him first. She doesn't even flinch. While this man's aggression disturbed me, she does not even seem concerned.

Around two o'clock, I take my little plastic container of vegetables out and begin to eat my lunch. She calls me a Rasta and tells me that's why I like to go to the UVA, because I am a Rasta. While I am eating, Miss Z., with whom she will be traveling, comes by. I introduce myself to her. The goosekiller comes back inside saying that nothing is going on out there. He leans over on the drum container and begins to stare at me. He picks up another style of shoe and leaves. She begins to tease me about not being able to use the cell phone again. Then she asks me when will I be coming back to do her nails. I promise to return the next day. It must be around four. I start to get frustrated with the darkness of the arcade, the noise, the smoking. I need a break. I leave and go to the African Caribbean Institute of Jamaica.

Day 3. I arrive at the arcade an hour later today. It is around noon and I will stay until 5 p.m. Miss T. is happy that I remembered to bring the nail polish. I sit down on the little stool that has become my seat and give her a manicure. The whole time I am there, she only has one customer. However, several friends stop by. The first is a tall, dark ICI with gray natural hair. She is dressed fashionably. She tells Miss T. she has just returned from declaring her goods and wants to borrow her pulley to take her stuff from her pickup to the stall. Miss T. asks the goosekiller, who is leaning on the drum, to get the lady the pushcart. I continue with her nails. Again today there are no interactions between Miss T. and the traders across from her. Another woman comes by. I notice her black shoes and ask her where she has bought them. She does not tell me. In fact, she completely ignores me and does not talk to me. Before she leaves, she tells Miss T. that the shoes are in the catalogue. I am not sure why she does not talk to me, but I am not surprised. Miss T. pulls out the catalogue and tells me this is one of the stores we will go to on the trip to Miami. I take a look at it. Another customer comes in and asks about a pair of shoes. I notice that Miss T. really doesn't interact with customers, unlike both Miss B.s, who always chat and ask customers how they are. When I asked about it, she said she comes here to sell and that is what she does. She adds, "If they come to buy, they buy." I finish her nails. She sits and lets them dry. One of her sons comes by, and she asks me if I want him. I said, "Me don't need no man with pickney" (children). She just laughs and says that's good. I eat my lunch. Just before I leave, another person stops by whom I recognize as the "pardner" man who comes to her house on Sundays to collect the money.[15] Money exchanges hands. She counts it, and then she dates and signs the list. I hang out a bit longer, then head back home to my cozy apartment.

My Uptown/Downtown Crossings

During fieldwork in 1995–1996, I traveled downtown mostly by taxi. In 1993 and 1994, I had experienced the bus system enough to recognize it as yet another marker of class identity, which I had to mediate. The bus is a space with specified social boundaries that are primarily crossed by outsiders, mainly Peace Corps volunteers, foreign students, and anthropologists. Over the years, my bus experiences have ranged from fun and silly moments to tense verbal and physical threats. The stress, fear, and awkwardness I experienced on buses were not worth the money I saved. Knowing that I would be going downtown on a regular basis, I opted to hire a regular taxi driver. This would also allow me to minimize the continuous negotiations over the tourist price that locals often charge foreign visitors. In the beginning, I found a driver, a Rasta (who had cut off his locks) who agreed to drive me to the arcade. All started well. He even began to teach me Jamaican words and drive me around different routes so I could get to know different areas of Kingston. As soon as he knew I was single (because I told him), he started to ask me to cook for him, etc. I politely declined. My politeness, however, only worsened the situation. Eventually, I gave up and found another driver. My tactic with this driver was to quickly establish that I was engaged and that my fiancé visited every month. That fiction allowed me to establish boundaries in such a way as to minimize continuous harassment.

Eventually, I learned the best arrangement was to have several drivers so I would not be dependent on any single one. My main reason for wanting a regular driver was the fear of being stuck downtown after hours. Over the years since I began this project, I heard enough stories about being caught in the wrong place at the wrong time and what could happen. Indeed, most downtown taxis will not drive uptown during evening rush hour, because the half hour ride could take as long as two hours. Since the fare is not metered and is based on distance as opposed to time, they earn less. A regular driver will pick up a regular customer regardless of the time because of the assurance of continuous fares. The few times I was stuck downtown, I quickly paid the exorbitant fare to get myself uptown. At the beginning of fieldwork, my anxieties about being stranded were many. First, I remained highly conscious of the fact that I hold a Haitian passport, as I am a Haitian citizen first and a U.S. resident second in Jamaica. I dared not take any risks, knowing that if something happened to me, finding me would simply not be a priority to my country's embassy. In that sense, my complex positioning was a hindrance and a challenge, especially given the depreciating value of local black lives. Since I can only partially pass for local with my butchered, U.S.-accented patois, my North American accent could be helpful. Or not. Also, I did not know downtown well enough to find my way around. Most of my network of traders (the ICIs profiled) lived some distance from the arcade.

At the UVA office where I volunteered, I was comfortable. Right outside on the lane, which ran behind the arcade, there were several cooking tables where for most of the morning a number of young men cooked food that ICIs and pedestrians purchased at lunchtime. In the first couple of months, these men often looked at me suspiciously. By the middle of the following year, we greeted each other, and once in a while, when I brought my camera, they sometimes asked for a picture, which I developed and always returned along with the negative. On the left of the UVA office and at the back entrance to the PC arcade, there was a music sound system that consisted of several oversized speakers that blasted dancehall and roots music from 11 a.m. until after 5 p.m., when the arcade closed. On Fridays, different ICIs sponsored parties on the lane with the Original Sowa sound system selectors presiding over the spin tables (for DJ records). On the left side of the office a couple doors down were a small restaurant and a hair salon where several traders got their hair done during the day. The daughter of an ICI operated the business. I walked up and down the lane cautiously, though always feeling safe, because my facilitators were within reach.

Within a couple months, my sense of safety downtown began to extend further, well beyond the purview of my network. I began to branch out of my immediate field site. I started to go to Coronation Market several times a week to buy fresh herbs, because I had started to sell flavored olive oil (mostly to upper-class friends) to fund my additional expenses. On my first visit, I went with a part-time ICI. I returned the following week to explore the different parts of this market. Coronation Market is located a few feet away from Tivoli Gardens, the JLP stronghold. I soon became a regular at the market and would walk the long way, crossing King Street by the Jubilee Market to and from the arcade. I also visited several of the other arcades within that area.

My ease downtown was quickly disrupted the day I came upon a confrontation between two sidewalk vendors near the fish market. A tall man had a cutlass up above his head, while with his left hand he was holding his would be victim by the neck of his shirt. They were both shouting.

Several people tried to disengage these men. I stood there staring, praying for the man with the cutlass to calm down. The would-be victim kept shouting. I crossed the street, and then continued to walk towards the market, deciding I did not have to witness this event. Several weeks before this incident, a man had pulled a machine gun, an AK-47 (I have seen them on TV), on a road worker, right outside my living room window in New Kingston. The worker would not let him drive across the freshly laid asphalt. He stepped out of his SUV and went to talk with the worker. Angry, he walked back to his SUV and returned armed with the AK-47. The road worker backed down, and he drove across the fresh asphalt. The following week, I returned to Coronation somewhat awkwardly, yet, ironically, even more at ease knowing that violence cannot be predicted and knows no spatial boundaries in Jamaica.

Violence is a gendered concept, an integral part of local definitions of masculinity in Jamaica (Harrison 1997b). Several weeks later, the son of an ICI was beaten by several goosekillers from the arcade. At around the same time, in the UVA office, a male ICI was stabbed up—in other words, stabbed repeatedly—because he was trying to steal "his" woman. I heard the story the next morning when I arrived for work, and I noticed the dried pool of blood by the display case. It turned out that the victim was the son of someone I know. When I asked her about it, she calmly stuped (kissed her teeth with disgust) and noted, "Him should know better. Him shouldn't run after another man's woman." Indeed, it was a fait accompli; he should have respected another's man's property, and he got exactly what he deserved.

I was most struck by how calmly and matter-of-factly they talked about these incidents. This response was similar to that of several uptown ladies who simply asked me whether the man on my street had fired the machine gun: "Did he shoot? Then why are you getting so excited?" It was through both subtle and overt forms of violence that I became increasingly conscious of my local outsider and North American middle-class identities in Jamaica and downtown.[16] These events highlighted the persistent threat of and actual violence as an integral part of life for everyone in Kingston.[17] The stabbing incident was in no way typical of events that occurred at the UVA, but it was not strange for the downtown area. Indeed, since the 1980s violent incidents in Kingston (especially downtown) have steadily increased. In a notable number of these, class taboos were crossed as wealthy businessmen were also killed in 1994 and 1995. As a result, the government deployed the military.

I was in the field during the series of shootings in 1996, which were, in one way or another directly related to traders in the arcade or their families and/or not-so-distant relatives. I often read about these events in the newspaper. Upon arrival at the office or the arcade, sometimes it was mentioned that there had been a shooting. These statements never turned into discussions or went beyond abstractions. I never probed. When I began to spend more time downtown, an ICI I had just met had simply told me that there are things that happen here that I wouldn't want to know about. She noted, "If you know, you don't talk because people will kill you for that." I took her advice because I wasn't interested in these things. During the research years, however, I could barely ignore the fact that these occurrences may be unspeakable but they had tremendous impact on everyone, including the ICIs who occupied this space. Indeed, ignoring this persistent violence would be another form of silencing.

While I learned of ICIs coping strategies, I became cognizant of my own inability to manage as my levels of discomfort revealed gender, national, and class-specific habitus.[18] When uptown friends sympathetically admitted "I couldn't do what you do" and exclaimed they didn't understand how I could go there and be part of that world every single day, I thought nothing of it, until time went by and the violence soared. Then I began to recognize the limits in my sense of ease and the extent of my adaptation. I was able to tolerate downtown mostly because of the ICIs and because of my political commitment to the project. At the end of the day, I returned to my studio apartment with cable TV and all the comforts of home that had weighed down my suitcases in October. Despite these, there were days when I just had to escape or simply not go downtown. As I developed the project, I overlooked the demands the environment would place on me. The fact is that violence and the threat of violence informed the broader context within which I conducted this phase of the research. Yet, I could always leave. For the ICIs, it was an everyday reality. The gang wars, the government's lack of response, and extrajudicial executions by the police were constant reminders of the depreciating value of blackness, black bodies, and black lives.

Managing the emotions produced by my context was one of the most difficult aspects of research for me to adjust to.[19] As Ahmed writes, "emotions are effects of circulation ... they make and shape bodies [as well] as stick and move" (2004:1–8). Every time I returned to Jamaica to continue this work, I was moved by the hope and visions of ICIs who quietly expressed rage about the acts of aggression in the area. Many among them invoked the name of God as comfort and strength. Their churches offered them solace. I admired their sheer determination to live by their rules, in a world without guarantees (Hall, Gilroy, Grossberg, and McRobbie 2000). What ICIs sought was the autonomy to create different lives for themselves. As they usually referred to their genealogies, they would stress wanting to give their children and grandchildren even more opportunities than they had. I often read this as their commitment to not re-create certain structures.

Female Attitudes and Masculine Domination

I mapped out historical and contemporary sketches of downtown for two reasons. First, I wanted to show the extent to which masculine domination pervades this area. Second, my aim was to draw attention to the continuities and discontinuities of both the overt and symbolic violence—as exemplary of this domination—that permeate the downtown environment. One could argue that the consistent eruptions of violence that characterize life in Kingston are so explicit that they should not be considered symbolic. However, since these are at times random—even when it was to settle a score between rivals—I argue that the threat of violence looms large. It is this impending possibility and the habitus that it creates that I am concerned with. That I was repeatedly shocked by these occurrences reaffirmed the socioeconomic distance between us. Among Kingstonians, accounts of stabbings, gun toting, and murder (especially in politically charged areas) are also met with performances that range from indifference to horror. These reactions have their gender and class specificities.

Whereas masculinity is realized through the gun, female tuffness is expressed through embodiment of protective shields. I first noticed the female tough attitude in 1992. The smile or relaxed look that I was accustomed to seeing on women's faces in Ann Arbor was totally absent. In its place was a facade—an almost impenetrable veneer of toughness. Hoisted shoulders. Chin held up high. Walking languidly, yet always with a sense of purpose. Soon I would learn that this toughness was an armor, a survival mechanism of sorts worn mostly in public, especially on the street, used to rebuff or discourage any unwanted interaction, especially commentaries from men hanging out on corners, posing, and/or engaged in street vending activities. On the streets, these men are gatekeepers. They police those who cross boundaries demarcating racial/class/spatial orders.

The tuff attitude distinguished the tourist from the local, the lady from the woman, the approachable from the unapproachable, and the harassable from the unharassable.

This toughness is also a class marker. It is characteristic of females who must occupy public space for any reason in their everyday lives. To successfully navigate public space, they must develop various gendered, embodied strategies (such as tuffness) that amount to a reputation.[20] I became aware of this demeanor within the context of street harassment. Indeed, in Jamaica, there are females who are to some extent unharassable, and they include young schoolgirls. Even though men would leer and gaze at them, they were less likely to comment on them, at least not loud enough for them to hear. If men did comment and were heard, these females would respond with a cut eye, stupe, or cast of their eyes directly on the man in question. They would deliver a riposte of expletives, which would either silence him or force him to recant and apologize. In the worst-case scenario, he could get angry and shower her with insulting remarks. A battle of words would ensue. Or not. This is a perfect example of the overt symbolism of which I spoke.

In 1993, I saw this attitude and its power in action at the Reggae Sunsplash festival during dancehall night. Our study abroad group attended the event. Another student (Kim) and I were standing away from the concert crowd near a couple of young men who were in a corner posturing. Two young women walked by in full dancehall gear. Both were wearing bustiers and lycra batty riders with multicolored Doc Martens. They also wore colored condom packets as earrings and on a string as necklaces. One of the young men made a comment; I did not hear what he said. Both girls stopped in their tracks and turned back. Physically, they were small in stature—under five feet four inches and petite. One of them approached the young men, poked the one who spoke with her finger and asked him to repeat what he had said to her face. She proceeded to assault him with a series of words that I had come to learn had purely derogatory meanings: bloodclaat, pussyhole, etc.[21] Her friend stood there prepared for conflict, as she let her companion handle the situation. The girl said, "Watch yourself! And nuff respect ya hear" and stuped as she slowly walked away. The men fell silent and looked intimidated.

In the remaining months of that visit I learned about the importance of this tuffness, as I eventually realized that surviving Kingston depended upon my adopting the attitude, or a version of it, as long as I continued to walk everywhere. As it was, I was continuously harassed on the streets, from the moment I left my gate to the time I returned home. I became quite anxious about being on the streets, because the daily misogynistic comments and class hostility could be disturbing. That I received these comments as assaults in itself reflected my class position; many females in Kingston rebuffed such comments with the attitude or disavowed them with shrugs. Some comments were even welcomed.

A month before my departure for Ann Arbor in late December 1993, however, things changed as I adopted a version of this attitude. I was walking home from the university when I noticed a large woman dressed in an orange gauze (transparent) shirt and matching orange mid-thigh tights. She walked past the roundabout that I normally dreaded. The men sitting on the wall raised their brows; the brave ones just whispered to themselves. No one made a comment to her. I was wearing my palazzo pants and a long sleeveless vest. As soon as I approached the wall, a chorus of annoying remarks serenaded me. At that moment, I realized that in some ways clothing had little to do with who gets harassed and, at the same time, it had everything to do with it, especially because clothing is a signifier of class. The more I hid my body, the more I hinted at a class position that does not belong on the streets, hence, the more susceptible I was to their cat calls.

That day, I decided that this was the last time I would be harassed on the street. I stopped covering myself up and walked out of my apartment everyday ready for any confrontation. Ironically, the day I was to give a presentation on radical feminism in my gender and development class, a tall man began to follow me, mumbling that he wanted to talk to me. Soon he began to shout, insisting that when he talks to me I must stop and listen to him. After several minutes, I grew increasingly annoyed and turned to face him. "And why should I listen to you?" I demanded. Without hesitation, he replied, "I'm a man and you're a woman." "Oh, yeah? Well fuck off!" I retorted, shutting out my mother's childhood instructions on politeness. I turned around and kept walking. Inside I was terrified. I kept my shoulders back, chin up high, and tried not to walk fast to project an appearance of composure. What if he follows me or throws a rock at me, like the man at the bus stop several weeks earlier to whom I had said nothing at all, I wondered. By the time I made it to the university compound, I felt triumphant because this simulated response becomes the real response. It makes me appear as I wish to be. Prior to coming to Jamaica on the first study abroad program in 1992, Dr. Haniff had prepared us by saying we had to perform toughness. In addition, she gave us countless instructions on various ways to deal with harassment. I simply refused to embody this persona; when I finally did, I resented having to act this way. I shared the experience with a middle-class colleague, Althea Perkins. At the time, we were both graduate students at UWI. She said, "That's what you have to do, you know, if you want to keep walking on the street and not be bothered."

Perkins, now a lecturer in UWI's department of gender studies, and I had countless conversations about how we felt on the streets of Kingston. She asserted that outside, on the streets, a female body became the object of a male gaze. Perkins says that this is why she dresses as she pleases and cuts her hair so low. Let any of them even try to say something, anything about it, she dared. I had taken another route; I retreated from the gaze instead of challenging it. In the beginning, even Miss T. teased me about my big dresses, which I wore downtown. It began as a question of taste, as long flowing items were in style in the U.S. that year. Then, the clothes were my resistance against gendered ideals, and later, they became my attitude. However, they could be easily read as signs of middle-class conservatism, which is characteristic of uptown ladies' aesthetics. Moreover, these coverings reaffirmed my outsider and foreigner status, and even ascribed to me what Jamaicans call "stoosh" status.

According to Caribbean performance artist and playwright Jean Small, "stoosh" is a term used to describe an individual or a group that assumes the dress, verbal and nonverbal language, and general behavior of a higher or more acceptable social class. It is a performance of class, as in "putting on airs" or "acting uppity." From that perspective, she notes that "stoosh" always has a negative connotation, especially when this label comes from someone of a lower social position. Simultaneously, stoosh can be seen as an enviable characteristic from an upper-class viewpoint, where it is recognized as a natural presentation of class. Jamaican documentary filmmaker Mary Wells notes that stoosh can be interpreted as "classy" or "well put together." Black middle-class stoosh ladies belong in cars; they do not hang out in arcades, walk on the streets, or ride on the back of trucks to conduct research. By entering this public space, I was crossing class boundaries. Inevitably, there were consequences. In this case, the outcome of the transgression was a loss of power that had to be openly negotiated through attitude. The embodiment of this attitude, in turn, implies another class and subjective transgression, as a lady becomes a woman.

In June 1994, after I met Miss B., we were walking through the arcade when I asked if she knew anyone in that part so I could take a picture of that person's clothing display. She said, "Oh, don't worry, just take a picture." I aimed the camera up at the clothing on view and clicked. A male vendor, who assumed I had taken his picture, came up to me and began to berate me for taking his photo. "Give the camera," he yelled. Miss B., who had been walking ahead of me to the UVA office, heard the commotion and turned back. Soft-spoken a moment earlier, she now shrilly asked the man "What you want? Did you see her take your picture? She not interested in your picture." He insisted I did, and then he said I should watch myself when I come to the arcade. Miss B. walked up to him, squarely faced him and said he better be careful about what he says. Then she softened up a little and added "She mi pickney, man, no worry, she mi pickney"; She's my child, don't you worry. As with Miss T., I had become her daughter the minute I was entrusted in her charge. Like a mother, she protected me.

Miss B. is small in stature and very thin. Similar to the girls at Sunsplash, Miss B. has what Jamaicans call a magga body. According to white anthropologist Elisa Sobo, among the lower class in rural Jamaica, the magaw or thin body often carries a negative connotation. It is seen as meager and powerless and is associated with frailty and vulnerability (1993:34). ICIs who are average or large-sized are less easily intimidated. Those with magaw bodies are seen as at a disadvantage and must compensate with a tough attitude (including cussing skills and some kind of weapon) to avoid being exploited or bullied.

In my first interview with Miss B., I asked if she was afraid for her safety, especially given the increasing violence downtown.[22] She sells her goods outside the arcade in a van by a taxi stand where there is continuous traffic, directly across from the entrance to Old Wolmers arcade. "No man! Why me be fraid for?" She stooped, then pulled up her flower printed dress to reveal a pair of short leggings. "This is where me keep me change," she said, pointing to a small bundle on her thigh. She then pulls out a small knife from beneath the lycra. "You see this... You see this. I work too hard for what me have. If anybody think dem can take it from me they have to deal with this." She puts it away. "No, man, me not afraid. Me a warrior," she laughed.

Miss B. is a devout Pentecostal. She keeps her hair natural, wears no makeup and loves to quote the Scriptures. She will begin an informal sermon while buying U.S. dollars from a passerby or when selling to her dancehall regulars (who buy packets of fake hair from her because she gives a fair price and always sells quality material.) If anyone questions her fairness, she quickly sends him/her to other ICIs, because she does not haggle over prices. She is devoted to her family, friends, and peers. I took a liking to her immediately because she is so outspoken. I visited her frequently. I would sit with her inside the hot van among the plastic packets of hair and we would talk about the persistence of the violence that plagues the downtown area. When I became increasingly disturbed by a series of shootings that occurred close to the arcade, Miss B. told me I needed to get a boyfriend because things are too rough these days. You have to have love in your life. When things get rough, she told me, "I call up my husband, say, honey, I love you." But when it comes to her business, don't even think of crossing her. When I returned for fieldwork in 1995, I spent more time with Miss B. Almost everyone knows her. Her van/stall was often surrounded with individuals who stop by just to talk about the latest event in the arcade or to catch up on family news. She still quotes the Bible in response to any question or doubt about the role and importance of God in life. She has a positive outlook and is grateful for her good fortune. Her personal motto is "Work hard and never give up."

Miss B.'s Tuffness

Miss B.'s tough composure requires little reflection on her part. It is a posture she assumes whenever necessary, a learned disposition of her habitus. She code switches competently to adapt to conditions of the moment. In all these instances, she is responding appropriately to something that is situational, as she has been socialized to do. Nonetheless, she and others like her are often viewed as naturally tough. This association is yet another continuity of stereotypical qualities ascribed to black females. As Stuart Hall asserts, stereotyping is a signifying practice that constrains through a strategy of splitting, which also symbolically fixes the person (1997a). Where gender is concerned, this fixity has posited black females in opposition to white females, constructing the latter as feminine and the former as masculine or unfeminine. That masculinity or unfemininity has been read and labeled as applying to the black superwoman. It is this characteristic imposed on black females that I wish to deconstruct, as it forces black females into limited categories that, in turn, account for the continuous erasure of their attempts to remake new subjectivities.

Feminists in the black diaspora have sought to demystify this construction and its local variations (Bakare-Yusuf 1997, Cooper 2004a, Hill-Collins [1991] 2000, Noble 2005, Reynolds 1997) as it continues to be reinscribed through discursive practices and to influence official reports and public policies. Whether it is the market woman who overcharges, or the emasculating matriarch who marginalizes black males or the "welfare queen" who siphons resources from the state, black females' attempts at self-making occur in tandem with these persistent images. As black activist Angela Davis (1971) contends, these stereotypes stem from, and are reinforced by, socioeconomic structures of both colonialism and slavery that continue to have real impact. According to Carla Freeman and Donna Murdock, Caribbean feminist ethnography tends to eschew these connections, as the enduring traditions, particularly among social science feminist scholars, are driven by Marxist approaches and emphasis on development, which assumes rather than interrogates the specificity of experience and identity (2001). Symbolic analysis is more commonly practiced in the humanities, in the fields of literary and cultural studies. That disciplinary separation, also a discursive practice, maintains the naturalization of these aforementioned categories and the characteristics associated with them. In other words, the focus on the material has been at the expense of the symbolic. Yet it is precisely at these crossroads that challenges to historical representations must be plotted to further deconstruct such ontological essentialisms.

Toughness is a defining characteristic that black females embody, celebrate, manipulate, mediate, and reappropriate, as survival depends on performing some version of it. While it is part of a socially constructed corporeal performance, toughness is lived and felt and has actual implications. The experience of the absence or presence of toughness in everyday life reveals its complex significance. It is yet another false binary that upholds the gendered polemic. Indeed, "woman" is not to "lady" as "toughness" is to "weakness" any more than "uptown" is to "downtown" as "civilized" is to "vulgar." Yet such demarcations persist, as they serve purposes of control, difference, and domination. They are further evidence of a need to mark difference, which is itself often enticed by desire. So then, are ladies not tough? Where do they perform their toughness? In what ways do their interlocutors determine their performances? Needless to say, the masculine domination that surrounds them is far from abstract. While it has its rhetorical aspects, it is very real and occurs within a historical set of gender relations. In recent times, these relations have been getting more and more tense and desperate, as it is their sons, lovers, fathers, and other relatives who often embody the male power they confront. Their toughness, in that sense, often begins at home before expanding onto the city streets they must navigate. Ironically, in the literature on "men at risk" in Jamaica, it is mothers who are blamed for badly rearing their sons and emasculating them (Ulysse 1999). From that angle, the toughness ascribed to black females (which counters the good/true female as passive and controlled) is naturalized and seen as a threat to male power. Moreover, this toughness is also demonized precisely because it is a form of active agency that is seen as a theft of a naturally masculine prerogative.[23]

Uncontested toughness re-creates what black feminist historian Darlene Clark Hine calls a culture of dissemblance. She argues that southern black females, who were themselves blamed for their own rapes and violations because they were coded as hypersexual, retreat within to not disclose their vulnerability to others. More specifically, she notes that they responded with "behavior and attitudes...that created the appearance of openness and disclosure but actually shielded the truth of their inner lives and selves from their oppressors" (1994:37). What Hine proposes is a theory of black female performance of silence, another example of what James Scott (1987) calls "weapons of the weak." Indeed, it is not that they do not suffer or are not impacted by rapes; rather, they practice self-censorship to keep these issues private. In doing so, they hope to negate the prevailing stereotypes of themselves. They achieve this in part by using an impenetrable veneer or by performing a toughness that masks and privatizes their pain (James 1993). Historically, black female survivalist practices depended on re-creating this disposition and variations of it. As black feminist science historian Evelynn Hammonds found, there were class elements to this strategy. Drawing on two literary black feminists, Ann duCille and Hazel Carby, Hammonds clarifies that while black middle-class females practiced this silence or dissemblance, among the lower classes, especially blues singers, gendered stereotypes of sexuality were both defied and appropriated (1997).

The same can be said of Jamaican females. Carolyn Cooper gives evidence of a female slave not only reveling in her sexuality, but commodifying it (1993a). Barbadian historian Hilary Beckles supports Cooper's work with examples from Barbados (1989). This appropriation reinscribes this natural characteristic, rendering lower- and working-class black females as one-dimensional subjects exuding sexuality and/or tuffness, depending on the stereotype. While there may be strength in this construction for black female subjects, it can be constructed by others in ways that reinforce their objectification. Tricia Rose puts it very well by saying that other stories must be told about black people to "rewrite widely held de-humanizing ideas about black people" (2004:9). In other words, stereo-types must be debunked. Indeed, Miss B. is not just tough. She expressed her vulnerability, commented on her weakness time and time again when I asked her about the business, and recited her reasons for hanging on despite the brutal environment and an international context that devalues her person even more than this country where her citizenship is flexible. Her fear of the violence and that of other traders are articulated in com-plex ways. They cannot be directly voiced. Given downtown's code, Miss B. is required to adapt. To use Audre Lorde (1984), it is her silence that is transformed into language and action. She gives sermons and speaks of God and love as a counterpoint (Ortiz 1995).

From that perspective, I expand upon Hine's notion of performing dissemblance to include a multilayered array of concerns that applies dif-ferently to subjects depending on their location and their contexts. Our inability to capture this complexity stems from the fact that global cap-italist structures of power maintain a "possessive investment" in stereo-types. They are not only socially entrenched, but have exchange and use value as well. Relations of domination are characteristically multilevel with material and symbolic components. For example, the government's consistent extraction of duties from ICIs is based on state legitimization of an anachronistic image, on a perception of traders as thieves who over-charge, and on the ethical marginalization of ICIs inherent in the official paradox of labeling them "informal." Effectively, these exemplify how globalization affects the economic conditions of ICIs. These consequences have their symbolic counterparts. That said, the argument simply cannot end here but must also engage the representational.

Much of the work done on market traders in the Caribbean follows strict disciplinary boundaries that uphold the division between the ma-terial and the symbolic, which reinforce these false chasms and, in the process, limit the scope of interrogation. Performativity is as much quo-tidian practice as a cultural text that is as relevant to the social sciences as the humanities.[24] As black females of lower, working, and upper classes, visible and invisible ICIs comprise the body and bodies onto which this late stage of capitalism is developing. Traders' responses are inevitably specific to their social location and economic positions. ICIs' perfor-mances of subjectivities and self-making practices are not simply re-ducible to cultural expressions but rather are manifestations of their dif-ferential contact with capitalist power and discipline, as Ong (1987) has shown with Malaysian factory workers.[25] Given the multiple levels and complexities of these local-global forces that impinge upon ICIs and structure their behaviors, their retorts will inevitably entail some form of code switching.

Our different capacities for adapting to the same milieu are significant and point to the differences we embody and inhabit. These dispositions reflect our attitudes and tastes. As forms of capital, they can be deployed but they also reveal how our experiences and responses to spaces vary. Self-making will inevitably be contradictory, as this ability to code switch from one habitus to another itself depends upon a habitus of code switching. Integral to this notion is W. E. B. Du Bois's double consciousness in action. Formulations of this concept as advocated by Kelley (1996), Gilroy (1993), Harrison (1991b), and Hill-Collins (1990) stress the need to further refract consciousness to encompass the multiplicity of intersections and matrices they reflect. My ability to pass through customs, for example, not as an ICI but as a middle-class female smuggling electronics is worth revisiting. My traveling companions could not pass in the same way, as their bodies are inscribed with ICI. While I had some success at the airport, on the streets and in the arcade I faced more limits. The arcade became a maze through which I lost all confidence in an unknown territory that operates under its own set of economies. The ICIs, on the other hand, shift back and forth within the arcade knowing the details of boundaries, many of which to this day I remain clueless about. Such strategies require a particular set of learned tools.

Another example is Miss B.'s tuffness and sweetness. These are the embodied responses of a dynamic person. There are times, indeed, when she is exasperated and simply tired. Others, like herself, persevere in the trade and continue their work downtown having learned how to mediate their bodies in an environment that assaults all of their senses, where violence and criminality are everyday trading commodities with which they must cope. Despite this context, in many instances, ICIs like Miss B. not only persist, but also manage to succeed. Their accomplishments are based on considerable skills.

Shopping in Miami: Globalization, Saturated Markets, and the Reflexive Political Economy of ICIs

I like the travel... shopping. I get to choose things that customers will like. —Miss M.

Sometimes all mi sell is one pair of shoes all day. —Miss T.

Miami Day 1: Shopping

It is 4:25 a.m. "Gina... Get up! Get Up!" It was Miss T. I had spent the night at her house because we were leaving for Miami in the morning. "We have to pick up Miss M. at 5," she tells me. I rush to get ready while she has coffee. Our flight is at 6:30 a.m. She is already dressed and ready to go. It is still dark and not quite 5 a.m. when we arrive at Miss M.'s gate. Her husband kisses her good-bye at the gate, and we drive off towards the Norman Manley International Airport. Miss T.'s son, Mr. R., also her apprentice, is driving the pickup and starts to talk to me about how rough these trips are. "Some ICIs are thieves, you know! Dem do all kinds of business... so you be careful and listen to my mother." He is being protective of his mom. He is nervous as I am a novice, a complete liability to a planned project that needs to go according to plan. Before stopping he adds, "Do what she says." Miss T. proceeds to instruct him on how to take care of things in her absence. He drops us off at the airport and leaves.

We enter the Air Jamaica terminal, which is quite busy so early this Wednesday morning. It is full, almost entirely with females, mostly ICIs.

You can sometimes tell who they are by their clothing and accessories. There is also their baggage—many large empty suitcases and boxes of Jamaican products, such as Jamaican cheese, Betty condensed milk, crackers, and mints. Miss M. has several boxes of Betty milk piled together and tied with a rope, which she has checked as luggage. While in line, several of the traders greet each other. Miss T. seems to know a few. The airline workers are pleasant and helpful. This flight is known as the ICI flight. It was added by Air Jamaica in response to demand by the traders.

On the plane, I sit between Miss T. and Miss M. Miss T. does not talk to me. Miss M. soon falls asleep. I begin to write in a small green notepad. I am excited about this trip, which I feel is finally "real" fieldwork. I soon fall asleep and wake up to the captain's announcement that we are landing. It's about 9:15 a.m. We get our bags from the overhead bins and leave the plane. We then we make our way through immigration separately and regroup at the luggage carousels to get our belongings. Miss T. and Miss M. pick up their empty suitcases. Miss M. hands the cartons of condensed milk she had checked in to another ICI. They say good-bye to each other. By then, Miss T. is already leading the way out of the airport. She is walking fast and barely says a word. The van man is waiting outside by the door. We quickly get into the van and drive off. She introduces us while we are on the way and tells him I am doing some research and want to know more about the trade. He doesn't seem pleased that I am here. That morning, Miss T. tells him, she had asked me to put the gallon of sorrel that she brought for him into my carry-on. He loosens up a little as we drive to the wholesale district in the northwest section of Miami and the first store. It takes over a half hour.

First stop. We arrive at a men's sportswear and shoe store. Already several other traders looking at the merchandise. The owner is speaking Spanish to several other buyers. There are several young male clerks who work there whom I quickly recognize as Haitian by their accents. They speak several languages. I walk around the store and take some brief notes while Miss T. tries to negotiate better deals. She uses the word "fuck" in every single sentence.[1] She asks for a discount and a Christmas present, because this is her first trip since the New Year. She informs me that she has been shopping in this store for over fifteen years. Miss M., on the other hand, has been coming here for two years. She selects several different styles of shoes. The merchandise is quickly brought out from the storeroom and taken out of boxes and put into a giant plastic bag to go. I ask the van man why they do this. He tells me that the boxes will take too much space in the van and they have to make a lot of stops. Also the boxes won't fit properly in the drum that they use for shipping. In the meantime, Miss T. and Miss M. are paying at the register. As we get ready to leave, I eavesdrop on several conversations between three other traders who are arguing about whether they are being overcharged for a jersey sport shirt. Miss T. asks the owner for a shoeshine brush to dust off her shoes. He tells her that it will cost her two dollars. She puts it in her bag.

Second stop. As we drive to the next store, the van man points out the Miami Sun Hotel—a popular hotel right on the avenue where many ICIs stay. Miss T. says that in the old days she had stayed there but that it is not safe. ICIs come to buy with cash; people know this and they rob them. We drive up the street to another shoe store. They do not have what Miss T. wants to buy, so we leave.

Third stop. This next stop is the store with a catalogue that I had seen the week before. The showroom is empty. On display, there are mostly women's shoes. Some of the shoes are leather; others are synthetic. They ring a bell by the back room door. The owner comes out. Another man. He knows both Miss T. and Miss M. by name. He greets them, and they talk and decide on some merchandise. They will return to collect the goods at the end of the day.

Fourth stop. We leave for the next store. The van man proceeds to tell Miss M. what to buy, what is "in style," and what other traders are buying. They make me try on several pairs of platform shoes so they can see what the shoes look like on somebody. Most of them have leather uppers and synthetic bottoms. I tell Miss T. that I'll buy a pair when the shipment arrives. She says she'll give me a discount. Miss T. goes back to negotiate with the owner. I interview the van man. He informs me that the drivers usually receive about 5 to 6 percent of what the ICIs spend from the owner of the store, because they bring them buyers. They also charge ICIs a flat fee for the two days of driving. This fee includes packing and shipping help. I am already tired. I ask him when they take a break. He laughs and asks me if I am tired already. They don't take a break until around 2 p.m. We stop for gas, and I go to get us drinks and snacks. Miss T. makes a comment about my dried fruits, saying that I am a Rasta.

Fifth stop. We stop at another shoe store. The shoes are mostly made of synthetic material. There are several Haitian madansaras—market women—as well as people from other Caribbean islands buying. The saleswoman quotes Miss M. a price in French. I point out to her that Miss M. is Jamaican. The van man starts to get fresh. I ignore him. He is starting to get rude. I am continuing to ignore him. Then he makes some comment and asks me if I know how poorly the dollar is doing in Haiti. He tells me to go get him some water. I roll my eyes and walk away. I go to talk to the lady who spoke to Miss M. in French. She asks me what I want to buy. I tell her that I am not a trader. She asks if I am here to learn. I say yes. It turns out she is also Haitian. I wasn't sure because her nametag has a Spanish name on it. She says she was born in the Dominican Republic to Haitian parents. I tell her I am from Haiti. She gives me her card and tells me to look her up when I start my own business. She tells me that it is better that I am Haitian, better because the owner prices items differently for traders from different countries, depending on the dollar rate of that country. So, I would need less capital to get started on my own. I say, "OK, I'll keep in touch." I am impressed with these informal distribution systems.

Sixth stop. Several Asian workers (I am not certain of their specific background) operate an enormous warehouse that specializes in housewares and haberdashery. They sell plastic flowers, plants, bedding, towels, picture frames, kitchen supplies, and other household items. Neither of my companions buys anything. I ask them why. They tell me they are just looking. They'll come back tomorrow and then they'll buy.

Seventh stop. It is now 1:32 p.m. We are going to another shoe store. Miss T. goes inside and looks. She doesn't see what she wants. She talks with the salesman, then proceeds to walk out. Miss M. and I follow.

Eighth stop. We go next door to a sport shop where they sell T-shirts, pants, etc. I asked the Arabic-speaking man where he comes from; he answers that he is Egyptian. While Miss T. talks with the salesmen, I continue my interview with the van man. He has been in the business for the last fifteen years. As a child, he used to help sell goods in Kingston with his older brother. Their mother is an ICI. He migrated to the U.S., but he had some problems, so in 1985 he began to work with van drivers. A couple of years ago, he decided to go into the driving business for himself. We leave the store and go next door.

Ninth and tenth stops. Next door to the sport shop, Miss T. is looking for special styles of Fila socks and Nike shoes. We go into several other stores on the same street. The goods are too expensive, she insists, and proceeds to another store. We follow her in. She doesn't even talk to the sales help. She walks out. Miss M. says we should stop for now because we can't seem to find these shoes at a good price. Miss M. believes it is the actual style of the shoe we are looking for that is expensive.

Eleventh stop. It is 3:30 p.m. We take a lunch break in a Jamaican restaurant that is run by two sisters from the island. Miss T. tells me to hurry; we have only a half hour. The waitresses are quick. This is an ICI stop, the van man tells me. We finish eating our food quickly. We get back into the van to continue shopping.

Twelfth stop. We go back to the garment district. We have found the Fila socks. Miss T. talks to the salesman and buys several pairs. They are packed in a large plastic bag.

Thirteenth stop. Another shoe store. Miss T. is the nicest I have seen her all day. She introduces me to the owner and tells me she has known this man for twelve years and has been buying from him since they met. They are affectionate and sweet with each other. I am in total shock at seeing her this way, especially since she had been so tough before. And he seems to know just how to negotiate with her. "You're too rough with me," he coddles her. "I am giving you a break so you give me one." She purchases her goods and then we leave.

Fourteenth stop. Miss M. and I leave Miss T. and go to look for women's shoes. We find several styles she likes. Then we go back to meet Miss T. Miss M. tells her that there are some nice styles in the store we went to. We return there. Miss T. agrees. Miss M. buys the shoes she liked.

Fifteenth stop. We go to a clothing place. They look, but they are not interested in buying. I ask them why they bother to stop there. Their answer: so they can see what is selling. By then I can no longer hide the fact that I am dead tired. I ask them when they normally stop. "After we're done shopping, sweetheart," says Miss M.

Sixteenth stop. We leave together to go back to the place where they had left their shoes. Miss T. makes a fuss. She calls the man a "fucking tief" and pays him. The van man and stockroom man both pack the shoes in the van.

Seventeenth stop. The supermarket. It is around 6 p.m. They come to this place to shop for personal items. Things are cheaper in Miami, so they buy some food items and a lot of paper products. Miss T. suggests I do the same; that way I can save some of my money. My feet and my back are killing me. After this, we stop for dinner at a fast food restaurant, buy food for takeout, and go to the hotel.

At 7:30 p.m. we arrive at the hotel. There is a room reserved for us. They unpack their supermarket bags and pack the household items into their suitcases. Then we eat dinner. Miss T. jokes about how tough the business is and how I could never do it, as I get tired too quickly. I agree and tell her I really don't think I could do it. It's too much running around. Soon after dinner, she becomes very quiet and turns her back on us to write some things down on a piece of paper. I ask her what she is doing. Miss M. quickly tells me to leave her alone because she's figuring out her business. Miss M. uses this time to call her family members and other friends who live in the States. She bought a prepaid telephone card for that reason. They get ready for sleep. I call a friend to take me to the nearby bookstore, where I stock up on as many books as I can. Miss M. lets me in when I come back. Miss T. jokes that I need to sleep and not run around Miami because tomorrow is a busy day and she doesn't like to rush because haste makes waste.

Miami Day 2: Packing and Shipping

Miss T. wakes me up at 6 a.m. She tells me to get ready. The van man has arrived and has started to load the van. Miss T. goes to check out. It is 7:30 a.m. We drive towards the wholesale shopping district again. On the way, we stop near a shipping yard where a number of day laborers are sitting around waiting for work. The van man goes to talk to several of the workers. Soon, Miss T. gets out of the van and talks to them as well. They both get back in the van. We are going to find the Nikes, Miss T. says. Miss T. is determined to get these shoes we looked for yesterday. She needs to buy a pair for her grandson and a pair of soccer shoes for a nephew. First, we go to a haberdashery store, not the one we went to yesterday. They both buy things for their homes. We go to several shoe stores before we finally find the shoes, which both Miss T. and Miss M. buy. They drop me off for one hour on one of the main streets (so I can buy a new tape recorder and batteries as well as a fax machine for a friend). This is family time. They both go to visit Miss T.'s grandkids. Before the van takes off they remind me again that they have a schedule to keep. Be on time.

An hour later, I meet them at the street corner. The van is full of merchandise from the day before. We go to buy more shoes. Then we go to the packing place to get several boxes and barrels. Miss T. starts to worry about feeling rushed. "Haste makes waste," she keeps telling the van man, who assures her that there is a ship leaving tomorrow for Kingston and that we'll be able to get there on time. The men they spoke with in the morning are waiting outside the packing place. They quickly unload the van into the storage place. In one corner, there is a pile of merchandise that belongs to Miss T. and Miss M. It turns out the van man had left those things there after he dropped us off the evening before. There are several other clusters of ICIs and packers stuffing barrels. Everyone is rushing. I try to help but it is clear that I am in the way. I step aside and watch. As the van man tells me, the point is to fill up the barrels, to airpack them with as many pairs of shoes as possible. So they stuff them, then lift up the barrels and drop them in order to compress them and stuff them some more. This lasts about one hour. Miss T. pays the packers after they load the van, and we leave for the ship.

Throughout the ride to the shipping yard, Miss T. worries about getting the barrels on this ship. Apparently the next one is in two days time. She prefers to deal with this company because it is reliable. As she notes, "If they tell you your shipment is coming today, the things will be there and they won't tief you." We finally get to the shipping place. Miss M. and I stay in the van while Miss T. and the van man go out to negotiate fees. They return. We drive the van to one of the openings and the van is unpacked. We leave for the airport. We arrive at the airport an hour and a half before the flight. Miss M. goes to the ladies room and comes back dressed in a dressy blouse. We check our bags and suitcases in along with the other ICIs. We sit in the lobby until departure.

On the plane, several traders are talking about their trips. Miss T. goes to sleep saying she's tired. I am exhausted and soon fall asleep as well. I wake up more exhausted. We have a bumpy landing. Everyone claps. We get off the plane and go our separate ways through immigration. We meet again at the luggage carousels. All I had was two carry-ons. I can't believe how tired I am. My calves and ankles hurt. I am annoyed and sweaty, and just can't wait to get to my studio. We say good-bye and proceed through our respective customs sections. They line up at the ICI table behind several other traders. I go through a "nothing to declare" line and botch my attempt to pass through customs.

Nothing to Declare

I went through the nothing to declare line even though in my carry-on luggage were a fax machine and an answering machine, as well as numerous pieces of clothing I had bought to resell to a friend. I queued up in the long line. Then it was my turn. I faced the officer, who looked at me and asked me to open my bag. He rummaged through the top of the bag, and the bulky fax machine was soon discovered beneath layers of clothing. The answering machine, on the side of the bag beneath several books, went undetected. With a look of recognition, he handed me a form to take to the duty window. I left my luggage and walked to the window. The officer there proceeded to go through a number of bound lists and handbooks. She looked up the value of the fax machine and charged me a percentage. I had to pay this amount at another window, returning to her for a stamp. The entire tedious process took well over a half-hour. She took her time.

When I returned with the receipts, I was allowed to take my luggage and leave. What struck me was the fact that the officer was not remotely interested in the clothing in my bag. During previous trips, I remember always being asked if I had any electronic equipment. This question was seldom asked on shorter trips. Middle- and upper-class travelers, it seems, tend to import these items, which carry a 25 percent duty rate depending on their locally estimated worth. This incident clearly suggests that government operates on a particular notion of classed consumption of mobile technologies. It also made it clearer to me that they seek to collect revenue when they can rather randomly, that is by taxing items that are easily identifiable. There is a very practical aspect to this. Regulation would be virtually impossible to implement if the criteria for determining what is taxable were not simple. My interest in obtaining these guidelines was to gain an understanding of how decisions are made and what this could reveal about state regulation of the trade and its differential treatment of traders. However, the process of getting access to customs was a most difficult task.

During my year-long trip, 1995–96, I used my University of Michigan affiliation to try to gain entry to these government offices. This approach proved to be an automatic dead end. So I proceeded to use my more local affiliations, the University of the West Indies and the Institute for Social and Economic Research, but these also failed. I called numerous secretaries and assistants and made myself readily available and willing to meet with officials whenever their busy schedules permitted. I still had tremendous difficulty. Eventually, I acknowledged that time was not the real reason and became more aggressive. As I mentioned in the last chapter, policies are floating signifiers that became even more elusive whenever I mentioned the word "research." I was told that personnel are not available and would not be for months. This process was different with other government agencies, which were at least more cooperative, initially, on some levels. What was most striking about customs, however, was that I was sent on a wild goose chase that began at middle-management level and went all the way to the top. I finally gained some access at the lower level when I created a chain of the names of officials I had tried to contact and recounted the list to my new interviewee.

At the top level, I was successful when I used my last resort, the personal contacts of a very prominent businesswoman. Had it not been for her, I would not have gained this access. Though she facilitated my entry into this office, it did not guarantee that the interview would result in valuable information. My interest in customs was to comprehend the details of duties collection from ICIs and the regulation of taxes. In these interviews with top management in 1996, I didn't learn much that I didn't already know. I pressed for more details, about extra duties especially, but my persistence failed. I was most successful with lower-level employees from whom I attained a sense of the specificities of the collection process. It is likely that their willingness to share this information was partially prompted by feelings of class alliance with traders and perhaps less of an investment in the policies themselves and the ministries for which they work. Nonetheless, their revelation shows that duties and customs policies inevitably have different effects on different ICIs.

Duties and Taxes

Upon their return home from buying trips, ICIs have several options to claim and collect their merchandise. In Kingston, these include: the Norman Manley International Airport, the Norman Manley International Airport Container Service, and the Kingston Wharf and other independently operated warehouses. The container service and the wharf are most popular with visible ICIs and the invisible ICIs who import in greater volumes for themselves or department stores. These are used for barrels that are shipped while abroad. Otherwise, they can check carry their goods as personal or excess luggage by plane. After going through immigration, travelers must choose among three customs sections. These include a nothing to declare line, another line to declare goods, and a third line with a table that is specifically for ICIs. This table is to check the goods that are carried as personal or excess luggage. As in most other airports, individuals are expected to go to their respective lines. For ICIs, this process is similar at both of the national airports. In their lines, the goods are searched and appropriate duties are charged and paid. Merchandise is often held and sent to the container service when ICIs fail to produce all of the necessary documentation for declaration. They must produce their registration cards, BENO numbers, tax compliance forms, and the proper invoice and receipts for all purchases. Using these, officers will charge them customs duties and taxes.

Since trade liberalization occurred during the 1980s, one of the ICIs' chief complaints is that they pay too much duty. Over the years, this amount has been rather high, as it is calculated on the value of the shipped goods, to which various duties are added, including a value-added tax. Indeed, the duties and taxes on their commercial merchandise amount to nearly 45 percent of its value. This includes an initial 25 percent in customs duties (based on official price guidelines that determine the amount of duty to be paid on different goods). Another 15 percent General Consumption Tax (GCT) is added after the overall value of the goods total has been increased by 33.5 percent. This a different rate that is specifically for ICIs. According to the Commissioner of Customs, the 33.5 percent is charged because ICIs import counterfeit merchandise that is of lower value. In addition, he notes, they will recover the GCT since they overcharge for their products. The issue of ICI duty rates has been tricky since duties were instituted. They became even more problematic when the concessions given to ICIs were removed in 1991. As a result, these purported "informal" traders pay as much as, and sometimes more than, established merchants for their imported merchandise. The ICIs claim that they are in the highest tax brackets. Over the years, these claims have been made by both the UVA and the JHSVA. The government has consistently denied these charges. In addition, over the years, the government has failed to disclose the amount of revenue they collect from ICIs and how this contributes to the national economy.

In fact, within government, there is a general lack of transparency regarding any monetary issues (including how Metropolitan Parks and Markets spends the weekly stall fees, security fees, custom duties, etc.) concerning ICIs. During the high points of the relocation attempts in the mid-1990s, a trader explained how she has to negotiate with the MPM or government patrolmen charged with removing vendors from the streets. She says that sometimes they bother her and other times they do not. Her elaboration exemplifies how ICIs often view themselves in relation to the state: "The business is difficult enough these days. Government doesn't do its job. Instead, they are trying to squeeze the small man." Often, for this trader and others like her who do not occupy an official commercial spot, negotiations with these officials vary. There are many officers who do not harass them. They simply allow them to sell in these areas. There are those who not only confiscate their goods, but also require kickbacks to return these items, which are often damaged or tampered with. This is one of the primary reasons that many ICIs on the streets are highly suspicious of MPM officials, especially the metro men who patrol the street en masse during relocation times. The ideal situation, another told me, is to have a special arrangement with one officer. However, this hardly safeguards the vendor from other officers. In 1996, to combat the inconsistencies in the behavior of these officials, MPM began to rotate officers by sending them to different areas in order to discourage them from forming arrangements or relationships with vendors.

Such corruption extends all the way to the top, where the collection and distribution of fees and revenues from ICIs is also elusive. During the beginning stages of the project, it became clear to me that this was yet another area that would be difficult to examine. I asked both naïve and pointed questions concerning the allocation of stall fees and the failure of state-hired security agents to guard the property of ICIs in the PC arcade. Eventually, a former government employer warned me that I had better leave this topic unexplored. He noted that when he inquired about fees collected from the arcades he was told by a coworker outright, "You come here to drink milk, not to count cows." As a result of this warning and other more explicit threats that followed, he eventually left the agency. The metaphor points to the fact that appropriation of funds from this unregulated source is a common practice. It points to similar findings in other nations with proliferating informal economies (Seligman 2004).

Gracia Clark (1994) found the same thing in Ghana, where such funds are used to facilitate the clientelist system, which also constrains ICIs in various ways. For example, in Jamaica, because arcades were built by the JLP, they are likely to be neglected by the PNP; the neglect will last until the former returns to power. As a result, the 1990s were a particularly difficult decade for the vendors, who had been formalized under the JLP administration. The PNP, which came to power in the early 1990s, has had a contentious relationship with the ICIs. Twice a year—once before Christmas and once in the spring—the MPM attempts to relocate the ICIs. This often results in small clashes, and vendors often take to the streets in protest. In some instances, a number of vendors are removed only to soon return because they have no other location from which to sell and enforcement is ad hoc. Traders' grievances regarding arcade conditions, for example, and the need for other vending spaces have been more or less ignored. This remains a point of contention with the state. Arcades have come and gone. The Metropolitan arcade, for example, burned down in 2001 and has not been rebuilt. In addition to these local obstacles from government, ICIs are further constrained by the detrimental effects of globalization, mainly the saturation of the market and the exploding drug trade.

Saturated Markets

After the Miami trip, Miss T. and I had numerous conversations about the state of the market. I often asked her why she sells shoes when almost everyone in the arcade does the same. Her response was customer demand. Throughout different stages of fieldwork, I noticed that unsold shoes spent months on her shelves. She often took these items to Falmouth, where she sold them wholesale to other ICIs, or got rid of them at a much lower price in Kingston. On rare occasions, a pair or two would be undersold to people in need. The monetary loss on these goods was buffered by her other activities. When I pressed her about how she survives with the increasing number of people entering the business, she responded that she would soon leave the business. Several others said they would also leave. Yet every time I returned, most of them were in the arcade, often selling the same items. They continue to trade in the same commodities because they are "lucky" with them, and also because this is the market in which they participate. What these items provide for some is consistent income (no matter how low) on which they can depend throughout the year. In these cases, their informal commercial importing work is a means to sustenance.

Thus, most visible lower-class ICIs have become petty traders rather than entrepreneurs. The saturated market allows only those who began in the old days and/or who take greater risks to fare well. The rest are another class of traders with little to no possibility of expansion. In her examination of the experience of market traders in Bogota during the 1970s, Carolyn Moser (1978) found that the "poor remains poor" because of the various constraints that impede their economic expansion. Their informal economic activities are subsumed within a larger economy dependent on the purchasing power of customers who are also affected by failing economies.[2] The importing business may have its ups and downs, but the cycle itself allows traders room or cracks to go through (day to day and season to season) to have and enjoy the autonomy necessary to engage in their self-making practices. This is one reason that many often stress: "You can't let the system beat you down," or "you have to keep fighting." Those able to fight the system do so by engaging in other economic activities, while the ones who cannot fall by the wayside. For many within the arcade, operating the stall may be their primary job, but it is not their sole means of generating income. As a veteran ICI has told me, "You can't depend on the business... it would be foolish to put all your eggs in one basket." So they engage in occupational multiplicity (Comitas 1973) or what Charles Carnegie refers to as flexible maneuverability (1981).

Through diversification, many ICIs are able to remain in the trade and take fewer risks. Though they depend primarily on the income they earn from buying and selling, they are also involved in other activities, which serve as a buffer against the harsh realities of supply and demand in a depressed economy. Despite these constraints, many traders prefer the autonomy and independence of the trade, even as they lose their investments due to saturation and other factors. In conversation, several admitted that they are currently at an impasse. They now face additional competition from the new wholesalers from Hong Kong who moved to Jamaica when China took over the port city in 1997. These new wholesalers are undercutting ICIs, as they are bigger businesses that are able to import in greater volume. They no longer need to travel since they can go to warehouses in Kingston to purchase the goods once sold in Miami. Many of the ICIs insist that they have to find an alternative way to survive these new challenges because, as one noted, "I like being my own boss. I have to find a way to make things work." Another worried, "I don't know what else to do but I can't work for nobody."

For example, work in free trade zones or as a domestic pay the minimum wage or slightly more. In 1996, the minimum wage was about J$500 for a forty-hour workweek. (At the then-current exchange rate, that was less than US$30 a week.) In January 2005, the amount had increased to J$2,400. But with increasing devaluation of the Jamaican dollar, this amount equaled only US$38.40 (at an exchange rate of J$62.5 to US$1). As several interviewees (most were mothers of young children) stressed, this income can barely cover basic needs and education costs, let alone leisure activities. While many enter the trade with dreams of making it big, what they will attain is greater flexibility in their daily lives as self-employers. Their activities indicate awareness that it is structurally impossible for all of them to be equally successful in the business. This job allows them to "put food on the table," "send their children to better schools," "take care of family," "buy pretty things," "go to shows," or even "buy a home." They spend their money in ways that reflect their interest in making a life within their communities. They are often critiqued for remaining small and not expanding their businesses. In most cases, it seems that their intent is to maintain and manage small operations. A good indication of this is where traders choose to invest their profits. They get their pleasure from working with each other, vending, traveling, and manipulating foreign currency. For many, the business is about being a player, no matter how small, in the global market.

Indeed, they know that they are but one more worker among many. This is most evident in the various ways that they watch out for each other and in their sense of friendly competition. This camaraderie is nothing new. Other scholars have observed it among vendors throughout the region.[3] Ironically, although the ICIs interviewed often complained that too many people were getting into the trade, they were quick to say that everyone should have a chance to make a living. The growth of the business has been rather consistent since the 1980s, as the trade subsumes the dispossessed, unemployed, and others. When new recruits enter the business, it is a veteran that brings them on board and teaches them the trade. During their apprentice period, novices travel with this expert and make few or no decisions regarding purchases. Note that Miss M. did get an opportunity to select a few styles on this Miami trip. On these trips, apprentices establish a relationship with the van man, observe how to negotiate with storeowners, and learn the process of packing and shipping. When new traders travel on their own, they maintain the buying patterns they learned. After years in the trade, they too will take on apprentices. Among my network of traders, very few would trade in new products. I concluded that they were keen on minimizing their risks. McFarlane-Gregory and Ruddock-Kelly's study (1993) found similar results. A decade later, I also found that the ICIs who took the most risks tended to be younger and were often newcomers to the business or individuals with more start-up funds.

Over the years, when I asked ICIs why they purchased certain items, the answer was often "because it's what the people want." At other times, they talked about how they take a risk when they choose a particular item and are pleased when customers like it. A number of traders mentioned that they buy goods with which they have a history. For example, as discussed in chapter 2, an ICI, like Miss T., will specialize in shoes because that is what she sold when she began her activities. Miss T.'s apprentice Miss M. follows the same logic. When we left the Miami airport, I asked the van man where ICIs shop and why. His response was that Miss T. had been frequenting several stores since she began in the 1980s, but once in a while, he would take her to other places where they were selling different styles. When we arrived at the stores throughout the day, I noticed several of the ICIs from the airport also buying. In some of the stores, Miss M. and Miss T. bought the same goods, sometimes in the same exact style and color. Other times, they bought different colors and styles. Yet these two are but a row apart in the arcade. I wondered about the competition this would create. The van man quickly told me that they have different customers. Then, he added, "Besides, it's business; sometimes one sells and sometimes the other one sells." As I show below, the downside to the increasing saturation is an illegal drug trade that threatens to get (or actually is) out of control.

Adapting to the Boom

Since 1980, adaptation to the boom in informal commercial importing has become quite an exercise for ICIs. Traders openly admitted that things are not as easy as in the old days. While they continue to contest excessive taxes, relocation problems, and increasing bureaucratic regulation from government agencies, the main challenge confronting them is the impact of the burgeoning drug trade on their activities and their daily lives. While no ICI ever mentioned the issue when I first began the project, questions concerning drug trafficking constantly arose in my exchanges with other locals including government officials. I was repeatedly told that "a lot of ICIs are smugglers" who export drugs out of Jamaica to earn foreign exchange that they use to buy the goods they import back to the island. These accounts were usually hearsay. This popular narrative came predominantly from middle-class individuals who were usually anti-ICI. At the time, the population in question was relatively small. I overlooked trafficking and its potential impact on ICIs until it became evident that this avoidance compromised the integrity of the research.

Few ICIs ever discussed this issue with me. Those who did were vague, giving no details. They expressed concerns about the negative impact of this new obstruction on their livelihood and its power to further disgrace them. Indeed, drug smuggling impacts the lives of ICIs in the most inhumane ways both at home and abroad. By 1994, I was told that the biggest problem facing ICIs today is drug trafficking. When "dem get caught, dem say 'We ICI,'" she said. The silence was being broken, though in a limited way, because the implications for informing remained the same. Individuals were clearly afraid. I was warned to stay clear of this issue. One said, "You *don't have to know* about *that* to do your research..." By 1995, the drug problem had escalated and become difficult to ignore. My initial reluctance stems from the power of the word, of which traders are only too aware, hence their silence. Indeed, the mere mention (a speech act) of smuggling vis-à-vis ICIs only reinforces the association and coagulates the concomitant stigma. Equally important, drug smuggling is a sensitive topic that would entail creating and managing all kinds of risks to everyone in my network, including myself. I had to extrapolate information. There was lots of it in the media, as well as in the scholarship on criminality in Jamaica (Harrison 1989; Headly 1994; Griffith 1997, 2000).

The fact is that during fieldwork, trafficking was present both in the most explicit and the most subtle of ways. Cocaine, heroin, marijuana, and other drugs in great demand were constantly flowing in and out of Jamaica. Driven by an expanding market, drugs became just another ready-made source of income (known as fast money) for anyone willing to move them. Drug couriers, known as mules, increasingly shared spaces with ICIs. They too used various creative methods to smuggle their commodities. Some of these include strapping it to their bodies, hiding it in weaved hair, or ingesting pellets or condoms and latex gloves packed with cocaine, a practice known as stuffing or swallowing. Although a significant amount of drug trafficking occurs on private airstrips, commercial airlines are also frequently used. Those engaged in the drug trade reflect the desperate state of the local economy, which makes this dangerous activity so attractive. It must be noted that in addition to the disenfranchised who have been drawn into this business, as they have no other recourse, there are those who are tired of their position in the global political economy and want fast money. Nonetheless, individuals across the class and color structure are involved in this activity.

In April 1994, sons of Richard Bernal, the Jamaican ambassador to the U.S. and the OAS, were arrested and charged with drug trafficking. They attempted to smuggle compressed marijuana as canned juice to Washington, D.C. On July 21, 1996, a single mother arrived at Miami International Airport aboard an American Airlines flight from Jamaica. Upon examination by the Customs Service, it was discovered that her cardboard box containing three bottles labeled "Jamaican Rum" were filled with a total of 889.2 grams of cocaine. In June 1999, customs intercepted 2,464 kilograms of Jamaican marijuana and 141 kg of hash oil at Newark, New

Jersey, in a marine container bound for Montreal. In December 2001, twenty-two Jamaicans were charged with attempting to smuggle a class A drug after disembarking from an Air Jamaica flight to Heathrow. Five days earlier, sixteen Jamaicans were arrested on suspicion of swallowing cocaine packages after arriving in Gatwick on a British Airways flight. That same year forty-eight British citizens were held in Jamaican jails. As this practice escalated in the U.K., Air Jamaica became so notorious for trafficking that in 2001, London's *Daily Mirror* dubbed it "Cocaine Air." According to government officials, about 60 percent of the cocaine in the U.K. comes through Jamaica. In November 2003, twenty-six U.S. airport employees were arraigned in federal court on charges of smuggling tens of millions of dollars worth of cocaine to the U.S., mainly from Guyana and Jamaica (Worth 2003). The incidents listed here illustrate the broad scope of this business and the array of the positions of participants.

As Ivelaw Griffith notes, the consent and participation of officials from various state agencies is necessary to facilitate the movement of large amounts of illegal commodities (1997). A significant number of females (especially single mothers) are involved. Among ICIs, it seems that both young and old traders are smuggling, as the increasing number of arrests and detainment in Kingston jails confirms. They have different reasons for entering into the drug trade. There are those who turn to illegal commodity trading to recover investments lost due to the saturated market. Others are recruited to traffic because of their experience as traders. There are also new ICIs, who enter the occupation solely to gain the BENO number to facilitate their movement as traffickers.

In that sense, the illegal drug trade became just another structure of power with which ICIs had to contend. Its most disadvantageous effect was that it threatened to erode the already politically fragile solidarity that existed among traders. In 2002, when ICIs clashed with the government over relocation issues, the biggest hindrance to coalition building was distrust. It appeared that traders trusted each other less and were less likely to band together against opposing forces, whether these were government officials or members of civil society. I must stress that the majority of importers are simply looking to make a living, to be their own bosses while they manage their daily lives. As their livelihood intersects with this other nightmarish aspect of globalization, they adapt. Several of those who had been searched for drugs spoke of the humiliation. In one case, an ICI decided to stop traveling to Panama altogether. Another ICI sends her son to buy her merchandise instead. The worst aspect for another ICI was that she simply could not tell who was and who was not trafficking. In recent conversations, several traders revealed that the situation was grave. Given that at one time they would hardly ever mention this issue, I can only assume that things were getting worse. In 1998, when I asked her what was going on now, Mrs. B. proceeded to explain the current economic conditions and how these were affecting the trade. She noted:

> The trade is receiving competition from all sides. Big merchants with large capital have become importers who specialize in the goods that ICIs travel to acquire. People are traveling less. You can buy wholesale in Kingston. The local economy is in trouble like the rest of the world. Government policies are not working for the country. Big business and little business are in trouble. Whole heap of banks are crashing. People are losing their jobs now just like in the 1980s. For every one thousand who leave their jobs seven hundred enter the business because they believe there is money in it. There is more selling than buying going on and purchasing power is very low. The trade is getting a battering from all over. You have people falling out because that is business.

Always concerned with the future, another ICI worries that too many ICIs are choosing what she says is "the easy way out instead of fighting." Painfully, she elaborated:

> Most of our ladies are in prison all over the world. Plenty of people are throwing up hands. Some of us are still fighting. Some will be up and some will be down. Some people don't have the fighting spirit ... We in the business so long now that we must fight to the bitter end. We couldn't leave now, it's too late for that. We have to get around the problems. We have to organize ourselves and come back. Some will go but some will fight.

Her candor prompted me to ask why she does not trade in drugs. She replied, "I have my four kids and five grandchildren who I dearly love. I'll be with them till I die."

The impact of the burgeoning drug trade on the business warrants further attention for its own sake. Haitian sociologist Alex Dupuy writes that the expanding drug trafficking and money laundering booming in the region are consequences of neoliberal globalization policies that supplant local economies, undermine local production, and increase dependence on international financial institutions and migration as the region exports more of its labor force. These factors combined have made countries in the Caribbean region increasingly economically vulnerable (2001:524–526). Moreover, drug trafficking is literally destroying communities, and from the perspective of human rights concerns has rendered certain parts of Kingston war zones unevenly open to legitimized state violence on the poor. This trade also stigmatizes ICIs, who are already socially marginalized. It poses new sets of challenges that further undermine their attempts at self-making.

Globalization and ICIs' Reflexive Political Economy

At home and abroad, amidst all of these structures of power, ICIs manage to do their business and make a life. Not all of them fare equally well. Their success depends upon the scale of their activities, their investments, their overall goals and aspirations, and their awareness of the uneven spaces they occupy and of the scope and inconsistencies of their power as black females maneuvering in a "fragmented globality" that historically favored the North. This perception underscores what I call ICIs' reflexive political economy. This theory is grounded in ICIs' sense of their personal history as members of communities in a constant state of formation and forms the basis of traders' self-making practices as these relate to local, national, and global dynamics. It is in part an articulation of what Raymond Williams refers to as a "structure of feeling" or the making of "meanings and values as they are actively lived and felt." Williams emphasizes that the feelings of which he speaks are "affective elements of consciousness and relationships" (1977:132). While considering Williams, we note that this idea of reflexive political economy stems from the theoretical crossing of James Scott's moral economy and the aforementioned extensive black feminist contributions, with special attention to the works of Hill-Collins, hooks, and Lorde.

James Scott (1976) used the concept of moral economy to explain Southeast Asian peasantry's perception and response to exploitation from capitalist penetration of the countryside. However, it was first introduced by E. P. Thompson to explicate the behavior of English crowds in eighteenth-century riots.[4] He revised the term. Thompson noted that the market took on multiple meanings as "it turns out to be a junction-point between social, economic, and intellectual histories and a sensitive metaphor for many kinds of exchange" (1991:259). He elaborated that his use of the

term was "confined to the confrontations in the market-place over access
(or entitlement) to necessities-essential food" (Thompson 1991:337). Scott
argued that in their relationships with patrons, peasants prioritized both
social and material guarantees in the form of reciprocal exchanges and
customary rights. In that vein, when these systems failed, their particular
notion of (economic) justice justified their subordinate activities, which
peasants viewed as legitimate because they sought to secure the livelihood
of a community as opposed to individual interests.[5] According to Sivaramakrishnan, Scott was interested in "recovering the agency and ideologies
of the poor and lower class rural people to show how their political actions
in contexts of rapid agrarian change 'limited the types of economic relations and the intensity of exploitation that elites were able to impose'"
(2005:347).[6] This approach is applicable to informal commercial importing given the aforementioned history of contestation from which it stems
and the tensions that continue to affect the trade and its participants.

    Similarly, throughout this text, I have deployed various feminist criti-
ques to consider the black feminist anthropology within more conventional or elite anthropology. I used the collective works of Lorde, Harrison,
Hill-Collins, and hooks, who have argued that epistemic knowledge is situated not only along gender lines but also on the bases of race, class, sexuality, nationality, and other axes of difference that operate in tandem
with each other. I elaborated on black and transnational feminist perspectives, which stress that compounded experiences of those subject to
these intersecting multiaxial oppressions locates one as "outsiders-within"
(Hill-Collins [1991] 2000). This results in a complex understanding of the
social order and a particular set of insights into social relations that are
unavailable to those in power (Hill-Collins [1991] 2000). In pursuit of my
project, I have repeatedly argued both within and outside of the academy that black females have long "struggled to find alternative locations
and epistemologies for validating our own self-definitions" (Hill-Collins
[1991] 2000:269). This search for self-making has been central to both Lorde
and hooks, who write of the benefit of being situated on and writing from
the margins. This position, I propose, is comparable to that of ICIs in Jamaica. As a transnational black feminist anthropologist in white academe,
I occupy my own margin. It is the differences in our positions that inform
the ways we enact our respective reflexive political economy. In Scott's
model, peasants too have their own logic that differentiates among and
prioritizes various types of capital. I argue that the same can be said of
ICIs. Thompson's multiple meanings of exchange are evident both in the

arcade, where ICIs interact with each other and with their customers, the government, civil society, and their interlocutors abroad as well as in my maneuvering and negotiating in the academic market.

Indeed, as Jamaican citizens abroad, ICIs are only too aware of their contribution to local, regional, and global economies as buyers, distributors, and consumers of goods. Simultaneously, they experience being targeted as potential drug mules and must also mediate their identities to facilitate their businesses. These contradictions sensitize them to the incongruity of their positions. In gendering globalization, feminist analysts point to local responses to the omnipresent power of global economic forces that exploit those in the South. Their findings illuminate the cracks in globalization and the creativity and broader contexts within which subjects of capitalism attempt to make their own lives.[7] Such perspectives offer valuable insights into how historical enactments of power are dependent on articulation (Hall 1996).

On a daily basis, local-global relations are nothing but intersubjective encounters that are in a constant state of flux. In her recent ethnography, anthropologist Anna Tsing uses a metaphor of friction to characterize these moments of global connections that is useful here.[8] More specifically, she writes: "friction is the reminder of the importance of interaction in defining movement, cultural form and agency. Friction is not just about slowing things down. Friction is required to keep global power in motion ... it makes global connection powerful and effective. Meanwhile without even trying it gets in the way of the smooth operation of global power. Difference can disrupt, causing everyday malfunctions as well as unexpected cataclysms. Friction refuses the lie that global power operates as a well-oiled machine" (2005:6). In light of this definition, the Miami trip can be read as consisting of copious instances of friction. The various encounters between buyers and sellers, at all the different shopping stops, reveal the kinetic tensions of global connections. In one such encounter, a Dominican salesperson who assumed I was an ICI in training revealed that prices differ for buyers from different countries. Wholesalers do not have a set price for items; rather, they take the exchange rate of the buyer's country of origin into account and charge according to these values. Later, when I discussed this with Miss T. and Miss M., they were not at all surprised. That's just business. The Haitian dollar is much weaker than the Jamaican. In fact, they were shocked that I did not expect this, because to them it was just another fait accompli.

Another moment illustrative of Tsing's friction is Miss T.'s charged performance at the shoe store. Along with Miss M., Miss T. entered the shop with the intention of spending thousands of U.S dollars. Despite their purchasing power, however, the veteran ICI had to mediate her identity and perform toughness to avoid being taken advantage of. Miss T.'s presentation was an embodied response that may end in her desired result (to not be cheated by the shop owners), but in the process, it reinforced the black superwoman stereotype as well as the perception of ICIs, in particular, as rude gals. However, this is too simple an explanation of this abrasive moment. I argue that Miss T.'s response was also based on substantive engagement of the sensory to deploy what Audre Lorde refers to as power of the erotic (1984). Her repetition of "fuck" in the conversation with the Miami wholesaler is an important example of the complexity of the power that ICIs, like herself, now occupy as a buyer abroad.[9] I believe there are multiple hidden transcripts in her well-timed delivery of that chorus of expletives. Indeed, just what did it mean that this white man let a black female curse him out to the extent that she did and in the way that she did? That was playful at times and then tougher later. To what extent were these curses tolerated because the transaction was about the exchange of material capital? Her performance of toughness demarcated her boundaries. Don't fuck with me, she said quite literally. But at the same time what kind of erotic play was also taking place? How did her black body figure into this battle? How did she use it, or how was it being used?

Not all ICIs have nor manipulate their power over their bodies and/or choose to perform tuffness when they cross borders. For those who do, their performance and charismatic influence does not have unlimited use for countering state power. While abroad (whether in Cayman, Panama, or the U.S.), ICIs are at the mercy of other national policies that render some of their strategies inutile. While much has been said about globalization's effects on the economic conditions of ICIs, more attention is needed to explicate how these intertwine with the corporeal demands of such crossings. ICIs' bodies are central to this business, which is premised upon their movement. While on the move, they are economic agents who also contribute to the economies of their destinations. In the Cayman Islands, cargo companies note that business from ICIs is very lucrative. During their trips, ICIs also frequent and spend money at local shops and restaurants as well as hotels. In Miami, traders' feed the local economy and cross the lines between formal and informal (these include their wholesale purchases, their employment of day workers, and their use of shipping companies).[10] They have similar effects when they travel to free trade zones in Panama and wholesale districts and stores in Toronto, London, New York, and other destinations. Here, my findings diverge from those

of Carla Freeman, who argues that "contemporary higglers in the Caribbean engage in activities that are transforming practices of global capitalism" (2001:1008). I argue that as ICIs make their way in the world, they
collide and make contact with others; this contact has both momentary
and long-term influence. Their impact abroad is tenuous. At home, it may
have more lasting power in some arenas, especially in the ways they manage each other. Indeed, classed perceptions of them remain rigid rendering them outsiders within (Hill-Collins [1991] 2000).

For example, their apprenticeship system is a highly collaborative practice that is quite revealing about how some ICIs see and understand their
positions at home and in the world. This perspective does not extend to
all ICIs, but it does apply to several traders in this study. Though there
were others who tended to be less communal in their approach, as with
higglering, it is veteran importers who routinely train newcomers who are
likely to become would-be competitors. The nature of this relationship
is based on a sense of friendly competition. First, they view themselves
as being in the same situation. Second, the willingness to cooperate with
one another coalesces around ICIs' position vis-à-vis big business merchants, the government, and international monetary agencies that have
directly affected their livelihood. Third, they band together as black females who understand how they have been historically limited by capitalism and seek to surpass their mothers and better their lives and that
of their children. These are the basis of their imagined communities (Anderson 1991). What motivates their joint efforts is worthy of discussion as
similar observations have been made in cross-cultural studies of market
traders.[11] Miss M. carrying the condensed milk that she relinquished at
the luggage carousel is another example. She and other ICIs have mentioned that they carry items for each other when they travel. Nowadays,
with the pervasiveness of drug trafficking, this is a particularly poignant
and risky effort. Miss M.'s response to me was simple: "She mi friend I
want to help her." I have also observed moments where a veteran wholesaler will give items to a newcomer on credit to sell, because this person is
in a bind. The understanding is that they will take these goods away from
the premises and sell elsewhere so as not to interfere with the veteran's
business. These occasions were rare, but when they happened, the trader
would shrug her shoulders and admit they are all in this together.

This demonstration of unity also extends to customers and brings up a
crucial point concerning class alliance given the demographics of arcade
customers and traders' perceptions of their position. A number of the

ICIs interviewed identified themselves not just as sellers who respond to
the demand of the poor, but also as their protectors. Mr. C. has been an
ICI for over ten years. He apprenticed with his mother and now has his
own business. He defends the often-ignored role of ICIs as suppliers to
a specific market: "It's wi who watch out for the poor people you know.
Somebody have to watch out fer dem. It's wi who buy things they can afford. We have to buy things that last, you know. Dem don't have money."
Indeed, most of the clientele at the arcade is of a particular socioeconomic
bracket. While there are also those middle-class customers who frequent
arcades because they can consume more, most arcade customers are of
the working and lower classes.[12] These individuals cannot enter stores in
Half-Way-Tree or New Kingston and walk out with merchandise, whether
these are shoes, undergarments, notebooks, pens, or soaps. The arcade is
one of the places where they find what they need at affordable prices.

Once upon leaving Miss D.'s stall, a black shoe on the back shelf caught
my eye. I made my way back in and was about to reach for the item when
I realized that it wasn't leather. I retrieved my hand slowly. She asked
if I wanted to see it. I quickly responded: "No! They're really cute... I
just thought they were leather." She gave me a dumbfounded look then
dismissively stuped, and added, "Working-class people don't have money
to buy leather!" Indeed, they often don't. When they shop in the arcade,
they are restricted by their income. Whether these customers are satisfied or not, however, is a point that warrants inquiry. Those who protest
about the cost of and types of products sold by ICIs are often more vocal
and have opportunities to express their disapproval. They are usually members of the middle class. In the early years, newspapers published numerous letters from concerned citizens who were aghast by the excessive flow
of commodities that flooded the island. As I reveal in the following chapter, this narrative is loaded with incongruities and recalls scholarly debates about third world victims of consumption and the passivity of agents
in the periphery. Let me stress that this narrative obscures the fact that ICIs
not only supply the lower classes, most of whom are downtown dwellers,
but that these transactions occur within a particular cultural context.

That said, contact between importers and their customers highlights
the significance of the value ascribed to different types of capital. In many
instances, an ICI's response may seem illogical to market-driven observers seeking evidence of profit building. For example, Miss B. will turn down
a sale from a customer who questions her prices. It is worth losing a sale or
two, particularly from a customer who seeks to undermine her standing,

to maintain her reputation as someone who sells quality products and does not overcharge. The long-term effects of a damaged reputation are much costlier than those of a single sale. Moreover, for those engaged in occupational multiplicity, there are always other opportunities for material gain. This practice was most common among more successful ICIs, who are wholesalers. Their patterns of investment are dictated by their reflexive political economy, which does not always seem to affect their business directly. Beautification and other types of self-presentation expenses are good examples. The point of these investments is to perform class in a way that minimizes potential clashes with interlocutors and makes life easier, which in turn facilitates the conduct of their businesses. Vehicles are also key purchases. Those who are able to do so purchase trucks that their children drive; others also learn to drive themselves. There are also cases where mobility is forgone and traders reinvest their profits in property (homes, farms, and stores). These are the success stories that beckon newcomers to the trade. It is structurally impossible for all ICIs to make it big in the business; the number of successes is proportionately small.

What motivates them is the same reflexive political economy that underlies their commitment to downtown areas. Among the successful traders I encountered, most continued to sell at the arcade. They simply did not wish to relocate elsewhere even though they could afford to relocate. Among the influx of novices that began during the 1980s, there were numerous suitcase traders who eventually transitioned into store operations on the fringes of the uptown/downtown line or even uptown proper. These persons imported invisibly or even legally as registered ICIs. They slowly built their profit to afford the shop operator's licensing fee. They traveled as ICIs to build their stock, found a location in which to establish themselves, and eventually joined the formal business sector as shop owners. Many among them continue to stock their businesses in this way. This was most common among middle-class practitioners (school teachers, beauticians, and others) who could afford to make this crossing. In part due to the pervasiveness of this practice during the early 1980s, the JLP implemented a J$25,000 tax to obtain a shop operator's license and agency permit in 1986. This exorbitant fee was meant to be a deterrent. It restricted entrance into the formal economy to those who could afford it. Economist James Bovard notes that this tax policy had a "devastating effect on the creation of small businesses which, as most studies indicate, create far more new jobs than their larger competitors. The new shop operator's tax, equal to more than double the national per capita income, closes the doors of opportunity for all but the rich and upper middle-classes" (1987). There are old-timers who are not negatively influenced or deterred by the violence and scarceness of opportunities downtown. They regard it as a place that has potential, that can be turned around, and that they have no intention of abandoning.

Instead of looking toward uptown areas that had social value, one ICI decided to open a shop in Portmore, a lower middle-class area forty-five minutes southwest of Kingston, where there was greater demand. Another began to bankroll new recruits. Both continued to operate their stalls in the downtown arcades. When I asked them why they did not branch out or move uptown, they had different answers. The first stayed there because, as she said, "it's how mi get started." The other was keen on maximizing her profit and building capital to better the lives of her children. Another wanted to own a shop downtown. While she stands to gain financially, her other motive is purely positional. She is adamant that black business owners not only belong on the main shopping streets of downtown Kingston, but that they too can flourish there. As I discussed in chapter 4, historically it is nonblacks who have owned downtown businesses. This fact is not lost on traders who are continually reminded that the racial/spatial order restricts their place as business owners solely to the market or the arcade. One ICI was adamant about purchasing a building downtown to leave the extractive and unsafe arcade system. Attempts to form alliances and build a partnership with other ICIs failed for various reasons. In the end, she went into business with her sons.

These examples provide insight into both the social meaning of exchange for traders and the reflexive political economy that underscores their activities. They constantly consider their individual positions in relation to their broader communities. What I have shown in this chapter is that the shopping trip and its aftermath offer an opportunity to explicate the intricate web of meaning created by ICIs as they navigate structures in different localities. Not surprisingly, there is virtually no data available on the specifics of their economic contribution globally. Indeed, more extensive research in this area is needed. This lack of information is yet another method of erasing the gender of globalization.

However, this is nothing new. Black female labor has historically been obscured. Simultaneously, while their work may be rendered invisible and go unrecognized, their bodies remain hypervisible. Nowhere is this more apparent than in local responses to the impact of ICI-imported items that commodify blackness. As I conclude in the following chapter, when the material and symbolic components that are embedded in gendered class and color codes intersect with consumption of foreign styles, the result is a series of contradictions and paradoxes that confound the lady and the woman, thus further emphasizing the complexity and the depth of the local when it collides with the global.

CHAPTER SEVEN

Style, Imported Blackness, and My Jelly Platform Shoes

Style of dress has become associated with the status symbols of class and the escape from economic reality. —Michael Manley

Oh Gina! Get serious... These shoes are so common. —Miss Q.

A Return to Style

The implications of appearance in Kingston are evident in a myriad of ways, varying according to class. Newspapers have style sections. Society pages comment on who attended important events and what they were wearing. There is always the competing female gaze on the street, at the store, or in the office. Meant to demarcate social and spatial boundaries, this look assesses whether one is a possible contender. Nothing is more disarming than this sweeping look that starts at the top of one's head and then slowly scans every item on the body down to the shoes. Whereas the male gaze tends to uncover, this particular gendered scan ascertains positions and claims space. It is a cultural device that females use to keep each other in line. Across the social spectrum, self-presentation matters to Jamaicans though the motives differ. In search of respect, the very poor strive to look their best at church, the bank, the doctor's, in any public place. They sometimes borrow clothing from family members and friends because it is important to keep up appearances. A middle-aged female in a shiny cocktail dress in the middle of the day is a frequent sight in the metropolitan area. This dress may be the only stylish item this person possesses. Under the hot sun, she stands in line at the embassy, not caring whether her style of dress is appropriate for the occasion; it is simply her best dress. Schoolgirls walk together in starched and pressed uniforms, bows or jewelry in their hair, shoes shined, socks clean and bleached. Young men wearing checkered or plain button down shirts tucked into shorts or long pants and sport watches carry backpacks and distinctive school bags. Lower-level office workers wait for the bus in uniforms that separate them from top management. Bank tellers and administrators in high heels carpool with friends and family dressed in uniforms, always well put together in a look that emphasizes neatness. Style has its very own order.

Kingston has numerous finishing schools, modeling schools, gyms, beauty salons, and spas. Considerable capital can be expended on achieving one's perfection. There is also a parallel market where similar services can be obtained privately in one's home or in makeshift shops and salons operating without commercial licenses. Undoubtedly, Jamaica's beauty and fashion industries are highly lucrative. As the first visible marker of difference, appearance carries complex value. As white anthropologist Terrence Turner (1980) makes clear, the social skin or physical surface marks the boundary between social classes. This differentiation often works through class and color codes that counter racial homogeneity.

During the PNP period in the 1970s, political leaders attempted to disrupt the old (post)colonial order and refract class/color divisions through multiple social and economic programs. They brought public attention to the colonized aspects of one's social skin by encouraging African-inspired modes of dress. Manley and other PNP officials chose guayaberas over three-piece suits. This shirt, which has become synonymous with Cuba (though it is made in Mexico), symbolized populist and socialist politics.[1] In 1980, the new JLP administration came to power preaching deliverance with neoliberalist policies, including trade liberalization and deregulation, and wearing three-piece suits. The leaders obtained numerous loans and development aid from international lending agencies. If these moments did not signal a new era, what a *Gleaner* staff writer referred to as a "return to style," certainly did. That same year, in the June/July issue of the *Caribbean and West Indies Chronicle*, Prime Minister Edward Seaga was voted the best-dressed prime minister in the Caribbean. According to the commentator, "In 1980 on the wings of deliverance three-piece suits returned to the Jamaican scene. Before that a stroll at a state function or one of those after hours scenes, would reveal an abundance of bush jackets, karebas or shirts. I cannot forget attending a function at the Jamaica Pegasus Hotel (as a journalist) at which the men were dressed in the most ghastly colors and outfits, even though it had an international touch. That was the days of 'manners.' With a new Prime Minister and the return to style ... "[2]

Indeed, times had changed. The region was hit by a recession. With multimillion-dollar loans from the Caribbean Basin Initiative fueling the economy, growth seemed up. The Jamaican dollar was devalued and food prices reached an all-time high, increasing the poverty of the masses. Yet even during dire times, one must put one's best foot forward. Or, perhaps because of the direness of times, the return of the power suit was even more crucial. In Kingston, government officials and uptown businessmen were covering their bodies, suiting up. Downtown dancehall enthusiasts, on the other hand, began to shed some of their sartorial restraints. For females, the popular look revealed more skin. One such style, aptly called air-conditioned, consisted of strips of cloth sewn together strategically to cover or uncover different parts of the body. Tights and lycra tops were punctured and stretched to create holes of all sizes.

This striptease was facilitated in part by the boom in informal commercial importing that accompanied the explosion of dancehall (Ulysse 1999). This popular culture, which evolved with its own ideology and lifestyle, was a response to the Manley government's embrace of reggae in the 1970s. From its inception, dancehall celebrated the local. Norman Stolzoff asserts that with Bob Marley's death in 1981 dancehall rose as a "creative means of reasserting a distinctive black lower-class space, identity, and politics. Dancehall itself became a symbol of the division between uptown and downtown, between a music that was increasingly oriented to an international market (roots reggae) and one that spoke to the local sensibilities of a younger generation" (2000:103). The Jamaican gaze was shifting away from Zion (Africa). Music producer Maxine Stowe best describes this view: "The Rastafarian culture and Afrocentric talk started dispersing. Kids became less Afrocentric and more New York–centric" (quoted in Leland 1992:187). And I would add that this shift included everything New York City had to offer at the time: drugs, guns, hiphop, rock, and punk.

Responding to customer demands, ICIs imported Nike, Adidas, Cross Colours, and Karl Kani among other popular brands. Initially these items were knockoffs or counterfeits, but with the emergence of the price tag as symbolic of authenticity, some traders began to import the real thing. For females, they purchased spandex tights, leggings, shorts, lace tanks, organza tops, body suits, studded bustiers, laced and bubble gum dresses, and shirts. Specialty shops sold dominatrix patent leather boots, punk stilettos, Doc Martens, and studded shoes. ICIs became part of a huge distribution network that moved these items especially from Fulton Street and Pitkin Avenue in Bedford-Stuyvesant and the wholesale district in Manhattan to Kingston. At dancehalls, these items were worn together to create a mix. Rex Nettleford (1995) has argued that this penchant for creative ensemble is a historical continuity, a return of the "pitchy-patchy" popular at Jonkonnu festivals during slavery.[3]

Whether these goods were brought into the country by ICIs or were sent home by family members abroad, who shipped barrels to those "left behind," they were thrown together and personalized by individual taste. At dances and shows, outfits clashed ultrafemininity with a hard-core and edgy tuffness. While symbolically these compositions crossed gendered notions, materially this style reflected a self-assured female reveling in her sexuality and feminine power, proudly showing off her assets.[4] Economically, however, this look perpetuated the island's dependence on imports and the devaluation of locally manufactured products. Yet it was for another reason that this style spurred anxieties uptown: dancehall females' appearance signaled that the middle and upper classes no longer dictated standards of decency and respect.

While I was conducting my doctoral fieldwork (1992-1997), dancehall became pervasive, affecting more aspects of Jamaican life. The question of "appropriate" dress in public remained on the middle-class agenda, but was contested by supporters who called the middle class hypocritical for its scandalous attire and behavior during Carnival. The most notable defender of dancehall culture is UWI's Carolyn Cooper, whose lyrical arguments reveal the various classed agendas implied in persecutions of dancehall. She and other local scholars conclude that the middle and upper classes' panic is a response to the cultural war that they are losing (Cooper 2004a,b,c; Meeks 1997; Gray 2004). There was indeed a sound clash that was somewhat similar to the "moral panic" concerning "mugging" that gripped Britain during the 1970s. The response to dancehall bears enough parallel to be characterized as a crisis that also needed to be contained.[5] Dancehall followers were getting out of control with their slackness or "vulgar lyrics" and "sexually explicit" expression. The black masses had to be domesticated. Consequently, it was not surprising to hear of dress codes posted at malls, hospitals, or even police stations. Gatekeepers, fearful of encroachment upon their terrains, tried to suppress this upheaval and rein in their loss of social power. In efforts to halt this disorder caused by globalization, uptown's enforcement knew no boundaries. During the early years of dancehall, the fashion police stood guard everywhere, especially at funerals.

Policing the Fashion Crisis

In February 1992, the deaths of two West Kingston dons brought the dancehall fashion phenomenon into uptown living rooms. Jim Brown, the notorious don of Tivoli Gardens, one of West Kingston's most dangerous JLP garrison communities, was killed by an unexplained fire in his prison cell during his son Jah-T's funeral. Since both father and son were community leaders, Edward Seaga, the opposition leader, and other party officials attended their funerals. As a result, their interments were two of the most well-attended events to be held downtown in years, and both received full coverage by radio, TV, and newspapers, including the *Gleaner*, whose article on Jah-T's funeral devoted a great portion of the text to the appearance of those who attended, especially the females. The writer described the various styles of black dresses and heavy gold accessories that were worn by attendees, including Jah-T's girlfriend's tight-fitting dress and the deceased's own attire of a white satin shirt and a black velvet suit.

Several weeks later, the *Gleaner* published a two-page pictorial with a brief text on Jim Brown's funeral. Jamaica's leading fashion commentator and uptown designer, Norma Soas, authored the piece, titled "Mourning as Spectator Sport." Her elaboration on the variation of styles she saw and downtown people's fashion sense deserves to be quoted at length:

> The women seemed to wear every piece of fashionable item they owned—all at once. Baubles, bangles, beads abounded. This was a "let it all hang out" (literally) affair. No mini was too short, no tights too tight, and no chiffon too sheer, no lace too see-through. Hot pants were cheek-by-jowl with lace leggings. Feet were shod in everything from Roman sandals to studded boots. Breasts were encased in bustiers and worn with chiffon big-sleeved blouses. Ankles were wrapped in gold chains with longer thicker versions adorning the neck. Oversized earrings brushed the wearer's shoulders.
>
> Uptown people who might think the dress shown here is inappropriate for the occasion do not really understand the ghetto culture which is vibrant in its own right.

This is how a large segment of our female population dresses when they go to their fetes. The mourners were not dressing for a funeral. They were dressing for an occasion and this was one of the biggest in their community. This therefore was not inappropriate in their eyes. Rather, these styles are de rigueur for any situation for profiling as this undoubtedly was. This is street fashion, a more sophisticated version of which has been seen in Greenwich Village in New York or Carnaby Street in London. (Soas 1992:10A)

In her descriptions of these female representations, Soas reaffirms the lady/woman dichotomy. According to this designer, these women publicly and explicitly asserted their sexuality in clothing that left little to the imagination. In the second part of the text, she critiqued the appropriateness of wearing dancehall clothing to a burial. By highlighting their distinctive taste, she repeatedly set them apart from uptown readers. Arguably, through this tactical process of distinction, she engages in the project of representing downtown as the "other" and in the process reifies uptown superiority.

Later, in another article, Soas highlights the Jamaican racial/spatial order and the spatial dimensions of the lady/woman dichotomy. She notes that it was indeed this funeral that opened the eyes of the folks uptown (who rarely go downtown) to the phenomenon of dancehall fashions. She writes, "the middle-class marveled at the homage to bareness. Many envied the self-confidence of the wearers, most of whom gave lie to the saying that you should only wear clothes that flatter the figure" (1993:7). Uptown ladies must not bare their bodies in the same manner as downtown women, unless of course it is carnival. Moreover, uptown ladies envy this downtown self-confidence in part because those who do not possess svelte bodies refrain from wearing tight clothing, which is considered inappropriate as these accentuate their voluptuousness (read curvy downtown bodies). Ironically, Soas realizes that, for attendees, these funerals were about getting recognition as she starts the original article with the following statement: "This was not high fashion but fashion excess. This was mourning as spectator sport with the spectators and mourners as the main attraction" (Soas 1992:10A). Funerals, because they, like dancehall sessions, are arenas of public display in which self-representations matter, are spaces where individuals assert their identities. Furthermore, Jim Brown's notoriety guaranteed extensive media coverage and thus an opportunity to be seen, to gain recognition beyond and within one's community.

In 1997, after former Prime Minister Manley's death, an announcement with guidelines for the public at the state funeral appeared in the

Gleaner. It was recommended that, for purposes of conformity and correct procedure during the period of mourning, men should dress conser-
vatively and women should dress "appropriately correspondingly" (Needham 1997). Nine days later, in one of numerous articles that recounted the
successful grand procession that sent off the former prime minister, another example of fashion policing appeared in the *Gleaner.* In the middle
of this article, entitled "A Grand Procession," the writer notes, "The afternoon was not without humor despite the seriousness of the occasion."
She recounts the tale of a "lady" wearing a green velvet dress and high
heel shoes, who was overheard complaining that the shoes were burning
her feet. She asked her friend to exchange shoes but was refused. Apparently they had already exchanged shoes.

The next paragraph was devoted to an exchange between two females
who asked the person directly in front of her to remove her wig as it was
blocking her view. According to the writer, the bewigged mourner replied,
"This is not a wig," to which the first woman then asked, "How it so stiff,
only wig suppose to stiff so" (Young 1997). In the remaining paragraphs
of the article, the writer returned to the actual funeral. These anecdotes
reveal middle-class concerns about appropriate conduct in public settings. The shoe swapping and the stiff wig comments are amusing. Still,
one must ask what makes these funny? Who is doing the laughing and,
perhaps most importantly, what is the object of laughter? These articles
provide insight into classed sensibilities and even anxieties about self-
presentation and their need to maintain distinction therein. Below, I offer
two more examples of self-making practices of blacks of different classes
that resulted in public reactions by uptown's middle class. These moments
further revealed the extent of the terrain in which this cultural war is
fought.

Foreign Expletives and Hair

In 1994, a series of popular T-shirts among downtown youths caused an
uproar uptown. Oversized, in black or white, they were designed with large
block letters that spelled the words "fuck you" or "don't ask me 4 shit."
Throughout the city, especially in downtown areas, the shirts were easily
spotted on individuals. They became the subject of debate on talk radio
shows for months. Callers offended by these words campaigned for prohi-
bition of the shirts. One of the main complaints concerning them was that

they were imported (by ICIs) and contained foreign obscenities.[6] Because of an existing law, which fines the verbalization of expletives in public spaces, the T-shirts were eventually banned as the boldly printed words were seen as an assault on the public, who were apparently forced to see, and hence read, these blocks of obscenities.

In April 1996, an unambiguously black female, Andrea Hutchinson, sporting Nubian knots was guest hosting *Tuesday Forum*, a morning TV program on JBC. Nubian knots are a pan-African hairstyle in which the hair is separated in small squares; each section is then twisted to its full length, coiled, and tucked in. Within her first hour on the air, the television station received calls from viewers across the nation demanding the removal of that "dutty gal," "bumpy head gal," or "ugly black woman" from the screen. According to Hutchinson, another viewer said, "If my helper turned up to work like that, I'd send her home, she would have to go home. For such an intelligent and well spoken person, how could she come out much less appear on TV like that?"[7] This particular comment is noteworthy. Indeed, as an intelligent person, Hutchinson should have known better than to present herself in a manner that, according to the caller, would not even befit a servant.[8] This viewer's reference to her helper (re)positioned the TV hostess to reveal how she rendered herself out of place with this hairstyle. In my conversations with various respondents, the general feeling was one of indifference. Individuals, unfamiliar with this hairdo, did note that they thought her hair was not quite done, that the style seemed incomplete. The belief is that the hair was twisted as though she were wearing curlers and would eventually be let down. Television hostesses in Jamaica tend to represent gendered hegemonic ideals, regardless of color. Hutchison's natural Afrocentric hairstyle, which was quite popular in the United States at the time, was not a look that would be associated with middle-class ladies in Jamaica. From those who objected, I argue, the issue seemed to be that Hutchinson had blurred the lines demarcating class and color codes.

This event sparked even more controversy for several weeks in the media. That "bumpy head gal," as she became known, is a well-known poet who is considered to be the heir-apparent to Louise Bennett, the grand dame of Jamaican oral poetry. Again, this public expression of "Afrophobia" became a popular debate. Newspapers, radio shows, and TV programs addressed this issue in attempts to bring closure to the incident. That moment resulted in a wave of responses, which revealed that Afro-Jamaican females were determined to express their power of self-definition.

Within days, numerous black, downtown, dancehall females, and some from the middle class, adopted this new hairstyle and wore it proudly everywhere. I saw young girls wearing this hairstyle with their pressed school uniforms and white socks. Discussions about the incident highlighted the fact that in some schools on the island, and in other parts of the region, dreadlocks are still prohibited.

Historically, hair has always had symbolic value. As Kobena Mercer notes, hair functions as a key signifier because, compared with bodily shape or facial features, it can be changed more easily by cultural practices. Caught on the cusp between self and society, nature and culture, the malleability of hair makes it a sensitive area of expression (1994:103). In the black diaspora, hair has always been a site of identity formation. In the Caribbean, in general, and in Jamaica, in particular, it has also been a point of contention between and within the classes. Rastafarians' natural locks are viewed as unkempt and unsanitary (Chevannes 1998). As a Rastafari explains, "That they don't like the hair, it's because they are afraid of nature themselves. Hair play a very important part upon a man. Anyone who fight against the hair fight against the self" (quoted in Owens 1976:154). Hutchinson said she styled her hair in this fashion because it is one of the latest popular styles from abroad. Though the class position of individuals who objected to Hutchinson's hairstyle is not known, what the incident also reveals is a continuous rejection of blackness in a perceived natural state in Jamaican society.

Since the 1990s, the use of hair extensions, weaves, and wigs has been popular across the classes. Among the upper classes, hairstyles that incorporate extensions are made to look as close to natural as possible. People from this class use natural as opposed to synthetic hair. Insofar as emulation can be claimed, it is through these styles that they aspire to whiteness. They are meant to enhance a natural look (Pinnock 1997). Among the lower classes, particularly downtown, these hair accessories are used conspicuously. Among dancehall participants and younger ICIs, these synthetic wigs or hair extensions are worn in bright colors such as white, yellow, red, blue, or green. The artificiality of the wigs or weaves is obvious, and they are used to create elaborate styles that could not possibly be natural. The common critique of such styles is that they are emulations of whiteness. These styles are exaggerated statements of difference that are not meant to assimilate (Mercer 1987). Pinnock also found that such hairstyles are meant to shock, to attract attention rather than to pass and assimilate into the dominant culture (Pinnock 1997). During the early

1990s, these styles were part of dancehall ensembles worn mostly at night. Soon, they became part of everyday life, as they were spotted throughout both downtown and uptown. The carnivalesque (Bakhtin 1984) that is in dancehall was seeping into daily life as a result of the pervasiveness of this subculture. Dancehall became so popular abroad, and such a lucrative commodity, that it had to be endured at home. As happened with the reggae that preceded it, and caused a similar reaction from the middle class, the disdain was replaced with tolerance, because this cultural form had a high exchange value, which put Jamaica on the global map, especially in North American, European, and Japanese markets. Nonetheless, during 1995–1996, it was still uncommon, or out of place and shocking, to see individuals in full dancehall gear posing, posturing as they strolled into uptown establishments.[9] Back then, being fashionable or hip was referred to as "making a statement" among the middle class and "popin style" by the working classes.

Making a Statement

Sometime during mid-September 1993, I had to go to the main Citibank, on Knutsford Boulevard, to collect a wire from the Social Science Research Council (SSRC) to support my entire semester of study in Kingston. While conducting my transaction, the female bank teller seemed overly preoccupied. Several times, she pleasantly asked me to wait for her while she went to the back and up the stairs to talk to this "lady" who was roaming around freely in the paneled offices above. I could see this activity through the glass partition that separated them from me. When she was through, the teller returned and proceeded to notify me that the lady (note that she did not refer to her as an ICI) was going shopping abroad the next day. The teller had to speak with her now for a few minutes before heading home. She sought my understanding, stressing that she desperately needed to add new items to her wardrobe because "you know how important it is to make a statement here." At that time, I did not know, and given my fashion woes exposed in chapter 3, I did not care. It's fieldwork, so I nodded in agreement. Then she proceeded to tell me how to contact this individual. She handed me a piece of paper with the buyer's name and phone number, adding, "You'd like her things ... because she never brings more than three or four of the same pieces."

Since I had gone to the bank to collect a rather sizable wire transfer of U.S. dollars from SSRC, I wonder if the bank teller would have been as forthcoming had I not been automatically ascribed a specific class, based upon the details of this transaction (the bank from which the funds were drawn and the actual amount in dollars). Let's suppose for a moment: would she have automatically established rapport with another dark-skinned female who had gone to the bank to change a rolled up fifty dollar bill that a cousin sent her by way of Mrs. V. who just returned from abroad? Undoubtedly, it was my ascribed economic position that facilitated access to this much-coveted personal shopper's phone number. My appearance at the bank was slightly above my usual style. I was wearing a tunic and palazzo pants. I enunciated every single syllable of every word with my American accent. My performance was meant to signal clueless "foreigner." After several bank incidents during 1993, I learned to present myself in my absolute best whenever I headed to these institutions for any transaction. Below I present the scenario that resulted in my eventual domestication.

One Saturday morning in August of 1993, I headed to a branch of my bank on Knutsford Boulevard after a gym class. I was being practical, because I was on my way to the country for the weekend. My taxi driver picked me up. The plan was to get money before the bank closed at 12:00 and to return to Papine, where friends would pick me up and we would get on our way. To get into the teller area of the bank, I joined the line where a female attendant sitting at a desk asked customers their purpose. She sized me up with a slow-motion version of the female gaze described above, then proceeded to pick her nails before finally telling me I could go inside. After getting through her, the teller took one disapproving look at me in my gym shorts and T-shirt to say that it was not possible for me to make a withdrawal, as this is not my branch. I persisted, telling her that I had conducted transactions here in the past. She relented a little then began to proceed with the transaction. She attempted to call my branch to no avail. After this unsuccessful attempt, she admitted that she would not carry out this transaction, for how could she be sure that I had *that* much money in *my* account. Astounded, I gave her a cut-eye then insisted she call again. She returned to me with another negative response. I demanded to speak with the manager and asked for an explanation as to why I could not access my U.S. account. She told me that they did not have enough foreign exchange, but that she would call my branch in Liguanea to make sure that they did, because I could carry out the transaction there. I pointed to the time and to the fact that I had a driver waiting for me outside and reminded her that the reason I came to this branch was precisely because I would not have enough time to make it to the Liguanea bank before it closed at midday. After several moments of going back and forth, they proceeded with the transaction. At that time, I was incensed. I knew that this moment would have occurred in a completely different way if I had been dressed correctly and did not look like a lower-class female.

There were numerous such moments at the bank, the library, restaurants, and the supermarket. In my journal, I listed the various incidents of having been policed on the basis of class and color. I experienced these instances as brutal, especially when my interlocutor was another black female. These interactions are particularly illuminating of the significant ways that everyone participates in the policing of dissident behavior. It takes considerable effort and emotional labor to live through these moments. Properly domesticated, I wore an outfit that August afternoon that did not exactly correlate to the monetary value of the transfer, but coupled with the accent and identification that gave me a U.S. address, I was definitely not local. Without doubt, the size of the transfer trumped any aspects of my fashion sense (which spelled out "foreigner"). The teller may have read me as a student, but I was one with a hoard of U.S. dollars from a highly reputable institution. It is precisely for these reasons that I sought to acquire a particular wardrobe to make the necessary statement that would facilitate my movement and minimize the emotional work that would inevitably be part of my research in 1996.

In their own ways, ICIs also seek to make a statement with their appearances. There are multiple reasons for this. Their daily lives do not necessarily require that they don their best. Because everyday life at the arcade is physically demanding and sometimes dirty, most traders dress casually and in accordance with the climate. Work clothes often consist of separates (pants, shirts, blouses, T-shirts, skirts, etc.) The "tuffer" and younger traders dress more provocatively (in T-shirts, leggings that have been given a dancehall flair) as they sit in their stalls waiting for customers. The ones who dress up usually stand out and are often complimented by peers for their sense of style. In the arcade, the ICIs seldom wore the clothing they import. For others, their appearance adhered to their religious decrees. The two Pentecostals always wore dresses or skirts, since their practice forbids them from wearing pants. In other aspects of their business, such as travel and the declaring of goods, ICIs pay considerable attention to their dress. In fact, one of the ways I could tell if a trader had been to the wharf was through their dress. They often wore dressier ensembles to government offices, especially to declare their shipped goods.

Among those profiled in this work, a tremendous effort is made to distinguish one's self and to dress "proper," especially when they travel. One ICI told me about bringing a different set of clothing with her on the plane, into which she changed before landing. These alternate clothes are "respectable." At the airport, ICIs are easily identifiable by their appearance for several reasons. Foremost, their clothing of choice often consists of the same goods (sometimes in different styles) that they sell in the arcades. Second, despite the fact that they wear various styles and that these clothes are of a middle-class conservative standard (e.g., less revealing, more conventional or conservative), they are often of lesser quality. That iself is another signifier of class. The texture and denier of the linen from the free trade zones in Panama are quite different from the finer versions, such as the costlier handkerchief linen popular with the upper middle and upper classes. The clothes that ICIs wear remain but a version of a higher-class style. In that sense, they retain a capital sign, since upper classes can read them as less expensive items consumed by lower classes. The class of style is also as visible inside as outside of the arcade.

To achieve a distinctive look, several ICIs have dressmakers abroad, in the cities where they shop, who sew them one-of-a-kind outfits that no one else at home will have. As in dancehall, where the distinctiveness of one's outfit is a marker of status, their travel clothes not only reflect their economic position and, hence, give them access to certain resources, but also indicate their sophistication or awareness of fashion (of what is "in" at the moment). They are always au courant and sometimes ahead of everyone else. ICIs' deployment of style rebuffs the claims of "inappropriateness" and lack of "sophistication" that have been part of public discourses concerning their "out of placeness." This is the primary reason that my earlier observations at the airport were flawed. I was uncertain about whether several female travelers in the terminal were ICIs. I had difficulty identifying them because their clothing adhered almost completely to a middle-class style, which rendered them unidentifiable to me.[10] They wore neither bright tailored linen blouses nor pants or skirts, which were quite popular with the traders, nor the one-piece linen dresses with appliqués from Panama. These are the popular styles associated with the stereotypical ICI. Instead, many among them wore dresses, which they considered more "respectable," with understated prints and pleats and "dignified" ladylike shoes. Their handbags were not the latest fashionable styles. The physical surface was one of understatement, unassuming. Such ensembles are also popular among traders who observe their religion's codes of conduct and dress. I argue that this practice of adopting a different aesthetic is a form of social cross-dressing used to mediate their identities as working-class black female ICIs. In so doing, they ease some of the impeding class tensions to better facilitate different stages of their business.

An encounter with Miss B. is a telling example. I usually stopped by to see her in the morning. One afternoon, I found her dressed in a manner that did not adhere to her usual look. She was wearing a "proper" navy cotton dress with small printed pink flowers and a Peter Pan collar. On her head was a wig, which she had pushed back because of the heat. Since I have never seen her in anything but a T-shirt and a skirt, I asked her if she was going somewhere? "No, child," she answered. "This is my costume," she laughed. Then she added, "Just got back from New York." I asked her, "Why are you wearing a wig, I thought you were a Pentecostal?" She stuped, then added, "Of course me still natural, but I was in New York." All the while, she seemed annoyed with me for not understanding her subtext. This was her travel outfit. I discuss reasons for her costume later. This and the other examples show that for ICIs, style has a class. Later, I will show that style also has color and gendered dimensions that are evident in both self-making that are reinforced by different patterns of importing.

My Jelly Platform Shoes

In October 1995, I went to conduct field research in Kingston. One of my prized possessions was a pair of platform jellies. I had worn them the entire summer in Ann Arbor as I waited to go to "the field." The shoes were in. Throughout the U of M campus, students and even professors wore these jellies or some variation of them. In Jamaica, I wore them everywhere, because they were comfortable, especially during the rainy season. I wore them until the buckle broke. That day, a dark-skinned, Jamaican friend, Miss Q. (who is first-generation middle class), was visiting. She seemed relieved and expressed happiness that I would finally stop wearing my jellies. "Well, thank God! You won't have to wear these ghastly shoes ever again. They're going in the bin." Surprised, actually shocked, I asked her why. "Oh Gina! Get serious . . . These shoes are so common," she exclaimed.

I must admit that this was not my first shoe incident. In 1993, during the semester at UWI, I brought along a pair of Doc Martens that I wore especially on my way back and forth to the university from Papine. One evening, a male friend, obviously fed up with my continuous inattention to gender expectations and politics, exclaimed in a fit, "You will never get a man in Jamaica as long as you continue to wear shoes like that." Annoyed with his imposition and the emotional burden of everyone else's constant policing of my appearance, I admitted what I had been withholding for months. Like Miss T., I enunciated every syllable of every word. "I do not want nor need a man who could not deal with my taste in shoes." After including this moment in the journal, I wrote an ode to my Docs. In 1996, I did bring several ladies' shoes. These were part of my costume, to use Miss B.'s words. I wore them when I went to government offices and with officials and other individuals, where making a statement was crucial to obtaining information. Otherwise, I rejected the local dress codes. I failed to include my down time with friends within the parameter of fieldwork, which reveals a limited conception of "field site." These moments did not occur in a vacuum but rather within cultural borders with specific definitions of consumption and presentation that affected all interactions.

Before I begin an examination of this moment, let me note that historically, in Jamaica, shoes have been a marker of distinction, which at times separated a field hand from a house slave. The cleanliness of one's feet and the type and style of shoes that encase them are visible signs of position. Feet covered in dust differentiate someone who walks to and from a bus from one who rides in a car. Whether feet are sheathed in plastic, synthetic, or leather shoes, these coverings have various capital signs that both mark and reinforce difference. Contemporary anthropological research on shoes is limited.[11] The role of shoes in the making of gender has been explored more in cultural and literary studies, which have raised a plethora of questions concerning such things as desire, identity, feminism, and globalization. Thicker description of my platform shoes necessitates a broader field of examination that can ultimately provide knowledge that crosses various disciplines. This is particularly relevant to Caribbean anthropology, where issues of gender and feminism, until recently, were disparate and thus hardly focused on this intersection.[12] Yet, this theoretical crossroads is central to understanding color-, gender-, and class-based inequalities, as these do not rest solely on material differences, but are fully entrenched in the symbolic.

Let's get back to the platform jellies incident. Weeks earlier, I had another conversation with Miss Q. about Tommy Hilfiger. She showed vulnerability when she mentioned that she used to like his clothing, but she no longer felt that she could wear them "because these days every butu wears Tommy." The term "butu" has strong racial and class connotations. It refers to a black (to be read here as any shade of blackness), lower-class individual with little or no social dignity and character. This word entered my vocabulary in 1993, when Rex Nettleford, then the vice chancellor of the University of the West Indies, made a similar comment. In reference to the ostentatious display of wealth by the new bourgeoisie, he stated that "a butu in a Benz is still a butu." That statement caused a commotion that, as is often the case in Jamaica, resulted in rather extensive discussions in the media (especially on talk radio) about what was implied. In a commentary on the matter, Carolyn Cooper provided an etymology of "butu" (a word of West African origin that literally means to stoop) and defined its use in Jamaican parlance as "signify[ing] in the nominative a coarse person with refined social ambitions—though bereft of the requisite graces." She added that "Nettle-ford's reference to the term exemplifies the pejorative meaning of the word" (2004a:162). Finally, Cooper concluded that in contemporary Jamaica "money does not buy character."

Indeed, for dark-skinned, lower-class individuals, money buys character and, in the process, lightens one's color only when it is accompanied with other cultural capital that are determinants of class identities such as education, taste, and presentation. A good example is Rex Nettleford (who made the first comment on butu), who is himself dark-skinned and stems from humbler origins. He gained social acceptance and its economic rewards through his outstanding academic achievements (he was a Rhodes scholar) and involvement in the arts or high culture. Through processes of mobility, he achieved upper-class status and now, in some sense, *passes* as lighter.

Miss Q. proceeded to inform me of the depreciation of the value of Hilfiger, because it was mostly downtown people who wore his clothing. She stated that these days Hilfiger was mostly sold in arcades downtown by ICIs rather than in New Kingston shops. I declared that more than likely, in most cases, individuals were wearing seconds or copies, not originals. She insisted that the value had changed, especially because everybody was wearing Tommy, or some version of it. Indeed the *value* had changed. However, I argue that it had changed specifically for individuals like herself for whom *distinction* is utterly necessary to both highlight and maintain her newly ascribed middle-class identity and status. The value had changed especially because, in the Caribbean, gendered self-making practices are based upon and understood primarily within the context of presentation. Appearance or her social skin is the primary defining marker that distinguishes her from other dark-skinned lower-class females. In that sense, it is a mediator that can potentially lighten or darken her skin color. Or to put it crudely, her blackness must be neutralized. If she does not perform class "appropriately," in a way that mediates her skin color, her class position will be obscure.

Thus it appears that the social skin does not necessarily trump the value ascribed to one's actual skin, which is ever so present and has its own economy and significations. For that reason, feminist scholars Sara Ahmed and Jackie Stacey have called for the scholarly need to think through the skin (2001). That is to "interrogate how 'the skin' is attributed a meaning and logic of its own ... how the skin is assumed to contain either the body, identity, well-being or value" (2001:3). While Turner's concept (1980) works in this instance, the fact remains that one's skin itself contains memories of stigmatization (Prosser 2001), which ascribes it competing value that simply cannot be obscured by its social counterpart. Moreover, according to Shirley Tate, black skin almost requires some practice of what Kristeva calls "abjection" if difference is to be demarcated and alternative identities to stereotypes be made (2001:214). When blackness is not in its purported place, it creates disruptures. "Look a Negro!" Frantz Fanon writes (1967:109).[13] Whether vocalized or not, this articulation reinforces the permanence of some markings. They may be mediated but they simply do not go away. All the more reason they cause a sense of discombobulation, which stems from a preoccupation with hierarchy and the disorder caused by the very presence of the negro regardless of clothing. The negro-ness, if you will, continues to be troubling precisely because of the continuities in the symbolic markers history wrote on black bodies.

That color matters is evident in the local penchant for browning both personally and institutionally. While things have changed since independence and there is now a black middle-class, their position is relatively fragile compared to that of lighter-skinned individuals of the same socioeconomic status, who are automatically ascribed a higher social position by interlocutors. The increasing insidious use of bleaching creams and skin lighteners indicates this preference. This practice, read as an identity crisis (Kovaleski 1999), I believe reflects shades of an economic crisis. Color is not simply reducible to aesthetics and self-making (Bibi Bakare-Yusuf, cited in Cooper 2004a:139), though that is certainly a factor. I argue that bleaching pinpoints color's complex value and its concomitant socioeconomic benefits. With these dynamics, appearance works in conjunction with other indexes such as lineage, character, and manners. Depending on the gender and/or color of the individual and circumstance, these markers shift and take precedence over others in determining specific identities. I ascribe the gendered and class markers of the shoe to several factors articulated by Miss Q.

The jelly platform shoe with its thick platform, she argued, is not at all feminine. Her observations warrant more critical interrogation, as they present an excellent opportunity to explore not only how shoes are gendered and classed in this particular social context, but also the power with which high heels have been imbued. Shoes have long been considered a crucial component of dress. Their significance stems in part from the fact that they are the item that fashion stylists insist completes any outfit. Shoes that are viewed as feminine usually conform to several specific characteristics. According to white feminist journalist Susan Brownmiller such shoes must:

> make the foot look smaller, be light and flimsy in construction and must incorporate some stylish hindrance that no man in his right mind would put up with. None of this is accidental. A feminine shoe deliberately reverses the functional reason why people initially chose to wear shoes. A feminine shoe is not supposed to serve the foot, leg, and hip in a practical work of moving quickly without trouble or pain.... To the contrary, a feminine shoe insistently drains a certain amount of physical energy by redirecting a woman's movement toward the task of holding her body in balance. (1984:186)

Brownmiller makes an important point, because designs of "feminine" shoes are made specifically to socially differentiate genders where there is none in nature and to deemphasize the masculine. She specifies what happens to the body in high heels, noting that such shoes add an "extra wiggle in the hips, exaggerating a slight natural tendency, which is seen as sexually flirtatious while the smaller steps and tentative, insecure tread suggests daintiness, modesty and refinement" (1984:184). These observations further highlight the demanding corporeal aspect of this gendered performance.

A historical perspective offers more insight into the complex meanings of high heels. According to design historian Lee Wright, the gender difference in the styling of footwear was established early in the nineteenth century. During that period, she notes, "the heel as the component of the shoe which has become the most visible expression of gender... became 'female' footwear and was disallowed in a male sartorial code. Therefore, the high heel established itself as a part of female iconography and has since become a useful tool in the construction of a female image" (1989:8). Lisa Tickner notes, "the stilleto is seen as being exclusively female" (quoted in Wright 1989:8). The significance of this correlation is evident in transvestism, where mastering of the heel is a crucial component of femme cross-dressing. The allure of the heel is in its elevation and the fact that it not only requires the body to adapt to its form, but that it does so to accentuate the performance. In this process, heels both physiologically sexualize the body and commodify it as an object for gazes. Therein lie the pleasure and power of high heels. This is so particularly because in this environment, opportunity is scarce and having a man is central to social status; hence, a constant need to attract the male gaze. Over the years, different styles of heels have had their emblematic associations. In the 1960s, the stiletto was the rage, symbolic of extreme femininity. During the 1970s, the platform shoe became hip.[14] As Wright points out, platforms are actually the only exception to this rule of gendered heels (1989). Some male platforms were very high and sometimes even shared the same psychedelic designs as female versions. In many ways, this shoe crossed gender lines. The distinctive characteristic of platforms is that they elevate the instep and rest the ankle on a thick chunky heel. In the 1990s, variations of platforms came back.

In her continuous deconstruction of my platform jellies, Miss Q. said the plastic looked really cheap. This adjective is loaded, as it is often used to describe goods imported by ICIs, knockoffs or not. This is just another aspect of the ICI stereotype.[15] "These kinds of shoes," she added, "are sold downtown, in arcades." They are considered fashionable there and have mass appeal. The platforms' "in" status is more exemplary of the lower class's popin style than of middle- and upper-class concern with making a statement.[16] After my first discussion of shoes with Miss Q., I began to notice that most of the individuals who wore this particular style of shoes would be categorized as lower class. "Respectable" middle-class stores did not carry them.[17] Instead such stores carried mostly the stacked heels popular among middle-class ladies, including Miss Q. Plastic shoes such as my beloved platforms, on the other hand, were sold in arcades or stores catering to the masses.

The local meanings ascribed to this platform shoe reveal that it is also symbolic of differences in class constructions of gendered identities,

particularly that of the lady and the woman as well as uptown and downtown. With their clunky heel and wide rounded toe, my platforms were
far from being dainty or feminine. In addition, the clothing with which I
wore these did not reinforce the ideal lady in any way. Instead, my style
placed me in between, in a society where performing gender(ed) identities correctly meant upholding boundaries. I blurred this line and, given
my color, exacerbated my already vague class position. Located as an item
sold in arcades, this shoe became emblematic of the sociocultural meaning in different importing patterns. In that sense, over the course of its
travels, my platform shoe had acquired its social life (Appadurai 1986).
This revealed how commodities acquire their status through the buying
and selling process; that is, by who imports an item, how it is imported,
where it is sold, who consumes it and how. My jelly platforms had been
manufactured in China and were quite popular in the United States and
Europe. Several popular North American and European designers had
created variations of this style. The pair that I had, by Guess, had been
featured in the U.S. *Elle* magazine as well as the British *Vogue* issues of
winter 1995. But in Jamaica, they had low status, as they were associated
with common folk, more specifically with lower-class downtown women
and dancehall. Through their respective trading activities, both visible and
invisible informal commercial importers reinforce class differences that
maintain class identities.

Socioeconomic Disorder

Historically, gendered class identity has been color-coded. Despite recent
refractions in class and color hierarchies, distinction remains a necessary
practice that not only ascertains difference but assures the everyday benefits of class privilege. These include access to resources as well as basic
respect in a store or at the bank. This is due to the fact that the majority
population is predominantly black. Consequently, for a dark-skinned female, like Miss Q., Hilfiger can be a step towards downward mobility. In
some ways, it is a form of socioeconomic disorder that could be equated
with a form of class suicide because in Jamaica, as Michael Manley has
noted, the certainty of class status belongs only to the oligarchy and the
establishment. For these groups wealth is a natural right (1974). Indeed,
racial proximity causes anxieties and tensions that highlight the liminality of dark-skinned middle-class status. For the newest middle-class, this

uncertainty has been exacerbated by recent changes in working-class consumption patterns.

In the last two decades, global economic shifts and the boom in informal economies have both enabled and facilitated popular consumption of certain goods that seem to blur the existing lines that demarcate class positions and status, as the Hilfiger and platform shoe examples highlight. However, it seems that in this era of globalization, goods, people, and foreign exchange may flow freely, but meaning, as Hannerz (1992) and Friedman (1994) assert, is locally constructed.[18] Among these constructions are self-making practices that reveal the dynamics of color, class, and gender. From a feminist perspective, the platform shoe also highlights the social construction of the female category and the complexities in its performance. When the lady/woman polarity intersects with color and class, there are refractions. Yet the fragility of the position of the darker-skinned female becomes increasingly apparent. In that same vein, the shoe also shows the importance of social relations and the degree to which it influences self-making through one's perceived class position.

Indeed, part of Miss Q.'s anxiety also stemmed from my ambiguous class identity. I have attributes of a woman and both the cultural and material capital (education, grants) that could make me into a lady. I adhered to neither, despite the attempts of both middle- and working-class individuals. In addition, my self-making practices and style of presentation mixed many of the recognized class and color codes. As a result, materially and symbolically, my appearance fell somewhere between these markers of gender, class, and social color. In a sense, like the ICIs who don different clothing in part to deflect attention from their marked bodies, I too was engaged in a type of social cross-dressing. I had another motive; I dislike having to dress up (Ulysse 2006a). In addition, in doing this work, I became too cognizant of the fact that I had a choice in mediating my color by representing myself in ways that would be deemed acceptable. I simply did not want to re-create identities all the time. My refusal to conform to the existing rules stems from a sense of privilege. I did not live there. I was in Jamaica only for a period of time. Eventually I would return home, to the United States, where I confront similar restrictions but am more likely to call them out. Nonetheless, as I discussed in chapter 3, these interruptions always carried a price. The price would inevitably differ, as would the policing, had I been a white tourist or a light-skinned anthropologist. Yet, these instances of cross-dressing-across-class also challenged the existing order. ICIs, by making themselves in ways that trouble the stereotype, blur the boundaries that define the rigid lady/woman binary, along with its material and symbolic components. In so doing, ICIs highlight how this multiplicity of identities are socially constructed and depend upon various types of capital for these temporal crossings.

Along the same lines, I argue that ICIs with economic power represent a crisis in the category of class. They are not transitory, as they do not posses and cannot access the social and cultural capital that would allow them to move further within the existing middle class. They are yet another stratum in the hierarchy. While they may seek even better for their children, they do know that for themselves they have arrived. So when they pursue their beautification processes and dress to travel and to collect their merchandise, they go about their daily lives, enjoying the results of their hard work. In the process, they unsettle local configurations; and this is a social order, as Manley notes, in which social status not only implies access to wealth, but an open display of wealth that has to make itself known. Among newcomers, "it's a passport to be displayed prominently at the barrier...ostentation and extravagance are necessary. Without huge homes and flashy cars the neighbors might not notice" (1974:78). This still applies more than two decades later. Indeed, the uncertainty, which is the result of racial proximity, causes anxieties that highlight the liminality of new black middle-class status in Jamaica. This anxiety is exacerbated by changes in lower-class consumption patterns, which are closing the economic gap between the classes. To counter this encroachment of the lower class and new middle class on their terrains, traditional middle and upper classes are shifting the markers of status.

Since every butu can wear Tommy or buy a Benz, greater emphasis has been placed on conduct. Hence, class distinction is maintained through selective consumption and behavior. That butus can now transcend economic boundaries is due to the burgeoning informal economy and its illegal components, which have exploded due to neoliberal globalization. Upon closer examination, the discourse on butuism, which is meant to uphold distance, could be read as what Sara Ahmed refers to as the performativity of disgust. She explains: "Disgust is clearly dependent upon contact: it involves a relationship of touch and proximity between the surfaces of bodies and objects...it is manifested as a distancing from some object, event or situation, and can be characterized as a rejection" (2004:85). It is a speech act with the illocutionary consequence of sticking to its objects and symbolically locking the nouveau riche into a new category. This discourse also provides crucial insight into the articulation of the material and the symbolic during the process of class mobility. It also elucidates the complexity of the tension between class and color codes when these are applied to Bourdieu's concept of capital. Nettleford's statement was revelatory in two key ways. First, it pointed to the continuous importance of social capital to facilitate the social aspect of class crossings. Second, it revealed that in fact, middle-class anxieties about lower classes' encroachment upon their terrains are inutile. These newcomers are no real threat. They may seem to have arrived materially with their U.S. dollars, but symbolically they are still lacking. In other words, no need to be alert. In many ways the social position of the middle class is quite secure. From that perspective, this statement also brought into question the popular regional saying that money lightens.

Furthermore, this reference to the absence of the symbolic inadvertently injects history into this discursive analysis of class mobility. As Michael Manley noted above, it is one's heritage that ascertains one's place in society. In other words, certainty belongs only to those with established lineages, whether this is visible (or phenotypically evident, as in the color of the skin, hair and facial features, or popularity and fame) or invisible (as one's family name). Colonialism and slavery tightened the correlation between phenotype and class. For the latest newcomers, without the symbolic and cultural capital, there are no guarantees; their status must be consistently mediated. The boom in the informal economy since the 1970s resulted in the making of an even newer class who amassed some economic power rather quickly without possession of the symbolic capital. This is key, as the middle class policing this group made their own socioeconomic crossing as scholars and professionals who received elite education in the empire at the same time as the first wave of migrants arrived in Britain during the 1950s.[19] Cultured and refined, they returned home and were thus able to climb the socioeconomic ladder.

With globalization, even more lower-class persons are able to manipulate the hegemonic U.S. dollar. Their new economic power leads to sociocultural tensions within the old middle class. The result was what Brian Meeks (1997) refers to as a state of hegemonic dissolution and Deborah Thomas (2004) characterizes as expressions of modern blackness. That is, the old colonial order, which was replaced by the oligarchy after independence, was losing its power to maintain social control. Since the 1990s, this has been evident in the increasing power of internal hierarchies emerging in garrison communities. Among ICIs and downtown females, performances of identities and self-making practices are oftentimes in opposition to the old middle-class standards. The results of this cultural war point to yet another issue that is central to this project. While it has not been explicitly articulated until now, it has been the theme that underlies this story that I have told: change. What is change? How do ICIs perceive it? Or more poignantly, how much time does change take? Stuart Hall best articulates this view in reference to subaltern awareness of the persistence of hegemony:

> The subaltern class does not mistake itself for people who were born with silver spoons in their mouths. They know they are still second on the ladder, somewhere near the bottom. People are not cultural dopes. They are not waiting for the moment when, like an overnight conversion, false consciousness will fall from their eyes, the scales will fall away, and they will suddenly discover who they are. They know something about who they are. If they engage in another project it is because it has interpolated them, hailed them and established some point of identification with them. (1991:58–59)

In that same vein, I argue that among the visible ICIs, most are not even concerned with making a full crossing. They know who they are and where they fit in the social order. My point is best summed up by a comment from Mrs. B. In 1997, when I asked her why she did not dress in a way that would signal her economic power, she responded, "The difference between me and the brown man uptown is that him would go to Sovereign supermarket to buy his bread for one hundred dollars and I will go to coronation market and pay thirty dollars for it." This comment typifies Mrs. B.'s reflexive political economy as well as her rendition of Audre Lorde's statement that if she did not define herself, she would be crunched into other peoples' fantasies for her and be eaten alive (1984). Indeed, Mrs. B. exists as she is and engages in self-making practices that recognize and attempt to circumvent the limits imposed on her. She is not always successful. As her numerous statements indicate, she is driven by a desire to find and make spaces for herself and her family. These are not always in accord with societal expectations of someone in her position. She dresses up for church but does not work on keeping up appearances nor does she seek entry into the old social order that she knows would never consider someone like her. She knows who she is, where she comes from, and where she is going.

While others may complain of the crudeness and roughness and butuisms of this new middle class, these ICIs are engaged in their own processes of self-making. Their choices at times contradict identities that were and continue to be valued as sociocultural evidence that class lines have been crossed. For the brown or black individual who aspires to social mobility, having the right education and proper consumption patterns could eventually buy him/her some more acceptance. Mrs. B. and Miss T. know this, as they also know that for them such crossing is not possible. They are not interested in investing their profits in the pursuit of respectability. Rather, like Miss B., they choose to invest the seventy dollars they save from the bread elsewhere, where possibilities of return are more likely.

Since I began this research process as a second-year graduate student, I have seen numerous ICIs come and go. There are several old-timers who remain and are steadily making their day-to-day lives in the arcade. They travel when necessary and return home to carry out their business. One constant among the various traders profiled is that they operate differently, motivated in part by their own histories and goals. They evoke the past and reference where and how they got started in the business to indicate where they hope to be, especially for their children. Their subjective concepts of time and place are central to their activities. The banality of their daily lives hardly changes with time. They have survived hurricanes, tropical storms, new competitors, higher taxes, and new customs procedures, among other things. In addition, increasing saturation is clearly changing the face of the business. Yet in their day-to-day activities, it seems like very little has changed. However, in June 2004, I was surprised by changes that reinforced this concept of reflexive political economy. I offer three examples here of ICIs' perception of change over time, as these reveal how they view themselves in relation to the broader environment.

After the dissertation was completed, I arrived downtown and was shocked by the number of traders on the streets. I went to the arcade to see Miss T., and I asked her how she was. She said "not too bad." When I asked her how business was, she proceeded to tell me that she would soon leave the business because there is nothing in it. Too many people were becoming ICIs. She wasn't selling anything and she thought she should just stay home. I was struck by how familiar her words were. She basically repeated what she had told me throughout 1994, 1995, 1996, and 1997. I looked around her stall and saw different types of merchandise, all lined up in perfect rows on shelves. Behind her were toilet paper and cans of Scotchgard, which she had hardly ever sold before. To her right were several different styles of children's and women's shoes. I asked her how business was going again. This time I smiled because I had figured it out. She has been holding out on me, telling me only what she wants me to know. "Me don't sell a ting all day," she laughed. I laughed back in response. "Miss T., if it is so bad, why don't you get out of the business?" I asked her. "Gina, some days are good and some days are bad. Right now is slow season and me sell nothing yesterday and nothing today." "Well, do you think you'll sell something tomorrow?" I asked overly optimistically. She responded, "With God's help I will."

During the 1980s, once she amassed enough cash, Miss T. purchased a house in a middle-class neighborhood. When I first met her, she had been living there nearly ten years. When I asked her how she liked her neighbors, she said they're fine. After a little more probing, she told me that since she moved, her next-door neighbor (her house is on a corner) has never uttered a word to her. "Not even once?" I asked. "Never," she responded. She stuped so I knew that part of the conversation was closed. Subsequently, during every visit, I asked her about her neighbor. Naïvely, I hoped that eventually this lady would let down her guard and speak to Miss T. One year, Miss T.'s pup went missing. She could not find the dog, which had accidentally entered the neighbor's yard. The neighbor did not even tell her she was next door for a couple days. Every time I returned to Jamaica, I inquired about the neighbor hoping that as time passed, she would acknowledge Miss T. However, my questions were to no avail.

In 2004, I asked Miss T. how things were and we caught up on some recent developments and old problems with the business. I asked what the exchange rate was. She told me to hold on, she had to call her son. I returned from the bathroom to find him in her front yard. We said our hellos. She reminded him who I was. After a brief chat of mostly nods, he began to walk out towards the gate. He turned to the right and continued to walk next door. I raised my eyebrows and let my jaw drop. He lives next door? I asked her. I broke into laughter and asked again. Traces of a smile began to form on the corners of her mouth. He lives next door? I asked even louder this time. I shook my head in disbelief, honor, and respect. So you bought her out? "Nuhhhhhh," her voice trailed. "It's not me house.... that's his house." But you helped him pay for it? Didn't you? Didn't you? Didn't you? I hounded her until she finally broke into laughter.

Mrs. C., with the stall she passed on to her sons, invests in farming and sponsors other family members. Since I met her in 1993, she has remained focused on one goal: to better the lives of her children. Code switching between English and Jamaican, she notes, "It with a tray mi start. A tray. Mi want to leave a legacy for my children and grandchildren. I don't want them to go through what I went through." For this reason, she refused to let her daughter follow in her footsteps and become an ICI. Mrs. C. invested in her daughter's education, sending her to one of the best girls' schools and then to college. Upon graduation, her daughter worked in a government agency. Her sons became partners in her business. When I saw her again in 1997, she was adamant about getting out of the arcade, but she wanted to remain in the downtown area: "Gina . . . it's we who stay here you know. . . . We who stay when dem went to foreign . . . we who sell to the poor. We who are here in the arcade, on the street, because we cannot let the people down." She takes a breath. "We need to have stores too so we can leave legacies. The Jews dem . . . they leave legacies for dem children, the Chinamen dem, they leave legacies for their children . . . I want to leave a legacy for my grandchildren so they don't have to start where I did."

When I saw her in 2004, she had accomplished her goal. She went into business with people she could trust—her children—and bought a building. This meant she no longer depended on a nonresponsive government that received stall fees yet delivered few services in return. She was also quick to point out to me that the government continues to marginalize blacks in their business policies. "You see how much dem treat we. They give five-year trade agreements to duty free shop owners . . . five years incentive to open these shops, and they pass it on to their families, brothers, sisters, and other family members"; most of them are East Indian or Chinese, she continued. Yet "ICI must continually battle to keep our business afloat. If I told you what I went through to get this place . . . " She began to shake her head in exhaustion when she told me her story. She had to be quick and savvy to obtain this plaza. Though she succeeded, she notes, "It is tough. We will never have stores on King Street [downtown's main shopping street]. Gina, I tell you we will never have King Street . . . they won't let us." She proceeded to explain how her earlier attempts to secure a place were botched by various businessmen in the area, who would not stand for having an ICI as a neighboring proprietor. "They think we idiots . . . they promised to help us and would go behind our back and thief it from us." Once she caught on, she was able to circumvent their obstacles. She wants to expand her business and be an example for other ICIs. I asked her what she would name her new place. She responded with a smile, "Blessings Plaza." This is a reminder that church ladies, too, harbor capitalist dreams.

For Miss B., stationed outside of the arcade, the business has been good. But, as she said, "It has its ups and downs." In 1996, a bus, trying to beat a red light, hit and killed her niece, and several of her friends lost their sons to bullets. She gave her niece a grand funeral and then went on a buying trip abroad to replace the savings spent. Another time, her son was physically beaten by goosekillers. She returned every day to her spot and continued to sell from her van, as she has for the last ten years. In 1994, when I asked what it was like to be an ICI, she simply answered:

> The trade has been an occupation for many people because it makes you to be independent. It makes you to be self-reliant. It motivates you to be a person of substance. A person that...you lose you gain, you fall you raise, you fall you raise...It make you to be tough. So many times I have fallen by the wayside, I get up, brush up meself and start again.

When I returned in 2004, I crossed the street in search of Miss B.'s van and could not find it. I have been told that she retired to her house in the country and comes in only to check on her employees. Her sister minds her stall.

That same summer, I was also reminded that although some things have changed, others have not. For example, the concepts (mainly that of lady and woman) that preoccupy this book may *sound* dated. They are not. While the rhetoric used may be somewhat antiquated and preferred by older folk, the ideals and value ascribed to these persist. In August, a battle of words between two well-known females point to why a feminist analysis of political economies is still needed in this context.

Ladies-Madonna/Women-Whore Redux

On Sunday, August 22, 2004, the In-Focus section of the *Gleaner* contained a single article accompanied by a photograph and a legal notice. The notice from attorneys abroad delineated details for the class-action lawsuit being pursued in the U.S. on behalf of workers exposed to asbestos or asbestos-containing products made, distributed, sold, or possessed by Federal-Mogul Corporation and T&N Limited or their subsidiaries. The ad covered less than a quarter of the page. While it reminds us of the continuation of migrant labor patterns, it does not draw one's gaze. What is most noticeable on the page is a black-and-white photograph that features the close-up of the buttocks of a dark-skinned female clad in white shorts. She is leaning forward with a bejeweled hand with extended painted nails apparent between the legs. Her back is to the camera and so are both legs, which are straight. Her feet are encased in white sneakers. She is absorbed in her performance of a popular dance. To her left a male hand loosely holds a bottle of Red Stripe beer. To her right, the torso of another dark female is visible. She is wearing a tight striped jacket with a single button. In her movement, one breast is nearly exposed. One hand holds onto what appears to be a Fendi purse (could be fake?) while the other one grabs her denim-clad crotch. Behind her another female stands with her arms crossed beneath her chest. No faces are visible. Just toned body parts. The caption reads, "Women from the ghetto are often stereotyped by uptowners as having looser mores on sexuality."

This photo ironically accompanies the article, which is titled "Slam Bam: A Saga of Consorts and Madonnas," by Glenda Simms, the executive director of the Bureau of Women's Affairs, in response to a piece by a local columnist, attorney Joy Crawford, titled "Ghetto Slam," which was published in the rival paper (the *Jamaica Observer*). Crawford begins with a question on the mind of her friends:

> Have you ever wondered why men stray and not only stray but go for women of a certain class or status? How many times have you heard women complaining that their husband is not only fooling around but fooling around with a woman from the lower class? A lot of us women are prejudiced—to the point that we feel no other woman is good enough for our man and certainly not some woman from the inner city!
>
> We hear about it every day, well-to-do, upper class men who "slum" and have affairs with women from the lower class—helpers, office clerks, you name it—women who can barely string together a grammatically correct sentence. (Crawford 2004)

Crawford then proceeds to explain that men always want what they cannot have, as they seek satisfaction in the slum that they do not receive at home. She warns her sisters of the dangers of playing lady of the house and refusing to make love, let alone experiment. She chastises such women for their hang-ups, which she argues have led their men to stray. As "men love the bad girl image…they want the girl who will freely strip down to her g-strings." She then informs her readership that her crew calls it "the ghetto slam, giving the man what he can only get in the ghetto." She offers her reluctant audience more encouragement and then reminds them that "the ghetto slam is really our basest animal instincts being played out in the bedroom." All the more reason that she suggests watching the X-rated channel to get tips. She concludes that once he gets what he wants, you can "make him such a slave to your body that he wants no other mistress."

If there was any thought that the colonial underpinnings of the categories of lady and woman were obsolete, this article ripped any such ideas to shreds. While color was never mentioned, to some degree it could be assumed even though in these times, when access to material capital is so porous, color is no longer as fixed to class as it once was. But behavior, as the article points out, is more a determinant. Indeed, throughout the column, Crawford makes references to good and bad girls, and what it means to be nice and to be nasty. And as the aforementioned quotation reveals, the desired woman is one who is sexually uninhibited, less constrained by social mores and morals (i.e., the ghetto or downtown woman and not the uptown lady). Crawford identifies with her girls when she uses the pronouns "us" and "we." This is a competition between married ladies (or women) and the ghetto girls and barmaids who entertain their husbands. She reminds her crew of their responsibility to their men; they must not treat them with contempt, for that is what entices husbands to leave the home and go elsewhere. That the man of the house should be the center of a wife's world is nothing new. Such emphasis is central to self-making among ladies of a certain class. What is not, however, is the public discussion of dalliances that many have endured and overlooked as the social value ascribed to marriage has not depreciated over the years. Hence, Crawford's bold insistence that ladies should behave like ghetto women, when necessary, to keep their men. That said, I argue that Crawford is proposing a behavioral class transgression on the part of ladies to ensure that they maintain their men's attention.

Simms's riposte to Crawford was quite extensive and included a history lesson. After recounting her interlocutor's argument, she makes a rather acidic remark to the columnist: "I wondered to myself how this group of women who benefited so well from the social, economic and political development of their country can be rendered so incompetent in such a basic aspect of their life, their sexuality." Then she proceeds to make obvious to her nemesis the race and class history that underlines Crawford's narration. She deserves to be quoted at length:

> I also wondered if Ms Crawford's research could enlighten us about the factors that result in the heightened sexual competence of the women whom she discusses as mere lower-class slum folk whose slamming is so appealing to massa.

I wondered if this great sexual competence of the "ghetto women" was the same as that which was possessed by our ancestors who were chained in the filthy lower decks of the slave ships that plied the Middle Passage.

Was it our female ancestors' sexual versatility that encouraged backra massa [white master] to take them to his quarters for his regular rape sessions? And when we landed on these Jamaican shores, was it because we knew all the tricks in the book to keep massa happy why he left his "white wife on the pedestal" in the big house and came slumming in our slave quarters?

I think that writers such as Ms. Crawford ought to be careful how they reinforce the negation of our womanhood. Perhaps it would be instructive to find out if Ms. Crawford is consciously relegating women who live in the inner city to the categories of whore and slut that have been prescribed to different categories of women throughout the many historical periods that have characterized western societies. (Simms 2004:G4)

Simms elaborates and recounts conceptualizations of gendered sexualities under the subheading of "ghetto whores and uptown madonnas." She assures Crawford that there is no cause for worry, as gendered hegemonies are resistant to the combination of the two. In other words, becoming a whore is not the solution. And in the "unlikely case that a 'queen of slam' would ever displace an uptown lady, the former would have to quickly abandon her ways to no doubt adjust to her new setting to fit right in to become a replica of the lady who preceded her." Indeed, class crossings necessitate some form of code switching to be successful, no matter how temporary.

In the last section of her response, Simms assumes her role as executive director of the Bureau of Women's Affairs and makes a plea for a united womanhood that will come to recognize that it is the strength of the patriarchal system that is dictating the scope of this "deadly sexual competition"—that all women are in fact limited and "need to break free from the mentality that says we are merely sex objects to be used and abused." She explains in ways that portray the downtown girl, especially, as a victim who is trading on her sole commodity, her body. It should be noted that no agency is given to the inarticulate ghetto girl, who is represented solely as the uptown man's disposable toy. In that sense, both writers represent their very classed perspectives on this issue.

Nonetheless, as Simms concludes, "uptown nice ladies and downtown slam girls are locked in a slow waltz in the male power dance." In this appeal for sisterhood, Simm's response disregards Crawford's primary call.

This article was written to call her readership's attention to an abomination that must be stopped for its impropriety or illicitness and because in class crossings, uptown ladies should not lose out to ghetto women. And as Simms was quick to point out, boundaries have always been crossed. The reasons for these crossings matter less than they used to, as they only serve to reinforce the persistent impact of gendered class and color codes, as Simms was quick to reveal to Crawford. She also manages to remind Crawford of how uptown ladies came to be in the first place: miscegenation. Their social standing, which they guard oh so highly and which they use to distance themselves, is superficial, as all women are commodities who need greater awareness of their use and exchange value within and outside of the marriage market.

As this dialogue occurred in the newspapers, it also revealed the continual limits of gendered self-making within a male-dominated public sphere. The Simms article was undoubtedly undermined by the photo and its caption, which was yet another reminder that when it comes to countering gendered class/color codes, the struggle continues.

On October 7, 2005, the Pearnel Charles arcade suffered its fourth fire since it first opened. About 180 stalls in the Laws and Church Streets section of the building were destroyed. One hundred ICIs were displaced. Many were soon relocated by KSAC to Constant Spring Arcade. The fire caused millions of dollars in damages.

On March 15, 2007, Cable and Wireless (Jamaica's premiere cell phone company) donated J$10 million to rebuild the arcade. Cable and Wireless will work in conjunction with KSAC on this J$21 million project to improve the Kingston Corporate Area.

Written on Black Bodies: ICIs' Futures

I leave the arcade behind and go back to the market. I make this return because after a purchase, the customer can ask for and will sometimes receive a brawta from a higgler. ICIs, on the other hand, do not give brawtas. Most of the ones featured here will not negotiate. They will quickly tell you that they have paid a whole heap of money for their goods and this is not a market. Go to a higgler. A brawta is that little extra something (some parsley, an extra orange, or piece of ginger) that will entice the customer to come back to the same higgler and maintain a relationship over time. This book is but a first step in a much-needed process of recognizing and engaging with ICIs. Below, I offer my brawta—one segment or area that highlights future research directions. Possibilities of research are as extensive as they are urgent, given the rapid pace that this profession and business has changed over the years.

The tales of success that precede the continuities in ladies and women provide an excellent ending of sorts to this story about lower-class females confronting and outmaneuvering the state, big business, and civil society to make a life for themselves. In seeking to "be their own boss," ICIs deploy both creative and conventional strategies in spite of multiple restrictions placed on black female bodies. They attempt to transgress socioeconomic and political boundaries dependent on their movement and labor as necessitated by global restructuring. While they have achieved material success, their bodies remain inscribed with variations of gendered class and color codes from the past that affect their lives, sometimes in the most dehumanizing ways. Indeed, the practice of profiling, prodding, and exploiting black female bodies is deeply rooted in history and has fostered an outrage that has been silenced (out of shame, fear, and now patriotism) by various structures of power to covet material profits. Unquestionably, Miss B.'s travel costume was a direct response to what is written on her body as a working-class black female from a third world country. That afternoon in 1994, when I found her bewigged in her printed blue dress, she was flabbergasted and frustrated as she told me her story of being searched for drugs. She insisted that the government of Jamaica should do something about it; "They should not let this happen to us." In conversations with other ICIs, I found that this is not an isolated case. Not surprisingly, in 2000, the ACLU found that more than any other group, black females traveling from abroad were nine times more likely to be searched, X-rayed, and probed for drugs than white females. Yet black females were less than half as likely to be drug couriers.[1]

These instances reveal the position of ICIs within the local-global system. At home, in Jamaica, as lower-class black females who are not even considered representative of the nation, their status as citizens is questionable, given state response to their business activities. Abroad, Jamaica's power as a small nation-state in the Caribbean region to intervene on behalf of ICIs is limited. In 1994, when numerous ICIs were trapped in Haiti during the political clashes involving Raoul Cedras's junta, the government intervened and facilitated their return home. They were able to do so because it was Haiti. Not all of their problems are so easily rectified. Jamaica's government is powerless when confronted with a country like the United States. In some settings, ICIs are defenseless when they travel. Nothing indicates their vulnerability more than the policing of the global drug trade, which attracts and subsumes individuals from all classes. Yet as patterns of incarceration demonstrate, it is on darker and lower-classed bodies that part of this war on drugs has been waged. In those instances, their government (which is also policed by these more powerful nation-states) can hardly intervene or come to their rescue.

This juxtaposition shows the workings of power at various levels. It is in this context that ICIs navigate. The successes detailed in the previous chapter were not easily attained, and they continue to have a price. To achieve their goals, traders withstand numerous challenges and obstacles that I have only begun to discuss. Further examination of everyday damages experienced by black bodies would inevitably unearth the extensive use and exchange values marked "unmarked" skin is loaded with. Being unmarked is a social luxury that accounts for a different existence. This way of being in the world is inherent to the permanent three-piece suit that black female bodies do not possess. To account for its lack, and to attempt to receive some of its benefits, they must, in their respective ways, engage in a continuous process of mediation.

In mitigating the various codes, ICIs reveal perceptions of themselves as actors on the global stage that highlight the underpinnings of their reflexive political economy. They consider and ascribe value to their achievements as these relate to their broader socioeconomic and historical contexts. Yet it cannot be stressed enough how much they value the autonomy to counter the enactment of larger forces on their person. In numerous conversations, many ICIs referred to their actual situation in comparison to that of the "big man dem" for whom the system has always worked. These big men who are the economic elite possess stores throughout Kingston, hotels on the north coast, social power, and a historical monopoly on political clout. From their perspectives, it is these big men who inform their most immediate experience of globalization. Too often, the emphasis is placed solely on multinational corporations and conglomerates, thus erasing how the local elite function to facilitate these companies' and agencies' economic power and exploitation of the poor.[2] In that sense, traders' views are quite illuminating, as the local elite and upper classes historically uphold socioeconomic and cultural hierarchies. Indeed, it is also these classes that represent the cultural hegemony against which ICIs are continually defined. And it is that definition that simultaneously reinforces all of their positionalities.

This complexity has eluded researchers on female market traders in the Caribbean, who often split local subjects into either passive victims or active agents of globalization. The search for opposition to various aspects of globalization has often led to romantic notions of symbolic resistance that too often disregard material realities. When these intersect, however, what they create is much more nuanced. They offer an explication of going through the cracks that begs to be recognized. ICIs are far from localized subjects since their work literally depends upon their international movement to recirculate capital. Moreover, they are avid participants in the global market as contributors to local, national, and global economies. In Jamaica, they sustained the failing national airline until it was privatized in 1994. Their loyalty to Air Jamaica has been cited as being significant to the expansion of the company. In turn, when the airline was totally revamped, it sought to attract and accommodate this group that was once perceived and treated as "out of place" on airplanes and in need of proper behavior seminars. In recent years, to draw customers, Air Jamaica's new ads featured voyagers representing ICIs and offered champagne flights and a frequent flyer program during the late 1990s. In 1999, when the airline launched new flights to Curacao, the UVA received a number of complementary tickets complete with lodging courtesy of Butch Stewart (the CEO of the airline), for ICIs to accompany him and other dignitaries on the inaugural trip to the island.

Consequently, I argue ICIs are at once by-products and reproducers of globalization who have become avid players in the global circulation of capital. They move and cross multiple borders and facilitate the flow of commodities, ideas, and currency. Through their activities, they create new sets of images that at times allow them to get through the cracks, but these are based on existing stereotypes and often only further incarcerate them. With the exception of the relative few who fared well financially, they have had minimal impact on those economic forces that continue to structure them.

Despite this predicament, travel remains an important component of their self-making. Many regard travel as a form of social and cultural capital (something that they do that their parents never did) with its own pleasures. Many stated that abroad, they learn of upcoming styles, which they import to set fashion trends at home. For others, travel also offers them the opportunity to visit their children and families more frequently. Then there are those for whom traveling is just another part of the job that has become mundane; it no longer possesses the allure it had when they first began, or their health impedes them from partaking in this activity. Regardless, this component, which has been so central to ICIs, is on the verge of disappearing. Now one can buy directly from Miami-based wholesalers who have taken to traveling to Kingston to accommodate traders who can no longer afford the buying trip. They arrive with their laptops and boxes of samples, set themselves up in hotels, and take orders that get filled when they return to the States. I also learned that several ICIs pooled their resources to make a wholesale trip directly to the source, China. They made this trip in an attempt to minimize their overall expenditures, cut out middlemen, and make even larger profits by wholesaling to other ICIs throughout the island. This effort has proven to be unsustainable as they lack the infrastructural support to facilitate international connections, and the government does not assist the traders in this effort.

Since 1982, government (regardless of the party in power) has worked relentlessly to bring ICIs under increasing regulation as their commitment remains to big business, as opposed to independent traders competing with established merchants.

As new challenges come, ICIs continually adapt. They have dreams, which they may not realize, yet they continue to hope for better. Their livelihood and self-making depend on their flexibility and perception of who they are in the world. They entered this occupation knowing that it is without guarantees. In that sense, I would go as far as to say that in many ways, ICIs are exhibiting anarchic tendencies. With their stubborn refusal to not exchange their labor power, they are attempting to dictate the terms of their place within global capitalism. They do so consciously determined, and desperately seeking, an ultimate goal: to be their own boss. The value they ascribe to this autonomy is quite high and must be recognized on its own merit, regardless of how well traders fare economically. Their relationship with each other and their practice of the reflexive political economy highlight how they are actively engaged in living their lives in the moment, aware of the structures continuously impinging upon them and constructing them, but vigilant for the cracks in the foundation. As Mrs. B. pointed out, they will continue to find them, and then those who can will go right through them.

Notes

Introduction

1. I understand reflexivity as an approach in which the lens that aims outwards is turned back onto the self. That said, there is no limit to what one could reflect on. In that sense, it is an analytical framework that can encompass various components including ethnography, political economy or semiotics. Hence, autoethnography (with its emphasis on the biographical) is one genre of reflexivity. I choose the term "reflexivity" to ground my cultural and political economy precisely because of its myriad possibilities to extend reflection beyond narrative to include issues like structures of renumeration, informal forms of political agency, and the symbolic.

2. My education and informal education in the media especially contributed to what Paul Farmer (1994) aptly calls a narrative of blame. I explore the complexities of my conditional love in greater depth in an ethnographic memoir, *Loving Haiti, Loving Vodou* (2006b). For this reason, I did not return to Haiti for seventeen years. That absence alone should be cause to question the very native position I was ascribed.

3. As Hoetink notes, these discussions are based on a three-tiered class system, which include a white upper class, a colored middle class, and a lower class that is predominantly black (1985).

4. Definitions of color include: depth of skin tone, hair color, hair texture, and facial features. However, as these approaches acknowledge, color is a social construct. In Jamaica, Taylor (1955) has noted forty different terms from twenty-four informants whereas Alexander (1977) has cited twelve terms from nine informants. One of the most critical factors about color, as Alexander and Taylor have revealed, is that categories are based on a subjective racial classification system that is highly influenced by social markers. (See also Alexander 1977; Dominguez 1986; Henriques 1953 [1968], 1957; Sanjek 1971; Taylor 1955; Wade 1993; Whitten and Torres 1998).

5. The body of work on class struggles in anthropology is quite extensive. I remain highly influenced by the world-systems approach articulated by Immanuel Wallerstein (1976) and Eric Wolf's *Europe and the People without History* (1982); Wolf emphasized the social, economic, and political transformations, filling the lacunae in Wallerstein's approach. (For extensive discussion of the various formulations of world systems, see Coronil 1996 and Trouillot 1988.) When this literature intersected with development anthropology, feminist anthropology, and peasant studies, theorists uncovered the linkages between larger capitalist processes such as the international division of labor, increasing industrialization in peripheral countries, and global economic interdependency (Beneria and Roldan 1987; Fernandez-Kelly 1983; Harrison 1988; Nash and Fernandez Kelly 1983; Mies 1982; Mintz 1985; Stoler 1985; Taussig 1980). In Caribbean literature, there is a lack of substantive research on how these processes in their current modalities affect women who participate exclusively in the informal economy. This is important considering Jamaica's economy is driven by exports while remaining highly dependent on imports. The impact of this history of extraction is a society with a socially entrenched class system that has experienced some shifts in the midst of constant struggle.

In *The Prophet and Power: Jean Bertrand Aristide, Haiti, and the International Community*, Alex Dupuy (2006) offers one of the most integrative and nuanced analyses of class conflicts in Haiti. He emphasizes the interconnections of class relations at the local, national, and international levels. In so doing, he has provided a new way of theorizing class conflict in Haiti that does not ascribe class power solely to the elite, but instead understands it in terms of this group's relationship both to the state and to the international community. Such analysis has become rare in Caribbean studies, where multinationals and foreign governments are often viewed as the sole culprits, while less attention is paid to how the elite facilitates and maintains this economic struggle as the oligarchy and puppeteers of the State. Dupuy's take on class power is particularly useful in my analysis of the struggle of ICIs because, as he puts it: "Those who control the state regulate the conflicts between the classes, the organization and relations of production and the movement of goods, capital, labor within their respective jurisdictional boundaries for the purpose of the accumulation of capital within their respective nation-state and between states in the capitalist world system" (2006:23). While this project does not explicitly trace or engage these specific relations among various actors in Jamaica, I insist that they exist and as such play particular roles on various aspects of ICIs' lives.

6. At 1.3 percent, East Indians comprise the second largest population; they are followed by the Chinese and whites at 0.2 percent each.

7. Hannam, Sheller, and Urry define mobilities as "both the large-scale movement of people, objects, capital and information across the world as well as the more local processes of daily transportation, movement through public space and the travel of material things within everyday life" (2006:1). Immobility, then is the

opposite, that which is physical or fixed, such as a building. But, as Peter Adey argues, such a structure can be imagined in terms of its relational intensity and the fluidity it embodies (2006:78). Adey makes his point reasserting Doreen Massey's contention that "place is not necessarily tied to the notion of location, for 'place' must be distinguished from simple locatedness" (Adey 2006:78). That said, he concludes, immobility is relative, as it is profoundly relational and experiential (2006:84). See also Grewal 1996; Grewal and Kaplan 1994; Kaplan 1996.

Chapter One

1. I borrow the term racial/spatial order from anthropologist Jean Muteba Rahier (1998), who argues that Ecuadorian society is spatially constituted. He writes, "different ethnic groups (indigenous people, blacks, mestizos, white mestizos and whites) traditionally reside in specific places or regions" (1998:426). Blackness, he stresses, must therefore be viewed within the context of both time and space restrictions and expectations. The "cultural topography" (Wade 1993) of Jamaica is not as rigid, given the island's history and demography. Nonetheless, as I will show throughout this book, blackness and its class referents are also spatially organized.

2. My definition of performing identity is based on Goffman (1959) and Butler (1990). I draw from Judith Butler, who stresses that all identities are constituted through performance, which are a necessary survival strategy particularly for the female sex (Butler 1990). I am also influenced by John Jackson Jr.'s (2001) take on race and class performance in contemporary black America. Because of the historical specificities of the Caribbean, I argue that in the Jamaican context, the performance of identities is coded by color (a symbol of race), which is linked to class.

3. During slavery, the colonial order's differential restriction on the movement of the enslaved, freed, indentured, and white population can be characterized as enforcement of the expected racial/spatial order.

4. Indeed, they were seen as female, though of a particular kind. The males who "bred" them and exploited them and the females who regarded them as competitors and were jealous of them biologically and socially reinforced their gender. Needless to say, their identities have always had a sexualized component.

5. This binary exists in a larger field within which lady and woman are the extremes of two polar opposites. Within the continuum there are distinctions and similarities among "gal" and its variations, good and bad woman, and rebel woman, among others.

6. As Inderpal Grewal argues, "physical beauty [ascribed to ladies] was central to class formation, especially since working women, worn out by hard work, childbearing and undernourishment, could not possess the kind of beauty that the more comfortable life of upper-class women allowed" (1996:39).

7. Barbara Bush writes, "Of all the slaves, domestics exhibited the greatest duality of behavior and were in the most contradictory position. Though outwardly they were obliged to conform more than field slaves to European culture and values, they employed covert and subtle means to retain their cultural integrity and to protest their enforced enslavement" (1985:37). Or as Abrahams and Szwed contend, interpersonal performance was a countervailing force against enslavement (1983:30).

8. See Buckridge 2004, Robertson 1995 for examples in the Caribbean; for examples in the U.S., see Chin 2001, White and White 1998.

9. Contrary to popular beliefs, the enslaved population had access to material capital. Sidney Mintz discusses how provision plots and markets not only allowed slaves to make money and buy things, but over time, especially with the increasing development of the internal market system, the enslaved population owned 20 percent of the monies circulating in Jamaica (1974).

10. The literature critiquing sexual exploitation and illicit relations during slavery in the Caribbean is rather sparse. The dominant theme in the existing material tends to argue for sexual agency. See, for example, Beckles 2003, Cooper 1993a.

11. Verena Martinez-Alier makes a similar point regarding marriage practices in nineteenth-century Cuba. One's color and class identity was not based entirely on phenotype. Social practices were often determinants of one's position (1974:71–73).

12. See, for example, Brown 1979, Heuman 1981, Sheller 1999.

13. See, for example, Dominguez 1986, Henriques [1953] 1968, Hurston [1935] 1978, Martinez-Alier 1974.

14. Maxwell Owusu found that among the ruling groups and educated elite, and occasionally among segments of the working class, there is a "widespread view that any concession to the persistence or recovery of African historical consciousness implies a choice...between a more prestigious and technologically more powerful European civilization and a less prestigious, debased African savagery and barbarism" (1996:7). Because African and European traits pervade all aspects of Jamaican life, Owusu stresses that Jamaicans face the problem of "living with Africa in the Caribbean." This tension is apparent in local definitions of beauty.

15. The following is a complete list: Miss Apple Blossom (white European), Miss Allspice (part Indian), Miss Ebony (black), Miss Golden Apple (peaches-and-cream complexion), Miss Jasmine (part Chinese), Miss Mahogany (cocoa-brown complexion), Miss Pomegranate (white Mediterranean), Miss Lotus (pure Chinese), Miss Sandalwood (pure Indian), and Miss Satinwood (coffee-and-milk complexion) (Barnes 1994:478). According to Rudine Sims, descriptions of skin color correlated with food are meant to create a positive association. The same observation applies to plants. These foods and spices conjure pleasurable and highly sensuous images (Lindberg-Seyersted 1994:16). Indeed, this pageant reads like a smorgasbord menu. These titles and their descriptive associations are indicative of another factor, that of the female as object, prize, and possession.

16. Maureen Rowe (1998) and Obiagele Lake (1998) also critique Rastafari for its patriarchal and misogynistic practices. Ella Maria Ray (1999) offers a reading of Rastafari that considers the agency of female devotees. Ray argues for recognition of the particular ways in which females within Rastafari reconstruct their African identity and consciousness to renegotiate demeaning popular constructions of themselves. Carole Boyce Davies makes a similar argument concerning black females Filhas d'Oxum in Bahia carnivals in Brazil (1999).

17. I concur with Kobena Mercer, who contends that the Afro is only a representation of the natural since it has to be cut and picked to achieve the rounded effect (1987).

18. This celebration of brown-skinned feminine beauty as representative of the nation contradicts the whitening ideology known as *blanquemiento* that is popular in Latin America (Whitten and Torres 1998, vol. 2).

19. Spartan Health Club's association with the Miss World contest began in 1976. The club was offered the national franchise by Miss World Limited, along with a request that Cindy Breakspeare be their first representative. Cindy, who was then affiliated with Spartan and who was the recent winner of the national Miss Jamaica body-beautiful title as well as the international Miss Universe bikini title, then went on to win Miss World 1976. Lisa Hanna brought home the crown in 1993. Between these victories, there have been two third-place winners, two fourth-places, one fifth-place, and two sixth-places, as well as several winners of the Caribbean Queen of Beauty title. Prior to Spartan's staging of the contest, Jamaica had produced its first Miss World when Carol Crawford won that title in 1963. Jamaica has never won Miss Universe.

20. Although the Chinese intermarried (blacks and browns) more than any other minority group on the island, historically the relationship between blacks and Chinese has been one of antagonism. Initially, resentment was caused by the arrival of Chinese indentured servants and laborers at the turn of the century. By the 1920s, their economic activities (they have a monopoly on the grocery business) fueled tensions and conflicts. During the labor riots and later in the 1960s, tensions between Chinese merchants and the masses flared. In the 1970s, conflicts continued as downtown ICIs squatted in front of grocery stores in Chinatown to get customers. Many of these stores closed. However, more recently a new anti-Chinese discourse has begun downtown, silently protesting the arrival of wholesale merchants from Hong Kong (who are traditionally part of the merchant class). Many argue they are undercutting ICIs' business activities.

21. According to Walter Rodney, the similarities in the colonial experience of Indians as indentured laborers are the basis for more solidarity with blacks (1969). Hence, black affiliation with East Indians is due in part to the fact that they are somewhat closer to blacks in the local class/color order.

22. These concrete structures are not to be confused with the elaborate Parisian bourgeois "theatre" meant to encourage leisure and consumption that captivated Walter Benjamin ([1982] 2004).

23. Girls, particularly of the working class, have long been lured by glamour and have seen it as a vehicle for mobility. For more detailed arguments, see Beattie 2003; McRobbie 1990, 1994.

24. Elsewhere, I discuss Carlene, the reigning dancehall queen of the 1990s, who is phenotypically light-skinned and is considered brown but has a physical shape that is associated with black females (Ulysse 1999a,b). Years later, as dancehall queen contests proliferated, others began to rival Carlene. She hardly dances professionally and was finally socially dethroned in 2002 by a Japanese enthusiast. Junko "Bashment" Kudo, a hairdresser and beauty consultant, learned her moves watching the dancehall queen. She held on to the title for two years and became the new media darling. In 2004, Latesha Brown, a dark-skinned Kingstonian from Portmore, won. Brown, it is said, surprisingly won without being wicked on the dance floor. What this makes clear about the title "dancehall queen" is that its value increases well beyond its milieu, particularly when someone who is an "outsider" (whether brown or Japanese) wins it. I thank Ryan Williams for pointing this out to me.

25. Sociologists Mimi Sheller and John Urry (2003) argue that automobility both enables and constrains time schedules as well as contributes to the blurring of boundaries between public and private activities. In "Automotive Emotions: Feeling the Car," Sheller extends this argument. She contends that there are functional as well as expressive dimensions to one's relation to the car. She tracks a series of "feeling uses" for the automobile within various contexts. Sheller notes that the car has also been used to make up "for feelings of status injury and material deprivation through [what Gilroy calls] 'compensatory prestige' especially so long as high-income earners and professional elites continue to equate car worth with personal worth, the young and disempowered will continue to use cars for status compensation" (Sheller 2003:13). Indeed, within the Jamaican context, there is another expressive dimension of car use that needs further inquiry. For many, the car is also an encasement that facilitates the distance necessary to practice distinction. In a sense, it prevents class contacts that are otherwise deemed as social pollution.

26. Generally, white and brown Jamaicans do not use buses. Instead, they take taxis, which cost 200 percent more than bus fares but offer safety and privacy. It is a rarity to find a white Jamaican of means on the bus. The whites who use this system are usually tourists, Peace Corps volunteers, and anthropologists.

27. Deborah Thomas (2004) writes that the West Indian Royal Commission was so bent on "fixing" the family patterns of the poorer classes that during its rule it conceived of various projects to address this problem, including Lady Huggins's failed Mass Marriage Movement. Huggins, the wife of the then governor of Jamaica, spearheaded this effort in 1944; it lasted until 1955.

28. See, for example, Barrow 1986, Durant-Gonzalez 1976, Powell 1986.

29. That anachronistic image is revived time and time again both at home and abroad. It is the costume of the market woman that the beauty queen dons to

represent Jamaica in pageants. This juxtaposition of the brown lady as a black woman on the international stage is but another example of why the trompe l'oeil is an apt metaphor for national identity. I discuss this metaphor in the following chapter.

30. "Marchande" and "machanta" are literally translated as female market trader. "Madansara" is used to refer to market traders in Haiti. The term is also the Kreyol word for a spotted-backed weaver. The quickness with which this bird flies about and chirps is seen as representative of the behavior of market women.

31. The greater portion of agricultural produce sold in local markets is imported predominantly from the United States and has been since the early 1980s.

32. I contend that the displacement of the ICI as symbolic of the modern has been restricted to the local or at least regional settings. Indeed, popular images of the island as a tourist destination tend to favor portraits that are caught in a time warp. In that sense, I would say that certain representations of Jamaica and Jamaican life eschew the modern. For a more extensive argument of modern blackness in Jamaica, see Thomas (2004).

33. These words literally translate into a cunning Jamaican woman. This phrase is also the title of one of Bennett's well-known poems cited in Cooper (1993a).

34. According to Wilson's theory, English-speaking Caribbean societies are structured around oppositional value systems of respectability and reputation, which underwrite the constant competition among individuals within communities. Respectability, he wrote, "is the force behind coercive power of colonialism; the explicit value system of churches . . . subscribed to by the middle class and more vaguely by women" (1973:102). Reputation he ascribed to men and defined as "an existentially valid structure of relations by which men secure their identity more or less separately from women" (1973:149). For my purposes here, however, it is the practice of distrust and one-upmanship that these competing ideologies foster that is most central. Elsewhere, I have noted the usefulness of Wilson's insights particularly on lower-class females' rebuff of elite social standards of femininity (Ulysse 1999). Nonetheless, I disagree with the premise of his binary and its gendered dimensions. Other critiques of Wilson, such as Burton (1997), point to his failure to "confront the implications [of his dual model] for the sexual politics of the region" (160). Moreover, Jean Besson (1993) argues that working-class and peasant females have their own system of reputation. I discuss this in more detail in chapter 5.

35. See, for example, Clark 1989, 1994; Carnegie 1981; Mintz 1974; Sudarkasa 1973.

36. In the past, lower- and working-class females have had an unprecedented degree of economic autonomy. The definition of autonomy used here is based on Helen Safa's, which stressed that females have considerable control over their own resources, hence the freedom to make decisions about households, their economic activities, and their personal consumption. This autonomy certainly does not imply

sexual equality, because women still look to men for emotional and material support (1986:2).

37. Since they emerged in the 1970s, there has been increasing specialization among ICIs (Le Franc 1989, Witter and Kirkton 1990). Distinctions have emerged among those who are self-employed and those sponsored by senior ICIs or established businesspersons, or sell in Kingston (McFarlane-Gregory and Ruddock-Kelly 1993). Nonetheless, in the sparse literature on informal commercial importers, this variation tends to be confounded to obscure noteworthy differences among traders (Glaude 2003). Yet naming or the act of self-definition remains a significant component of self-making. It is one of the basic tenets of black feminist practice. This phenomenon is no different among market traders (Clark 1994). For example, Marisol de la Cadena (1996) has also documented the importance of naming in Peru. She found that traders preferred to call themselves "mestizas," referencing their ethnic identities, as opposed to "cholas," the preferred term widely used by social scientists.

38. I return to the issue of the significance and power of naming in chapter 2. I discuss how official and popular discourses that refer to ICIs as higglers are consequential speech acts that contribute to the unmaking of this trader as modern.

39. This narrative is part of a larger global discourse on participants in informal economies. De la Cadena (1996) finds this in Peru as well, as has Stoller (2002) in New York City.

40. See, for example, Weismantel (2001) for comparable findings in Peru.

41. In that sense, she has been racialized or blackened given the association of class with color in the region. Indeed, these same adjectives were used to describe higglers in nineteenth-century England, which shows the connection between constructions of class and race. Natasha Korda's work on women's informal commercial activities around the all-male Elizabethan stage offer even earlier evidence from the sixteenth century. She writes that the "women brokers" who sold their wares "in the streets" were accused of "disorder and other market abuses as forestalling." Korda contends that the popular view that "these hagglers, hawkers, hucksters and wanderers raised their prices for their own luck and private gain" (2007:265). These continuities in the use of these terms can be read as the racialization of class over time.

42. While it was hosted by the UVA, participants included Air Jamaica pilots and flight attendants as well as several private sector businesses (such as Grace Kennedy, a canning company) that offered workshops on international travel. In chapter 3, I return to this event and discuss its broader implications.

43. I thank Zil Jeager for making me articulate the specifics of this point.

44. This toughness is necessary to survive the daily life challenges at the arcade and every other aspect of this male-dominated business, including buying trips, shipping of goods, getting through customs, etc. Similarly, Gracia Clark points to this characteristic among traders in Ghana, where toughness is associated with maturity, determination, and body weight (1994).

45. Hammonds (1997) points to the politics of this recourse to stress that for black females the reconstruction of womanhood is a process. See, for example, Carby 1987, duCille 1996, Hill-Collins [1991] 2000, Hine 1997, Lorde 1984.

Chapter Two

1. This multiple pattern of labor, with its distinctive racial codes eventually gave rise to a colonial class-color hierarchy and culture, which to this day characterizes the social structure of the island.

2. The provision ground system was pervasive throughout the region, including the French and Dutch colonies. Practices, however, varied depending on several factors including the topography of the island and the planters' willingness. In Barbados, for example, the enslaved were not given grounds; rather they cultivated their "house spots." The surplus of provisions from these spots was then used for marketing purposes. For more specific arguments on the system, see, for example, Bolland 1993; Olwig 1985; Fick 1992; Gaspar 1985; Saunders 2001; Sheller 1998.

3. In 1711, slaves were forbidden to sell goods with the exception of their own remuneration, including provisions and fruits; the penalty upon conviction before a magistrate was thirty-one lashes (Long 1774:2:486–487).

4. See Bickell 1836, Cundall 1936, Edwards 1793, Leslie 1739, Lewis 1834, Long 1774, Madden 1835, Sewell 1861.

5. According to McDonald (1993), there seems to be a direct correlation between the administration's restrictions on the marketing activities of the enslaved and freedmen and the increased costs of manumission during the 1700s. Indeed, the enslaved's idea of capital and property had an impact on the system of slavery. With the money they earned from marketing activities, they sought to better their lives, and slaveholders were aware of this interest. In fact, even during the apprenticeship period, many of the enslaved sought to purchase their freedom (fearing reversal of the Abolition Act) instead of being granted freedom from the queen. There may have also been greater status associated with self-purchase as opposed to freedom decreed by the colonial office (Marshall 1993).

6. Mintz stresses that the slave with a better diet, small source of income, and a feeling of proprietorship in land was less discontented, less likely to run away, and less dangerous as a potential rebel (1974:192).

7. The slave code of 1792 actually extended legal entitlement of these grounds to women and the 1816 Amelioration Act prescribed the minimum number of days slaves could work on their grounds (Holt 1992:67).

8. The apprenticeship system required the previously enslaved population to work 40½ hours for their former masters without pay. The rest of the time they were free to pursue their own activities (Holt 1992:63).

9. According to Swithin Wilmott, "the estates declined under the pressures of free labour and free trade; the Assembly and the local vestries increasingly sought

to shift the incidence of taxation away from the larger landholders by increasing the tax burden of the black peasantry. When efforts were made to collect taxes or to levy goods for non-payment, the peasantry resisted violently" (1995:289).

10. Jamaica faced labor problems after slavery was abolished in 1807. The island had become dependent on slave biological reproduction, which fell by nearly 10 percent for a fourteen-year period. Concomitantly, sugar prices fell with the decrease in production. During the apprenticeship period (1834-1838), sugar production was 23 percent less than before abolition. Between 1838 and 1848, output was 49 percent of the pre-Abolition level (Holt 1992:119).

11. From 1840 to 1940, over 135,000 Chinese and nearly 500,000 East Indians were sent or came to the Caribbean. They were unevenly dispersed throughout the Guyanas, Trinidad, Cuba, and Jamaica (Mintz 1974:31).

12. The terms "Lebanese" and "Syrian" are used interchangeably to refer to the early Middle Eastern immigrants fleeing religious persecution who settled in Jamaica. At the time of their displacement, during the middle of the nineteenth century, current boundaries between Syria and Lebanon had not yet been recognized.

13. According to David Lowenthal (1972), the Chinese population, which was predominantly male, was the least segregated of the minority groups on the island. Though there were sharp differences among this group about endogamy, many married blacks and coloreds. Among East Indians, integration into black Jamaica was generally met with disapproval, especially from older family members. The Syrians and Jews, who were "socially white," strove to remain endogamous.

14. This issue has been debated by scholars refuting Sidney Mintz's (1974) early assertion that there is no evidence of women predominating the market before emancipation. See, for example, Higman (1976), Reddock (1985), Shepherd (1994), Sheller (1998), Wilmott (1992).

15. By the early 1850s, over 5,000 Jamaicans had emigrated to Panama to work on the railway. According to Gisela Eisner, the 1891 census reported an outflow of 27,682 persons between 1883 and 1887 to Panama and Costa Rica. At the turn of the century, Cuba also drew migrant workers. It is estimated that by 1930 there were 60,000 Jamaicans in Cuba, 25,000 of whom were domestic workers (1961:145–149).

16. Benoit (1980) notes that, by the late nineteenth century, nearly all the coachmen in Port-au-Prince were Jamaicans. This is an irony, since Haitian immigrants landing in Jamaica during the twentieth and twenty-first centuries are viewed as economic refugees. I thank Melynda Price for bringing this link to my attention.

17. Eisner shows that at the end of the apprenticeship period, there was a rapid increase in the number of small farm holders. There were 2,114 persons who owned under 40 acres of land. In 1841, there were 1,919; by 1845 that number had jumped to 19,397 (with holdings under 10 acres). She also estimates that during

that time over two hundred free villages were established with a total of 100,000 acres of land. The number of small farmers with holdings between 5 and 49 acres had increased from 13,189 in 1880 to 24,226 in 1902 and 31,038 in 1930. The peasantry rose from 11 percent of the total population in 1860 to 17.5 percent in 1890, and to 18 percent in 1930 (Eisner 1961:210–230).

18. Jamaican political scientist Carl Stone describes this system, pervasive in third world nations, as more than a device to win votes for competing parties. Clientelism is a mechanism to institutionalize a power structure when imperialist interests disengage from the management of state power, handing over the machinery of state to the emergent politically dominant petit bourgeois party leaders. This is distinguishable from the class-based politics of liberal democracy in advanced capitalist countries or authoritarian military rule in states and militarized one-party monopolies of communist states. Party leaders, regardless of their ideological persuasions, seek only to expand and deepen the mechanisms of clientelism (1986:93). In Jamaica, Stone stresses, party clientelism, which harnessed access to state power to compete with and eventually subordinate the power base of capital and property ownership, gave the traditional merchant ruling class its ascendancy in the domestic political arena under colonialism (ibid.). Stone convincingly argues that this system permeates the economic, political, and administrative spheres including party officials, functionaries, bureaucrats, economic managers and the lower echelons of society. See also Edie 1991:16.

19. According to Stone (1991), expanded opportunities for higher education in technical fields and areas related to management and the social sciences, both overseas and in Jamaica, helped change the social class structure. They allowed a cross section of middle-class individuals of black, brown, Chinese, Indian, white, Jewish, and Arab backgrounds to enter important leadership positions in the economy.

20. See, for example, Le Franc 1989, Taylor 1988, Abbensetts 1990.

21. One of the most difficult parts of researching this occupation is obtaining reliable data on the economic aspects of the trade. It is very unlikely that higglers would report exact figures to researchers or state officials, since this information would affect the regulation of their activities. For example, in 1987 the Ministry of Agriculture estimated a higgler's average weekly intake as J$1,000 (about US$46). As Le Franc (1989) noted, this information, which was used to calculate profit, is highly questionable for several reasons. First, formal methods were used to assess these informal activities; second, given the variations in scale in the individual activities of higglers, profit margins were not as likely to be systematic. Because of the sensitivity of the issue of income, I avoided direct questions concerning the specific monetary value of their businesses with most traders. Also, this information is not relevant to my research and can be supplemented with other data, such as their consumption patterns or the volume of the goods they buy and sell.

22. Le Franc seems to have conflated Katzin and Durant-Gonzalez. Still, according to her definition there are seven distinctive types of higglers: ICIs, sellers

of locally purchased manufactured goods, fish and meat vendors, farmer-vendors, farmer-cum-higglers, country-higglers, and town-higglers. In addition to these, there are traders who are difficult to categorize (1989:104).

23. Local agricultural production has been on the decline for several decades. The sugar and the banana industries suffered from inefficient and outdated systems of production that could not compete internationally (Stephens and Stephens 1986). Farmland was scarce and new generations were less interested in working the land (Thomas 2004).

24. Between 1960 and 1964, exports from Jamaica to England increased by 22 percent, from 18 million to 22 million pounds; exports to the U.S. increased by 66 percent, from 15 million to 25 million pounds (Edie 1991:13).

25. Economic and Social Survey of Jamaica 1960-1980, Yearbook of Jamaica 1960-1980.

26. Between 1943 and 1960, Kingston's population nearly doubled to 375,000. That number comprised over a quarter of the entire population of the island. Within six years, Kingston's population was a third of the national total (Small 1995: 37).

27. Witter's hustling economy includes mostly illegal and some informal economic activities including robbery, theft, drug trafficking, financial scams, tax fraud, smuggling, begging, and petty trade or service under one rubric (1977). In the following chapter, I briefly explain the impact of hustling downtown as these affect informal commercial importing. This provides a context for a discussion of space and class and the social politics of locating the arcades in certain areas.

28. They imposed a bauxite levy tax. Locally, they also enforced a property tax and introduced the National Housing Trust (Beckford and Witter 1980:87).

29. In Trinidad, where a similar policy was in affect, the list of items was known as "negative list." I thank Dr. William M. Bridgeford for bringing this to my attention.

30. This move was primarily the result of lobbying activities by Lucille Mair and Mavis Gilmour, two professional women who presented a paper to the party on the roles and status of women in Jamaica and the absentee relationship between the state and the majority of the population.

31. Since its inception in 1973 the Women's Bureau has been shifted from one ministry to the next. After 1980, it was downgraded to a desk.

32. The national minimum wage recognized the work of domestic servants and gave them the new title of "helpers" (Girvan, Richard, and Hughes 1980:117).

33. Foreign investments declined from J$161.7 million in 1970 to J$24 million in 1978 (Sander 1992).

34. These included a reduction in bauxite production by foreign companies, the credit blockade by the U.S., and the foreign press attack (which gravely affected tourism), as well as social destabilization by the CIA (Beckford and Witter 1980:91).

35. Historically, women have suffered from unemployment more than men. Women's employment dropped more drastically than that of men. For example, from 1960 to 1978, the number of women employed in the manufacturing sector plummeted from 43,865 to 19,400. Male employment during that period increased from 45,658 to 58,000 (Bolles 1981:85).

36. According to Witter, 70 percent of the higglers during this period had lost formal jobs, and could find no alternative to higglering (1989:6).

37. One of the main objectives of the EPP was to spread income and employment opportunities to the base of society and democratize ownership of the economy (Girvan 1998). This self-reliance ideology to which they were committed was based on the Puerto-Rican "by your own bootstraps" model that stressed individual initiative, which the PNP was trying to instill among the population.

38. The Caribbean Basin Initiative provided Jamaica with duty-free trade provisions such as softened tariffs and quotas for a twelve-year period and special tax concessions to U.S. corporations investing in the area (Harrison 1991a).

39. Items allowed were quite specific. These included dress shields, belts, muffs, sleeve protectors, pockets, elastic stockings, collars, tuckes, fallals, jabots, cuffs, flounces, yokes and other trimmings for women's and girls garments.

40. For example, in 1988, out of the US$424 million that was issued from the Bank of Jamaica, ICIs bought only US$10 million.

41. According to Brackette Williams, in rural Guyana, among the Cockalorums, "make a life" refers to "one's assessment of the individual interest in the socioeconomic well being of others and his inclination to balance work and sociability—the enjoyment of life through participation in organized and casual forms of socializing, on the one hand, conspicuous consumption on the other" (1991:56). Similarly, Lynn Bolles uses the concept of "making do," that is, using social and cultural traditions and economic practices to manage, maneuver, and manipulate one's situation in light of larger politico-economic structural constraints (Bolles 1996:61).

42. The details surrounding this event (the arson) are rather sketchy. ICIs who occupied stalls in the arcade lost their investments. Initially the government refused to reimburse them for their losses. Traders had the support of the Chamber of Commerce, led by Sameer Younis, a well-known businessman, who fought to get ICIs recognition. His intervention and that of others (including several UWI professors) eventually produced results. In most cases, however, ICIs were not fully compensated.

43. This issue of ownership is also about who gets to tell the story of ICIs first. Indeed, during the research years and thereafter, I encountered tensions and even hostility from Jamaicans who have asked why I did not study Haiti. Conversations with other black anthropologists attest that this is not an isolated problem. Such conflict is not unrelated to competition between local and foreign scholars; the former view the latter as having greater access to academic resources that will lead to research and publication. As I discuss in detail in the next chapter, foreign

researchers are indeed part of a history of silencing and disavowal of local scholarship. Many local scholars, in turn, often engage in this battle by not engaging
or citing work produced abroad in order to be the first to publish it, a decision
which ultimately results in a lack of dialogue that reinforces the primacy of insider knowledge. In the larger academic field that tokenizes scholars of color, this
practice only fosters competition within the margins.

Chapter Three

1. I use a series of ethnographic moments to create a narrative or, if you will,
to make a quilt. I employ the analogy of quilting here both to follow Carole
Boyce Davies's adoption of this perspective as opposed to disjointed fragments
([1990] 1994) and to resonate historian Elsa Barkley-Brown's womanist formulation, which recognizes African-American women's historiography through quilting (1989).

2. See, for example, Hymes 1974, Harrison 1991b, Fox 1991.

3. Indeed, every time I returned to Kingston, individual participants deepened
their commitment to me by increasing my access to information. At the institutional level, however, things were quite different. During my fieldwork year, the
African Caribbean Institute of Jamaica suspended a fellowship I was awarded just
before I arrived, in part because previous researchers who benefited from their
support consistently failed to honor their commitments to the institute. After com-
pleting the dissertation, I returned to Jamaica and did a presentation at ACIJ. The
director was shocked that I submitted the required research paper and even chose
to present my work. After that presentation, the UVA founders presented me with
tons of minutes from their annual meetings. Prior to this point, they withheld this
information, though I had asked for the minutes repeatedly. This is not specific to
Jamaica. Other anthropologists have addressed similar concerns. See, for example,
Harrison 1991b, Page 1988.

4. Fabian defines what he calls the "denial of coevalness" as an anthropological
practice of distancing the self (researcher) from others (subjects) through charac-
terizations that fix certain societies in a particular time (e.g., primitive societies).
More specifically, he argues that this denying the other the same temporal existence is part of a murky and, ultimately, politically motivated practice (1983:35)
that maintains global cultural hierarchies. As more natives became researchers,
the distance between self and other needed addressing. Others such as David Harvey have argued that it is the spatial and temporal compression of the condition of
postmodernity that has compelled anthropology to cope with having native subjects and researchers in our midst (1989:240).

5. For detailed arguments in the feminist literature on women writing culture,
see, for example, Abu-Lughod 1991, 1993; Behar and Gordon 1995; Harrison 1997b;

McClaurin 2001a; Bolles 2001; Slocum 2001; Rodriquez 2001; Page 1988; Wolf 1997.

6. At the time, I was a permanent resident in the U.S. I possessed an alien registration card and traveled with my Haitian passport, which often proved to be a bureaucratic nightmare. Visas are always required, and lower-class Haitian citizens have to wrestle with perceptions of them as potential refugees. I needed a visa to stay in Jamaica for fieldwork, whereas with a U.S. passport this would not have been necessary.

7. JUTA (Jamaica Union Taxi Association) is the national taxi company, which operates mainly at airports and hotels to serve tourists and businesspersons. It charges its fares in U.S. dollars.

8. Trompe l'oeil is an artistic technique that creates the illusion of three-di-mensionality. Art historian Celeste Brusati's discussion of this technique focuses on three types of painted deceptions during the seventeenth century. The first were designed to be mistaken for real objects before being discovered as painted coun-terfeits; the second type confronted viewers with illusory views rather than objects, a feigned perspective; and the third included pictures of counterfeit trophies, as well as feigned paintings that re-present painted deceptions (1999:59-61). It is with the latter that I align Jamaica.

9. David Nicholls makes a similar argument about the white elite in Haiti. He refers to this phenomenon as a politics of la doublure (1979).

10. According to Richard Wilk, direct broadcast transmission of U.S. television programs had an impact on Belizean society. The immediacy of these programs not only reduced the lag time between center and periphery, but also affected who controlled the conduits of power. For example, television soon became a source of new ideas, which rivaled the elite as trendsetters of the latest fashions abroad (1990).

11. Between 1992 and 1998, visa applicants were required to provide evidence that they had substantial savings in their personal bank accounts and intended to return home by providing statements from their places of work and confirmation of familial ties.

12. Though I identify as Haitian-American because I have lived in the U.S. most of my life, in Jamaica my Haitian identity was constantly foregrounded and engaged.

13. For a black feminist critique of academic relations of production, see Har-rison 1999.

14. There have been several studies of ICIs that have cited the difficulties of es-tablishing a rapport with traders, as they are highly suspicious of individuals seek-ing information about their businesses. See, for example, Wyatt et al. 1995, Glaude 2003, Le Franc 1989, McFarlane-Gregory and Ruddock-Kelly 1993, Sander 1992. Indeed, the question of whether I was a spy arose on several occasions. Downtown individuals, as well as uptown liberals who identified with the masses, questioned

whether my research was to reveal ICIs' secrets to Babylon. It took several months to dispel the suspicion. Although I was invited to meetings and was privy to information regarding the problems the organizations faced with the government, this was passed on to me with the oral admonitions that I use it for the greater good of the traders.

15. As several feminist scholars have argued, there is a politics to doing reflexive work in a discipline where dominant theoretical approaches consider admission of the personal disruptive and nonprofessional (Behar 1996, McClaurin 2001b, Viswewaran 1994). I would add that this is coupled with a political economy of reflexivity that dictates differential value to such work based on the position of the scholar. The point at which one is reflexive and the extent of one's reflections is often an indicator of one's professional security. Indeed, women who dare to tell what undergirds the structure of anything are regarded as bad girls who air dirty laundry in public. Given the position of women of color, in general, and black women, in particular, within the discipline, forays into the reflexive are still treated with reluctance. Indeed, as Bruce Knauft argues, within anthropology, multicultural voices tend to be regarded as exemplary of identity politics (1996).

16. In Jamaican lore, a "duppy" is the shadow of a dead person, a roving spirit, or a ghost that can be manipulated through "obeah" for destructive as well as protective spiritual work. Elsewhere (Ulysse 2002), I use the metaphor of the duppy and the duppy conqueror to decipher fieldwork negotiations and elaborate on my changing positions as the researcher who has to be alternatively both ghost and ghostbuster at various stages of research. For another interpretation of disciplinary ghosts and European bias within a Guyanese context, see Williams 1990.

17. This notion, of course, ties into racial and racist ideologies that associate hard work with whiteness and laziness with color. I thank Melissa Johnson for insisting I make this point.

18. Reactions to my chosen profession varied by the class of my interlocutors. Downtown participants initially questioned the applicability of a Ph.D. then praised me for wanting to make something of myself. Uptown, among middle- and upper-class browns and whites, disbelief was often couched in polite interest that I was engaged in such an esoteric project. What was not said but was implied was "what is a black girl like you doing in a place like this?"

19. For specific arguments see, for example, Aggarwal 2000, Behar 1996, Enslin 1994, Wolf 1996b.

20. I received such responses from students when I taught contemporary anthropological theory. Similar reactions are documented by scholars whose work and/or pedagogical approaches challenge eurocentrism and androcentrism in various disciplines. See, for example, Bannerji 1995, Carty 1992, James 1993.

21. One's surname is an important marker of status, as it is symbolic of socioeconomic position. For example, the local elite is often referred to as the "twenty-one families." They include several Syrians, Jews, and members of the former British plantocracy. The latter have become even more elusive and less public

than the newcomers. These "big men" and their extended families own and operate commercial and residential properties and wholesale and retail outlets. They also constitute the stock market. According to locals, they have government at their fingertips. Individuals within this group are especially identifiable to each other. They use the "name game" to situate their parentage and lineage as being historically privileged. I refer to the twenty-one families here keeping in mind Lisa Douglass's argument about the myths of this grouping (1992). Indeed, the twenty-one families have become a signifier of white wealth and power (associated with an old plantocracy that is not and never was an entity), which further obscures class differences and the material realities of individual whites.

22. For more specific discussions of similar issues in other contexts, see for example, Silvio Torres-Saillant in the Dominican Republic (1998), Arlene Torres in Puerto Rico (1998), and Michael Hanchard in Brazil (2000).

23. The place of emotional labor in fieldwork as par for the course is often relegated to special articles and not necessarily included in ethnographies. Johnnetta Cole (1998) insists that ethnographers place ethical concerns at the forefront of their work.

24. A slow lowering of eyelashes, used to express contempt. It is considered rude in Jamaica (and elsewhere in the black diaspora) and is in some places viewed as a classed mannerism.

25. According to Alex Dupuy, this term, which was evoked by Cabral (1969) and Rodney (1969), refers to aligning oneself with the working class and the peasantry to defend their interests against the forces of imperialism and neocolonialism (1997:314). I use it here to refer to a process of ostracization that can occur among the middle class as a result of identification with the masses.

26. She asked where I grew up, where I went to school, my family background, why I talk like I do (as I did not speak like an African American), among other questions. At the end of this conversation, she informed me that in 1993, I behaved neither like a black American nor like a West Indian.

27. See, for example, Browne 2004, Freeman 2000, Stolzoff 2000, Smith 2001. In her monograph, Lisa Douglass (1992) reflected on some of her negotiations and constant policing by the white elites who were the subjects of her dissertation. I especially thank Melissa Johnson (Belize) and Kate Ramsey (Haiti) (both white females) for their frank and extensive discussions with me about their fieldwork experiences while working in the region.

28. Contemporary black reflexive anthropologists are few and far between and are commonly females. In the past, black female anthropologists who blurred different genres of writing, such as Zora Neale Hurston and Katherine Dunham, were relegated to the humanities because of the interdisciplinary aspects of their projects.

29. Black feminist anthropologists have used their "native" status in many complex ways. Kimberly Simmonds (2001) and Karla Slocum (2001) took different approaches to their fieldwork, deploying their identities in culturally specific ways to reveal the heterogeneity of this category.

30. Anthropologist Elizabeth Chin (2001) deconstructs the practice of purchasing power. In her monograph, she provides a complex reading of black kids' patterns of consumption and argues for structural understanding of pragmatic mediations of stigma in a wealthy society such as the United States.

31. These nicknames are important as they point to yet another characterization of black femininity. Even in my low hair phase, I was still referred to in those terms. I believe they were given to me precisely because of my penchant for long skirts and natural fabrics, etc. My aesthetic was the antithesis of the downtown/dancehall enthusiast, but I also did not conform to the conventional middle-class lady's code. I was also often asked by men who did not know me if I was Christian. These classifications, I argue, stemmed from a recognition that I chose to identify with the Jamaican masses. In "Ethnography as Politics," Faye V. Harrison discusses various aspects of her dissertation fieldwork experience in downtown Kingston during the 1980s. In terms of gender dynamics, our experiences varied as her light skin color complicated her story to show the persistence and ruptures of gendered class and color codes. In addition to being sexualized in a different way, she was "labeled 'white' or 'brown'–or sometimes 'red'–viewed as representative of 'Babylon,' the Rastafarian designation for Black Jamaicans' domestic and foreign oppressors" (1997a:99).

32. This is a rampant practice among anthropologists in the field. Cross-dressing-across-class is also common in the U.S., especially on some college campuses, where students do not dress up. The University of Michigan, a state university located in a town with a liberal past, is generally more relaxed in terms of appearance than Williams College, a private liberal arts college, or Howard University, a historically black college. Self-presentation practices at these institutions vary according to the demographics.

33. The term pitchy-patchy is a reference to the costume worn at the Jonkonnu Festival that was made of scraps and patches of fabric strategically sewn together. The costume was made of various cloths including burlap from the sugar and flour sacks from abroad as well as locally produced fabrics (Nettleford 1995). This term is analogous to Claude Levi-Strauss's "bricolage" (1966) and Jean-Francois Lyotard's "pastiche" ([1979] 1984).

34. Like di Leonardo (1991) and Haraway (1991), who argue that at the level of ethnography, no one can claim privileged access to knowledge, I believe that this process and the information acquired through it is situated knowledge.

35. I believe that within the Caribbean context, fieldwork methods are not as limiting for men. They can go native in ways that women cannot because certain aspects of female life are bound by constructions of class-specific gendered identities (such as lady and woman with qualifiers such as good and bad), which are premised upon the occupation of certain localities, that is, "inside" as opposed to "outside" or private as opposed to public.

36. Besides, the notion of the participation of the participant-observer is one-sided. "Participant" implies some sort of contribution and reciprocity. In the field, participation is on the researcher's terms. She/he is always on the receiving end. She/he is being taught how to participate by the subject (Nesha Haniff personal communication).

37. I would have had to pretend to be someone I am not, which is disrespectful to the traders because the pretense denies them knowledge and agency. As Haniff continually reminded me, respect is integral to conscious and responsible research. My motive was already an issue, especially with the UVA and several traders who thought I was in the CIA. In the downtown context that kind of suspicion is potentially dangerous because it is linked to greater concerns and different interests in the traffic of contraband, as well as local and national sovereignty and security. Another more plausible option would be for me to become a middle-class ICI.

38. ICIs and their organizations have been rather suspicious, since several studies conducted by researchers have been used to inform government policies that were detrimental to this group. See, for example, Le Franc 1989, Taylor 1988.

39. Despite a history of competition, my goal from the onset was to engage Jamaican and other Caribbean scholars in conversation. Trouillot rightly argues that the native has never been a full interlocutor in anthropological projects. Indeed, ethnographers tend to dismiss local scholarship as elitist, while engaging with Western scholarship as authoritative. In so doing, ethnographers determine which of the natives belong to the savage slot (Trouillot 2003).

40. See, for example, Williams (1991), Bolles (1985), McClaurin (2001b), Harrison (1991b).

41. See Baker (1998) on Du Bois and Harrison (1999) on Drake.

42. Irma McClaurin (2001b) recently asserted that indigenous and marginal voices have once again been banished to the margins with the exception of the token few. Lynn Bolles (2001) and Faye V. Harrison (1999) make a similar argument.

43. See, for example, Appadurai (1991), Basch, Glick-Schiller, and Blanc (1994).

Chapter Four

1. This phenomenon is new insofar as it appears that a significant number of middle-class and upper-class persons are engaging in plural occupations simultaneously. Lambros Comitas has referred to this practice as occupational multiplicity (1973). Historically, such activities have been detected among lower- and working-class rural Jamaicans, where Comitas conducted his study.

2. I thank Kendra Ing for pointing this out.

3. When the category of peasant was in vogue, there was more scholarly interest and work on market traders. During the last two decades, anthropological

interest in this area has waned. More recently, several projects on this activity in the region have been undertaken. See, for example, Browne 2004, Mantz 2003, Mulero Diaz 2000.

4. See, for example, Browne 2004; Chickering and Salahdine 1991; Cross 1998; Portes, Castells, and Benton 1989; Smart and Smart 2005.

5. A number of lower-class women frequently shift between foreign higglering and domestic work, depending on market demands and their ability to raise the necessary capital for the buying trip.

6. While it would be advantageous to know how these factors might change if the ICI was a man, I did not focus on this aspect as I carried out my research.

7. I thank Kristen Olson for pointing this out.

Chapter Five

1. Comportment is a signifier of difference, which quickly reveals foreigners to locals. Those who have lived abroad are also marked as foreign by their lives, lifestyles, and socialization.

2. Government and development researchers often conduct quantitative analysis that requires spending little, if any, time with traders. During the research years, studies conducted on ICIs did not involve the arcade in this study. Traders in general are not used to seeing researchers pass through the arcade. I, on the other hand, lingered.

3. Grant Farred has argued that the very names and location of these areas are literally disempowering for dwellers. He notes, "Dung Hill (also known as the Dungle) and Back O' Wall were located on a municipal garbage dump and behind a cemetery respectively" (2003:226).

4. Jonathan Xavier Inda refers to such areas as "post-national zones." By this he means a "space that once belongs and now does not belong to the nation-state. The nation-state is not in complete control" (2000:92).

5. A don (a reference to the Italian Mafia system) is the leader of a demarcated geographical area who oversees everything, from finding and allocating work for residents and local fund raising to petty crime and/or drug trading; dons also participate in the redistribution of these resources and provision of safety to their communities.

6. According to Carl Stone's seminal study, the export of ganja also allowed importers to earn foreign exchange abroad, which facilitated their buying for imports (1989).

7. According to Obika Gray, in Jamaica, this term "refers to a distinct dramaturgy in which claimants to respect and social honor employ intimidation and norm disrupting histrionics to affirm their right to an honor contested or denied." Moreover, he writes that badness-honor can be seen as a "mundane but ubiquitous

weapon of the weak . . . It is a cultural style, which consists of a repertoire of facial gestures, body poses, assertive mien, menacing or histrionic gestures to compel rivals or allies to grant power, concede respect, accord deference or satisfy material want" (2004:129). Also, see Sives (2002).

8. Historically, during election times such activities escalate. This pattern is sustained, though in recent years the death toll from election-related violence has decreased considerably.

9. http://www.jamaicansforjustice.org/jfj_website.php?section2=aboutus&section1=aboutlink.

10. http://www.jamaicansforjustice.org/jfj_website.php?section2=aboutus&section1=aboutlink.

11. The CBI was a tax incentive program that allowed all goods except textiles and apparel produced in the Caribbean Basin to enter the U.S. duty-free for twelve years. Many argued that this initiative benefited multinationals and exploited the core workforce of predominantly female workers in these free trade zones (Bolles 1996). It must be noted that the program also included a military component (Harrison 1987, Stephens and Stephens 1986).

12. These began in 2003. Prior to that, after-parties were always held downtown for a select few who dared to cross the divide. With Passa Passa, this event became more open and legitimate.

13. There are a couple of arcades in uptown areas or at least on the borders away from residential neighborhoods. The first was built in Constant Spring to accommodate traders who had squatted there. The conditions of this arcade are far better than that of those located downtown. Eventually, social divisions emerged among traders. The ICIs in the Constant Spring arcade are represented by the Jamaican Higglers and Sidewalk Vendors Association (JHSVA), which distinguishes itself from the United Vendors Association (UVA), which represents mostly downtown traders. Recently, another arcade was built in the Crossroads area as well. Lower- and lower-middle-class customers frequent both.

14. Generally, spatial class boundaries are crossed mostly by middle- and upper-class men. Towards the latter part of fieldwork in 1997, I recall going near Coronation with two Jamaican white male friends. I was surprised that they had never been to these areas. They were in awe of my having "conquered" a part of their own culture from which they were expelled. However, as we walked through the streets, several of the vendors actually called them tourists. These vendors interacted with me so that I could facilitate interactions with these men. Through my black presence these white Jamaican men actually became foreigners. As a result, I became Jamaican, perhaps even a downtown woman, though my appearance and demeanor could have presented a conflict.

15. "Partners in Martha Brae fits the basic model of the structure, organization, and function . . . identified by Margaret Katzin [1959], though the associations are now larger. Katzin described partners as consisting of a 'banker' and from

ten to twenty 'throwers,' called a 'round' in Martha Brae. The Banker initiated and organized the partners, which lasted for the same number of weeks as there were throwers. Contributions to the fund varied among groups, ranging from a few shillings to a pound sterling or more per week at the time of Katzin's study, but were consistent within a given group. (Early in my fieldwork, the usual weekly contribution in Martha Brae was one pound [Besson 1974:1:209].) The banker consulted each thrower as to his or her position for receiving the 'draw.' The banker, who usually received a gratuity from throwers, was also responsible for ensuring that each thrower met his or her obligations. Throwers who drew late in the rotation were prevented from defaulting by the fact that they could not retrieve the contributions already paid. Sanctions for those who drew early were the knowledge that their default would become widely known and prevent them from being admitted to other partners and the fear of court prosecution or physical reprisals. All but the last to draw received credit" (Besson 2002:228). Partners is a very common practice in the region, where it is known as sou-sou, throwing box, or meeting turn among English-speaking people (Besson 2002:230).

16. Two days after the stabbing, the bloodstain had dried on the office floor. I asked for a bucket to clean it. I could not stand it any longer; several of the young traders who were in the office at the time laughed at me and said "why bother?" I told them I simply could not sit next to the dried blood. I went to another worker in the office whose response was similar to the traders'.

17. Homes and apartments are secured behind wrought iron gates that are often double-locked. Within these, bedrooms are usually sequestered by rape gates. In recent years, gated apartments and condo communities have been, and continue to be, built throughout the capital, especially in uptown areas.

18. Also at times I abhorred the darkness in the stalls or offices, the noise, the senseless acts of aggression, and the men who would grab me because, in that context of spatial transgression, I had to negotiate boundaries. All of these discomforts in many ways are culturally specific class markers.

19. There is a trend especially among white male anthropologists to romanticize fieldwork in volatile areas. These rarely reflect on how white privilege operates in these situations. In my case, like Miss B., I was simply tired of having to be so alert, and having to embody toughness in a way that I was unaccustomed to. As it was unnecessary in Ann Arbor, a place that, Melynda Price rightly notes, "dulls the senses," I became increasingly aware of my frustrations with being in Jamaica especially when others would point out these differences to me. Price's first observation upon arriving in Kingston was: "women do not smile here. They have no expression on their faces." This helped me to confirm that I wasn't crazy.

20. In her work on Martha Brae, anthropologist Jean Besson refutes Peter J. Wilson's (1973) theory of reputation and respectability. Besson found that peasant and working-class females "did not subscribe to Eurocentric respectability" as Wilson has argued. Rather, like men, they sought to compete and establish reputations (1993:27–30).

21. The worst of local expletives almost always makes some reference to female anatomy or something in relation to a female condition. "Bloodclaat," for example, is blood cloth or menstrual pad, and "pussyhole" is vagina.

22. That year, drug-related crimes were escalating. In addition, several prominent uptown businessmen were killed, which prompted the government to deploy the army in downtown areas.

23. I thank Betsy Traube for pointing this out.

24. See Barnes 2006, Cooper 1993a, Edmondson 2003.

25. See Freeman 2000 and Yelvington 1995 for examples specific to the Caribbean region.

Chapter Six

1. By the end of the trip, I learned that Miss T.'s continuous use of expletives was in many ways intended as an affront. It was part of the attitude, the toughness, that she used to earn respect and deter merchants from attempting to cheat her. She pointed out that in the past both she and Miss M. had lost a considerable amount of money at one of the stores they frequent. In the old days, wholesalers used to ship them the wrong type or incorrect volume of goods. This is one of the reasons that they now ship goods on their own. Other ICIs have reaffirmed the need to be tough when they travel abroad, because they are continually robbed or cheated. Pickpockets, the van man, and even friends who they stay with during the buying trip have robbed them of their cash when they arrive at their destination.

2. Anderson (1987) and Portes, Castells, and Benton (1989) make similar arguments regarding other regions.

3. See Edwards 1980; Mintz 1974, 1993; Katzin 1959, 1960; Durant-Gonzalez 1976.

4. Thompson himself thinks that the term comes from the eighteenth century. He could not find references until the mid-nineteenth century (1991:336–37).

5. Critiques of Scott pointed to his romanticization of the peasant and his characterization of them as mere noble savages. The perception of peasants as noncapitalists also reified east/west Orientalist perspectives. This view only re-creates the hierarchy among nations. It ignores the fact that, historically, in societies where exchange has been an integral feature of life and market, traders may have their own logic of capital. Popkin (1979) responded to Scott with Popkin's creation of the rational peasant.

6. For Scott, Sivaramakrishnan notes, "much of the politics of subordinate groups falls into the category of everyday forms of resistance. He further asserts that this is definitely a high level of tacit cooperation among resisters and . . . everyday forms of resistance being loosely coordinated, have to rely on venerable popular cultures of resistance" (2005:347).

7. See, for example, Alexander 2006, Grewal and Kaplan 1994, Freeman 2001, di Leonardo 1991, Marchand and Runyan 2000, Mendez 2005, Mohanty 2003, Tsing 2005, Wolf 1997.

8. Mary Louise Pratt's formulation of contact zones is similar to Tsing's, with greater emphasis on more immediate spaces of colonial encounters. As Pratt writes, "I use this term to refer to social spaces where cultures meet, clash, and grapple with each other, often in contexts of highly asymmetrical relations of power, such as colonialism, slavery, or their aftermaths as they are lived out in many parts of the world today" (1991:33).

9. Baubie Paschal pushed me to expand this point, as I was in danger of desexualizing Miss T.

10. More recently, Miss T. ceased this practice of hiring day laborers and began go to a shipping company that handles both the packing and the shipping of her barrels of goods.

11. See, for example, Clark 1994; de la Cadena 2000; Seligman 2001, 2004.

12. Several middle-class consumers admit to purchasing goods in arcades that allow them to be up to date with fashion trends. Because these items are cheaper, they are able to purchase new styles more frequently and keep up with fads.

Chapter Seven

1. According to Marilyn Miller, "various political leaders–former presidents Carlos Prio in Cuba (1948-52) and Luis Echeverria Alvarez in Mexico (1970-6), the late farm worker activist Cesar Chavez in California and Hugo Chavez in Venezuela and Vicente Fox in Mexico have all conducted much of their national and international business dressed in a guayabera. . . . The breezy shirts call attention to the wearer's role as a mediator between economic classes, local and global economies, between mass production and custom preparation, between national and transnational ideologies, and between negotiations of cultural difference and belonging" (2005:218–219).

2. The article mentions the contest organizers and the rules and concluded with brief paragraphs on the most snappy dresser, Seaga, and the least snappy dresser, Michael Pilgrim, an interim prime minister of St Lucia (*Gleaner* 1982).

3. I also use the term "pitchy-patchy" to show that historically styles are created by mixing local with foreign items and to stress that consumption patterns have been import driven.

4. In *Toward an Anthropological Theory of Value*, white anthropologist David Graeber writes that "formal male dress is designed to hide the body . . . rendering him abstract and in a certain sense, invisible. Clothing for women [on the other hand] not only reveals more of the body (or at least hints at revealing it: it transforms what is revealed into a collection of objects of adornment–body parts

becoming equivalent, as such, to clothing, makeup, jewelry–that together define the wearer as a sight, and by extension, as relatively concrete and material" (2001:96).

5. As Hall et al. have argued, mugging was an imported social construction (1978). I characterize it as a crisis because of the hysteria about decency that pervaded the popular media. Their subsequent attention could be read as a hysteric response to perceived public indecency. Since it was black bodies that were revealed and being targeted, this raced class and only reinscribed racial stereotypes.

6. These shirts were seen as symbolic of North American power. That is, they were exemplary of the ability of a powerful country like the United States to "pollute" small local markets, like Jamaica, with its foreign expletives. During the fiasco over these shirts, talk radio shows such as Barbara Gloudon's and Wilmot Perkins's held call-ins to discuss this issue.

7. http://www.reggaeshow.com/index.html.

8. This reference to servants was a form of classification. Servants are considered to represent "the people" (Clifford 1988).

9. Jamaican cultural studies scholar Sonjah Niaah Stanley suggests that the penchant for crisscrossing of [symbolic and material] spaces is inherent to dancehall's philosophy of boundarylessness (2004).

10. There are some advantages to being unrecognizable including less harassment from customs abroad as well as at home. In recent years, ICIs have been the target of customs officials because they are perceived as drug smugglers. By presenting themselves in a more "acceptable" manner, traders avoid such harassment and humiliation. Another benefit is the ability to pass through customs undetected, without having to pay duties.

11. Studies of feet tend to focus on cultural preoccupation with feet from the point of view of fetish and or gender oppression, especially foot binding practices in China. See Hong 1997, Ko 2001, Levy 1966.

12. See, for example, Freeman 2000, Thomas 2004.

13. I thank Demetrius Eudell for our discussions of Frantz Fanon.

14. Platforms can be traced all the way back to fifteenth-century Venice. Known then as chopines, or overshoes, these were slipped over dainty shoes to protect them from mud and dirt. According to historian Andrea Vianello, chopines were "characterized by thick soles made of cork or wood, which could be up to twenty inches tall.... were worn in the streets of early modern European cities by both noblewomen and commoners... they were used differently by persons of different social classes to define themselves and their social relations and to give expression of their vision of Venetian society" (2006:89-91). It must be noted that even then females who donned chopines were actually perceived as "depraved and dissolute women" (Brownmiller 1984) and as "prostitutes and courtesans" (Vianello 2006). Vianello argues that this notion was a misrepresentation that ignored class differences among women and the fact that such shoes were also symbols of status.

Platforms eventually disappeared. Then they made their comeback during the 1930s in wood and cork. They were worn mostly on the beach and came back again forty years later.

15. Prior to independence, Jamaica had a thriving shoe industry. A number of English styles and brands were actually made on the island. During the early 1970s, thirty-six companies were manufacturing safety boots, galoshes, and genuine leather shoes. The free market system opened, major companies such as Bata and Hush Puppies left, respectively, in 1983 and 1986. ICIs have been blamed for the decline of this industry as well. Bryan John, managing director of Gator Limited (one of the companies that still exists) notes, "Those ICIs precipitated the exodus of giants like Bata, which was an established name in the Jamaican community, by flooding the market with cheap, imported shoes. The companies were swamped and some were forced to leave because of the economic situation" (*Gleaner* 1996, 10:28:C7). While major European and Canadian manufacturers have suffered, sandals made by Rastafarians continue to be sold in Half-Way-Tree and other areas mostly to socially conscious customers seeking to support local creativity. Other establishments include Bridget Sandals, a middle-class former-model-turned-shoemaker, who designs and sells distinctive styles mostly to high income individuals and visitors from abroad.

16. This distinction in self-representation and consumption is also exemplary of the hegemonic struggle between the opposing cultural forms of high and mass culture that is prevalent in Britain (Gledhill 1997). The tendency among upper classes is to consume distinctive pieces and replicate or recycle existing styles rather than quickly adopt the "new."

17. Similarly in Haiti, these plastic shoes, known as fabvac, are sold in the popular downtown markets and associated with the poor.

18. In *Cultural Complexity*, Hannerz refutes earlier arguments that stress passive ingestion of global flows. His analysis of the difference in the flow of communications between center and periphery highlights the extent to which local responses to these are determined by local contexts (1992).

19. I thank Rupert Lewis for highlighting this distinction.

Brawta

1. http://www.cnn.com/2000/LAW/05/12/aclu/.

2. The documentary *Life and Debt,* an antiglobalization film, focused solely on the impact of multinational companies in Jamaica. It completely disregarded the role that the local elite (many featured in the film) play in the exploitation of their own workers. I thank Opal Linton for being adamant about this point in our discussion of this film.

Bibliography

Abbensetts, Joanne M. E. 1990. *International Higglering in Jamaica: An Informal Sector Study*. Master's thesis in Development Economics, Dalhousie University, Halifax, Nova Scotia.

Abrahams, Roger D., and John Szwed. 1983. *After Africa: Extracts from British Travel Accounts and Journals of the Seventeenth, Eighteenth, and Nineteenth Centuries Concerning the Slaves, Their Manners, and Customs in the British West Indies*. New Haven: Yale University Press.

Abraham-Van Der Mark, Eva. 1983. "The Impact of Industrialization on Women: A Caribbean Case." In *Women and Men and the International Division of Labor*, edited by June Nash and Patricia Fernandez-Kelly. Albany: State University of New York Press.

Abu-Lughod, Lila. 1993. *Writing Women's World: Bedouin Stories*. Berkeley: University of California Press.

———. 1991. "Can There be a Feminist Ethnography?" *Women and Performance* 5:7–27.

———. 1990. "The Romance of Resistance: Tracing Transformations of Power through Bedouin Women." *American Ethnologist* 17:41–55.

Aggarwal, Ravina. 2000. "Traversing 'Lines of Control': Feminist Anthropology Today." *Annals of the American Academy of Political and Social Science* 571 (September):14–29.

Ahearn, Laura M. 2001. *Invitations to Love: Literacy, Love Letters, and Social Change in Nepal*. Ann Arbor: University of Michigan Press.

Ahmad, Aijaz. 1992. *In Theory: Classes, Nations, and Literature*. New York: Verso Books.

Ahmed, Sara. 2004. *The Cultural Politics of Emotion*. London: Routledge.

Ahmed, Sara, and Jackie Stacey. 2001. *Thinking through the Skin*. London: Routledge.

Alcoff, Linda. 1988. "Cultural Feminism versus Poststructuralism: The Identity Crisis in Feminist Theory." *Signs* 13(3):405–436.

Alexander, Jack. 1977. "The Culture of Race in Middle-Class Kingston, Jamaica." *American Ethnologist*. 4:413–435.

Alexander, M. Jacqui. 2006. *Pedagogies of Crossing: Meditations on Feminisms, Sexual Politics, Memory, and the Sacred*. Durham: Duke University Press.

Anderson, Benedict. 1991. *Imagined Communities: Reflections on the Origin and Spread of Nationalism*. New York: Verso Books.

Anderson, Elijah. 2003. *A Place on the Corner*. Chicago: University of Chicago Press.

Anderson, Patricia. 1987. "Informal Sector or Secondary Labour Market: Towards a Synthesis." *Social and Economic Studies* 36(3):149–176.

Antrobus, Peggy. 1989. "Gender Implications of the Development Crisis." In *Development in Suspense*, edited by George Beckford and Norman Girvan. Kingston: Friederich Ebert Stiftung.

Antrobus, Peggy, and Lorna Gordon. 1984. "The English Speaking Caribbean: A Journey in the Making." In *Sisterhood Is Global*, edited by Robin Morgan. New York: Anchor Books.

Anzaldua, Gloria. 1990. *Making Face, Making Soul/Hacienda Caras: Creative and Critical Perspectives by Women of Color*. San Francisco: Aunt Lute Books.

———. 1987. *Borderlands/LaFrontera*. San Francisco: Spinsters/Aunt Lute.

———. 1983. "Speaking in Tongues: A Letter to Third World Women Writers." In *This Bridge Called My Back: Writings by Radical Women of Color*, edited by Cherrie L. Moraga and Gloria Anzaldua. New York: Kitchen Table: Women of Color Press.

Appadurai, Arjun. 1991. "Global Ethnoscapes: Notes and Queries for a Transnational Anthropology." In *Recapturing Anthropology*, edited by Richard Fox. Santa Fe: School of American Research Press.

———. 1986. Introduction. *The Social Life of Things*, edited by Arjun Appadurai. Cambridge: Cambridge University Press.

Aptheker, Bettina. 1989. *Tapestries of Life*. Amherst: University of Massachusetts Press.

Austin-Broos, Diane J. 1997. *Jamaica Genesis*. Kingston: Ian Randle Publishers.

———. 1994. "Race/Class: Jamaica's Discourse of Heritable Identity." *New West Indian Guide* 68(3–4):213–233.

———. 1984. *Urban Life in Kingston, Jamaica: The Culture and Class Ideology of Two Neighborhoods*. New York: Gordon and Breach Science Publishers.

Babb, Florence. 2001. "Market/Places as Gendered Spaces: Market Women's Studies over Two Decades." In *Women Traders in Cross Cultural Perspective: Mediating Identities, Marketing Wares*, edited by Linda Seligman. Stanford: Stanford University Press.

———. 1989. *Between the Field and the Cooking Pot: The Political Economy of Market Women in Peru*. Austin: University of Texas Press.

Bakare-Yusuf, Bibi. 1997. "Raregrooves and Raregroovers: A Matter of Taste, Difference, and Identity." In *Black British Feminism*, edited by Heidi Safia Mirza. New York: Routledge.

Baker, Lee. 1998. *From Savage to Negro: Anthropology and the Construction of Race 1896–1954*. Berkeley: University of California Press.

Bakhtin, M. M. 1984. *Rabelais and His World*. Translated by Helene Iswolsky. Bloomington: Indiana University Press.

Bannerji, Himani. 1995. *Thinking Through: Essays on Feminism, Marxism, and Anti-racism*. Toronto: Women's Press.

Bannerji, Himani, Linda Carty, et al. 1991. *Unsettling Relations: The University as a Site of Feminist Struggle*. Toronto: Women's Press.

Banton, Buju. 1995. "I.C.I.," track 4, *Cell Block*, vol. 2. Penthouse Records, CBCD2032.

Barnes, Natasha. 2006. *Cultural Conundrums: Gender, Race, Nation, and the Making of Caribbean Cultural Politics*. Ann Arbor: University of Michigan Press.

———. 1994. "Representing the Nation: Gender, Culture, and the State in the Anglophone Caribbean." *Massachusetts Review* 35:471–492.

Barrett, Leonard. 1977. *The Rastafarians: Sounds of Dissonance*. Boston: Beacon Press.

Barriteau, Violet Eudine, ed. 2003. *Confronting Power, Theorizing Gender: Interdisciplinary Perspectives in the Caribbean*. Kingston: University of the West Indies Press.

Barriteau-Foster, Eudine. 1992. "The Construct of a Post-modernist Feminist Theory for Caribbean Social Science Research." *Social and Economic Studies* 41(2):1–43.

Barrow, Christine. 1986. "Finding the Support for Survival." *Social and Economic Studies* 35(2):131–177.

Barry, Tom, Beth Wood, and Deb Preusch, eds. 1984. *The Other Side of Paradise*. New York: Grove Press.

Barthes, Roland. 1985. *The Fashion System*. London: Cape.

Basch, Linda, Nina Glick-Schiller, and Cristina Szanton Blanc. 1994. *Nations Unbound: Transnational Projects, Postcolonial Predicaments, and Deterritorialized Nation-States*. New York: Gordon and Breach.

Beattie, Julie. 2003. *Women without Class: Girls, Race, and Identity*. Berkeley: University of California Press.

Beckford, George. 1972. *Persistent Poverty: Underdevelopment in Plantation Economies of the Third World*. London: Zed Books.

Beckford, George, and Michael Witter. 1980. *Small Garden, Bitter Weed: The Political Economy of Struggle and Change in Jamaica*. Morant Bay: Maroon Publishing House.

Beckles, Hilary. 2003. "Perfect Property: Enslaved Black Women in the Caribbean." In *Confronting Power, Theorizing Gender: Interdisciplinary Perspectives in the Caribbean*, edited by Eudine Barriteau. Kingston: University of the West Indies Press.

———. 1995. "Sex and Gender in the Historiography of Caribbean Slavery." In *Engendering History: Caribbean Women in Historical Perspective*, edited by Verene Shepherd, Bridget Brereton, and Barbara Bailey. Kingston: Ian Randle.

———. 1991. "An Economic Life of Their Own: Slaves as Commodity Producers and Distributors in Barbados." *Slavery and Abolition* 12(1):31–47.

———. 1989. *Natural Rebels: A Social History of Enslaved Black Women in Barbados*. New Brunswick: Rutgers University Press.

Behar, Ruth. 1996. *The Vulnerable Observer: Anthropology that Breaks Your Heart*. Boston: Beacon Press.

————. 1995. "Writing in My Father's Name: A Diary of Translated Woman's First Year." In *Women Writing Culture*, edited by Ruth Behar and Deborah A. Gordon. Berkeley: University of California Press.

————. 1993. *Translated Woman*. Boston: Beacon Press.

————. 1989. "Rage and Redemption: Reading the Life Story of a Mexican Marketing Woman." *Feminist Studies* 16(2):223–258.

Behar, Ruth, and Deborah A. Gordon, eds. 1995. *Women Writing Culture*. Berkeley: University of California Press.

Bell, Diane. 1993. "Introduction: The Context in Gendered Fields." In *Women, Men, and Ethnography*, edited by Diane Bell, Pat Caplan, and Jahan Karin. London: Routledge.

Beneria, Lourdes, and Martha I. Roldan. 1987. *The Crossroads of Class and Gender: Homework, Subcontracting, and Household Dynamics in Mexico City*. Chicago: University of Chicago Press.

Benjamin, Walter. [1982] 2004. *The Arcades Project*. Translated by Howard Eiland and Kevin McLaughlin. Cambridge: Harvard University Press.

Bennett, Louise. 1982. "Colonization in Reverse. "In *Selected Poems*, edited by Mervyn Morris. Kingston: Sangster's.

Bennett, Tony, Michal Emmison, and John Frow. 1999. *Accounting for Tastes: Australian Everyday Cultures*. New York: Cambridge University Press.

Benoit, Joachim. 1980. *Les Racines du Sous-Development en Haiti*. Port-au-Prince: Imprimerie H. Deschamps.

Berlin, Ira, and Philip D. Morgan. 1991. "Introduction." *Slavery and Abolition* 12(1):68–91.

Besson, Jean. 2002. *Martha Brae's Two Histories: European Expansion and Caribbean Culture-Building in Jamaica*. Chapel Hill: University of North Carolina Press.

————. 1993. "Reputation and Respectability Reconsidered: A New Perspective on Afro Caribbean Peasant Women." In *Women and Change in the Caribbean: A Pan-Caribbean Perspective*, edited by Janet Momsen. Kingston: Ian Randle; Bloomington: Indiana University Press; London: James Currey.

————. 1974. *Land Tenure and Kinship in River Village Jamaica*. Ph.D. dissertation in Anthropology, University of Edinburgh.

Best, Lloyd. 1989. "West Indian Society One Hundred and Fifty Years after Abolition: Elements of an Interpretation." Wilberforce Lecture presented at the University of Hull. Spring.

Bettie, Julie. 2003. *Women without Class: Girls, Race, and Identity*. Berkeley: University of California Press.

Bickell, Reverend R. 1836. *The West Indies As They Are*. London: Hatchard and Son.

Bigelow, J. [1851] 1970. *Jamaica in 1850*. London: George Putnam.

Black Public Sphere, ed. 1995. *The Black Public Sphere*. Chicago: University of Chicago Press.

Blair, Colin, and Glenroy Sinclair. 1995. "PM Promises to Saturate Downtown Area with Security Personnel." *Gleaner*, pp. 1, 3A.

Bolland, Nigel. 1993. "Systems of Domination after Slavery: The Control of Land and Labour in the British West Indies after 1838." In *Caribbean Freedom:*

Economy and Society from Emancipation to the Present, edited by Hilary Beckles and Verene Shepherd. Kingston: Ian Randle.

Bolles, Lynn. 2001. "Seeking the Ancestors: Forging a Black Feminist Tradition in Anthropology." In *Black Feminist Anthropology: Theory, Politics, Praxis, and Poetics*, edited by Irma McClaurin. New Brunswick: Rutgers University Press.

———. 1996. *Sister Jamaica: A Study of Women, Work, and Households in Kingston*. Lanham: University Press of America.

———. 1986. "Economic Crisis and Female Headed Households in Jamaica." In *Women and Change in Latin America*, edited by June Nash and Helen Safa. South Hadley: Bergin and Garvey.

———. 1985. "Of Mules and Yankee Gals: Struggling with Stereotypes in the Field." *Anthropology and Humanism Quarterly* 10(4):114–119.

———. 1983. "Kitchens Hit by Priorities: Working Class Women Confront the IMF." In *Women and Men and the International Division of Labor*, edited by June Nash and Patricia Fernandez-Kelly. Albany: State University of New York Press.

———. 1981. "Household Economic Strategies in Kingston, Jamaica." In *Women and World Change: Equity Issues in Development*, edited by Naomi Black and Ann Baker Contrell. London: Sage Publications.

Bordo, Susan. 1990. "Feminism, Postmodernism, and Gender Skepticism." In *Feminism/Postmodernism*, edited by Linda Nicholson. London: Routledge.

Bourdieu, Pierre. 2001. *Masculine Domination*. Stanford: Stanford University Press.

———. 1986. *Distinction: A Social Critique in the Judgment of Taste*. Cambridge: Harvard University Press.

———. 1986. "The Forms of Capital." In *Handbook of Theory and Research for the Sociology of Education*, edited by John Richardson. New York: Greenwood Press.

Bovard, James. 1987. "Jamaica: No Free Market, No Miracle." *Freeman: Ideas on Liberty* 37(12). http://www.fee.org/publications/the-freeman/article.asp?aid= 2394. Accessed April 3, 2007.

Boyne, Ian. 1997. "Decadent Dancehall Mirrors Society." *Gleaner*, January 5, A8.

Brana-Shute, Gary. 1979. *On the Corner*. Alssen, The Netherlands: Van Gorcin and Comp.

Brathwaite, Edward Kamau. 1971. *The Development of Creole Society in Jamaica 1770–1820*. Oxford: Oxford University Press.

Brenner, Neil. 2004. *New State Spaces: Urban Governance and the Rescaling of Statehood*. Oxford: Oxford University Press.

Brodber, Erna. 1986. "Afro-Jamaican Women at the Turn of the Century." *Social and Economic Studies* 35(3):23–46.

Brody, Jennifer DeVere. 1998. *Impossible Purities: Blackness, Femininity, and Victorian Culture*. Durham: Duke University Press.

Brown, Aggrey. 1979. *Color, Class, and Politics in Jamaica*. New Brunswick, New Jersey: Transactions Books.

Brown, E. M. 2000. "Learning to Love the IMF." *New York Times*, April 18.

Brown, Elsa Barkley. 1989. "African-American Women's Quilting: A Framework for Conceptualizing and Teaching African-American Women's History." *Signs*. Chicago: The University of Chicago Press.

Brown, Lynette. 1994. "Crisis, Adjustment, and Social Change: The Middle Class under Adjustment." In *Consequences of Structural Adjustment: A Review of the Jamaican Experience*, edited by Elsie Le Franc. Kingston: Canoe Press.

Browne, Katharine. 2004. *Creole Economics: Caribbean Cunning under the French Flag*. Austin: University of Texas Press.

Brownmiller, Susan. 1984. *Femininity*. New York: Linden Press/Simon and Schuster.

Brusati, Celeste. 1999. "Capitalizing on the Counterfeit: Trompe L'Oeil Negotiations." In *Still Life Paintings from the Netherlands 1550–1720*, edited by Alan Chong and Wouter Kloek. Zwolle: Waanders Publishers.

Buckridge, Steeve O. 2004. *The Language of Dress: Resistance and Accommodation in Jamaica, 1760–1890*. Kingston: University of the West Indies Press.

Burman, Jenny. 2001. *Economies of Nostalgia and Yearning: Traveling the Route Between Toronto and Jamaica*. Ph.D. thesis in Philosophy, York University, North York, Ontario.

Burton, Richard. 1997. *Afro-Creole: Power, Opposition, and Play in the Caribbean*. Ithaca: Cornell University Press.

Bush, Barbara. 1990. *Slave Women in Caribbean Society, 1650–1838*. Bloomington: Indiana University Press.

———. 1985. "Towards Emancipation: Slave Women and resistance to Coercive Labour Regimes in the British West India Colonies, 1790–1838." In *Abolition and Its Aftermath: The Historical Context 1790-1916*, edited by David Richardson. London: Frank Caas.

———. 1981. "White Ladies, Colored Favorites, and Black Wenches; Some Considerations on Sex, Race, and Class Factors in Social Relations in White Creole Society in the British Caribbean." *Slavery and Abolition* 2(2):245–262.

Butler, Judith. 1997. *Excitable Speech: A Politics of the Performative*. New York: Routledge.

———. 1990. *Gender Trouble: Feminism and the Subversion of Identity*. New York: Routledge.

Cabral, Amilcar. 1969. *Revolution in Guinea*. London: Stage 1.

Campbell, Andrew C. [aka Tuffie]. 1997. "Reggae Sound Systems." In *Reggae, Rasta, and Revolution: Jamaican Music from Ska to Dub*, edited by Chris Potash. New York: Schirmer Books.

Campbell, Horace. 1980. "Ras Tafari: Culture and Resistance." *Race and Class* 22:1–22.

Carby, Hazel. 1987. *Reconstructing Womanhood: The Emergence of the Afro-American Woman Novelist*. New York: Oxford University Press.

Carley, Mary. 1962. *Jamaica: The Old and the New*. New York: Praeger.

Carmichael, A. C., Mrs. 1833. *Domestic Manners and Social Condition of the White, Coloured, and Negro Population of the West Indies*. London: Whittaker Treacher.

Carnegie, Charles V. 1981. *Human Maneuver, Option-Building and Trade: An Essay on Caribbean Social Organization*. Ph.D. diss. in anthropology, Johns Hopkins University.

Carty, Linda. 1992. "Black Women in Academia: A Statement from the Periphery." In *Unsettling Relations: The University as a Site of Feminist Struggles*, edited by Himani Bannerji, Linda Carty, Kari Dehli, Susan Heald, and Kate McKenna. Toronto: Canadian Scholars Press.

Chancer, Lynn. 1998. *Reconcilable Differences: Confronting Beauty, Pornography, and the Future of Feminism*. Berkeley: University of California Press.

Chevannes, Barry. 1998. *Rastafari and Other African-Caribbean Worldviews*. New Brunswick: Rutgers University Press.

———. 1994. *Rastafari Roots and Ideology*. Syracuse: Syracuse University Press.

Chickering, Lawrence, and Mohamed Salahdine, eds. 1991. *The Silent Revolution*. San Francisco: International Center for Economic Growth.

Chin, Elizabeth. 2001. *Purchasing Power: Black Kids and American Consumer Culture*. Minneapolis: University of Minnesota Press.

Ching, Barbara, and Gerald W. Creed, eds. 1997. *Knowing Your Place: Rural Identity and Cultural Hierarchy*. New York: Routledge.

Christian, Barbara. 1987. "The Race for Theory." *Cultural Critique* 6:51–63.

Chude-Sokei, Louis. 1997. "Post-national Geographies: Rasta, Ragga, and Reinventing Africa." In *Reggae, Rasta, and Revolution: Jamaican Music from Ska to Dub*, edited by Chris Potash. New York: Schirmer Books.

Clark, Gracia. 2001. "'Nursing Mother Work' in Ghana: Power and Frustration in Akan Market Women's Lives." In *Women Traders in Cross-Cultural Perspectives: Mediating Identities, Marketing Wares*, edited by Linda Seligman. Stanford: Stanford University Press.

———. 1994. *Onions Are My Husband*. Chicago: University of Chicago Press.

———, ed. 1989. *Traders versus the State*. Colorado: Westview Press.

Clarke, Colin. 2006. "Politics, Violence, and Drugs in Kingston, Jamaica." *Bulletin of Latin American Research* 25(3):420–440.

———. 1975. *Kingston, Jamaica: Urban Development and Social Change, 1692–1962*. Berkeley: University of California Press.

Clarke, Edith. 1957. *My Mother Who Fathered Me*. Kingston: University of the West Indies Press.

Cliff, Michelle. 1985. *The Land of Look Behind: Prose and Poetry*. Ithaca: Firebrand Books.

Clifford, James. 1988. *The Predicament of Culture: Twentieth-Century Ethnography, Literature, and Art*. Cambridge: Harvard University Press.

———. 1986. "Introduction: Partial Truths." In *Writing Culture: The Poetics and Politics of Ethnography*, edited by James Clifford and George E. Marcus. Berkeley: University of California Press.

Cole, Johnnetta. 1988. "Introduction." In *Anthropology for the Nineties: Introductory Readings*, edited by Johnnetta Cole. New York: Free Press; London: Collier Macmillan.

Comaroff, Jean. 1985. *Body of Power, Spirit of Resistance*. Chicago: University of Chicago Press.

Comitas, Lambros. 1973. "Occupational Multiplicity in Rural Jamaica." In *Work and Family Life: West Indian Perspectives*, edited by Lambros Comitas and David Lowenthal. New York: Anchor Books.

Cooper, Carolyn. 2004a. *Sound Clash: Jamaican Dancehall Culture at Large*. New York: Palgrave.

———. 2004b. "Lady Saw Cuts Loose: Female Fertility Rituals in the Dancehall." *Jamaica Journal* 27(2–3):13–19.

———. 2004c. "Enslaved in Stereotype: Race and Representation in Post-Independence Jamaica." *Small Axe* 16 (8) 2:154–169.

———. 1994. *Splash*. September 23–25. 5d.

———. 1993a. *Noises in the Blood: Orality, Gender, and the "Vulgar" Body of Jamaican Popular Culture*. London: Macmillan.

———. 1993b. "Las Lick." *Lifestyle Magazine*. July–August.

Coronil, Fernando. 1996. *The Magical State*. Chicago: University of Chicago Press.

Crapanzano, Vincent. 1984. "Life-Histories." *American Anthropologist* 86(4):953–960.

Craton, Michael. 1977. *Searching for the Invisible Man: Slaves and Plantation Life in Jamaica*. Cambridge: Harvard University Press.

Crawford, Joy. 2004. "Ghetto Glam." *Jamaica Observer*. August 9, p. 11.

Crenshaw, Kimberle Williams. 1991. "Mapping the Margins: Intersectionality, Identity Politics, and Violence against Women of Color." *Stanford Law Review* 43(6):1241–1299.

Cross, John C. 1998. *Informal Politics: Street Vendors and the State in Mexico City*. Stanford: Stanford University Press.

Cundall, Frank. 1936. *The Governors of Jamaica in the Seventeenth Century*. London: West India Committee.

Curtin, Philip. 1955. *The Two Jamaicas: The Role of Ideas in a Tropical Colony, 1830–1865*. Cambridge: Harvard University Press.

D'Amico-Samuels, Deborah. 1991. "Undoing Fieldwork: Personal, Political Theoretical and Methodological Implications." In *Decolonizing Anthropology: Moving Further toward an Anthropology for Liberation*, edited by Faye Harrison. Washington, DC: Association of Black Anthropologists, American Anthropological Association.

Davies, Carol Boyce. 1999. "Re-/Presenting Black Female Identity in Brazil: Filhas d'Oxum in Bahia Carnival." In *Representations of Blackness and the Performance of Identities*, edited by Jean Rahier. Westport: Bergin and Garvey.

———. [1990] 1994. *Out of the Kumbla: Caribbean Women and Literature*. Trenton: African World Press.

Davis, Angela. 1971. "Reflections on the Black Woman's role in the Community of Slaves." *Black Scholar* (December): 2–15.

Deere, Carmen Diana. 1977. "Changing Social Relations of Production and Peruvian Women's Work." *Latin American Perspectives* 4(1–2):38–47.

Deere, Carmen Diana, et al. 1990. *In the Shadows of the Sun*. Boulder: Westview Press.

de la Cadena, Marisol. 2000. *Indigenous Mestizos: The Politics of Race and Culture in Cuzco, Peru, 1919–1991*. Ann Arbor: University of Michigan Press.

———. 1996. "'Women Are More Indian': Ethnicity and Gender in a Community near Cuzco." In *Ethnicity, Markets, and Migration in the Andes: At the*

Crossroads of Anthropology and History, edited by Brooke Larson and Olivia Harris. Durham: Duke University Press.

De Soto, Hernando. 1989. *The Other Path*. New York: Harper and Row.

di Leonardo, Micaela. 1998. *Exotics at Home*. Chicago: University of Chicago Press.

———. 1991. "Introduction: Gender, Culture, and Political Economy: Feminism in Historical Perspective." In *Gender at the Crossroads of Knowledge: Feminist Anthropology in the Postmodern Era*, edited by Micaela di Leonardo. Berkeley: University of California Press. Dominguez, Virginia. 1986. *White by Definition: Social Stratification in Creole Louisiana*. New Brunswick: Rutgers University Press.

Douglas, Mary. 1966. *Purity and Danger: An Analysis of Concepts of Pollution and Taboo*. London: Penguin Books.

Douglass, Lisa. 1992. *The Power of Sentiment: Love, Hierarchy and the Jamaican Family Elite*. Boulder: Westview Press.

Drake, St. Clair. 1991. *Black Folk Here and There*. Volume 2. Berkeley: University of California Press.

duCille, Ann. 1996. *Skin Trade*. Cambridge: Harvard University Press.

Dupuy, Alex. 2006. *The Prophet and Power: Jean Bertrand Aristide, Haiti, and the International Community*. New York: Rowman & Littlefield.

———. 2001. "The New World Order, Globalization, and Caribbean Politics." In *New Caribbean Thought: A Reader*, edited by Brian Meeks and Folke Lindahl. Kingston: University of the West Indies Press.

———. 1997. "Race and Class in Post-Colonial Caribbean: The Views of Walter Rodney." In *Ethnicity, Race, and Nationality in the Caribbean*, edited by Juan Manuel Carrion. San Juan: Institute of Caribbean Studies.

Durant-Gonzalez, Victoria. 1985. "Higglering: Rural Women and the Internal Market System in Jamaica." In *Rural Development in the Caribbean*, edited by P. I. Gomes. New York: St. Martin's Press.

———. 1976. *Role and Status of Rural Jamaican Women: Higglering and Mothering*. Ph.D. diss., Anthropology Department, University of California, Berkeley.

Economic and Social Survey of Jamaica 1960–1980. Kingston: Planning Institute of Jamaica.

Edie, Carlene. 1991. *Democracy by Default: Dependency and Clientelism in Jamaica*. Colorado: Lynne Reinner.

Edmondson, Belinda. 2003. "Public Spectacles: Caribbean Women and the Politics of Public Performance." *Small Axe* 13 (vol. 9 no. 1):1–16.

Edwards, Bryan. 1793. *The History Civil and Commercial of the British Colonies in the West Indies*. London: John Stocksdale.

Edwards, Melvin R. 1980. *Jamaican Higglers: Their Significance and Potential*. Swansea: University College of Swansea, Centre for Development Studies.

Eisner, Gisela. 1961. *Jamaica 1830–1930*. Manchester: Manchester University Press.

Enslin, Elizabeth. 1994. "Beyond Writing: Feminist Practice and the Limits of Ethnography." *Cultural Anthropology* 9(4):537–568.

Entwistle, Joanne. 2000. *The Fashioned Body: Fashion, Dress, and Modern Social Theory*. Cambridge: Polity Press.

Erskine, Marcia. 1983. "Government Treatment of ICIs Irks Businessmen." *Gleaner*, September 8, pp. 1, 16.

Escobar, Arturo. 1995. *Encountering Development: The Making and Unmaking of the Third World*. Princeton: Princeton University Press.

Fabian, Johannes. 1983. *Time and the Other: How Anthropology Makes Its Object*. New York: Columbia University Press.

Fanon, Frantz. 1967. *Black Skin, White Masks*. New York: Grove Press.

Farmer, Paul. 1994. *The Uses of Haiti*. Monroe, ME: Common Courage Press.

Farred, Grant. 2003. *What's My Name?: Black Vernacular Intellectuals*. Minneapolis: University of Minnesota Press.

———. 1998. "Wailin' Soul: Reggae's Debt to Black American Music." In *Soul: Black Power, Politics, and Pleasure*, edited by Monique Guillory and Richard C. Green. New York: New York University Press.

Fernandez-Kelly, Maria P. 1983. *For We Are Sold, I and My People*. Albany: State University of New York Press.

Ffrench, Jennifer. 1983. "Frustrating the Higgler." *Gleaner*, February 15, p. 6.

Fick, Carolyn. 1992. *The Making of Haiti: The Saint Domingue Revolution from Below*. Knoxville: University of Tennessee Press.

Firth, Raymond, and B. S. Yamey, eds. 1964. *Capital, Saving, and Credit in Peasant Societies*. Chicago: Aldine Publishing Company.

Fischer, Sibylle. 2004. *Modernity Disavowed: Haiti and the Cultures of Slavery in the Age of Revolution*. Durham: Duke University Press.

Fluehr-Lobban, Carolyn. 2000. "Anténor Firmin: Haitian Pioneer of Anthropology." *American Anthropologist* 102(3):449–466.

Ford-Smith, Honor. 1991. "Women and the Garvey Movement in Jamaica." In *Garvey: His Work and Impact*, edited by Rupert Lewis and Patrick Bryan. Trenton: Africa World Press.

Foucault, Michel. 1980. *Power/Knowledge: Selected Interviews and Other Writings 1972–1977*. Edited by Colin Gordon. New York: Pantheon Books.

Fox, Richard G. 1991. *Recapturing Anthropolgy: Working in the Present*. Santa Fe: School of American Research Press.

Franck, Harry A. 1920. *Roaming through the West Indies*. New York: Century Company.

Fraser, Peter D. 1990. "Nineteenth Century West Indian Migration to Britain." In *In Search of a Better Life*, edited by Ransford W. Palmer. New York: Praeger Publishers.

Freeman, Carla. 2001. "Is Local:Global as Feminine:Masculine? Rethinking Gender of Globalization." *Signs* 26(4):1007–1037.

———. 2000. *High Tech and High Heels in the Global Economy: Women, Work, and Pink-Collar Identities in the Caribbean*. Durham: Duke University Press.

Freeman, Carla, and Donna Murdock. 2001. "Enduring Traditions and New Directions in Feminist Ethnography." *Feminist Studies* 27(2):423–458.

Friedman, Jonathan. 1994. *Cultural Identity and Global Process*. London: Sage Publications.

———. 1990. "The Political Economy of Elegance: An African Cult of Beauty." *Culture and History* 7:101–125.

Garber, Marjorie. 1992. *Vested Interests: Cross-Dressing and Cultural Anxiety*. New York: Routledge.

Gaspar, Barry. 1985. *Bondsmen and Rebels: A Study of Master–Slave Relations in Antigua*. Baltimore: Johns Hopkins University Press.

Gaunst, Laurie. 1995. *Born Fi Dead: A Journey through the Jamaican Posse Underworld*. New York: H. Holt.

Geertz, Clifford. 1976. "'From the Native's Point of View': On the Nature of Anthropological Understanding." In *Meaning in Anthropology*, edited by K. Basso and H. Selby. Albuquerque: University of New Mexico Press.

———. 1973. *The Interpretations of Cultures*. New York: Basic Books.

Giddens, Anthony. 1982. "Structuration and Class Consciousness." In *Classes, Power, and Conflict*, edited by Anthony Giddens and David Held. Berkeley: University of California Press.

Gikandi, Simon. 1997. *Maps of Englishness*. New York: Columbia University Press.

Gilman, Sander. 1985. *Difference and Pathology: Stereotypes of Sexuality, Race, and Madness*. Ithaca: Cornell University Press.

Gilroy, Paul. 1993. *The Black Atlantic: Modernity and Double Consciousness*. Cambridge: Harvard University Press.

Girvan, Norman. 1991. "The Political Economy of Race in the Americas: The Historical Context of Garveyism." In *Garvey: His Work and Impact*, edited by Rupert Lewis and Patrick Bryan. Trenton: Africa World Press.

———. 1998. "Not for Sale: Three Episodes in the Life of Democratic Socialism, 1997–1980." Paper presented at symposium on Jamaica in the 1970s. University of the West Indies, Kingston, August 24–26.

Girvan, Norman, and George Beckford, eds. 1989. *Development in Suspense*. Kingston: Friedrich Ebert Stiftung Press.

Girvan, Norman, Bernal Richard, and W. Hughes. 1980. "The IMF and the Third World: The Case of Jamaica." *Development Dialogue* 20(2):113–155.

Glaude, Winnifred Brown. 2003. *Female Micro-Entrepreneurs in the Jamaica Urban Semi-Formal Economy: The Impact of Race/Color, Class, and Gender*. Ph.D. thesis in Sociology, Temple University, Philadelphia.

Gleaner. 1990. Caption. January 18, p. 1.

———. 1983a. "Import Quotas for Higglers." February 6, p. 1.

———. 1983b. "215 Higglers Receive Import Quotas under New Licensing System." February 10, p. 2.

———. 1983c. "Higglers Have Status—They Are Small Business People Says PM." September 10, pp. 1, 16.

———. 1982. "Seaga Best Dressed PM in the Caribbean." September 19, p. 17.

Gledhill, Christine. 1997. "Genre and Gender: The Case of Soap Opera." in *Representation: Cultural Representations and Signifying Practices*, edited by Stuart Hall. Thousand Oaks: Sage.

Glick-Schiller, Nina, and Georges Fouron. 2001. *Georges Woke Up Laughing: Long Distancce Nationalism and the Search for Home*. Durham: Duke University Press.

Goffman, Irving. 1959. *The Presentation of Self in Everyday Life*. New York: Doubleday.

Goldstein, Donna M. 2003. *Laughter Out of Place: Race, Class, Violence, and Sexuality in a Rio Shantytown*. Berkeley: University of California Press.

Gordon, Derek, Patricia Anderson, and Don Robotham. 1997. "Jamaica: Urbanization during the Years of the Crisis." In *The Urban Caribbean: Transition to the New Global Economy*, edited by Alejandro Portes, Carlos Dore-Cabral, and Patricia Landolt. Baltimore: Johns Hopkins University Press.

Graeber, David. 2005. "The Auto-ethnography That Can Never Be and the Activist's Ethnography That Might Be." In *Auto-Ethnographies: The Anthropology of Academic Practices*, edited by Anne Meneley and Donna J. Young. Peterborough, Ontario: Broadview Press.

———. 2001. *Toward an Anthropological Theory of Value: The False Coin of Our Dreams*. New York: Palgrave.

Gray, Obika. 2004. *Demeaned but Empowered: The Social Power of the Urban Poor in Jamaica*. Kingston: University of the West Indies Press.

Green, Cecilia. 2007. "'A Civil Inconvenience'? The Vexed Question of Slave Marriage in the British West Indies." *Law and History Review* 25(1):1–61.

———. 1998. The Asian Connection: The U.S.-Caribbean Apparel Circuit and the Evolution of a New Model of Industrial Relations. *Latin American Research Review* 33(3): 7–47.

Greene, Dennis. 1997. "Immigrants in Chains: Afrophobia in American Legal History." *Oregon Law Review* 76.

Gregory, Stephen, and Roger Sanjek. 1996. *Race*. New Brunswick: Rutgers University Press.

Grewal, Inderpal. 1996. *Home and Harem: Nation, Gender, Empire, and the Cultures of Travel*. Durham: Duke University Press.

Grewal, Inderpal, and Caren Kaplan, eds. 1994. *Scattered Hegemonies: Postmodernity and Transnational Feminist Practices*. Minneapolis: University of Minnesota Press.

Griffith, Ivelaw, ed. 2000. *The Political Economy of Drugs in the Caribbean*. New York: St Martin's Press.

———. 1997. *Drugs and Security in the Caribbean: Sovereignty under Seige*. University Park: Pennsylvania State University Press.

Grosz, Elizabeth. 1994. *Volatile Bodies: Toward a Corporeal Feminism*. Bloomington: Indian University Press.

Guinier, Lani, Michelle Fine, and Jane Balin. 1997. *Becoming Gentlemen: Women, Law School, and Institutional Change*. Boston: Beacon Press.

Gunning, Sandra. 2001. "Traveling with Her Mother's Tastes: The Negotiation of Gender, Race, and Location in *Wonderful Adventures of Mrs. Seacole in Many Lands*." *Signs* 26(4):949–981.

Gupta, Akhil, and James Ferguson. 1997. "Discipline and Practice: The Field as Site, Method, and Location in Anthropology." In *Anthropological Locations: Boundaries and Grounds of a Field Science*, edited by Ahkil Gupta and James Ferguson. Berkeley: University of California Press.

Guy-Sheftall, Beverly, ed. 1995. *Words of Fire: An Anthology of African-American Feminist Thought*. New York: New Press.

Gwaltney, John. 1980. *Drylongso: A Self-Portrait of Black America*. New York: Vintage Books.

Habermas, Jurgen. 1989. *Structural Transformation of the Public Sphere*. Cambridge: MIT Press.

Hall, Catherine. 2002. *Civilizing Subjects: Metropole and Colony in the English Imagination 1830–1867*. London: Polity Press.

———. 1995. "Gender Politics and Imperial Politics: Rethinking the Histories of Empire." In *Engendering History: Caribbean Women in Historical Perspective*, edited by Verene Shepherd, Bridget Bereton, and Barbara Bailey. Kingston: Ian Randle.

Hall, Stuart. 1997a. "The Spectacle of the 'Other.'" In *Representation: Cultural Representations and Signifying Practices*, edited by Stuart Hall. London: Sage Publications.

———. 1997b. "What Is This 'Black' in Black Popular Culture?" In *Stuart Hall Dialogues in Cultural Studies*, edited by David Morley and Kuan Hsing Chen. New York: Routledge.

———. 1996. "Negotiating Caribbean Identities." *New Left Review* 209 (January–February): 3–14.

———. 1991. "The Local and the Global: Globalization and Ethnicity" and "Old and New Identities, Old and New Ethnicities." In *Culture, Globalization, and the World System: Contemporary Conditions for the Representation of Identity*, edited by Anthony D. King. Binghamton: State University of New York Press.

———. 1977. *Pluralism, Race, and Class in Caribbean Society: Race and Class in Post-colonial Society*. Paris: UNESCO.

Hall, Stuart, Chas Critcher, Tony Jefferson, John Clarke, and Brian Roberts. 1978. *Policing the Crisis: Mugging, the State, and Law and Order*. London: MacMillan Press.

Hall, Stuart, Paul Gilroy, Lawrence Grossberg, and Angela McRobbie, eds. 2000. *Without Guarantees: In Honour of Stuart Hall*. New York: Verso.

Hammonds, Evelynn. 1997. "Toward a Genealogy of Black Female Sexuality: The Problematic of Silence." In *Feminist Genealogies, Colonial Legacies, Democratic Futures*, edited by M. Jacqui Alexander and Chandra Talpade Mohanty. New York: Routledge.

Hanchard, Michael. 2000. "Racism, Eroticism, and the Paradoxes of a U.S. Black Researcher in Brazil." In *Racing Research, Researching Race: Methodological Dilemmas in Critical Race Studies*, edited by France Winddance Twine and Jonathan W. Warren. New York: New York University Press.

———, ed. 1999. *Racial Politics in Contemporary Brazil*. Durham: Duke University Press.

Haniff, Nesha. 1988. *Blaze a Fire*. Ontario: Sister Vision Black Women and Women of Color Press.

Hannam, Kevin, Mimi Sheller, and John Urry. 2006. "Editorial: Mobilities, Immobilities and Moorings." *Mobilities* 1(1):1–22.

Hannerz, Ulf. 1992. *Cultural Complexity*. New York: Columbia University Press.

———. 1989. "Culture between Center and Periphery: Toward a Macroanthropology." *Ethnos* 54:200–216.

Haraway, Donna. 1991. "Situated Knowledges: The Science Question in Feminism and the Privilege of Partial Perspective." In *Simians, Cyborgs and Women: The Reinvention of Nature*, edited by Donna Haraway. New York: Routledge.

———. 1989. *Primate Visions: Gender, Race, and Nature in the World of Modern Science*. New York: Routledge.

Harding, Sandra. 1991. "Whose Science? Whose Knowledge? Thinking Women's Lives." In *What Is Feminist Epistemology?*, edited by Sandra Harding. Ithaca: Cornell University Press.

Harris, Cheryl. 1991. "Whiteness as Property." *Harvard Law Review* 106(8):1710–1791.

Harrison, Faye. 2005. "Introduction: Global Perspectives on Human Rights and Interlocking Inequalities of Race, Gender, and Related Dimensions of Power." In *Resisting Racism and Xenophobia: Global Perspectives on Race, Gender, and Human Rights*, edited by Faye V. Harrison. Walnut Creek, CA: AltaMira Press.

———. 2002. "Global Apartheid, Foreign Policy, and Human Rights." *Souls: A Critical Journal of Black Politics, Culture, and Society* 4(3):48–68.

———. 1999. "New Voices of Diversity, Academic Relations of Production, and the Free Market." In *Transforming Academia: Challenges and Opportunities for an Engaged Anthropology*, edited by Linda Basch, Lucie Wood Saunders, Jagna Wojcicka Sharf, and James Peacock. Washington, DC: American Anthropological Association.

———. [1991] 1997a. "Ethnography as Politics." *In Decolonizing Anthropology: Moving Further Toward an Anthropology for Liberation*, 2nd ed., edited by Faye V. Harrison. Fairfax: American Anthropological Association.

———. 1997b. "The Gendered Politics and Violence of Structural Adjustment: A View from Jamaica." In *Situated Lives: Gender and Culture in Everyday Life*, edited by Louise Lamphere, Helena Ragone, and Patricia Zavella. New York: Routledge.

———. 1995. "The Persistent Power of Race in the Cultural and Political Economy of Racism." *Annual Review of Anthropology* 24:47–74.

———. 1991a. "Women in Jamaica's Urban Informal Economy." In *Third World Women and the Politics of Feminism*, edited by Chandra Mohanty Talpade, Ann Russo, and Lourdes Torres. Bloomington: Indiana University Press.

———. 1991b. *Decolonizing Anthropology*. Washington, DC: American Anthropological Association.

———. 1990. "Jamaica and the International Drug Economy." *TransAfrica Forum* 7(3):49–57.

———. 1989. "Drug Trafficking and World Capitalism: A Perspective on Jamaican Posses in the U.S." *Social Justice* 16(4):115–131.

———. 1988. "The Politics of Social Outlawry in Urban Jamaica." *Urban Anthropology and Studies in Cultural Systems and World Development* 17(2–3):259–277.

———. 1987. "Gangs Grassroots Politics, and the Crises of Dependent Capitalism in Jamaica." In *Perspectives in U.S. Marxist Anthropology*, edited by David Hakken and Hanna Lessinger. Boulder: Westview Press.

———. 1982. *Semiproletarianization and the Structure of Socio-economic and Political Relations in a Jamaica Slum*. Unpublished dissertation, Stanford University.

Harrison, Ira E., and Faye V. Harrison, eds. 1999. *African-American Pioneers in Anthropology*. Urbana: University of Illinois Press.

Hart, Keith, ed. 1989. *Women and the Sexual Division of Labour in the Caribbean.* Kingston: Consortium Graduate School.

———. 1973. "Informal Income Opportunities and Urban Employment in Ghana." *Journal of Modern African Studies* 2(1):61–89.

Harvey, David. 1989. *The Conditions of Postmodernism: An Enquiry into the Origins of Cultural Change*. London: Blackwell Publishers.

Headly, T. 1994. *The Jamaican Crime Scene: A Perspective*. Mandeville: Eureka Press Limited.

Hearn, Lafcadio. 1890. *Two Years in the French West Indies*. New York: Harper and Brothers.

Hebdige, Dick. 1989. *Subculture the Meaning of Style*. London: Methuen.

Hecht, David, and Maliqalim Simone. 1994. *Invisible Governance: The Art of African Micropolitics*. New York: Autonomedia.

Hendrickson, Carol. 1995. *Weaving Identities: Construction of Dress and Self in a Highland Guatemala Town*. Austin: University of Texas Press.

Hendrickson, Hildi. 1996. *Clothing and Difference*. Durham: Duke University Press.

Henriques, Fernando. [1953] 1968. *Family and Colour in Jamaica*. London: MacGibbon and Kee.

———. 1957. *Jamaica: Land of Wood and Water*. London: MacGibbon and Kee.

Heuman, Gad. 1981. *Between Black and White: Race, Politics, and the Free Colored in Jamaica 1792–1865*. Westport: Greenwood Press.

Higman, B.W. 1976. *Slave Population and Economy in Jamaica 1807–1834*. Cambridge: Cambridge University Press.

Hill-Collins, Patricia. [1991] 2000. *Black Feminist Thought: Knowledge, Consciousness, and the Politics of Empowerment*. New York: Routledge.

Hine, Darlene Clark. 1997. *Hine Sight: Black Women and the Reconstruction of American History*. Bloomington: Indiana University Press.

Hoetink, H. 1985. "'Race' and Color in the Caribbean." In *Caribbean Contours*, edited by Sidney W. Mintz and Sally Price. Baltimore: Johns Hopkins University Press.

———. 1971. *The Two Variants in Caribbean Race Relations: A Contribution to the Sociology of Segmented Societies*. London: Oxford University Press.

Holt, Tom. 1992. *The Problem of Freedom: Slave Emancipation in Jamaica*. Baltimore: Johns Hopkins University Press.

Hong, Fan. 1997. *Footbinding, Feminism, and Freedom: The Liberation of Women's Bodies in Modern China*. London: Frank Cass.

hooks, bell. 1990. *Yearning: Race, Gender, and Cultural Politics*. Boston: South End Press.

———. 1981. *Ain't I a Woman? Black Women and Feminism*. Boston: South End Press.

Hull, Gloria T., Patricia Bell Scott, and Barbara Smith. 1982. *All the Women Are White, All the Blacks Are Men, But Some of Us Are Brave: Black Women's Studies*. New York: Feminist Press.

Hurston, Zora Neale. [1935] 1978. *Mules and Men*. New York: Perennial Books.
———. 1942. *Dust Tracks on a Road*. Philadelphia: J. B. Lippincott.
Hymes, Dell. 1974. *Reinventing Anthropology*. New York: Vintage Books.
Inda, Jonathan Xavier. 2000. "A Flexible World: Capitalism, Citizenship, and Postnational Zones." *POLAR: Political and Legal Anthropology Review* 23(1):36–102.
Inda, Jonathan Xavier, and Renato Rosaldo, eds. 2002. *The Anthropology of Globalization: A Reader*. London: Blackwell Publishers.
International Monetary Fund. 2003. *Balance of Payments Statistics Yearbook 2002*. Washington: IMF Publications Services.
Jackson, J. L., Jr. 2001. *Harlemworld: Doing Race and Class in Contemporary Black America*. Chicago: University of Chicago Press.
Jacobs-Huey, Lanita. 2002. "The Natives Are Gazing and Talking Back: Reviewing the Problematics of Positionality, Voice, and Accountability among 'Native' Anthropologists." *American Anthropologist* 104(3):791–804.
James, Joy. 1993. *Spirit Space and Survival: African American Women in White Academe*. New York: Routledge.
Jefferson, Owen. 1972. *The Post-war Economic Development of Jamaica*. Kingston: University of the West Indies, Institute for Social and Economic Research.
Jones, Delmos. 1970. "Toward a Native Anthropology." *Human Organization* 29:251–259.
Jordan, June. 1997. *Kissing God Goodbye*. New York: Anchor Books.
Kahn, Aisha. 2001. "Journey to the Center of the Earth: The Caribbean as Master Symbol." *Cultural Anthropology* 16(3):271–302.
Kaplan, Caren. 1996. *Questions of Travel: Postmodern Discourses of Displacement*. Durham: Duke University Press.
Katzin, Margaret Fisher. 1960. "The Business of Higglering in Jamaica." *Social and Economic Studies* 9(3):297–331.
———. 1959. "The Jamaican Country Higgler." *Social and Economic Studies* 8(4):424–429.
Keith, Nelson W., and Novella Z. Keith. 1992. *The Social Origins of Democratic Socialism in Jamaica*. Philadelphia: Temple University Press.
Kelley, Robin D. G. 2003. *Freedom Dreams: The Black Radical Imagination*. Boston: Beacon Press.
———. 1997. *Yo Mama's Disfunktional*. Boston: Beacon.
———. 1996. *Race Rebels: Culture, Politics, and the Black Working Class*. Northampton, Massachusetts: Free Press.
———. 1993. "We Are Not What We Seem: Rethinking Black Working-Class Opposition in the Jim Crow South." *Journal of American History* 80:75–112.
Knauft, Bruce. 1996. *Genealogies for the Present in Cultural Anthropology*. New York: Routledge.
Knight, Franklin. 1978. *The Caribbean: The Genesis of a Fragmented Nationalism*. New York: Oxford University Press.
Knight, Franklin, and Colin A. Palmer, eds. 1989. *The Modern Caribbean*. Chapel Hill: University of North Carolina Press.
Ko, Dorothy. 2005. *Cinderella's Sisters: A Revisionist History of Footbinding*. Berkeley: University of California Press.

Kondo, Doreen. 1990. *Crafting Selves: Power, Discourse, and Identity in a Japanese Factory*. Chicago: University of Chicago Press.

Korda, Natasha. 2007. "Women's Informal Commerce and the 'All-Male' Stage." In *The Impact of Feminism in English Renaissance Studies*, edited by Dympna Callaghan. New York: Palgrave Macmillan.

Kovaleski, Serge. 1999. "In Jamaica, Shades of an Identity Crisis; Ignoring Health Risks, Blacks Increase Use of Skin Lighteners." *Washington Post*, August 5, A15.

Kuper, Adam. 1976. *Changing Jamaica*. London: Routledge & Kegan Paul.

Lake, Obiagele. 1998. *Rastafari Women: Subordination in the Midst of Liberation Theology*. Durham: Carolina Academic Press.

Lamming, George. 1970. *In the Castle of My Skin*. London: Longman Group Limited.

Larsen, Nella. [1929] 1997. *Passing*. New York: Penguin Books.

Leacock, Eleanor, and Etienne Mona, eds. 1980. *Women and Colonization*. New York: Praeger Publishers.

Le Franc, Elsie, ed. 2001. Consequences of Structural Adjustment: A Review of the Jamaican Experience. Kingston: University of the West Indies Press.

———. 1989. "Petty Trading and Labour Mobility: Higglers in the Kingston Metropolitan Area." In *Women and the Sexual Division of Labour in the Caribbean*, edited by Keith Hart. Kingston: Consortium Graduate School.

Leland, John. 1997. "When Rap Meets Reggae." In *Reggae, Rasta, Revolution: Jamaican Music from Ska to Dub*, edited by Chris Potash. New York: Schirmer Books.

Leo-Rhynie, Elsa. 1993. "The Jamaican Family: Continuity and Change." Kingston: Grace Kennedy Foundation.

Leslie, Charles. 1739. *A New History of Jamaica*. London: J. Hodges.

Lessinger, Johanna. 1988. "Trader Versus Developer: The Market Relocation Issue in an Indian City." In *Traders versus the State: Anthropological Approaches to Unofficial Economies*, edited by Gracia Clark. Boulder: Westview Press.

Levi-Strauss, Claude. 1950. "Introduction a l'Oeuvre de Marcel Mauss." In Marcel Mauss, *Sociologie et Anthropologie*. Paris: Presses Universitaires de France. (Also available as "Introduction to the Work of Marcel Mauss." London: Routledge and Kegan Paul, 1987).

———. [1962] 1966. *The Savage Mind*. Chicago: University of Chicago Press.

Levitt, Kari Polanyi. 1991. *The Origins and Consequences of Jamaica's Debt Crisis 1970–1990*. Kingston: Consortium Graduate School of the Social Sciences.

Levy, Howard S. 1966. *Chinese Footbinding: The History of a Curious Erotic Custom*. New York: John Weatherhill.

Lewin, Ellen, and William L. Leap, eds. 2002. *Out in Theory: The Emergence of Lesbian and Gay Anthropology*. Urbana: University of Illinois Press.

Lewis, Linden. 2003. "Caribbean Masculinity: Unpacking the Narrative." In *The Culture of Gender and Sexuality in the Caribbean*, edited by Linden Lewis. Gainesville: University Press of Florida.

Lewis, Matthew. 1834. *Journal of a West India Proprietor*. London: John Murray.

Lewis, Rupert. 1987. "Garvey's Forerunners: Love and Bedward." *Race and Class* 28(3):29–40.

Lindberg-Seyersted, Brita, ed. 1994. *Black and Female: Essays on Writings by Black Women in the Diaspora*. Oslo: Scandinavian University Press.

Lipsitz, George. 1998. *The Possessive Investment in Whiteness: How White People Profit from Identity Politics*. Philadelphia: Temple University Press.

Long, Edward. 1774. *The History of Jamaica*. 4 vols. London: T. Lowndes.

Lorde, Audre. 1990. "Is Your Hair Still Political?" *Essence* 21 (September): 40, 110.

———. 1984. *Sister Outsider*. Trumansburg, New York: Crossing Press.

Lowenthal, David. 1972. *West Indian Societies*. Oxford: Oxford University Press.

Lowenthal, David, and Lambros Comitas, eds. 1973. *Consequences of Class and Color: West Indian Perspectives*. Garden City: Anchor Books.

Lutz, Catherine. 1995. "The Gender of Theory." In *Women Writing Culture*, edited by Ruth Behar and Deborah A. Gordon. Berkeley: University of California Press.

Lyotard, Jean-Francois. [1979] 1984. *The Postmodern Condition: A Report on Knowledge*. Minneapolis: University of Minnesota Press.

MacGaffey, Janet, Vwakyanakazi Mukohya, Rukarangira wa Nkera, Brooke Grundfest, and Walu Engudu, eds. 1991. *The Real Economy of Zaire: The Contribution of Muggling and Other Unofficial Activities to National Wealth*. Philadelphia: University of Philadelphia Press.

Madden, R. R. 1835. *A Twelve Month's Residence in the West Indies*. London: James Cochran.

Mair, Lucille Mathurin. 1977. "Reluctant Matriarchs." *Savacou* 13:1–6.

Manley, Michael. 1982. *Jamaica: Struggle in the Periphery*. London: Third World Media, in association with Writers and Readers Publishing Cooperative Society.

———. 1974. *Politics of Change*. London: Deutsch.

Mantz, Jeffery W. 2003. *Lost in the Fire, Gained in the Ash: Moral Economies of Exchange in Dominica*. Ph.D. dissertation in Anthropology, University of Chicago, Chicago.

Marchand, M., and A. S. Runyan. 2000. *Gender and Global Restructuring: Sightings, Sites, and Resistances*. New York: Routledge.

Marcus, George. 1994. "After the Critique of Ethnography: Faith, Hope, and Charity, But the Greatest of These Is Charity." In *Assessing Cultural Anthropology*, edited by Robert Borofsky. New York: McGraw Hill.

Marshall, Woodville K. 1993. "'we be wise to many more things': Blacks' Hopes and Expectations of Emancipation." In *Caribbean Freedom: Economy and Society from Emancipation to the Present*, edited by Hilary Beckles and Verene Shepherd. Kingston: Ian Randle Publishers.

———. 1991. "Provision Ground and Plantation Labour in Four Windward Islands Competition for Resources during Slavery." *Slavery and Abolition* 12(1):48–67.

———. 1985. In *Rural Development in the Caribbean*, edited by P. I. Gomes. New York: St. Martin's Press.

Martin, Tony. 1991. "Women in the Garvey Movement." In *Garvey: His Work and Impact*, edited by Rupert Lewis and Patrick Bryan. Trenton: Africa World Press.

Martinez-Alier, Verena. 1974. *Marriage, Class, and Color in Nineteenth Century Cuba*. Cambridge: Cambridge University Press.

Mascia-Lees, Frances, Patricia Sharp, and Colleen Cohen. 1989. "The Postmodernist Turn in Anthropology: Cautions from a Feminist Perspective." *Signs* 15(1):7–33.

Mason, Beverly J. 1986. "Jamaican Working-Class Women: Producers and Reproducers." In *Slipping through the Cracks*, edited by Margaret Sims and Juliane Malveaux. New Brunswick: Transactions Books.

Massey, Doreen. 1994. *Space, Place, and Gender*. Minneapolis: University of Minnesota Press.

Massiah, Joycelin. 1989. "Women's Lives and Livelihoods: A View from the Commonwealth Caribbean." *World Development* 17(7):965–977.

———. 1986. "Work in the Lives of Caribbean Women." *Social and Economic Studies* 35(2):177–239.

Mathison, Gilbert. 1811. *Notices Respecting Jamaica, in 1808–1809–1810*. London: Printed by J. Stockdale.

Mathurin, Lucille. 1975. *The Rebel Woman in the British West Indies during Slavery*. Kingston: Institute of Jamaica.

Maurer, Bill M. 2000. *Recharting the Caribbean: Land, Law, and Citizenship in the British Virgin Islands*. Ann Arbor: University of Michigan Press.

McAfee, Kathy. 1991. *Storm Signals: Structural Adjustment and Development Alternatives in the Caribbean*. London: Zed Books Ltd.

McClaurin, Irma, ed. 2001a. *Black Feminist Anthropology: Theory, Politics, Praxis, and Poetics*. New Brunswick: Rutgers University Press.

———. 2001b. "Theorizing a Black Feminist Self in Anthropology: Toward an Autoethnographic Approach." In *Black Feminist Anthropology*, edited by Irma McClauren. New Brunswick: Rutgers University Press.

———. 1991. "Incongruities, Dissonance, and Contradiction in the Life of a Black Middle Class Woman." In *Uncertain Terms*, edited by Faye Ginsberg and Anna Tsing. Boston: Beacon Press.

McClintock, Anne. 1995. *Imperial Leather: Race, Gender, and Sexuality in the Colonial Contest*. New York: Routledge.

McDonald, Roderick A. 1993. *The Economy and Material Culture of Slaves: Goods and Chattels on the Slave Plantations of Jamaica and Louisiana*. Baton Rouge: Louisiana State University Press.

McFarlane-Gregory, Donna, and Thalia Ruddock-Kelly. 1993. *The Informal Commercial Importers of Jamaica*. Research Project on Jamaican Micro-Enterprises presented at the Macro Policy Conference. Kingston, June 28–30.

McGaffey, Janet, and Remy Bazenguissa-Ganga. 2000. *Congo-Paris: Transnational Traders on the Margins of the Law*. Bloomington: Indiana University Press.

McLean Petras, Elizabeth. 1988. *Jamaican Labor Migration: White Capital and Black Labor, 1850–1930*. London: Westview Press.

McMillan, Mona. 1957. *The Land of Look Behind*. London: Faber and Faber.

McRobbie, Angela. 1994. "Shut Up and Dance: Youth Culture and Changing Modes of Femininity." In *Postmoderism and Popular Culture*, edited by Angela McRobbie. London and New York: Routledge.

———. 1990. "Fame, Flashdance, and Fantasies of Achievement." In *Fabrications: Costume and the Female Body*, edited by Jane Gaines and Charlotte Herzog. New York : Routledge.

Medicine, Beatrice. 2001. *Learning to Be an Anthropologist and Remaining "Native": Selected Writings*. Edited by Sue-Ellen Jacobs. Urbana: University of Illinois Press.

Meeks, Brian. 1997. "The Political Movement in Jamaica: The Dimensions of Hegemonic Dissolution." *Race and Reason* 3:39–47.

Mendez, Jennifer Bickham. 2005. *From the Revolution to the Maquiladoras: Gender, Labor, and Globalization in Nicaragua*. Durham: Duke University Press.

Mercer, Kobena. 1994. *Welcome to the Jungle: New Positions in Black Cultural Studies*. New York: Routledge.

———. 1987. "Black Hair/Style Politics" *New Formations* 3:33–54.

Mies, Maria. 1986. *Patriarchy and Accumulation on a World Scale*. London: Zed Books.

———. 1982. *The Lace Makers of Narsapur: Indian Housewives Produce for the World Market*. London: Zed Books.

Miller, Daniel. 1994. *Modernity, An Ethnographic Approach: Dualism and Mass Consumption in Trinidad*. London: Berg Publishers.

———. 1990. "Style and Ontology in Trinidad." *Culture and History* 7:49–77.

Miller, Errol. 1988. "The Rise of the Matriarchy in the Caribbean." *Caribbean Quarterly* 34(3–4):1–21.

Miller, Marilyn. 2005. "*Guayaberismo* and the Essence of Cool." In *The Latin American Fashion Reader*, edited by Regina A. Root. New York: Berg.

Min-Ha, Trinh. 1990. "Not You/Like You." In *Making Face, Making Soul = Haciendo Caras*, edited by Gloria Anzaldua. San Francisco: Aunt Lute Books.

Mintz, Sidney W. 1993. "Black Women, Economic Roles, and Cultural Traditions." In *Caribbean Freedom*, edited by Hilary Beckles and Verene Shepherd. Kingston: Ian Randle Publishers.

———. 1985. *Sweetness and Power*. New York: Viking.

———. 1981. "Economic Role and Cultural Tradition." In *The Black Woman Cross-Culturally*, edited by Filomina Chioma Steady. Cambridge: Schenkman Publishing Company.

———. 1974. *Caribbean Transformations*. New York: Columbia University Press.

———. 1971. "The Caribbean as a Socio-Cultural Area." In *Peoples and Cultures of the Caribbean: An Anthropological Reader*, edited by Michael Horowitz. Garden City: Natural History Press.

———. 1965. "The Jamaican Internal Marketing Pattern: Some Notes and Hypotheses." *Social and Economic Studies* 14(1):95–105.

———. 1959. "Internal Marketing Systems as Mechanism of Social Articulation." *Proceedings of the American Ethnological Society* 20–30.

Mintz, Sydney, and Sally Price, eds. 1985. *Caribbean Contours*. Baltimore: Johns Hopkins University Press.

Mirza, Heidi Safia, ed. 1997. *Black British Feminism: A Reader*. London: Routledge.

Mohammed, Patricia, ed. 2002. *Gendered Realities: Essays in Caribbean Feminist Thought*. Kingston: University of the West Indies Press.

————. 1998. "Towards Indigenous Feminist Theorizing in the Caribbean." *Feminist Review* 59:6–33.

————. 1994. "Nuancing the Feminist Discourse in the Caribbean." *Social and Economic Studies* 43(3):135–167.

Mohanty, Chandra T. 2003. *Feminism without Borders: Decolonizing Theory, Practicing Solidarity.* Durham: Duke University Press.

Mohanty, Chandra Talpade, Ann Russo, and Lourdes Torres, eds. 1991. *Third World Women and the Politics of Feminism.* Bloomington: Indiana University Press.

Momsen, Janet. 1988. "Gender Roles in Caribbean Agricultural Labour." In *Labour in the Caribbean,* edited by Michael Cross and Gad Heuman. London: McMillan.

Moore, Henrietta. 1988. *Feminism and Anthropology.* Oxford: Basil Blackwell.

Moraga, Cherrie, and Gloria Anzaldua, eds. 1981. *This Bridge Called My Back: Writings by Radical Women of Color.* New York: Kitchen Table: Women of Color Press.

Morrissey, Marietta. 1989. *Slave Women in the New World: Gender Stratification in the Caribbean.* Lawrence: University Press of Kansas.

Moser, Caroline, O. N. 1980. "Why the Poor Remain Poor: The Experience of Bogota Market Traders in the 1970's." *Journal of Interamerican Studies and World Affairs* 22(3):365–338.

————. 1978. "Informal Sector or Petty Commodity Production: Dualism or Dependence in Urban Development." *World Development* 6(1):1041–1064.

Mulero Diaz, Maria D. 2000. *Strategies for Survival in a Changing Economic Structure: Puerto Rican Women in the Informal Economy.* Doctoral Thesis in Philosophy, Temple University, Philadelphia, Pennsylvania.

Mullings, Leith. 1997. *On Our Own Terms: Race, Class, and Gender in the Lives of African American Women.* New York: Routledge.

Murphy, Joseph. 1994. *Working the Spirit: Ceremonies of the African Diaspora.* Boston: Beacon Press.

Narayan, Kirin. 1995. "How Native Is a 'Native' Anthropologist?" *American Anthropologist* 95:671–686.

Nash, June, and Maria Patricia Fernandez-Kelley, eds. 1983. *Women and Men and the International Division of Labor.* Albany: State University of New York Press.

Needham, Merrick. 1997. "Mourning for Manley...Guidelines for the Public." *Gleaner,* March 10, p. A2.

Nettleford, Rex. 1995. "Fancy Dress and the Roots of Culture: From Jonkunnu to Dancehall." *Gleaner,* July 18, 1D, 16D.

————. 1979. *Caribbean Cultural Identity: The Case of Jamaica.* Los Angeles: Latin American Center Publication, University of California.

————. 1972. *Identity, Race, and Protest in Jamaica.* New York: Morrow Books.

Nicholls, David. 1979. *From Dessalines to Duvalier: Race, Colour, and National Independence in Haiti.* New Brunswick: Rutgers University Press.

Noble, Denise. 2005. "Remembering Bodies, Healing Histories: The Emotional Politics of Everyday Freedom." In *Making Race Matter: Bodies, Space, and Identity,* edited by Clare Alexander and Carline Knowles. New York: Palgrave.

Nugent, Maria. 1904. *Lady Nugent's Journal.* Edited by Frank Cundall. London: Adam and Charles Black.

Nurse, Keith. 2005. *The Masculinization of Poverty and the Poverty of Masculinism: Gender, Geoculture, and Violence.* Occasional Paper Institute for International Integration Studies, University of Dublin, Ireland.

Oliver, Cynthia. 2003. *Queen of the Virgins: Queen Shows, The Popular Women's Theatre of the U.S. Virgin Islands.* Ph.D. diss., Department of Performance Studies, New York University, New York.

Olivier, Lord. 1942. *Jamaica: The Blessed Island.* London: Faber & Faber.

Olwig, Karen Fog. 1985. *Cultural Adaptation and Resistance on St. John: Three Centuries of Afro-Caribbean Life.* Gainesville: University of Florida Press.

Olwig, Karen Fog, and Kirsten Hastrup, eds. 1997. *Siting Culture: The Shifting Anthropological Object.* New York: Routledge.

Omi, Michael and Howard Winant. 1994. *Racial Formation in the United States: From the 1960s to the 1990s.* New York: Routledge.

Ong, Aihwa. 1999. *Flexible Citizenship: The Cultural Logics of Trasnationality.* Durham: Duke University Press.

———. 1987. *Spirits of Resistance and Capitalist Discipline: Factory Women in Malaysia.* Albany: State University of New York Press.

Ortiz, Fernando. 1995. *Cuban Counterpoint: Tobacco and Sugar.* Durham: Duke University Press.

Ortner, Sherry B. 1997. "Identities: The Hidden Life of Class." *Journal of Anthropological Research* 54(1):1–17.

———. 1990. "Gender Hegemonies." *Cultural Critique* 14:35–80.

Owens, Joseph. 1976. *Dread: The Rastafarians of Jamaica.* Kingston: Sangster.

Owusu, Maxwell. 1996. "Inside of History: Roots and Redemption: Reflections on the Paradoxes of Synthetic Nationalism in Jamaica." Paper Presented at the International Conference on Caribbean Culture in Honour of Professor the Honorable Rex Nettleford, OM, University of the West Indies at Kingston, March 3–6.

Page, Enoch. 1999. "No Black Public Sphere in White Public Space: Racialized Information and Hi-Tech Diffusion on the Global African Diaspora." *Transforming Anthropology* 8(1–2):111–128.

———. 1988. "Dialogic Principles of Interactive Learning in the Ethnographic Relationship." *Journal of Anthropological Research* 44(2):163–181.

Paquet, Sandra Pouchet. 1992. "The Enigma of Arrival: The Wonderful Adventures of Mary Seacole in Many Lands." *African American Review* 26:651–663.

Parrenas, Rhacel Salazar. 2001. "Transgressing the Nation-State: The Partial Citizenship and 'Imagined Global Community,' of Migrant Filipina Domestic Workers." *Signs* 26(4):1129–1154.

Parry, John H. 1955. "Plantation and Provision Ground: An Historical Sketch of the Introduction of Food Crops into Jamaica." *Revista de Historia de America* 39:1–20.

Patai, Daphne. 1992. "U.S. Academics and Third World Women: Is Ethical Research Possible." In *Women's Words,* edited by Daphne Patai. New York: Routledge.

————, ed. and trans. 1988. *Brazilian Women Speak: Contemporary Life Stories.* New Brunswick: Rutgers University Press.

Patterson, Orlando. 1969. *The Sociology of Slavery: An Analysis of the Origins, Development, and Structure of Negro Slave Society in Jamaica.* Ruthford: Fairleigh Dickinson University Press.

Phillips, Evelyn Newman, ed. 2003. Special issue of *Transforming Anthropology* on "Black Hair and Beauty in the African Diaspora." 11(2).

Pierce, Paulette, and Brackette F. Williams. 1996. "And Your Prayers Shall Be Answered through the Womb of a Woman: Insurgent Masculine Redemption and the Nation of Islam." *Woman Out of Place: The Gender of Agency and the Race of Nationality*, edited by Brackette Williams. New York: Routledge.

Pinnock, Amillah. 1997. *The Roots of the Problem: An Exploration of the Social Politics of Hair in Contemporary Jamaica.* Honors thesis, Anthropology Department, Harvard University, Cambridge, Massachusetts.

Polanyi, Karl. 1957. "The Economy as Instituted Process." In *Trade and Markets in the Early Empires*, edited by Karl Polanyi, C. Arensburg, and H. Pearson. New York: Aldine.

Popkin, Samuel L. 1979. *The Rational Peasant: The Political Economy of Rural Society in Vietnam.* Berkeley: University of California Press.

Portes, Alejandro, M. Castells, and L. A. Benton, eds. 1989. *The Informal Economy: Studies in Advanced and Less Developed Countries.* Baltimore: Johns Hopkins University Press.

Portes, Alejandro, Carlos Dore-Cabral, and Patricia Landolt, eds. 1997. *The Urban Caribbean: Transition to the New Global Economy.* Baltimore: Johns Hopkins University Press.

Post, Ken. 1978. *Arise Ye Starvelings: The Jamaican Labour Rebellion of 1938 and Its Aftermath.* The Hague: Martinus Nijhoff.

Powell, Dorian. 1986. "Caribbean Women and Their Response to Familial Experiences." *Social and Economic Studies* 35(2):83–130.

Pratt, Mary Louise. 1992. *Imperial Eyes: Travel Writing and Transculturation.* London: Routledge.

————. 1991. "Arts of the Contact Zone." *Profession* 91:33–40.

Pred, Allan, and Michael Watts. 1992. *Reworking Modernity: Capitalisms and Symbolic Discontent.* New Brunswick: Rutgers University Press.

Price, Charles. 2004. "What the Zeeks Uprising Reveals: Development Issues, Moral Economy, and the Urban Lumpenproletariat in Jamaica." *Urban Anthropology* 33(1):73–113.

Price, Richard. 1996. *Maroon Societies: Rebel Slave Communities in the Americas.* Baltimore: Johns Hopkins University Press.

————. 1990a. *Alibi's World.* Baltimore: Johns Hopkins University Press.

————. 1990b. *Ethnographic History and Caribbean Pasts.* Working paper no. 9. College Park: Department of Spanish and Portuguese, University of Maryland.

Price-Mars, Jean. [1928] 1983. *So Spoke the Uncle.* Washington, D.C.: Three Continents Press.

Prosser, Jay. 2001. "Skin Memories." In *Thinking Through the Skin (Transformations)*, edited by Sara Ahmed and Jackie Stacey. New York: Routledge.

Rahier, Jean Metuba. 1999. *Representations of Blackness and the Performance of Identities*. Westport: Bergin and Garvey.

———. 1998. "Blackness, the Racial/Spatial Order, Migrations, and Miss Ecuador 1995–6." *American Anthropologist* 100(2):421–430.

Ramsay, Alva. 1969. "Jamaica Will Become a Fundamentally Black Society." *West Indian Sportsman*. November–December, 28.

Ray, Ella Maria. 1999. *Standing in the Lion's Shadow: Jamaican Rastafari Women Reconstructing Their African Ancestry*. Ph.D. diss., Department of Anthropology, John Hopkins University, Baltimore.

Reddock, Rhoda. 1998. "Contestations over National Culture in Trinidad and Tobago: Considerations of Ethnicity, Class, and Gender." In *Caribbean Portraits: Essays on Gender Ideologies and Identities*, edited by Christine Barrow. Kingston: Ian Randle.

———. 1985. "Indian Women and Indentureship in Trinidad and Tobago: 1845–1917." *Economic and Political Weekly* 20(43):79–87.

Reid, Egbert. 1989. "The Informal Commercial Importers: Their Origins and Their Problems." In *Proceedings of the Symposium on Higglering in Jamaica, Higglering/Sidewalk Vending/Informal Commercial Trading in Jamaican Economy*. Kingston: Department of Economics, University of the West Indies.

Reynolds, Tracey. 1997. "(Mis)representing the black (super)woman." In *Black British Feminism*, edited by Heidi Safia Mirza. New York: Routledge.

Richardson, Laurel. 1990. *Writing Strategies: Reaching Diverse Audiences*. Newbury Park, CA: Sage Publications.

Rigby, Peter. 1996. *African Images: Racism and the End of Anthropology*. London: Berg.

Risech, Flavio. 1995. "Political and Cultural Cross-Dressing: Negotiating a Second Generation Cuban-American Identity." In *Bridges to Cuba/Puentes a Cuba*, edited by Ruth Behar. Ann Arbor: University of Michigan Press.

Robertson, Glory. 1995. "Pictorial Source for Nineteenth Century Women's History: Dress as a Mirror of Attitudes of Women." In *Engendering History: Caribbean Women in Historical Perspective*, edited by Verene Shepherd, Bridget Brereton, and Barbara Bailey. Kingston: Ian Randle.

———. 1987. "Advertisements of Clothes in Kingston: 1897–1914." *Jamaica Journal* 20(4):32–38.

Robotham, Donald. 2001. "Blackening the Jamaican Nation: The Travails of a Black Bourgeoisie in a Globalized World." *Identities* 7(1):1–37.

———. 1985. "The Why of a Cockatoo?" *Social and Economic Studies* 34(2):111–151.

———. 1980. "Pluralism as Ideology." *Social and Economic Studies* 29:69–89.

Rodney, Walter. 1969. *The Grounding with My Brothers*. London: Bogle-Louverture Publications.

Rodriguez, Cheryl. 2001. "A Homegirl Goes Home: Black Feminism and the Lure of Native Anthropology." In *Black Feminist Anthropology*, edited by Irma McClauren. New Brunswick: Rutgers University Press.

Rosaldo, Renato. 1989. *Culture and Truth: The Remaking of Social Analysis*. Boston: Beacon Press.

Roscoe, Paul. 2003. "Margaret Meade, Reo Fortune, and Mountain Arapesh Warfare." *American Anthropologist* 105(3): 581–591.

Rose, Tricia. 2004. *Longing to Tell: Black Women Talk about Sexuality and Intimacy.* New York: Picador.

———. 1994. *Black Noise: Rap Music and Black Culture in Contemporary America.* Hanover: Wesleyan University Press.

Ross, Andrew. 1998. *Real Love in Pursuit of Cultural Justice.* New York: New York University Press.

———. 1991. "Head to Toe: On Tribalism in Effect." *Art Forum* 30 (November):22–24.

Roumain, Jacques. 1978. *Masters of the Dew.* Portsmouth, New Hampshire: Heinemann.

Rouse, Roger. 1991. "Mexican Migration and the Social Space of Postmodernism." *Diaspora* 1(1):8–23.

Rowe, Maureen. 1998. "Rastawoman as Rebel: Case Studies in Jamaica." In *Chanting Down Babylon: The Rastafarian Reader,* edited by Nathaniel Samuel Murell and William D Spencer. Philadelphia: Temple University Press.

Safa, Helen I. 1995. *The Myth of the Male Breadwinner: Women and Industrialization in the Caribbean.* Boulder: Westview Press.

———. 1986. "Economic Autonomy and Sexual Equality in Caribbean Society." *Social and Economic Studies* 35(3):1–21.

Salzman, Philip Carl. 2002. "On Reflexivity." *American Anthropologist* 104(3): 805–813.

Sander, Kirsten. 1992. *Action and Reaction: The Linkages between Structural Adjustment Programs and the Informal Economy in Jamaica.* Masters thesis, Queens University, Kingston, Ontario.

Sanjek, Roger. 1971. "Brazilian Racial Terms: Some Aspects of Meaning and Learning." *American Anthropologist* 73(5):1126–1143.

Sassen, Saskia. 1991. *The Global City.* Princeton: Princeton University Press.

Satchell, Vernon. 1992. "Government Land Policies in Jamaica during the Late 19th Century." In *Plantation Economy, Land Reform, and the Peasantry in a Historical Perspective 1838–1890,* edited by Claus Stolbert and Swithin Wilmot. Kingston: Friedrich Ebert Siftung.

Saunders, Gail. 2001. "Slavery and Cotton Culture in the Bahamas." In *Working Slavery, Pricing Freedom: Perspectives from the Caribbean, Africa and the African Diaspora,* edited by Verene Shepherd. New York: Palgrave.

Saunders, Pat. 2003. "Is Not Everything Good to Eat, Good to Talk: Sexual Economy and Dancehall Music in the Global Market Place." *Small Axe* 7(1):95–115.

Scheper-Hughes, Nancy. 1992. *Death without Weeping: The Violence of Everyday Life in Brazil.* Berkeley: University of California Press.

Scott, David. 2000. "The Permanence of Pluralism." In *Without Guarantees: In Honour of Stuart Hall,* edited by Paul Gilroy, Lawrence Grossberg, and Angela McRobbie. New York: Verso.

Scott, James. 2005. Afterword to "Moral Economies, State Spaces, and Categorical Violence." *American Anthropologist* 107(3):395–403.

———. 1990. *Domination and the Arts of Resistance*. New Haven: Yale University Press.

———. 1987. *Weapons of the Weak: Everyday Forms of Peasant Resistance*. New Haven: Yale University Press.

———. 1976. *The Moral Economy of the Peasant: Rebellion and Subsistence in South East Asia*. New Haven: Yale University Press.

Scott, Joan. 1986. "Gender: A Useful Category of Historical Analysis." *American Historical Review* 91(5):1053–1301.

Scott, Michael. 1852. *Tom Cringle's Log*. Edinburgh: William Blackwood.

Scott, Rebecca J. 1985. *Slave Emancipation in Cuba: The Transition to Free Labor, 1860–1899*. Pittsburgh: University of Pittsburgh Press

Seacole, Mary. [1857] 1988. *The Wonderful Adventures of Mrs. Seacole in Many Lands*. New York: Oxford University Press.

Seligman, Linda J. 2004. *Peruvian Street Lives: Culture, Power, and Economy among Market Women of Cuzco*. Urbana: University of Illinois Press.

———, ed. 2001. *Women Traders in Cross Cultural Perspective: Mediating Identities, Marketing Wares*. Stanford: Stanford University Press.

Senior, Olive. 1991. *Working Miracles: Women's Lives in the English-Speaking Caribbean*. Kingston: Institute of Social and Economic Research (Eastern Caribbean); London: James Currey; Bloomington: Indiana University Press.

Sewell, William G. 1861. *The Ordeal of Free Labour in the British West Indies*. New York: Harpers Brothers.

Sharpley-Whiting, T. Denean. 1999. *The Black Venus: Sexualized Savages, Primal Fears, and Primitive Narratives in French*. Durham: Duke University Press.

Shaw, Carolyn Martin. 1995. *Colonial Inscriptions: Race, Sex, and Class in Kenya*. Minneapolis: University of Minnesota Press.

Sheller, Mimi. 2005. "Citizenship and the Making of Caribbean Freedom." *NACLA* 38(4):30–33.

———. 2004. "Automotive Emotions: Feeling the Car." *Theory, Culture, and Society* 21:221–242.

———. 2003. *Consuming the Caribbean: From Arawaks to Zombies*. London: Routledge.

———. 1999. *Democracy after Slavery: Black Publics and Peasant Radicalism in Haiti and Jamaica*. London: MacMillan Press.

———. 1998. "Quasheba, Mother, Queen: Black Women's Public Leadership and Political Protest in Post-emancipation Jamaica." *Slavery and Abolition* 19(3):90–117.

Sheller, Mimi, and John Urry. 2006a. "Introduction: Mobile Cities, Urban Mobilities." In *Mobile Technologies of the City*, edited by Mimi Sheller and John Urry. London: Routledge.

———. 2006b. "The New Mobilities Paradigm." *Environment and Planning A* 38(2).

———. 2003. "Mobile Transformations of 'Public' and 'Private' Life." *Theory, Culture, and Society* 20(3):107–125.

Shepherd, Verene A. 2001. *Working Slavery, Pricing Freedom: Perspectives from the Caribbean, Africa, and the African Diaspora*. New York: Palgrave Press.

———. 1994. *Transients to Settlers: The Experience of Indians in Jamaica, 1845–1950*. Leeds: Peepal Tree Books.

Shepherd, Verene A., and Glen L. Richards, eds. 2002. *Questioning Creole: Creolisation Discourses in Caribbean Culture*. Kingston: Ian Randle Publishers.

Silverblatt, Irene. 1991. "Interpreting Women in States: New Feminist Ethnology." In *Gender at Crossroads of Knowledge: Feminist Anthropology in the Postmodern Era*, edited by Micaela di Leonardo. Berkeley: University of California Press.

Simmonds, Kimberly. 2001. "A Passion for Sameness: Encountering a Black Feminist Self in Fieldwork in the Dominican Republic." In *Black Feminist Anthropology: Theory, Politics, Praxis, and Poetics*, edited by Irma McClaurin. New Brunswick: Rutgers University Press.

Simmonds, Lorna. 1985. "Higglers, Hucksters, and Hirelings: Urban Female Slaves in the Internal Market System in Jamaica 1778-1834." Paper presented at Women and Society, Social History Workshop, Kingston, University of the West Indies, November 8-9.

Simms, Glenda. 2004. "Slam Bam: A Saga of Consorts and Madonnas." *Gleaner*, August 22, p. G4.

Sims, Rudine. 1982. *Shadow and Substance: Afro-American Experience in Contemporary Children's Fiction*. Urbana: National Council of Teachers of English.

Sistren with Honor Ford-Smith. 1987. *Lionheart Gal: Life Stories of Jamaican Women*. Toronto: Sister Vision Press.

Sivaramakrishnan, K. 2005. "Some Intellectual Genealogies for the Concept of Everyday Resistance." *American Anthropologist* 107(3):346–356.

Sives, Amanda. 2002. "Changing Patrons, from Politician to Drug Don: Clientelism in Downtown Kingston." *Latin American Perspectives* 29(5):66–89.

Skeggs, Beverly. 2004. *Class, Self, Culture*. London: Routledge.

———. 1997. *Formations of Class and Gender: Becoming Respectable*. London: Sage Publications.

Skelton, Tracy. 1998. Doing Violence Doing Harm: British Media Representations of Jamaican Yardies. *Small Axe* 2(3):27–48.

Slocum, Karla. 2001. "Negotiating Identity and Black Feminist Politics in Caribbean Research." In *Black Feminist Anthropology: Theory, Politics, Praxis, and Poetics*, edited by Irma McClaurin. New Brunswick: Rutgers University Press.

Slocum, Karla, and Deborah Thomas. 2003. "Rethinking Global and Area Studies: Insights from Caribbeanist Anthropology." *American Anthropologist* 105(3):553–565.

Small, Geoff. 1995. *Ruthless: The Global Rise of the Yardies*. London: Warner Books.

Smart, Alan, and Josephine Smart. 2005. *Petty Capitalists and Globalization: Flexibility, Entrepreneurship, and Economic Development*. Albany: State University of New York Press.

Smith, Jennie Marcelle. 2001. *When the Hands Are Many: Community Organization and Social Change in Rural Haiti*. Ithaca: Cornell University Press.

Smith, M. G. 1984. *Culture, Race, and Class in the Commonwealth Caribbean.* Kingston: Department of Extra-Mural Studies, University of the West Indies.

———. 1965. *The Plural Society in the British West Indies.* Berkeley: University of California Press.

Smith, Raymond T. 1973. "The Matrifocal Family." In *The Character of Kinship,* edited by J. Goody. Cambridge: Cambridge University Press.

Soas, Norma. 1993. "Fashion of the Times." *Lifestyle* no. 27 (July–August): 7.

———. 1992. "Mourning as a Spectator Sport." *Gleaner,* March 15, 10A.

Sobo, Elisa Janine. 1993. *One Blood: The Jamaican Body.* Albany: State University of New York Press.

Spivak, Giyatri. 1988. "Can the Subaltern Speak?" In *Marxism and the Interpretation of Culture,* edited by Cary Nelson and Lawrence Grossberg. Urbana: University of Illinois Press.

Stacey, Judith. 1988. "Can There Be a Feminist Ethnography?" *Women's Studies International Forum* 11(1):21–27.

Stallybrass, Peter, and Allon White. 1986. *The Politics and Poetics of Transgression.* Ithaca: Cornell University Press.

Stanley, Sonjah Niaah. 2004. "Making Space: Kingston's Dancehall Culture and Its Philosophy of 'Boundarylessness.'" *African Identities* 2(2):117–132.

Steady, Filomina Chioma, ed. 1981. *The Black Woman Cross-Culturally.* Cambridge: Schenkman Publishing Company.

Steedman, Carolyn. 1985. *Landscape for a Good Woman: A Story of Two Lives.* New Brunswick: Rutgers University Press.

Stephens, Evelyne Huber, and John D. Stephens. 1986. *Democratic Socialism in Jamaica: The Political Movement and Social Transformation in Dependent Capitalism.* London: Macmillan.

Stewart, John. 1823. *A View from the Past and Present History of the Island of Jamaica.* Edinburgh: Oliver and Boyd.

———. [1808] 1971. *An Account of Jamaica and Its Inhabitants.* London: Black Heritage Library Collection.

Stoler, Ann L. 2002. *Carnal Knowledge and Imperial Power: Race and the Intimate in Colonial Rule.* Berkeley: University of California Press.

———. 1996. *Race and the Education of Desire: Foucault's History of Sexuality and the Colonial Order of Things.* Durham: Duke University Press.

———. 1985. *Capitalism and Confrontation in Sumatra's Plantation Belt: 1870–1979.* New Haven: Yale University Press.

Stoller, Paul. 2002. *Money Has No Smell: The Africanization of New York City.* Chicago: University of Chicago Press.

———. 1989. *The Taste of Ethnographic Things.* Philadelphia: University of Pennsylvania Press.

Stolzoff, Norman C. 2000. *Wake the Town and Tell the People: Dancehall Culture in Jamaica.* Philadelphia: Duke University Press.

Stone, Carl. 1991. "Race and Economic Power in Jamaica." In *Garvey: His Work and Impact,* edited by Rupert Lewis and Patrick Bryan. Trenton: Africa World Press.

———. 1989. *Politics versus Economics: The 1989 Elections in Jamaica.* Kingston: Heinemann.

———. 1986. *Class, State, and Democracy in Jamaica.* New York: Praeger.

———. 1980. *Democracy and Clientelism in Jamaica.* New Brunswick: Transaction Books.

———. 1974. *Race, Class, and Politics in Urban Jamaica.* Kingston: University of the West Indies, Institute for Social and Economic Research.

———. 1973. *Class, Race, and Political Behaviour in Urban Jamaica.* Kingston: University of the West Indies, Institute of Social and Economic Research.

Stone, Carl, and Aggrey Brown, eds. 1977. *Essays on Power and Change in Jamaica.* Kingston: Jamaica Publishing House.

Straight, Bilinda. 2007. *Miracles and Extraordinary Experience in Northern Kenya.* Philadelphia: University of Pennsylvania Press.

Sturge, J., and T. Harvey. 1838. *The West Indies in 1837.* London: Hamilton Adams and Company.

Sudarkasa, Niara. 1973. *Where Women Work: A Study of Yoruba Women in the Marketplace and in the Home.* Ann Arbor: University of Michigan Press.

Sutton, Constance. 1987. "The Caribbeanization of New York City and the Emergence of a Transnational Socio-Cultural System." In *Caribbean Life in New York City: Socio-cultural Dimensions,* edited by Constance Sutton and Elsa Chaney. New York: CMS.

Tarlo, Emma. 1994. *Clothing Matters: Dress and Identity in India.* Chicago: University of Chicago Press.

Tate, Shirley. 2001. "'That Is My Star of David': Skin, Abjection, and Hybridity." In *Thinking through the Skin (Transformations),* edited by Sara Ahmed and Jackie Stacey. New York: Routledge.

Taussig, Michael. 1980. *The Devil and Commodity Fetishism in Latin America.* Chapel Hill: University of North Carolina Press.

Taylor, Alicia. 1988. *Women Traders in Jamaica: The Informal Commercial Importers.* Paper prepared for the Economic Commission for Latin America and the Caribbean. Port of Spain, Trinidad.

Taylor, Charles. 1955. *Colour and Class: A Comparative Study of Jamaican Status Groups.* Ph.D. diss., Yale University.

Taylor, Frank. 1993. *The Hell with Paradise.* Pittsburgh: University of Pittsburgh Press.

Thomas, Clive E. 1997. "On Reconstructing A Political Economy of the Caribbean." In *Ethnicity, Race, and Nationality in the Caribbean,* edited by Juan Manuel Carrion. San Juan: Institute of Caribbean Studies, University of Puerto Rico.

———. 1988. *The Poor and the Powerless.* London: Latin American Bureau.

Thomas, Deborah A. 2004. *Modern Blackness: Nationalism, Globalization, and the Politics of Culture in Jamaica.* Durham: Duke University Press.

Thompson, E. P. 1991. *Customs in Common.* London: Merlin Press.

———. 1971. "The Moral Economy of the English Crowd in the Eighteenth Century." *Past and Present* 50:76–136.

————. 1963. *The Making of the English Working Class*. London: Vintage Books.

Thornton, Sarah. 1996. *Club Cultures: Music, Media, and Subcultural Capital*. Hanover: Wesleyan University Press.

Tokman, Victor. 1992. *Beyond Regulation: The Informal Economy in Latin America*. Boulder: Lynne Rienner Publishers.

Torres, Arlene. 1998. "La Gran Familia Puertorriquena 'Ej Prieta de Belda' (The Great Puerto Rican Family Is Really Really Black)." In *Blackness in Latin America and the Caribbean*, edited by Arlene Torres and Norman Whitten. Bloomington: Indiana University Press.

Torres-Saillant, Silvio. 1998. "The Tribulations of Blackness: Stages in Dominican Racial Identity." *Latin American Perspectives* 25(3): 126–146.

Transberg, Karen Hansen. 2000. *Salaula: The World of Secondhand Clothing in Zambia*. Chicago: University of Chicago Press.

Trollope, Anthony. 1860. *The West Indies and the Spanish Main*. New York: Harper and Brothers.

Trouillot, Michel-Rolph. 2003. *Global Transformations: Anthropology and the Modern World*. New York: Palgrave McMillan.

————. 1995. *Silencing the Past: Power and the Production of History*. Boston: Beacon Press.

————. 1992. "The Caribbean Region: An Open Frontier in Anthropological Research." *Annual Review of Anthropology* 21:19–42.

————. 1991. "Anthropology and the Savage Slot." In *Recapturing Anthropology*, edited by R. Fox. Santa Fe: Schooldr of American Research Press.

————. 1988. *Peasants and Capital: Dominica in the World Economy*. Baltimore: Johns Hopkins University Press.

Tsing, Anna Lowenhaupt. 2005. *Friction: An Ethnography of Global Connection*. Princeton: Princeton University Press.

————. 1993. *In the Real of the Diamond Queen: Marginality in an Out-of-the-Way Place*. Princeton: Princeton University Press.

Tuhiwai Smith, Linda. 1999. *Decolonizing Methodologies: Research and Indigenous Peoples*. New York: Palgrave, St. Martin's Press.

Turner, Terrence. 1980. "The Social Skin." In *Not Work Alone*, edited by Jeremy Cherfas and Roger Lewin. London: Temple Smith.

Twine, France Winddance. 1998. *Racism in a Racial Democracy*. New Brunswick: Rutgers University Press.

Ulysse, Gina A. 2006a. "Papa, Patriarchy, and Power: Snapshots of a Good Haitian Girl, Feminism and Dyasporic Dreams." *Journal of Haitian Studies* 12(1):24–47.

————. 2006b. *Loving Haiti, Loving Vodou*. Unpublished manuscript.

————. 2003. "Cracking the Silence on Reflexivity: Negotiating Identities, Fieldwork, and the Dissertation in Ann Arbor and Kingston." In *Decolonizing the Academy: Diaspora Theory and African New World Studies*, edited by Carole Boyce Davies. Princeton, NJ: Africa World Press.

————. 2002. "Conquering Duppies in Kingston: Miss Tiny and Me, Fieldwork Conflicts and Being Loved and Rescued." *Anthropology and Humanism* 27(1): 10–26.

————. 1999a. "Uptown Ladies and Downtown Women: Female Representations of Class and Color in Jamaica." In *Representations of Blackness and the Performance of Identities*, edited by Jean M. Rahier. Westport, Connecticut: Bergin and Garvey.

————. 1999b. *Updown Ladies and Downtown Women: Informal Commercial Importing and the Social/Symbolic Politics of Class and Color in Jamaica.* Doctoral dissertation, Department of Anthropology, University of Michigan.

Valentine, Betty Lou. 1978. *Hustlin' and Other Hard Work: Life Styles in the Ghetto.* New York: Free Press.

Vianello, Andrea. 2006. "Courtly Lady or Courtesan? The Venetian Chopine in the Renaissance." In *Shoes: A History from Sandals to Sneakers*, edited by Giorgio Riello and Peter McNeil. Oxford: Berg.

Vigil, James Diego. 2003. "Urban Violence and Street Gangs." *Annual Review of Anthropology* 32:225–242.

Visweswaran, Kamala. 1994. *Fictions of Feminist Ethnography.* Minneapolis: University of Minnesota Press.

Wade, Peter. 1993. *Blackness and Race Mixture: The Dynamics of Racial Identity in Columbia.* Baltimore: Johns Hopkins University Press.

Wallerstein, I. 1974. *The Modern World System.* New York: Academic Press.

Waters, Anita. 1985. *Race, Class, and Political Symbols: Rastafari and Reggae in Jamaican Politics.* New Brunswick: Transactions Books.

Weiner, A., and J. Schneider, eds. 1989. *Cloth and the Human Experience.* Washington, DC: Smithsonian Press.

Weismantel, Mary. 2001. *Cholas and Pishtacos: Stories of Race and Sex in the Andes.* Chicago: University of Chicago Press.

Wekker, Gloria. 1997. "One Finger Does Not Drink Okra Soup: Afro-Surinamese Women and Critical Agency." In *Feminist Genealogies, Colonial Legacies, Democratic Futures*, edited by M. Jacqui Alexander and Chandra Talpade Mohanty. New York: Routledge.

Weston, Kath. 1997a. "The Virtual Anthropologist." In *Anthropological Locations: Boundaries and Grounds of a Field Science*, edited by Akhil Gupta and James Ferguson. Berkeley: University of California Press.

————. [1991] 1997b *Families We Choose.* New York: Columbia University Press.

White, Shane, and Graham White. 1998. *Stylin': African-American Expressive Culture from Its Beginnings to the Zoot Suit.* Ithaca: Cornell University Press.

Whitten, N. E., Jr., and A. Torres. 1998. "To Forge the Future in the Fires of the Past." *Blackness in Latin America and the Caribbean: Social Dynamics and Cultural Transformations.* Vols. 1 and 2. Bloomington: Indiana University Press.

Wilk, Richard. 1996. "Introduction." In *Beauty Queens on the Global Stage: Gender, Contests, and Power*, edited by Colleen Ballerino Cohen, Richard Wilk, and Beverly Stoeltje. New York: Routledge.

————. 1990. "Consumer Goods as a Dialogue about Development." *Culture and History* 7:79–100.

Williams, Brackette. 1996. *Women Out of Place: The Gender of Agency and the Race of Nationality.* London and New York: Routledge.

————. 1995. "The Public I/Eye: Conducting Fieldwork to Do Homework on Homelessness and Begging in Two U.S. cities." *Current Anthropology* 36 (February):45–47.

————. 1991. *Stains on My Name, War in My Veins: Guyana and the Politics of Cultural Struggle.* Durham: Duke University Press.

————. 1990. "Dutchman Ghosts and History Mystery: Ritual, Colonizer, and Colonized Interpretations of the 1763 Berbice Slave Rebellion." *Journal of Historical Sociology* 3(2):133–165.

Williams, Eric. 1984. *From Columbus to Castro: The History of the Caribbean.* New York: Viking Books.

Williams, Raymond. 1977. *Marxism and Literature.* New York: Oxford University Press.

Wilmott, Swithin. 1995. "Females of Abandoned Character? Women and Protest in Jamaica 1838–65." In *Engendering History: Caribbean Women in Historical Perspective*, edited by Verene Shepherd, Bridget Bereton, and Barbara Bailey. Kingston: Ian Randle.

————. 1993. "Emancipation in Action: Workers and Wage Conflict in Jamaica 1838–1840." In *Caribbean Freedom: Economy and Society from Emancipation to the Present*, edited by Hilary Beckles and Verene Shepherd. Kingston: Ian Randle.

————. 1992. "Black Space/Room to Maneuver: Land and Politics in Trelawny in the Immediate Post-emancipation Period." In *Plantation Economy, Land Reform, and the Peasantry in a Historical Perspective 1838–1890*, edited by Claus Stolbert and Swithin Wilmot. Kingston: Friedrich Ebert Siftung.

Wilson, Peter. 1973. *Crab Antics: The Social Anthropology of English Speaking Negro Societies in the Caribbean.* New Haven: Yale University Press.

Witter, Michael. 1989. "The Role of Higglers/Sidewalk Vendors/Informal Commercial Traders in the Development of the Jamaican Economy." In *Proceedings of the Symposium on Higglering in Jamaica, Higglering/Sidewalk Vending/Informal Commercial Trading in Jamaican Economy.* Kingston: Department of Economics, University of the West Indies.

————. 1977. *Hustle Economy: Essay in Conceptualization.* Mimeo. Kingston: Department of Economics, University of the West Indies.

Witter, Michael, and Claremont Kirkton. 1990. *The Informal Economy in Jamaica: Some Empirical Exercises.* Working paper no 36. Kingston: University of the West Indies, Institute for Social and Economic Research.

Wolf, Diane L., ed. 1996a. *Feminist Dilemmas in Fieldwork.* Boulder: Westview Press.

————. 1996a. "Situating Feminist Dilemmas in Fieldwork." In *Feminist Dilemmas in Fieldwork*, edited by Diane L. Wolf. Boulder: Westview Press.

Wolf, Eric. 1997. *Europe and the People without History.* Berkeley: University of California Press.

Worth, Robert F. 2003. "20 Airport Workers Held in Smuggling of Drugs for Decade." *New York Times*, November 26, http://select.nytimes.com/search/restricted/article?res=F50710FC3D5E0C758EDDA80994DB404482#.

Wright, Lee. 1989. "Objectifying Gender: The Stiletto Heel." In *A View from the Interior: Feminism, Women, and Design*," edited by J. Attfield and P. Kirkham. London: Women's Press.

Wyatt, G. E., et al. 1995. *Female Low-Income Workers and AIDS in Jamaica.* Women and AIDS Research Program Research Report Series no. 14. Washington, D.C.: International Center for Research on Women.

Yearbook of Jamaica 1960–1980. Kingston: Statistical Institute of Jamaica.

Yelvington, Kevin A. 1995. *Producing Power: Ethnicity, Gender, and Class in a Caribbean Workplace.* Philadelphia: Temple University Press.

Young, K., C. Wolkowitz, and R. M. Cullagh, eds. 1981. *Of Marriage and Market: Women's Subordination in International Perspective.* London: CSE Books.

Young, Y. 1997. A Grand Procession. *Gleaner*, March 19, p. A15.

Index

Page numbers in italics refer to figures.